Computing across the Curriculum

EDUCOM
Strategies Series
on Information Technology

Computing across the Curriculum: Academic Perspectives

William H. Graves, Editor

Academic Computing Publications, Inc.

EDUCOM was assisted in the development of this book
by grants from the following Corporate Associates:
Apple Computer, Inc.
Digital Equipment Corporation
International Business Machines Corporation
NeXT, Inc.

International Business Machines Corporation
and Apple Computer, Inc.
are EDUCOM Corporate Leadership Sponsors.

Academic Computing Publications, Inc.
McKinney, Texas 75069

The opinions expressed in this book are those of the individual authors and are not
intended to represent policy statements of EDUCOM, the contributing institutions,
the supporting corporations, or Academic Computing Publications, Inc.

Library of Congress Cataloging-in-Publication Data

Computing across the curriculum : academic perspectives / William H.
    Graves, editor.
        p.   cm. — (EDUCOM strategies series on information
    technology, ISSN 1046-2317)
        Includes bibliographical references.
        1. Education, Higher–United States–Data processing. 2. Computer
    -assisted instruction–United States.   I . Graves, William Howard,
    1940-   . II. Series.
    LB2395.7.C66   1989
    378.1'734—dc20   89-27343
                                                                      CIP

Printed in the United States of America

CONTENTS

Contributors

Kamala Anandam
Associate Dean, Educational Technologies
Miami-Dade Community College

George F. Badger
Director, Computing Services
University of Illinois at Urbana-Champaign

Diane P. Balestri
Assistant Dean, Office of the Dean of the College
Princeton University

Thomas E. Byrne
Director of Operations, Support and Services
Kiewit Computation Center
Dartmouth College

Michael P. Carter
Director, Education Research
Apple Computer, Inc.

Ruth Chabay
Senior Research Scientist, Center for Design of Educational Computing
Carnegie Mellon University

Michael R. Cheney
Dean, School of Journalism and Mass Communication
Drake University

Frank Dominguez
Professor of Spanish
University of North Carolina at Chapel Hill

Brian Gallagher
Professor of English
LaGuardia Community College, CUNY

Gordon L. Galloway
Director of Academic Computing
Cornell University

Nina Garrett
Visiting Associate Professor of Modern Languages
Carnegie Mellon University

Ladnor D. Geissinger
Professor of Mathematics
University of North Carolina at Chapel Hill

George Gerhold
Associate Dean, College of Arts and Sciences
Western Washington University

William H. Graves
Director, The Institute for Academic Technology
University of North Carolina at Chapel Hill

Antony S. Halaris
Vice-President, Computing and Information Services
Iona College

Margret Hazen
Director, Instructional Computing
University of North Carolina at Chapel Hill

Robert W. Hendersen
Associate Professor of Psychology
University of Illinois at Urbana-Champaign

Loretta L. Jones
Associate Director of the General Chemistry Program
University of Illinois at Urbana-Champaign

Nancy Kaplan
Director, Writing Workshop
Cornell University

Elizabeth Kean
Associate Professor, Center for Curriculum and Instruction
University of Nebraska-Lincoln

Eric T. Lane
Professor of Physics
University of Tennessee

Lawrence M. Levine
Director, User Services
Kiewit Computation Center
Dartmouth College

Carolyn Chappell Lougee
Professor of History
Stanford University

Robert W. Lutz
Director of Computing and Telecommunications
Drake University

Richard A. Meiss
Professor of Physiology & Biophysics and OB/GYN
Indiana University School of Medicine

Joseph J. Moeller, Jr.
Vice-President for Information Systems
Stevens Institute of Technology

Christine M. Neuwirth
Assistant Professor of English
Carnegie Mellon University

James Noblitt
Professor of Linguistics
Cornell University

Anne Parker
Director, Microcomputing Support Center
University of North Carolina- Chapel Hill

Helen J. Schwartz
Professor of English
Indiana University-Purdue University at Indianapolis

Lynda W. Sloan
Director, Computing Center
Iona College

Stanley G. Smith
Professor of Chemistry
University of Illinois at Urbana-Champaign

Lawrence P. Staunton
Associate Professor and Chairman, Department of Physics and Astro-mony
Drake University

Richard F. Wilson
Associate Chancellor
University of Illinois at Urbana-Champaign

George L. Wolford
Professor and Chair, Department of Psychology
Dartmouth College

Introduction

William H. Graves
University of North Carolina at Chapel Hill

Picasso proclaimed: "Computers are useless. They can only give you answers." Were he alive today and attuned to higher education's lively interest in personal computing, he might recant and admit that computers have evolved from a technology that empowers numerical computation and structured data manipulation into a catalytic agent that is transforming teaching and learning with a vigor approaching Gutenberg proportion. He might recognize that computers extend the horizon of human curiosity and achievement by encouraging both visceral and cognitive experimentation with the coloring and shading of intellectual activity. This book addresses the practical aspects of this fanciful and polemical revision of Picasso's proclamation. It does so through a collection of contributed articles representing a variety of academic perspectives and experiences. The rationale for soliciting these articles from leaders in the silicon "evolution" rested on two propositions:

- Affordable interactive technologies can add value to the curriculum and fundamentally alter its form and content.

- Academe's traditional tentativeness in matters of curriculum revision and innovation argues for a national dialogue on the nature/nurture issues inherent in the complexity and cost of developing and employing such technologies.

This book, then, is an attempt to move educational concerns from the background into the foreground of the silicon-and-system vistas that, though they are of central importance to those who manage computing services and resources, too often are only a partial picture of the technological challenge facing the nation's campuses. *Curriculum* is thus a key word, but what is *curriculum?* Is it a body of content and pedagogy describing a disciplinary or professional course of study, or does it connote the broadest long-term outcomes of a higher education? This question was surely on the collective mind of several national panels recently reporting on the problems of baccalaureate education in American colleges and universities.[1] These problems include the following, to name just a few:

- Problems of "articulation" between the public schools and higher education.

- A confused baccalaureate mission as evidenced by academic fragmentation and an overemphasis on professional training at the expense of general education.

- Structures and practices of institutional and professional governance that discourage change and innovation in the curriculum and that even place faculty and institutional commitment to undergraduate education at risk.

Reports on undergraduate education are seldom best sellers, either in the population at large or in the nation's collective faculty. Individual authors occasionally pique widespread faculty and public interest, but their efforts provoke intellectual posturing on the part of stylish literary reviewers more often than institutional action.[2] Indeed, one problem of undergraduate education is the national absence of a concerned community of faculty willing to address current educational issues. One exception, however, is the issue of how to tap the educational potential of interactive technology to strengthen the undergraduate experience. On this front, many scholars are ahead of the aforementioned reports, which envision a contributing role for interactive technologies but offer little more than an intriguing hint of an educational environment enriched by technology. Indeed, the opportunity for technology-based curricular repair and innovation has captured the imaginations and efforts of thousands of faculty. There may not yet be a concerted and organized national faculty effort to exploit the educational opportunities inherent in interactive technologies, but these opportunities have attracted a national critical mass of faculty interest and experience and thus make it feasible to attempt to cohere interest and experimentation into direction. But from which constituency of higher education should guidance and action come? From individual scholars? From the disciplines, professions, and academic departments? From campus computer support organizations? From the highest academic or executive levels of colleges and universities? From the government and interested private foundations? From corporate vendors of interactive technologies? At a time when many observers argue that the nation's ability to compete in a technologically paced global economy depends on educational reform, I believe that the answer should be, "All of the above." This book, then, targets all of the above constituencies and describes a variety of ways to encourage and to support computing across the curriculum. It draws on a national cross section of experience, which is reported in three parts representing three intertwined academic perspectives: faculty, curriculum, and institutional.

FACULTY PERSPECTIVES: In this part of the book, the seven winners of EDUCOM/NCRIPTAL's "Best" awards for 1987 describe their experiences, thus lending a distinct faculty perspective to a variety of pedagogical, institutional, personal, and professional issues inherent in developing and using software to add value to education. I solicited the "stories" of these winners through a series of questions (recorded in appendix A) that should be considered by any scholar/teacher interested in developing (or using) instructional software and by any institution planning to involve its faculty in instructional computing.

CURRICULUM PERSPECTIVES: In their contributed essays, two national faculty groups representing two keystone curricula in higher education, writing programs and foreign language programs, assess technology's current impact on their respective fields and explore its future role. I invited leaders — several of whom have won EDUCOM/NCRIPTAL awards — in both areas to form working groups that would meet periodically with the goal of preparing position papers. In the first essay, the foreign language group develops the three themes of *authenticity* (of source materials technologically available to students and scholars), of *empowerment* (through powerful technological tools for analyzing source materials), and of *integration* (of research and teaching). They describe these three ideas as technological bridges that integrate the academic islands of literature, linguistics, and language teaching and that shape a "new humanism." In the second essay, the writing group constructs a practical blueprint for integrating the process-oriented advantages of word processing into writing instruction and practice. The group builds its case on the widely accepted premise that writing should be an across-the-curriculum responsibility, and its recommendations address the difficult issues of access and equity as well as faculty and curriculum development in the English department.

INSTITUTIONAL PERSPECTIVES: This cross section of nine institutional case studies indicates how various institutions are supporting instructional computing. The variables include institutional type and mission, faculty support programs, multivendor versus one-vendor environments, vendor support, student ownership, "computing-czar" positions, and academic reward structures. I asked the contributing authors to focus on academic issues at an institutional level, and I posed a series of questions (appendix B) to guide their responses. Several authors cited the questions and the writing assignment as very useful planning mechanisms for their campuses.

To help the reader understand my concerns and how they shaped the book, I introduce each of these three parts of the book with remarks designed to amplify this general introduction. The book thus moves from an individual (faculty) academic perspective to a collective (committee) focus on key areas of the curriculum and finally to an institutional perspective that reports on both technological and academic infrastructures. The picture that emerges is not a tidy landscape that can be replicated by others in a paint-by-the-numbers approach. Yet, several themes run through most of the contributions, and I would be remiss not to state these at the outset to help guide the reader through the rich and individually styled reports that compose the book.

- Those individual scholars whose accomplishments are reflected in all three parts of the book are dedicated to improving their teaching and their students' education. This, above all else, has motivated them to develop and use instructional technologies.

- Developing software requires an enormous commitment of a scholar's time, even with support. Without support from an institution, a vendor, or some combination of these and other sources, sustaining a project requires Herculean energy and persistence. Vendor support, in particular, has played a major role in progress to date.

- Evaluating the results of using instructional technologies is an important but difficult agenda that is seldom supported with institutional resources.

- Academic governance and reward structures are inhospitable to developing and using instructional technologies.

- The various vendor-specific flavors of technology and their constant changes present a moving, chaotic target for academe, which by its incremental nature and its budgeting mechanisms cannot allow change to dominate stability for very long in the curriculum. This and the high costs of the human talent behind technology-based curriculum development projects make it difficult to sustain such projects over time.

- Developing software that can be adapted to the individual instructional needs of others is difficult.

- Making software available to others across institutional boundaries is often difficult in today's review and distribution environments.

- The in-class use of technology is an important component of instructional computing. Because the associated costs of equipment and staff support are high, it is often an absent "luxury."

These observations reflect my general interpretations of the contributions to this book. They present few surprises to seasoned observers of the instructional computing scene in higher education, and they await response from those of us who believe that technology can play an increasingly beneficial role in teaching and learning. In a concluding part of the book, "A National Perspective?" I will take the editorial liberty of offering my response. My premise will be that the task before us is too important and too complex to be tackled solely at the traditional grassroots level or only within existing institutional frameworks. I will elaborate on the above observations to provide a rationale for creating a national program for advancing the promise of instructional technologies. I will say more on this, however, after the reader has had a chance to examine

at first hand the experiences and reflections of the other contributors to
this book.

Notes

1. Association of American Colleges (AAC), *Integrity in the College Curriculum:
   A Report to the Academic Community* (Washington, D.C.: Association of American Colleges, 1985); The Carnegie Foundation for the Advancement of
   Teaching, *College: The Undergraduate Experience in America* (New York:
   Harper and Row, 1987); National Institute of Education (NIE), *Involvement in
   Learning, Realizing the Potential of Higher Education* (Washington, D.C.: Na-
   tional Institute of Education, 1984).
2. A. Bloom, *The Closing of the American Mind* (New York: Simon and Schuster,
   1987); E. D. Hirsch, Jr., *Cultural Literacy: What Every American Needs to Know*
   (Boston: Houghton Mifflin Co., 1987).

Part One:

Faculty Perspectives

Faculty Perspectives

The role of computing in the curriculum cannot be clarified and advanced without the interest and effort of individual scholar/teachers. This is a compelling reason for expanding EDUCOM's agenda to reflect faculty interests and for changing its organizational structure to strengthen academic participation significantly beyond current levels. The EDUCOM Software Initiative (ESI) has taken a tentative first step in this direction. It is a volunteer effort to expand EDUCOM's and higher education's vision beyond the traditional (and important) technical concerns of the computation center and the disciplines and professions traditionally associated with computing—engineering, computer science, and the numerical sciences. The interests of ESI volunteers derive largely from issues that constrain the potential of interactive technology to strengthen teaching and learning. Organized into task groups to address various aspects of the *software issue*,[1] the Software Initiative has become a focal point for several projects, including three that directly influence the vantage point for this part of the book:

- The EDUCOM/NCRIPTAL Annual Software Awards Program is a joint project of the ESI and the National Center for Research to Improve Post-Secondary Teaching and Learning (at the University of Michigan). Winners are selected on the basis of both content (peer review) and instructional design. The case studies that follow this introduction were drawn from the seven "best" technology-based curriculum development projects, announced at the conclusion of the first competition in 1987.

- *Ivory Towers, Silicon Basements (ITSB)* is a report from the FIPSE Technology Study Group.[2] Its authors are faculty members and administrators from a variety of colleges and universities. They are innovators who understand not only the promise of bringing computers into the classroom but also the potential disruption and cost. They make recommendations for supporting faculty, increasing educational equity, devising useful evaluations, and improving the infrastructure for making hardware and software available.

- *Facilitating Academic Software Development* (*FASD*) is a
  resource for individuals and institutions interested in developing
  academic software.[3] *FASD* does not argue for a unique
  paradigm for software development. Instead, it offers an
  overview of several major development programs and from
  these synthesizes seven "core" issues that in some combination
  appear to be critical factors in the development of academic
  software.

These three ESI projects reveal considerable progress from several vantages, to include the teacher/scholar's. On the one hand, *ITSB* argues for a learner-centered perspective while *FASD* describes several productive development environments across the range of institutional types, from community college to research university. On the other hand, the EDUCOM/NCRIPTAL awards confirm the existence of exemplary academic software. Recounting their software development experiences in the articles that follow, the 1987 EDUCOM/NCRIPTAL "best" winners revisit and extend many of the issues discussed in *FASD* and *ITSB*.

The small but growing corpus of EDUCOM/NCRIPTAL award-winning software is neither representative of every discipline and profession nor a reason to abandon the effort to understand and encourage academic software development. It is, however, a lens of excellence through which to focus the cradle-to-grave spectrum of development *and* use issues. What campus infrastructures, for example, can support the extensive use of good academic software? What are the barriers to the widespread use of exemplary software? Do these barriers vary with factors such as subject area, institutional type, or technology itself — to list only a few of many possibilities? In this part of the book, the EDUCOM/NCRIPTAL winners address these questions by reflecting on the environments in which they developed and use their software, how those environments might be improved, and whether they would undertake such projects again. They offer teacher/scholars' viewpoints on an activity that, because it is usually resource-intensive and not traditionally a faculty responsibility, is typically and with considerable justification discussed from an institutional perspective. In this sense, the articles in this part of the book offer specifics to complement the institutional case studies in the third part. Indeed, four of the articles that follow report individual experiences at institutions (Illinois and North Carolina) represented in the third part of the book.

The contributing authors were asked to read this introduction, focusing especially on the issues raised by the questions listed in appendix A, as a means to reflect on how their institutions, their disciplines or professions, hardware vendors, and software distributors or "publishers" might better contribute to computing in the curriculum. They were asked to write from their own experiences and priorities and to allow the remarks and questions in appendix A at most to guide and provoke, rather than prescribe, their reflections or the format of their articles. I hope that their reflections will prove useful to EDUCOM's multiple constituencies by imparting a faculty perspective to the continuing dialogue on the role of interactive technologies in higher education.

Notes

1. Steven W. Gilbert, "Academic Software—Vision and Perspective," *EDUCOM Bulletin* 20 (Summer 1985): 18-21; Steven W. Gilbert and Kenneth C. Green, "New Computing in Higher Education," *Change* (May/June 1986), 33-50; William H. Graves, "Personal Computing and Liberal Education: A Higher Education Case Study," *Education & Computing* 2 (1986): 215-22; idem, "CAI: Computer-Assisted Involvement," *Academic Computing* 1 (Spring 1987): 6-9, 57-60; D. L. Smallen, "Infusing Computing into the Curriculum: Challenges for the Next Decade," *Academic Computing* 3 (April 1989): 8-12, 32-35.

2. Diane Pelkus Balestri, ed., *Ivory Towers, Silicon Basements: Learner-Centered Computing in Postsecondary Education,* EDUCOM/Academic Computing Software Initiative Monograph Series, vol. 1 (McKinney, Tex.: Academic Computing Publications, 1988).

3. Jerry W. Sprecher, ed., *Facilitating Academic Software Development,* EDUCOM/Academic Computing Software Initiative Monograph Series, vol. 2 (McKinney, Tex.:Academic Computing Publications, 1988).

Chapter 1

Microcomputer-Based Instructional Computing in Psychology: Where, What, When, Why, and Who?

Robert W. Hendersen
University of Illinois at Urbana-Champaign

Where

The University of Illinois teaches introductory psychology to more than four thousand undergraduates each year, and more than eleven hundred students are psychology majors. To meet the challenge of this heavy instructional load, the Department of Psychology at the University of Illinois has continually experimented with new teaching technologies. For example, the department was an early developer of videotaped teaching materials, and it participated in some of the initial stages of experimentation with mainframe-based tutorial software. The use of these earlier teaching technologies has steadily decreased over the past decade, a decrease that reflects the costliness of developing and using high-quality videotapes and mainframe-based software.

The microcomputer-based materials described herein were therefore developed in a locale in which there is a great deal of entrenched skepticism, based on lengthy experience, about the long-term cost-effectiveness of emerging instructional technologies. This wariness shaped the strategies I followed in developing microcomputer-based instructional tools. For example, I decided early in the process to do very little in the way of developing tutorial-based software of the sort that had dominated the earlier, mainframe-based experiments in instructional computing. This decision reflects ingrained doubts about whether the effort required to produce effective tutorial software is proportional to the benefits.

Another aspect of the locale that helped to shape our microcomputer-based instruction is the extensive degree to which faculty depend on computers in their research. Virtually all the research laboratories in the Psychology Department at the University of Illinois are computerized, and faculty have come to rely heavily on computers as tools in all aspects of their research activities. This reliance on computers in research labs meant that when this project began three years ago, there was a large and growing gap between the tools faculty used in their own research and the tools they placed in student hands in labs and demonstrations. Teaching laboratories, unlike research laboratories, were not heavily computerized, and as a result, students did not receive a representative notion of how psychological research actually is conducted. The focus of my project became the narrowing of this gap, with the explicit goal of lessening the distance between what faculty do in their research laboratories and what students do in teaching laboratories. The slogan of Stewart Brand's *Whole Earth Catalog* — "Access to Tools" — became the guiding theme of our development of instructional microcomputing.

Facilities and course organization specific to the University of Illinois permitted a stepwise progression in the development and testing of instructional software. For example, exercises that were initially developed in a relatively small, laboratory-based introductory course, using networked computers in a highly supervised setting, were subsequently made available (through the undergraduate library) to a much larger student base in another introductory course that does not include a laboratory. By using the laboratory course as a development site for materials that were subsequently released for use in less tightly monitored settings, we were able to evaluate, revise, and tune the materials extensively before students had to face them without readily available human help. Students in the lab course are encouraged to find ways to make the instructional software fail, and some of our materials are now in their twelfth version, benefiting from a long series of improvements spurred by the close monitoring of student use that was possible in the laboratory sections.

What

The program responsible for my invitation to participate in this volume is *Eventlog*, which received the EDUCOM/NCRIPTAL award in 1987. This program is but one component of the project in instructional computing that I directed, but it is a good example of how we have tried to develop research-quality tools whose ease of use makes them appropriate for undergraduates in psychology courses.

Eventlog is a software package designed to be used as a tool for recording real-time events. Data are entered through the standard keyboard, and precise times of keyboard entries, including the time each key is pressed and the time each key is released, are recorded for subsequent analysis. *Eventlog* runs on all members of the IBM PC family, and it runs on other machines that are PC-compatible. It is intended for use primarily by students and researchers who score and record observational data.

For example, an ethologist may need to record the behaviors of animals engaging in social contact. A psychologist may need to record patterns of facial expression by scoring muscle movements from videotapes of people reacting to various situations. A safety engineer may need to record observations of traffic patterns at a dangerous intersection. Wherever human observers must log their observations in real time, *Eventlog* is an appropriate tool. The observer simply presses the appropriate coding key for as long as the observed event occurs.

Eventlog can easily be customized to a wide range of different applications, and key assignments can be tailored to particular applications and to particular observers. No background in computer programming is required of the user. Simple, menu-driven procedures permit the novice user to customize an application quickly and easily.

To use *Eventlog*, the user first creates a customized Keyboard Configuration, using a menu-driven editing procedure. The user can choose which keys to activate, and the user can assign an understandable label to each activated key. The user can also define timers, to time intervals while observations are being made. Once a Keyboard Configuration has been created, it can be used repeatedly, without requiring redefinition. It can also be modified or used as a template for creating a new, different configuration.

The Event Logger records data, with the role of each key determined by the customized Keyboard Configuration. The observer enters the data by pressing the appropriate keys. The Event Logger records in a data file the precise time that each key is pressed and the precise time that each key is released. Several keys can be pressed simultaneously if several observed events occur concurrently. While the Event Logger is in operation, the user can monitor the recording of data by watching the display screen. The display screen also provides a variety of timing information, and it gives the user access to a listing of key assignments.

The user can interrupt the data-recording process at any time to add typed notes to the data file. Once a note has been completed, the program will resume recording key-based, real-time data. Students are strongly encouraged to use the notes facility to record anything they think might be relevant to the exercise they are conducting.

Students use the program in several ways. Sometimes they use keyboard configurations that have been prepared by the instructor for a specific purpose. For example, students in our introductory lab course do an experiment in animal social memory in which the social interactions between an adult rat and a juvenile are recorded at different intervals following the adult's first exposure to the juvenile; the encoding categories in this exercise are determined by the instructor. Subsequently, the students participate in other exercises, using the flexibility in key assignment permitted by the program to vary the coding categories used. An example of such an assignment, involving the observation of the behavior of squirrels, is described below.

Tools Rather Than Tutorials: Evaluation Results

The decision to focus on giving students access to the tools of psychological research has been supported (vindicated?) by the results of formal evaluations of the pedagogical effectiveness of the materials. Three separate evaluations of different groups of exercises have been conducted in the laboratory course in which these materials were first made available to students. In these evaluations, I compared the effectiveness of the instructional software with that of conventional, noncomputerized means of teaching the same materials. Each evaluation had several features in common. The laboratory sections under study were matched for laboratory instructor, a matching that was made possible by assigning two sections to each instructor. Each section participated in both the computerized and the conventional exercises, but in different orders. Between the two sets of exercises, a quiz was administered, and performance was compared between those sections that had just completed the computerized exercises and those that had just completed the conventional exercises.

Performance was assessed with quiz items drawn exclusively from materials used in the course before the computerized laboratories were introduced; this was to insure that the quiz items were not biased toward showing beneficial effects of the computerized exercises. Questions were drawn from previous years' exams and from test-banks provided with textbooks; questions that tapped the content areas covered by the exercises were used, and in each case the content areas were also covered in the lecture portion of the class and in the textbook. Laboratory instructors sorted the questions into two subsets: those whose content was covered by both the conventional and the computerized labs, and those whose content was covered by the computerized labs but not by the conventional labs.

Results were consistent across all three evaluations. When quiz questions addressed content that was tapped by both the conventional and the computerized exercises, performance was about the same. There was nothing magic about doing things on the computer that could be done using other, noncomputerized techniques. However, whenever the computerized exercises were able to do something that could not be done with the conventional exercises, there was a significant improvement in the pedagogical effectiveness of the laboratory. To the extent that the computer allowed the content of the laboratory to be expanded by giving students access to a more powerful tool, the students learned more.

When

This project has been under way for three years, and it has succeeded in placing microcomputer-based tools into the hands of students at all levels. Students with no background in either psychology or computers can begin using computer tools in the first week of their first course in psychology, and the level of access to computerized tools increases as the student becomes more experienced. We have developed software for four different levels of student accessibility. The student encounters different levels of access at different times in his or her education.

First-Level Access

This level of accessibility is for students who have no background in psychology, who have never used a computer, who do not know how to type, and who require software tools that are very forgiving if a mistake is made. The exercises we have developed at this level are very constrained, each demonstrating a particular phenomenon and each leading the student through the exercise in a stepwise, systematic fashion.

Students in Psychology 103, a laboratory-based introductory psychology course, participate in a series of twenty computer-based exercises, each an experiment that the student conducts on himself or herself. Just as a student in an introductory biology class might use dissection tools to explore the internal structure of a frog, students in this introductory psychology class use computer-based tools to explore the structure of their own mental operations. Each exercise is an adaptation of a classic experiment in psychology, and each is designed so that the students can see the phenomena under study in their own performances, without having to aggregate their data with those of the others in the class. Students staple printouts of the data they generate in the computer-based exercises to a worksheet that asks leading questions about the interpretation of those data; these printouts and worksheets are then given to the instructor for critique and evaluation.

Second-Level Access

As soon as a student has a bit of experience with the techniques of psychological research, the narrow constraints imposed by first-level exercises become limiting and even misleading. Real research, as opposed to calcified laboratory exercises, requires flexibility and creative decision making. The sooner the student can be introduced to the kind of thought required in scientific exploration of the unknown, the better.

Second-level tools are designed to have this flexibility. They are intended to be customized by their users for specialized use, but their use requires no extensive training or study. Whereas the tools collect data that are accurate to stringent, professional standards, the ease of use makes it possible for students to use such tools very early in their careers.

Eventlog is an example of a second-level tool. I have used it successfully with students in their first course in psychology, loaning them laptop computers equipped with *Eventlog* to record the behavior of gray squirrels on campus. The students were required to develop, modify, and hone the categories in which they encoded the behavior of the animals they observed. Because each student encoded behavior according to his or her own system, using the flexible key assignments permitted by the program, each student's project produced an idiosyncratic product. These data files were used as a basis for a class discussion of what constitutes good encoding categories in observational research, and the students then explored different ways of analyzing the data they had collected.

Third-Level Access

The more sophisticated the capabilities of a computerized research tool, the more likely it is that successful use of the tool will require specific training in its use. Undergraduates in advanced laboratory classes and in independent study projects need access to tools that are more flexible and powerful than is possible with tools designed to be used without prior training. The third-level tools in our project meet this need. Each is a software package designed to be used by undergraduates, but each assumes that between five and twenty hours can be devoted to instruction, training, and practice in the use of the package before the student uses it for his or her own project.

One example of a third-level tool is a package I call *Status*. This is a package for the real-time, interactive control of experimental devices external to the computer station itself. For example, the package can be used to control and monitor psychophysiological experiments with animals in which the contingencies of a training regimen and the recording of the resulting data are all handled by the computer. The package is programmed using a state-descriptive language; the student programs an experiment by filling out a series of on-screen forms describing the component states of the experiment. Although it takes several hours to teach a student how to use the package, the nature of the instruction requires the student to analyze the target experiment in careful detail. Thus the student learns how to break an experiment into its component parts in the process of learning how to use *Status* to achieve computerized control of the experiment.

Another example of a third-level tool is a package I call *SCOPE* (Simple Creation of Psychology Experiments). One component of the package is a screen editor specifically designed to make it easy to produce the kinds of screen displays required in psychology experiments. A second component controls the sequencing and the timing of the screen displays that have been produced by the editor. Although students must receive some particular instruction in how to use the package, the overhead does not outweigh the advantages of letting students develop and conduct experiments of their own design.

The needs of most advanced undergraduates and of most graduate students can be met with third-level, general-purpose software tools.

Fourth-Level Access

No matter how flexible and capable general-purpose packages are designed to be, there will always be experiments that fall outside their scope. It is inherent in the nature of the research endeavor that new, unforeseen demands will be placed on computerized tools. Even though we are trying to make it possible to do very wide ranges of psychological research using the computerized tools provided by general-purpose packages, there will always be students (particularly at the graduate level) and faculty whose requirements cannot be met by such packages. Fourth-level access requires that the user have access to a programmer (sometimes the user, sometimes someone else) who has some skill in laboratory applications.

For these users we have developed a tool kit of Pascal routines that deal with the kinds of display timing, response timing, and data handling problems that are commonly encountered in psychological experimentation. Even if an experimenter has to turn to *ad hoc,* limited-purpose programming to meet the demands of a particular research program, the tool kit provides each investigator with a set of available tools for many of the more difficult problems.

Why

There is nothing more dispiriting for an instructor than being forced, by limited laboratory facilities, to teach students out-of-date, unrepresentative examples of how research is conducted. This is the fundamental source of my own motivation for wanting to provide software tools that can give students access to the tools of contemporary psychology. I was teaching a course whose laboratories gave little sense of the excitement and promise of modern psychological research.

Shortly after I had obtained, through university instructional equipment funding, two PCs for use in the lab course, the pace of the computerization was boosted enormously by an Advanced Educational Projects grant from IBM to the University of Illinois. This grant supported projects throughout the Illinois campus. In my own department, it provided us with enough equipment to install several networked teaching laboratories specifically designed to make it possible to closely monitor the use of instructional materials. Matching monies provided by the university were sufficient to support a small programming staff. Because the programming resources were very limited, we strongly desired to design the project in such a way that programming would not have to be duplicated unnecessarily. This led to the development of the fourth-level tool kit and the third-level, general-purpose packages that I have already described.

Involvement in instructional computing, even when there is a programming staff available, is time-consuming and demanding. External rewards are not sufficient to induce a reasonable person to devote substantial energy to such an undertaking, nor should they be. In my own case, I wanted to provide students with access to scientific tools, and doing so has proved very rewarding, in and of itself. Instructional computing does not fit neatly into the existing reward structure of a research university such as the University of Illinois; like textbook writing, it is viewed as slightly less suspect than, say, working weekends pumping gas, but it is tolerated.

Part of the tolerance the University of Illinois shows toward instructional computing is formalized in its copyright policy. Authors who use university resources in the development of instructional packages can market their software, with the important proviso that the university retains a site license to any software so developed.

However, the marketing of software is very different from the marketing of more-familiar instructional materials. Acquisitions editors from major publishing houses have told me that they are interested in instructional software only because their customers demand it, and usually the demand is for ancillary materials to be provided when a textbook is adopted. Publishers are reacting to customer demands, rather than actively exploring the full potential of instructional software. Just as a successful textbook must have a bank of test items, so must it now have a software package. The problem here is that publishers have little experience in evaluating software in its own right, and much of the software that is given "free" to textbook adopters is worth exactly its purchase price.

There are signs that this is changing. I find that in the last year publishers have proved far more responsive to the idea of letting instructional software stand on its own merits, rather than simply tying it to a textbook. This is a major shift in perspective, and it bodes well for the future distribution of instructional software.

Who

I have focused in this paper on those projects that I directed. I hired the programming staff, assigned projects, designed the software, and wrote detailed specifications for each package. Throughout the projects, I have insisted that my role stop just short of programming. The design of software and its implementation through programming are very different skills, and I suspect that both are better served by letting different people play these distinct roles. I myself know enough about programming to let programming constraints inform the way I design a program, but it was useful to be able to dream about what ought to be done, instead of worrying constantly about just how it would be implemented.

This project thus required several very skilled and very creative programmers. Most of these were students in (or recent graduates from) engineering programs at the university. Most worked part-time, on a particular component of the project. Several of the programmers have continued to participate in instructional activities after completing their work for my projects. Coordinating programming efforts and monitoring adherence to stringent documentation standards were handled by a chief programmer, Nancy Sampson, who decided which part of the project would be assigned to each programmer.

The project also required the extensive cooperation, if not the full sympathy, of a remarkable group of teaching assistants: the laboratory instructors in the course in which most of the software was first tested. Particularly in the early stages of the testing and evaluation, these instructors bore the brunt of any failures or weaknesses of the software. That they did so while maintaining good cheer is testimony to their flexibility, resiliency, and capability.

Chapter 2

Case Study:
Exploring Chemistry

Loretta L. Jones

and

Stanley G. Smith
University of Illinois at Urbana-Champaign

Background

The University of Illinois at Urbana-Champaign is one of the nineteen universities that formed partnerships with the Academic Information Systems division of IBM in the Advanced Educational Projects (AEP) program. In the AEP program, IBM provided hardware and software for projects designed to explore the educational applications of advanced technologies. The universities provided the remaining funds. The first year, we requested and received two IBM XT microcomputers, two videodisc players, and the funds to produce a videodisc. In succeeding years we received the equipment and funds to set up a thirty-station interactive video learning center for chemistry. We have since added nine more microcomputer-based student stations.

Since 1981 we had been working on a plan to develop interactive video instruction in chemistry. We were in a unique position to perform this work, since at that time Stan Smith had thirteen years of experience creating and using instructional software and Loretta Jones had seven years experience producing and using videotaped chemistry instruction. In 1980, Jones had produced several interactive videotapes that were controlled by a classroom instructor using a hand-held control. However, we wanted to enhance the interaction between individual students and the videotaped experiments with the power of a computer. Lack of funds kept us from investigating the more powerful, but more expensive, interactive videodisc. We had just decided to pool our money to buy one of the $500 controllers when in 1984 we learned about the AEP program and applied for funding that would allow us to pursue the project with videodiscs.

Part of the success of the AEP program at Illinois is due to the leadership of the people involved in its administration. Richard F. Wilson, Associate Chancellor, set appropriate guidelines for investigators and helped us to design meaningful evaluation plans. He also set up procedures to provide investigators with assistance in project completion and evaluation. IBM assigned program support personnel to each campus, a farsighted move that greatly expedited work on the projects. Mary Marshall, IBM Regional AEP Manager, and Ed Meisenheimer and Ed Pinheiro, IBM Project Managers for the campus, were readily available to answer questions, solve technical problems, and obtain needed information.

We developed the interactive video lessons to address certain instructional problems in chemistry. Among the most serious are concerns such as safety hazards, costs, and time constraints. Another is the difficulty of relating the theoretical, invisible concepts of chemistry to things that the student can see and manipulate, or to things that might already be in the experience of the student. Often chemistry is taught as interactions between energy levels, involving atoms, ions, and molecules. These ideas are very difficult for students to grasp without a context, especially since the students in our non-majors course must take chemistry before courses in their majors and do not understand how chemistry relates to their interests. Interactive lessons containing video images can integrate discussions of theory with visible examples. In addition, simulated video experiments and tutorials allow students to perform and repeat experiments and to see the results of trying different experimental parameters without getting hurt.

We are also able by this means to give students feedback on errors at the time they are made, something otherwise difficult to do in a class of two thousand. Because our weekly introductory labs are three hours long, a teaching assistant (TA) with twenty-five students has an average of seven minutes per student per week for individual attention. As a result, many student errors are missed and the students may not learn from them. The interactive video lessons allow the students to make mistakes and to receive feedback before performing related experiments, thus filling a real need in our labs.

Production and Implementation

The courseware we have produced is the initial part of a first-year videodisc course in chemistry. It is being used in all the first-semester regular chemistry courses on our campus (about two thousand students per semester) and is now available to other schools through a commercial publisher, Falcon Software. The authoring team consisted of only the two of us. After selecting the topic for a set of lessons, we explored possible experiments to develop the concepts. All parameters were tested, and a general plan for the content of the lesson and approximate screen layouts were designed. Then the video was shot, followed by programming and refinement of the instructional strategies. Most of the video on the first two discs was produced with the help of a campus video production facility run by the Instructional Media and Technology Division of Instructional Management and Services.

In the first two years of this project we spent about 3,000 hours on courseware development alone. Because the computer code is an integral part of the material, we did not use student programmers. We did not work with instructional designers because of our own extensive experience and training in instructional design. In any case, instructional designers with the necessary grasp of chemistry are rare.

Getting the interactive video classroom ready took a great deal of additional time. We had to make decisions about lighting, air conditioning, layout, security, and even paint. Smith also spent many months writing and setting up the networked classroom management system.

The first hardware that we obtained, in December 1984, was an IBM XT microcomputer, an LD-V1000 Pioneer Video Disc player, a Video Associates Laboratory MicroKey overlay card, and a SONY monitor. The Microkey card mixed CGA graphics from the PC with video from the videodisc player for display on the SONY monitor. To provide maximum flexibility in instructional strategies, we used a general-purpose programming language supplemented with a special machine-language character generator written by Hank Krejci of HFK Software. This character generator made it easy to produce superscripts, subscripts, proportional spacing, and colored text. Because subscripts overwrite text in the next line when standard line spacing is used, the character generator also provided variable line spacing. MicroKey drivers were used to control the videodisc player. Program development was done in interpreted BASIC because of the ease of seeing on the screen the results of changes in wording and video window size.

In 1986, the lessons were adapted to run on the IBM InfoWindow system, with its touch-sensitive screen. This required major changes in the way lessons were written because the InfoWindow drivers for controlling the videodisc player, mixing video and computer graphics, and using the touch screen worked only with compiled code. The additional time required for compiling before the result of each change in code could be seen was unacceptably long; therefore, the development work was switched to Microsoft QuickBASIC. This required considerable changes in the code because of the differences in the way BASICA and Quick-BASIC treat color codes that control video windows. A great deal of programming time was required to deal with changes in authoring languages associated with changes in the hardware. In addition, replacing keyset input with touch required a considerable redesign of the lessons.

The thirty-nine microcomputers are networked with the IBM PC Local Area Network, using a PC/AT as a file server. Another PC/XT microcomputer is used by the proctors for authorizing students to take quizzes, thereby allowing instructors to check student progress and scores. A hard-copy summary can also be made.

The School of Chemical Sciences and the Chemistry Department, under the direction of Professors Jiri Jonas and Larry Faulkner, secured funds for the remodeling of a laboratory to accommodate the interactive videodisc equipment. By combining two existing facilities (a tutoring center and a PLATO facility) into the new learning center, we were able to set up a room that is open eighty-four hours a week and is staffed by chemistry tutors during the day and proctors in the evenings. The room is supervised by Jennifer Karloski, a teaching associate who has responsibility for staffing, instructor interface, and security. Since Ms. Karloski has a background in both chemistry and education, she has been able to assist with evaluations and to identify problems in the operation of the courseware.

The successful implementation of new technologies into an instructional program is facilitated by the support of colleagues. Our initial development work was encouraged by Gilbert Haight, who was then Director of the General Chemistry Program. In addition, Professor Haight was an invaluable source of ideas and information. Professor Elizabeth Rogers also made important suggestions and allowed a pilot study of the materials to be conducted in her course. The incorporation of the lessons into the introductory chemistry courses was facilitated by Steve Zumdahl, Director of the General Chemistry Program, and Roxy Wilson, Assistant Director. Dr. Zumdahl secured staff and funds for the operation of the center, and Dr. Wilson chaired a committee to consider how best to integrate the interactive video lessons and how to revise existing experiments to take advantage of the new instructional medium.

Outcomes

We incorporated evaluations of the materials into every step of the project. Using the initial inexpensive check videodisc, which contained video for only two lessons, we observed individual students and small groups complete the lessons, taking notes on comments and on the kinds of errors made. Other subject matter experts also reviewed the materials. After revisions and the completion of additional lessons, the first videodisc was mastered, and a pilot study of the materials was conducted on groups of fifty to one hundred students.[1] Later Jones conducted additional studies of the effectiveness of the courseware as compared to laboratory work and to written instructions.[2] Student attitudes toward the materials were surveyed by means of a questionnaire.[3] In each study, the interactive video lessons were shown to be an effective and efficient means of teaching concepts and introducing students to laboratory procedures. In addition, the majority of the students enjoyed using the courseware and rated it more positively than other aspects of their laboratory work.

The success of the courseware has had an effect on the general chemistry courses. The curriculum has been enhanced by replacing part of the laboratory work with interactive video lessons. Now we are designing new and more ambitious types of laboratory experiences to take advantage of the individualized preparation the computer offers. We are also examining how best to use laboratory time. A lab is very expensive to run, and if some topics can be better taught with interactive video, we need to find out what the unique benefits of hands-on laboratory experiences are and how to make them available to large numbers of students. The success of computer-assisted videodisc courseware has encouraged us to rethink the course structure as well as the curriculum.

Recommendations

The development of this courseware can be regarded as a two-stage process. The first stage was initially undertaken as a research project and was an attempt to explore the limits of applying the technology to instruction. Only when the potential of the medium became apparent did we make a commitment to the second stage, the production of courseware.

The ongoing production of courseware is closely akin to the authoring of a textbook and requires incentives different from those found in the initial exploration of the medium. The most important is the direct satisfaction of observing its use by students. Consequently, we believe that providing facilities for students to use courseware will encourage faculty members to develop computer-based materials. In addition, if they are to generate significant quantities of instructional courseware suitable for distribution, they must be allowed to retain ownership and distribution rights to their work. That is, the intellectual property rights of faculty creating instructional software should be protected in the same manner as are those of faculty in other creative endeavors such as writing books or producing works of art. Although some faculty authors may benefit from campuswide software-distribution programs, it does not seem appropriate to require college and university administrators to act as middlemen between authors and publishers.

It is very difficult for schools to stimulate the creation of instructional materials from the top down. Even faculty support groups seem to be most successful when initiated by the faculty themselves. However, there are three roles that colleges and universities might play to encourage the development of good courseware. First, they should make a commitment to the use of quality materials by supporting the installation of computer learning centers or other accessible campus facilities. Second, authors should be allowed to own their work and to control its distribution. Third, advanced degree programs and other efforts oriented toward instructional research and development at the college level should be encouraged. An example is the Doctor of Arts degree, which is granted within the discipline of interest. Jones's D.A. training in instructional design, curriculum development, classroom research methods, and instructional technology as applied to a chosen discipline proved to be a valuable preparation for courseware development.

Colleges and universities are generally dependent on outside funding for major instructional improvements. However, such funding is usually difficult to obtain, and cooperative efforts with industry can offer one solution. IBM's AEP program was successful in stimulating the production of a large amount of material for undergraduate instruction.

Notes

1. S. G. Smith, L. L. Jones, and M. L. Waugh, "Production and Evaluation of Interactive Video Disc Lessons in Laboratory Instruction," Journal of Computer-Based Instruction 13 (1986): 117-21.
2. L. L. Jones, "Enhancing Instruction in the Practice of Chemistry with the Computer-Assisted Interactive Videodisc," Trends in Analytical Chemistry 7 (1988): 273-76.
3. L. L. Jones, "Videodisc Laboratory for Chemistry," Proceedings of the Optical Information Systems Conference (December 1987), 157-65.

Chapter 3

The Development of *Exploring Small Groups:* A Tool for Learning Abstract Algebra

Ladnor D. Geissinger
University of North Carolina at Chapel Hill

Motivation

Most junior- or senior-level students in the mathematical sciences are required to take a course that introduces them to abstract algebra. Typically this means that class discussion centers on elementary properties of binary operations and the algebraic structures called groups, rings, and fields. Almost invariably students find this difficult and frustrating, and instructors are perplexed and disappointed with student performance. After one semester with a particularly trying algebra class, I spent some time reviewing the course topics, other texts, the assigned exercises, and the students' difficulties, attempting to identify some components of the pedagogical problem and looking for ways to aid the students. It seemed to me that extensive use of an appropriate computer program might help the students with two of the main problems. First, they must learn precise definitions of many technical terms and must understand the terms well enough to know what has to be checked to decide if a term applies in a given situation. A computer could repeatedly remind students of the relevant definitions and could show them many step-by-step calculations; it could do the routine computation, leaving them free to think about what needs to be done and about the computed results. Second, students have had no previous experience dealing with specific finite examples of the abstract structures about which they are now supposed to reason. It's hard to abstract without a familiar set of reasonably varied examples. A computer could provide access to many examples; it could be a laboratory instrument for experimenting. With it students could quickly gain hands-on experience. These were my hopes for what would eventually become *Exploring Small Groups (ESG)*.

Other mathematicians have stressed how important it is for students in algebra and discrete mathematics to see and work with many examples. In a recent review in the *American Mathematical Monthly,* Professor Nijenhuis, of the University of Pennsylvania, remarks on his disappointment with teaching an abstract algebra class. The difficulty, he says, is the generality of the concepts and the need to dispel the students' feeling that "the subject is just thin air. To make it more concrete, you have to do lots of examples: permutations, Rubik's cube, and what-have-you. But time does not permit that. So, we deal with only a tiny handful of examples. ...[A student] also learns about centers of groups, but how many centers does he get to see?"

Software for Abstract Algebra

When development of *ESG* began I knew of only two earlier uses of computers in undergraduate abstract algebra classes, both of which required that the students learn a new programming language. I wanted to avoid that kind of overhead, so *ESG* is a complete, stand-alone, easy-to-use package requiring no programming. It is menu driven, with on-screen prompts for everything. Others have since experimented with computers in abstract algebra, but there is still very little microcomputer software available for use in such a class. If you consult the latest edition of the mathematics software database created by R. Cunningham and D. Smith, published in the May 1988 *College Mathematics Journal,* you will find that although there is quite a lot of available software supporting undergraduate mathematics instruction, almost none deals with abstract algebra.

Design

ESG was designed to help students visualize some algebraic structures and decompositions and to give them a tool for easily doing many computations so that they can see what it really means for a property to hold. The program uses color and screen layout to help clarify fundamental computations and theorems, and it reminds students of the basic definitions whenever they are used. Its libraries of operations provide many examples for exploration, and the program makes such exploration easy to do. Some of the operations are derived from modular arithmetic and so are concrete and quite ordinary, whereas others are more exotic and represent perhaps the most abstract way of presenting an operation to a student. The program has two principal components. The first does elementary property checking. When students are comfortable with this, they can go on to the second, which does computations with group operations. This component can calculate, among other things, the centers of many groups.

ESG is also intended to be useful to an instructor, both for preparing class material and for classroom demonstrations. With a portable PC and a large color monitor or video projector in a classroom, you can use ESG to demonstrate to a class many things that are not possible or that are too time-consuming using just a blackboard or an overhead projector. An instructor can give larger and more- interesting examples of operations, can run through more-explicit checks of properties showing where things may fail, and can illustrate, in color, difficult ideas such as cosets and quotient groups.

Development

The development of *Exploring Small Groups* was made possible by a contract/grant from IBM's Academic Information Systems division awarded to the College of Arts and Sciences of the University of North Carolina at Chapel Hill. William H. Graves, Professor of Mathematics and Associate Dean of General Education at the time, wrote the grant proposal, organized the campus Courseware Development Project (CDP) when the proposal was approved, and was the chief UNC administrator of the grant. Over the past five years he has been the university's principal champion of the use of computers in education. Under the aegis of the CDP, over forty instructional software packages have been produced. Indeed, the CDP has been so successful that it is now viewed by some as a national model for academic software development.

IBM supplied hardware, software, and funds to hire necessary support staff for the CDP. Faculty developers and programmers generally used IBM XTs, and the student micro labs received standard IBM PCs. CDP staff evaluated programming languages, software development tools, and productivity tools for suitability to the proposed projects, and in some cases they wrote needed graphics software tools. The programming languages used by the various project teams were IBM PILOT, Borland Turbo Pascal, Logitech Modula-2, and IBM Compiled BASIC. In addition, almost everyone involved in the CDP used Microsoft Word as a standard writing tool. Those of us who struggled with the design and construction of programs benefited in many ways from the expertise of both the CDP director, Dr. Margret Hazen, who had much previous experience with CAI, and the instructional designer, Maria Ilgen-Lieth.

Most of the programming on the projects was done by students. In some cases they received credit for a programming practicum, and in other cases they were hired for the summer. The chief CDP technical consultant, Steve Griffin, trained and supervised the student programmers and also did some of the programming.

In the case of *ESG*, the project team consisted of one student programmer and myself. (When the first student graduated, a second came on board.) We met once or twice a week to copy disks, exchange printouts, and discuss modifications or the next section to be worked on. Not surprisingly, it worked best when I had my ideas and/or instructions already printed out for the programmer so that we could go over them together. In the later stages of development, when the program was quite large and it was tedious to quit and later return to the same place, I found it very convenient to write programming notes using Sidekick, a utility from Borland International. Sidekick was loaded first and remained memory-resident while *ESG* was running. Then, whenever I found something that didn't work or that I thought should be changed, I would switch to the Sidekick notepad and write a note to the programmer. I could also import into the note blocks of text from the *ESG* screen display so that the programmer could immediately see to what my note was referring. With two keystrokes, *ESG* would be back running at the point in the program where I had left it. (This was only possible because ESG upon in at mode, not graphics mode.) The programmer met regularly with Steve Griffin for a technical review of progress on the project and occasionally also with the instructional designer. These reviews frequently resulted in useful suggestions for improvements.

Before beginning work on *ESG*, I had played with microcomputers for several years and had used a few instructional programs in some of my classes. Also, I had written small programs in interpreted BASIC and so had a pretty good idea what was technically possible with the IBM PC. *ESG* was written in BASICA and was then compiled with the IBM BASIC Compiler so that it would run much faster. Later we switched to the more flexible and portable Microsoft QuickBASIC. From Steve Griffin and the student programmers I learned more about programming, including compiling and splitting programs into modules. I am quite sure that without the support of the CDP my ideas for *ESG* would not have developed very far. With CDP support, and specifically with the excellent work of two student programmers, *ESG* was eventually developed to commercial standards.

Costs and Rewards

Developing instructional software is expensive. The student programmers spent about 2,000 hours on the development of ESG. At $25 per hour (which includes some overhead costs), that adds up to $50,000. I have no records of the time I spent on the project, but I estimate that it was at least 800 hours. At $40 per hour, that comes to $32,000. I knew when I started that the project would take a lot of time. But other than time not now available for research interests, I did not think involvement in the project had any professional risks for me. Since winning the EDUCOM/NCRIP-TAL award I have certainly gained some recognition in my department, on campus, and nationally in my profession. This has resulted in invitations to speak about and to demonstrate *ESG*. It has not so far produced any noticeable financial rewards, except of course for the award prize money!

The incentives for participation in the project were twofold. First, I received IBM equipment and software for use during program development, with the understanding that if I satisfactorily completed the project,

I would be allowed to keep the equipment in my office and to continue to use it for my research and instruction. Second, if my project resulted in software that was eventually published, I would receive an 80 percent share of the residual royalties received by UNC as holder of the copyright. These conditions were part of the IBM/UNC CDP contract/grant. Professor Graves also negotiated a contract among IBM, UNC, and the publishing company Harcourt Brace Jovanovich to publish the courseware packages that were developed to reasonable commercial standards.

The development work on the *ESG* program and its user's manual would be roughly equivalent, I imagine, to the writing of a one-course junior/senior-level textbook.

Using *ESG*

ESG does not constitute an entire stand-alone course. It is a tool intended to supplement a text and is appropriate for about two-thirds of a typical beginning abstract algebra course. Both a colleague of mine and I have employed it while teaching such a course. We did many classroom demonstrations with *ESG*, and our students experimented with operations and did assigned homework problems with it. We still are testing ways to use it and are constructing exercises for students. No attempt was made to measure the educational effectiveness of introducing *ESG*. However, informal feedback indicates that students found the program easy to use and that they were helped by having many types of examples to explore, examples provided by *ESG*. We are pleased with the effect the program has had on our classes, and both of us plan to use it more extensively the next time we teach this class. There have also been enthusiastic responses from several other schools where *ESG* has been used.

Chapter 4

Development of Teaching Software: Some Hindsights

Richard A. Meiss
Indiana University School of Medicine

Software development requires a thirty-six-hour day. This may help to explain its relative scarcity in the context of medical education, since most other endeavors in the area of medicine likewise devour time as greedily as do a glowing display screen and a well-worn keyboard. In my case, the challenge of exploring a new way of communicating knowledge to medical students won out, at least temporarily, over other academic concerns and has resulted in the development of both some useful software and some useful insights (or hindsights).

The development of *Mechanical Properties of Active Muscle* occurred within a number of related contexts. Examining each of them in turn may, I hope, provide some direction to others who find themselves involved in similar efforts.

The first context is the discipline in which my subject matter finds its home. Physiology, which may be broadly defined as "how living things function," is integral to the study and practice of medicine. It is a science compounded from anatomy, biochemistry, physics, and mathematics, with dashes of engineering and basic biology thrown in. It seeks to provide mechanistic explanations for the way in which the many systems and components of living beings work together to make up a whole functioning organism. Since the many interactions involved are grounded in well-defined physical, chemical, and mathematical principles, the subject lends itself to descriptions that can take the form of mathematical expressions. Often these mathematical formulations can become the basis of a computer simulation of some process or interaction. Computer models have long been used in physiological research to extend the limits of an investigation into inaccessible areas or to predict outcomes not readily apparent. Just as such models can lead to new insights for researchers, they also hold the potential for allowing students to rediscover for themselves many complex processes that are critical to their understanding of physiology. All too often, students view a problem in the context of a textbook description or a traditional lecture and are not able to sort out the important variables in a process and to discover how a change in one area will affect many related functions. The power of computer simulations to pose and answer "what if" questions is such that their value in teaching should be obvious. Unfortunately, several things have worked against making computer simulations accessible to medical students.

First among these is the nature of the simulations themselves. Although the physiological literature abounds with mathematical models addressing numerous topics, most of these simulations have been developed with an eye towards mathematical rigor and numerical precision. As such, they are often cumbersome, slow, idiosyncratic, and have other attributes that make them very poorly suited to teaching students who are unfamiliar with a subject. For a computer simulation to be developed as an effective teaching tool, pedagogical factors and efficient student/machine interfaces must weigh as heavily as does the mathematical correctness of the model in question.

In many cases, elaborate and very powerful computing machinery is needed to realize such simulations. Until now such machinery has been far beyond the resources allocated to the task of teaching. With the advent of the microcomputer as an effective and affordable alternative to the mainframe computer, however, a "cottage industry" has grown up within the discipline of physiology, and a number of teachers have spent a great deal of time developing teaching software based on mathematical models of physiological processes. Most of this work has been done as a sideline to the regular duties of the faculty member, and the software arising from these efforts has been shared on an informal basis. Although much of this software is of excellent quality, the lack of uniform standards (for both hardware and software) has been a stumbling block since the beginning of the efforts. During the course of the development of my own teaching software, I was made aware of a number of other pitfalls, which will be treated in due course.

The software that I developed grew out of the context of a larger project. Realizing the potential value of using computer simulations as teaching tools in Physiology, Dr. R. A. Rhoades, chairman of the Department of Physiology and Biophysics at the Indiana University School of Medicine, decided to seek some outside assistance for a departmental effort in this area. A responsive chord was struck with the IBM Corporation, which agreed to enter into a joint venture and provide computing equipment (IBM PCs) and expert advice. The goal of the project was to construct simulations of laboratory teaching experiments that would extend the laboratory experience of first-year medical students into areas that, for one reason or another, were not readily accessible. I was asked to serve (with Dr. Rhoades) as the codirector of the project. As is often the nature of such academic ventures, the project functioned as a loose association of independent developers of software who shared advice and problems as the need arose. While the intent was to develop software that could be used in other institutions without modification, our primary goal was the teaching of our own students. For this reason, the effort was looked on as an extension of the usual teaching duties, and no special "release time" arrangements were made.

Although the foregoing describes the external context in which my software was developed, my own situation and background must be described to complete the picture. I agreed to become seriously involved in the project for several reasons, some of which are hinted at above. The potential usefulness of the computer as a teaching tool had long intrigued me; I had been using microcomputers in my own research since 1977 and had become a rather adept programmer. Unfortunately, my own laboratory computers lacked any graphics capabilities, and I was unable to work out the implementation of a number of ideas on which I had spent considerable mental effort. When I was presented with the opportunity to have a state-of-the-art graphics engine at my disposal, I decided that I was in a position to invest the time to make a serious attempt at working out some of the ideas that had lain fallow for so long. An important consideration was my academic position. Since I was a tenured full professor, I no longer needed to be heavily concerned with the preoccupations familiar to all who are climbing the academic ladder. I had been teaching physiology for a number of years, and I had a firsthand knowledge of some problem areas related to my teaching and research specialties. Students often had trouble sorting out the mechanical and temporal variables involved in muscle contraction, and a grasp of this subject is a prerequisite for understanding the pumping and self-regulating functions of the heart. The mechanical properties of muscle are well understood and have been described mathematically for many years. All that stood between this raw material and an effective teaching simulation was time — as it turned out, a huge amount of time.

The teaching simulation that was developed as a result of this effort is a set of six programs addressing several related aspects of the contraction of skeletal muscle. All the programs are graphically oriented and are designed for a maximum of student interaction and operational flexibility. Initially they were written in interpreted BASIC, but when the Microsoft QuickBASIC compiler (Version 2.0) became available, all the programs were redone in this language, as were all subsequent revisions. This compiler makes BASIC a very effective development language and enables the production of programs having surprising speed and complexity. Since the compiler can produce executable files that do not depend on a particular implementation of BASIC, the programs have proven to be quite portable among computers using the MS-DOS operating system. A conscious effort was made for all the software developed in the program to run on a "standard" IBM PC with one disk drive, 256 kilobytes of memory, and a color graphics adapter. Several versions of the simulations have been used by our freshman medical students as laboratory exercises. Student evaluation questionnaires were used to provide guidance for revision and improvement.

In its current state of development, the muscle simulation software is finding use in several areas of our educational effort at Indiana University. The primary purpose of our departmental software effort was to provide students with the equivalent of a laboratory experience. As such, the programs were designed for either individual or small-group use, aided by the presence of a laboratory manual and an optional human instructor. In the current year of use in the teaching laboratory, students are using the programs ad lib. They are advised as to the date by which they should have finished with the programs; this date is prior to group conferences in which the students go over their experiences and have any remaining questions clarified. When the software is being used this way, students are free to borrow it to use on either university computers or their own compatible hardware. (The software is copy-protected by the publisher.)

In addition to its primary use, the software has found a second application in the teaching of physiology. The lectures on topics related to muscle in the Human Physiology course are delivered with the aid of commercially available presentation software (IBM PC Storyboard). A personal computer is connected to a video projector and serves the function of a slide projector, with the added features (such as animation) afforded by this medium. The muscle simulation software forms an integral part of the lecture presentation, providing immediate illustration of dynamic processes within the context of the flow of the lecture material. This allows for some immediate reinforcement of concepts that students can later examine at their own convenience.

Throughout our departmental effort in software development, we explored many avenues of publication and distribution of the work being produced. Within our own university system, the "software workshop" approach was tried; some interest was generated, but the word did not spread far beyond the institutional walls. Following this, we set up a booth in the educational exhibits area of the annual meeting of the Federation of American Societies for Experimental Biology (FASEB). The display was designed to allow a large national audience of scientists and educators to have a hands-on experience with the software. *Mechanical Properties of Active Muscle* was included in this presentation. To generate user evaluation and responses, we offered to make evaluation copies of the software available to interested persons; this was not a distribution method per se because we requested that the software not be copied and passed along. We actively solicited comments on user experience and included a detailed questionnaire with each program. Many copies of the programs were sent out in this way, but no evaluation forms were ever returned (there was some telephone contact from a few users). A lesson from this experience was that "free" software appears to carry little impression of its value to the recipient.

Whereas distribution of evaluation copies of the software turned out to be tantamount to a free distribution system, it also pointed out the large amount of time and labor involved in making such a distribution system work well. The most obvious solution to the distribution problem was to interest a commercial publisher in the programs. When we explored this avenue, we found that the usual academic channels that dealt with the college undergraduate and postgraduate market (i.e., textbook publishers) were at something of a loss as to how to publish and distribute teaching software. One suggested possibility was to package the software as ancillary (promotional) material with a textbook; it was apparent that advocates of this approach did not appreciate the special strengths inherent in simulation software. These strengths could be best utilized if there were a careful integration of the textbook material and the simulation software, but the labor involved in supporting a complete textbook with appropriate software promised to be overwhelming, and this approach has not been pursued. Fortunately, our association with IBM Corporation during the course of this venture opened up what proved to be an excellent outlet for the muscle mechanics software (and potentially, for other software as well). Through some key personnel in the IBM organization, contact was made with a publisher of educational software who was experienced in serving the audience for which this software was intended. This publisher, a division of the textbook publishing firm Wadsworth, Inc., was COMPress, of Wentworth, New Hampshire. COMPress proved extremely helpful in providing advice on revising and refining the programs so that they could "pass muster" in a commercial environment, and the publisher had the technical facilities and personnel required to work with an author to assist in the required revisions. The set of programs, under the title *Mechanical Properties of Active Muscle*, is now available from the publisher and from educational software distributors. The current price is $75.00, which includes a backup diskette and the user's manual.

A conservative estimate of the time spent developing and polishing the programs would be on the order of many hundreds of hours; some of this time was spent developing documentation for student use. Refining the software to a commercially acceptable level was perhaps the most time-consuming aspect of the writing, and guidelines provided by the publisher were quite valuable in directing this effort. When the software attained commercial status, the question of copyrights and royalties naturally arose. Pursuant to the agreement with IBM Corporation, the university retained the basic copyright to the work. Royalties were to be shared between IBM and the university, and the author was to be entitled to a portion of the university's share. This appears to have worked satisfactorily. Major revisions of the software are not presently contemplated because the physiological basis of the simulations is very well established scientifically; some further polishing of the presentation may be done in response to user comments, but at this stage (the current version represents a major revision of the original), the life expectancy of the software seems fairly well assured.

A number of issues became apparent during the development of the software. First, the time required to produce clean and bug-free programs was surprisingly great. A colleague referred to his own endeavors in the writing of teaching software as a "black hole of time." Unfortunately, in my case this time came from research activities and occasioned some loss of progress in this area. Second, whereas the writing of textbooks or portions thereof has a secure place in academia, the development of teaching software generally is not recognized as an equivalent scholarly endeavor. Software development is not well integrated into the institutional reward and incentive system; a faculty member desiring to rise in academic rank would not be able to afford the investment of significant time required for this type of software development. Little direct programming assistance was available locally while these programs were being developed, and the personal acquisition of the necessary skills could have taken as much time as did the writing itself. It is worth noting that the overall project did not add many faculty to the ranks of the "computer literate."

Lest this account convey a negative impression, I must hasten to add an affirmation of a generally positive outcome on my part. My programming skills were sharpened, I developed some commercial-quality software that appears to address a real educational need, and I learned some new teaching techniques. The satisfaction of winning the NCRIPTAL award was an obvious positive outcome; even without this, I had the satisfaction of mastering a difficult challenge while adding a further dimension to my teaching experience. As a spin-off from the development effort, I have used modified versions of the programs as classroom teaching tools by integrating them into a "slide show" development and presentation tool (IBM PC *Storyboard*). Perhaps the most telling outcome, however, is the fact that I have a second teaching simulation project now under way, and another one is planned.

Developing *Standing Waves*

Eric T. Lane
University of Tennessee at Chattanooga

Introduction

On the occasion of receiving the 1987 EDUCOM/NCRIPTAL "Best Physics Software, Best Simulation Software" award for *Standing Waves*, I have been asked to write about the history behind the software, the conditions under which it was developed, and the future possibilities for software development.

The Program

Standing Waves creates animated displays of standing and traveling waves and pulses on the screen of an Apple II microcomputer. It may be run by an instructor as a classroom demonstration or by a student in laboratory or for individual study. It demonstrates the basic wave concepts, which include frequency, wavelength, wave velocity, nodes, reflection from a boundary, and superposition. The program uses pulses to illustrate reflection from fixed and free ends. Also included are examples of the algebraic addition and cancellation of traveling waves and pulses. It displays triangular, square, trapezoidal, and Gaussian waves. For each wave, the user may specify the variables of frequency, number of nodes, and fixed or free ends as well as slow or stop motion and superimposed traveling and standing waves and pulses. To gain a unique sense of control over the simulated wave environment, the user may also choose from a number of interesting wave forms stored on the floppy disk or may even design a special wave to display in animation.

History

When I started developing educational software in 1978, people were using microcomputers primarily for experimentation, elementary programming, and some word processing. Little, if any, useful educational software was available for microcomputers, especially not the animation graphics that I recognized as possible on the new (at that time) Apple II microcomputer. Since then, many interactive animated games have been produced, but little in the way of interactive animations has been developed for microcomputers. This is because of the need to develop the programs in machine language. Few people have the combination of a physics background and technical knowledge of machine-language programming, both of which are required for the development of satisfactory interactive science and physics animations.

In the beginning, I found myself alone in the development of this specialized software. Subsequently, I was able to offer my assistance to several other individuals who wanted to develop their own projects. I continue to encourage anyone with the desire to develop good educational software, and I will help in any way that I can.

I undertook several software projects in the early years and have completed most of them, with no help at first. I worked mostly during summers, on weekends, and at night to complete the first few projects. I continue to work summers, etc., without support on the majority of my projects. On a few projects, I have been supported by the Center of Excellence for Computer Applications (CECA) at UTC. They have provided me with some equipment, with software, and, most important, with one-fourth release time for six of the last eight semesters to give me time off from teaching so that I could develop software.

CONDUIT, in Iowa City, has been very helpful and supportive of my work. They have provided me with a pipeline to the real world of publishing. They have also paid for two one-week stays in Iowa City so that I could complete a development project or revision. In addition, the faculty of the Physics Department at UTC has been especially supportive by encouraging my work, by providing an avenue for seminars on my software, and by exchanging classes when I needed to be out of town.

I have been and still am a faculty member with no responsibilities in the computing services organization or in administration. Even so, I continue to help other faculty members and individuals in the community with their computer-related problems. I continue to push for the development and publication of good educational software because I believe that this is the way good instruction can be preserved and instruction as a whole can be improved, through the evolution of the best.

Background

My project is a direct result of my own work. Physics teachers, high school science teachers, and many university, junior college, high school, and grade school students gave me valuable comments and suggestions.

When I decided to develop my software, I was "very technical," having a Ph.D. in Theoretical Physics from Rice University in Houston, Texas, and a wide range of programming experience from 1959 to 1978. Since I began programming microcomputers in 1978 my technical skills in programming have increased considerably. I spent a year in 1985 trying to learn Pascal, to develop transportable programs, but Pascal didn't allow me to get close enough to the machine for the animation programs I wanted to do. Since 1986, I've learned the C language to get closer to machine language for developing the animations. It works.

Motivation

I wanted to demonstrate dynamic physics concepts to my students to help in teaching. I could visualize the looks of understanding on the faces of the students when they saw the moving presentation of electron waves; I saw the blank looks on their faces when I tried to illustrate it on the chalkboard. I saw the need for good microcomputer software. I enjoy programming. I respond to the challenge of creating a new program from a vision of what can be. With my technical background in physics and in programming, I felt that I could make a significant contribution to educational software that few others could make.

I continue to develop expertise on new machines as they come out.

Standing Waves was developed with BASIC to control the menus, text presentation, and branching. The animations, of necessity, used machine language on the 6502 microprocessor. I wrote both the BASIC and the machine-language portions of the program myself. External support was relatively unimportant in the development of *Standing Waves*, since I did most of the work before I received significant support. I would have done the work anyway.

I ordinarily use a single stand-alone personal microcomputer system for software development.

Incentives

No incentives to programming development existed when I started. As far as I can tell, there are still no direct incentives for the production of software. Such incentives as promotion and salary increases are often implied but are never directly stated. Since salary increases are primarily tied to percentage changes in the budget and vary by little more than one percent about the average, little is available for incentive. One percent is not nearly enough to encourage the extensive time and effort necessary to develop a quality piece of software, especially when one considers the long- time learning curve of getting started. Working alone, without help from a computer center or any other sources, I spent five years getting *Standing Waves* to first publication. From my discussions with other developers, I estimate that one can expect it will take from three to five years to publish software, even under more favorable conditions.

Publishing contracts came much later, after I had already developed the program and nearly completed the documentation. Publishers view software at the level of commercial standards and needed changes to suit their standards. That's why it took me so long to develop the software. I wanted to do the best that I could with what I had to work with, the Apple II microcomputer.

In 1984, the Center of Excellence for Computer Applications was established at the University of Tennessee at Chattanooga by the state governing board. Based on competitive proposals, it gives some support to faculty developers in the form of $2,000 grants (maximum for each faculty member) per semester for release time, equipment, travel, expenses, etc. The emphasis of CECA is now on artificial intelligence, assistance for the handicapped, computer-assisted instruction ($20,000 budgeted for the entire faculty in 1987–88), and mainframe computer support.

Equipment

In developing my software, I have purchased several Apple II and several Macintosh microcomputers along with memory boards, and other equipment. These have been and still are the primary development systems that I use.

In 1984, when the Lupton Foundation provided interest-free loans to purchase microcomputers for university use, I purchased my first Macintosh system. The same year, CECA loaned the Physics Department a Lisa microcomputer to facilitate the development of software for the Macintosh, which is now coming to fruition. In 1985, Acorn Computer Corporation, a British company, provided the Physics Department with a BBC Acorn microcomputer on which to develop animation software. The *Standing Waves* package is now available for the Acorn. In 1986, Digital Equipment Corporation provided the Physics Department with two DEC Rainbow microcomputers and other equipment for which software is now being developed. I would not have been able to complete the Acorn or the DEC projects without the equipment those companies provided.

I initiated each of the above requests for equipment with written proposals and specific objectives. I also submitted proposals to IBM and to Apple for equipment, from whom I got no response. Most equipment was either loaned to the department or given to the university.

As a direct result of the EDUCOM/NCRIPTAL award, IBM, Apple, and AT&T all indicated great interest in supplying me with equipment to continue software development. As of April 1988, Apple has provided over $20,000 worth of equipment to convert software to the Macintosh. IBM has provided me with a manual.

I also do consulting work with CONDUIT and with NCASE, the National Center for Aquatic Safety Education.

Cost of Development

I estimate that I spent about 2,000 hours a year for five years; 10,000 hours at $20 an hour totals $200,000 for the development of *Standing*

Waves and the documentation. In comparison, if a professional software development company were asked to produce a comparable software package, it is estimated that they would charge $250,000 minimum.

Other direct costs to the project were equipment, supplies, software (assembly language), telephone calls, reproduction costs, travel to Iowa City (three times at my own expense, twice at theirs), and secretarial help.

Risk Factors

I already had tenure. So I wasn't worried about losing my job over software development. Promotion was a different matter. It has been observed that to get a promotion at UTC, much research and publication is needed. When I began my work, it was questionable whether software development and publication would satisfy the criteria for promotion. I continued because I had a vision of what good software could become. Standards have not changed, but the publication of good software by myself and others on campus has now allowed these items to be accepted for promotion considerations.

Microcomputers are still not supported at a level comparable with mainframes when relative contributions are taken into account.

Legal Considerations

I hold the copyright to my software.

I do all my critical development work at home on my own microcomputers on my own time to avoid legal questioning.

I get 15 percent royalties for my published software, which I plow back into the development effort. I give away much of my work as public domain or as free disks, to get the animations into the hands of the physics and science teachers who can make use of it.

Legal issues? I expect that others will want to use my animation modules in their own programs. I intend to encourage such use by faculty developers at no charge for nonprofit use. I expect a 50 percent share of the royalties on any profit made through such use. If developers don't wish to share their profits with me, I hope that they will at least place my name in a prominent place so that others will recognize the quality of my work. I do not intend to pursue any users of my modules through legal channels, since I want as many people as possible to learn from my work and since I have many, many ideas that can yield more profit than would legal battles.

Copy Protection Issues

I do not argue with my publisher about copy-protecting my programs because they know their business better than I. But I don't intend to copy-protect any software that I distribute personally. I write it for people to use, for them to get the benefit of my experience and teaching ability. The more the better, as far as I am concerned.

I feel that society provides me with more than enough comforts and necessities. I would prefer to spend my time and effort doing my utmost to improve that society rather than trying to get rich at its expense. Besides, if you have a quality product, you're going to make enough money along with everyone else.

Focus of Software

Standing Waves and similar programs target only a small portion of the body of knowledge of physics. My animations contribute to the student's understanding of those concepts that require an appreciation of dynamic behavior. Textbook pictures and chalkboard drawings fail to capture the essence of these action-oriented concepts. Microcomputers, with animation, can display such concepts easily, quickly, and efficiently.

Although a movie can display a fixed set of moving images and so improve understanding, the student has no control over the display and has a difficult time transferring his knowledge to the real world. Microcomputers, with their interactive capabilities, allow the student to explore a set of concepts in an artificial world that clarifies and highlights important ideas. After experiencing the microcomputer-mediated phenomena, the student knows better what to look for and is better prepared to react properly to real-world phenomena.

I want to use the microcomputer in the way that the student responds to it best and not try to make it be all things to all students. This means using it as a complement or supplement to class lecture, laboratory, and individual study, not as a replacement.

The microcomputer has many valuable capabilities that are not yet being utilized. People exhibit different learning styles. A microcomputer can be programmed to recognize these. For example, if a student begins to exhibit tiredness and decreased learning efficiency, the microcomputer can be programmed to suggest a rest and to come back later. It can also present material in the style most beneficial to the user, from extensive text for a student who needs lots of explanation to simulated worlds to explore for the action-oriented student. I want to develop these and other ideas to the benefit of students and ultimately of faculty who use my programs.

On the continuum of published materials, I view my animations as little pamphlets that illustrate a particular idea or concept. The highly visual nature of the animations makes them appealing to the whole range of students, from grade school to graduate school. Only the words used in the explanations and in the documentation limit the programs to the range of pre-college and undergraduate students. With support, I or others can revise the words to make them appropriate for grade-school students or university graduate students.

I would very much like to develop programs for use by grade-school students, using words at their reading level. I don't have the necessary background in educational theory and practice. Is anyone out there interested in working with me?

I don't see my animations being used primarily by specialists. I developed my earlier programs and continue to develop programs to run on the lowest-level microcomputer that is capable of displaying them properly. This maximizes the chance that they will be more widely distributed to students of all classes and ages, and to the general population who want to know something about science.

I view practical education as a triangle consisting of research, textbook writing, and teaching in practice. I see program development in the middle of the triangle. It has much in common with research, since one never really knows what will come out of a new project. Quality program development requires the dedication and perseverance of the textbook writer. And it requires an intimate understanding of students' difficulties — to know what is worth doing and how to arrange it in a useful package.

Presentation

I performed very extensive tests on the software to determine the best way to present the material, to control the animations, and to reduce possible misconceptions. During a three-year period, I asked just about every student, faculty member, and visitor to the university to try out my software. I asked them to catch bugs in the software, to tell me about inaccuracies in the text and documentation, and to suggest how to improve the presentation of the material.

I had already had several years experience in designing user-friendly software for the HP-2000 minicomputer. I was aware of the problems that the new user faces in dealing with a fresh piece of software. I knew that only through extensive and thorough testing would I develop a high-quality product.

I consider quantitative testing for educational effectiveness of my software to be a highly significant issue. I have not undertaken such testing only because of my lack of proper background and time. I have presented my work to many individuals and at educational meetings. In each case I have offered to help in any way that I could to encourage quantitative testing. To my knowledge, no educational research project has yet involved my software. I would be more than willing to help in any way I can to facilitate such research, for example by preparing special versions of my programs or incorporating record keeping.

Unfortunately, I do not have the time to develop the background necessary for valid quantitative educational testing. I feel strongly that I must concentrate in the area that I do best: animation graphics. Few people have the theoretical background and the programming knowledge to produce good real-time animations on the microcomputer. My animations show the tremendous possibilities of dynamic, interactive presentation of information. It's a wide-open field with great promise.

In Practice

Microcomputer programs offer a distillation of the best that a teacher can present. Their interactive nature makes them the next best thing to the educational ideal of a log with a teacher at one end and the student at the other. I believe that software will evolve so that the best will sift to the top, both in the educational environment and in the marketplace. This will provide society with a valuable feedback loop: in the long run, the best teacher/programmers will get their software in the schools. Students will increasingly benefit as high-quality software is developed and as the principles for optimizing good teaching are recognized and utilized.

One sidelight that might be noted here is that in at least two cases that I know of, my animations have been critical in the recognition by other developers of the possibilities of real-time animation on a microcomputer. They have said things like, "I didn't know it could be done until I saw your stuff. Then I went out and did something similar on a project that I was working on." Perhaps my work will plant the seeds for better-quality software development in other areas as well.

I use my software in my teaching at every opportunity, as demonstrations in the classroom, as a supplement to experiments in the laboratory, and as out-of-class assignments for individual study. I've used the software in the wave sections of the general science classes, in the introductory noncalculus physics classes, the introductory calculus-based physics classes, the intermediate physics electricity and magnetism classes, and the modern physics, relativity, and quantum mechanics classes. In each case, the students were able to see the important concepts better than they ever had with class discussions, textbook presentations, or chalkboard drawings. Only movies have the capability to show such concepts with equal clarity. But movies must optimize the presentation for a particular, rather narrow level. Only microcomputers allow the interactive flexibility to illustrate the significant concepts to the wide range of students that I show my software to, and to customize the presentation for each group.

The students also have access to my software through the campus microcomputer laboratory that is open during normal working hours five days a week and by special arrangement. This is especially valuable to education students, who rarely get to the physics building. They use my animations in their presentations to high school students as part of their practice teaching.

Many of my colleagues have used my software in their teaching, not only in the physics department but also in the art, music, chemistry, education, engineering, and other departments.

I've also given many workshops, both in this country and abroad, to encourage the use and the development of good educational software.

Software Lifetime

The useful life of software is apparently determined by the life of the microcomputer it runs on. The Apple II has shown surprising longevity because of its strong acceptance in high schools and grade schools. The large pool of Apple software will encourage the manufacturer to continue to produce machines with the capability of running the old software. I estimate that the Apple II or clones will still be around for at least another ten to fifteen years.

In any event, I am already revising *Standing Waves* for the Macintosh, the IBM PC, the PS/2, and others. It is already running on the BBC Acorn, a British machine similar to the Apple II.

I have in mind significant improvements for presentation of the material, expansions of the examples, and adaptations to use of the mouse or other pointing devices to improve the user interface. As further developments in microcomputer technology take place, I intend to use them in producing ever higher quality software consistent with the idea that it be available to the maximum number of people.

As *Standing Waves* evolves over the next few decades, it will take on forms that will make it unrecognizable to present-day users. Only the basic concepts will remain the same. Among other changes, I hope to incorporate personality-adaptive programming techniques, artificial intelligence procedures that optimize the presentation for the personality of the user.

My software has been used in high schools, colleges, and universities all over the world. I estimate that several hundred copies have been sold worldwide.

I don't plan to make much money from educational software development. Educators have little money, and so far, most of the computer budget has gone for hardware. This will change as microcomputer prices decrease and as people realize that software is part of the overall system for educational delivery.

Future Publishing

The most promising vehicle for distributing software are the telephone networks that are springing up all over the country. Once a method of royalty allocation has been developed, people will be able to try out demonstration versions of new software on the network before purchasing the complete version, either directly off the net or through mail order or from local dealers. Once this becomes the accepted method of distributing software, educational materials will be available to anyone who can get access to a network, which will be most everyone with a telephone and a television set.

Kinko's Academic Courseware Exchange also has a good idea: keep only one master copy of the software and documentation on the premises. When a customer wants to purchase a package, copy the software onto a new disk and photocopy the documentation. Records are kept to assure proper royalty distribution.

Software Use

Standing Waves was designed primarily for use by individual students in study projects or in the physics laboratory. It turned out to be even more useful in the classroom for demonstration. Even though it is quite difficult for everyone in a fifty-student class to see the small television screen, the students usually sit riveted to their seats during the presentation. (Riveted may sound a little strong, but you will see that it is an accurate descriptor if you come to one of my demonstrations.) I know that I'm getting across to the students because I often hear comments like, "I really didn't understand those ideas before, but after seeing Dr. Lane's demonstration, I can really see what's going on." (As an interesting sidelight, a chemistry instructor told me of a student who suffers from dyslexia. The student told him that for the first time he understood the concepts because he could see what was going on at the same time that it was being explained.)

We need a microcomputer with a large-screen projector to use in the classroom on a daily basis. We need the large screen because my classes usually number at least fifty. I know that I could easily develop problem solutions, simple demonstrations, class interaction exercises, and many other ways to use the in-class microcomputer on a daily basis. I have done this for the smaller advanced physics courses that I teach, including thermodynamics, relativity, electricity, and modern physics. I feel it would make my classes more effective. I would also be encouraged to put all my class notes on the microcomputer text processor. Thus, the notes would

be available to students who miss a class for some reason. In-class micro
computers would also allow the weaker students to catch difficult concepts more easily. This in turn would allow the class as a whole to move at
a more uniform and faster pace. With effective organization supported by
in-class microcomputers and other modern technology, I estimate that we
could introduce about 50 percent more material in the regular class, or
the students would have to spend 30 percent less time studying the same
material we now teach. For example, York College, in Queens, New York,
uses such a system in everyday lecture. When I presented my work there,
in March 1987, it felt great to be able to use the microcomputer as an
extension of the regular chalkboard, with dynamic illustrations ... a real
electronic chalkboard.

With large numbers of microcomputers available at all times, we could
automate testing and problem grading. This would increase the amount of
time available for class discussion as well as improve student performance by requiring weekly or even daily testing. Some universities are
already experimenting with such systems. They don't presently do as well
as they could because appropriate software has not yet been developed to
take advantage of the many real capabilities of microcomputers.

Advice for hardware vendors: Students grow up to be consumers. The
hardware that they use in high school and college is what they will be
most familiar with when the time comes to purchase their own. Brand
loyalty has a significant effect on buyer behavior.

Support of educational software development contributes in three
ways. One, the more direct support given to faculty developers, the more
high-quality software is developed. Two, just as books have served in the
past, software is the reference medium of the future. It will provide the
amplifying feedback loop for improving the distribution of quality teaching. Three, individual faculty members will improve through their efforts
to develop good software.

Needs for the Future

We need direct and continuous support for faculty software development. We shouldn't have to beg for small sums of money to get release
time to do software development. We need the support of several full-time
programmers to help faculty with their projects. The faculty have plenty of

good ideas that could ultimately improve the university through better reputation, more students, more money from the students, etc.

Personally, I want to push for a microcomputer software development laboratory to support faculty all over campus. My efforts have already gained us five different types of microcomputers. I expect to obtain at least five more as a direct result of the EDUCOM/NCRIPTAL award.

The university environment could become a center for the production of the highest-quality educational software in the world. As its reputation grows, it would attract young, creative developers who would grow up with the new technology, producing new and innovative ways to deliver education not only to university students but also to the mass of poorly educated people in the city, county, state, and world. This would produce a synergistic effect; the better educated the populace becomes, the more industry would be attracted to move into such areas, thus improving the overall quality of life.

Future Plans

Microcomputers offer immediate feedback. For all their other advantages — such as good color graphics, animation, high-speed calculation — I feel that the concept of feedback will prove critical in the long-term use of microcomputers in education.

I want to work toward using that feedback to advantage. I have spent most of my life studying feedback systems in an effort to understand human behavior. Some simple principles have come out of this study, such as quasistable state formation for strongly interacting amplifying feedback systems. I feel that these principles can also directly apply to the interaction of a person with a computer in the appropriate situations.

I foresee the use of these principles in the design of very powerful educational computer programs, such as Personality Adaptive programs. PA programs would detect the user's personality type — for example, anxious or aggressive — and would present material appropriate to his needs — detailed explanation, free exploration of the phenomena, or reassurance. These programs would also look for fatigue effects and would suggest that the user go on to something else when his learning efficiency drops below some threshold. Many simple, basic educational principles, such as distributed learning, closure, etc., can be implemented in computer software, thus improving the overall educational environment.

Using these and other already known principles, I expect a break-through in computer interaction that will, within the next ten years, revolutionize computer-mediated instruction as we know it!

Probabilities

It is said that the ideal learning situation is a log with a teacher at one end and the student at the other. The microcomputer can give us this ideal. By providing a medium for recording and maintaining good teaching procedures, computers allow the evolutionary selection process to operate successfully, choosing the best presentations in each generation of software production. Computers also allow each generation to build on the successes of the previous generation. Thus we now have an amplifying feedback mechanism that will encourage the development of good educational software. And the software will be around long enough to find its niche in the educational environment.

We must take care with this feedback mechanism because such amplifying feedback has no will of its own. If it is allowed to grow without guidance, we cannot predict where it will end up. Without guidance, it probably won't end up where we want it to. We must have stabilizing feedback as well. The EDUCOM/NCRIPTAL award program is one such stabilizing influence. By recognizing those software packages that come closest to the goals that we set for good educational material, the awards provide a target that software developers can work toward to generate the highest-quality products possible.

Conclusion

Today, we are on the forefront of a revolution in educational technology. Microcomputers offer the graphics presentation and interactive capabilities to generate totally new ways to teach effectively and to learn effectively. The support given to educational software developers, such as the EDUCOM/NCRIPTAL award winners will determine the rate and the direction of this revolution.

Availability

Standing Waves is available for the Apple II, II+, IIe, IIc, and IIgs for $75.00 from CONDUIT and is available for use on networks and for large-class or campuswide use. CONDUIT also publishes the related programs, *Group Velocity* and *Animation Demonstration*. CONDUIT, a nonprofit educational software publisher located at the University of Iowa, has been publishing high school and college educational software since 1976 and has over one hundred microcomputer packages listed in their catalog. To order these packages, or to get a free catalog, write CONDUIT, Room 4557, Oakdale Hall, University of Iowa, Oakdale, IA 52319, or telephone 319-335-4100.

The Would-Be Gentleman: A Historical Simulation of the France of Louis XIV

Carolyn Chappell Lougee
Stanford University

and

Michael P. Carter
Apple Computer, Inc.

The Would-Be Gentleman simulation addresses a problem basic to teaching social history: the large-scale and long-term processes that social historians now consider the heart of the past are often difficult for undergraduate students to comprehend. Although the vital and flourishing research in our field over the past twenty-five years has given us important new ways of understanding these processes, it has not made teaching them any easier. Fluctuations and trends in demographic indices, market prices, interest rates, weather, and popular uprisings are too abstract to engage students easily; students often find such processes so remote from their own experience that they have little interest in understanding how they work. The same could be said of other unfamiliar features of the past such as patronage networks, court societies, and definitions of prestige or status in a hierarchical social structure. For these reasons, social history is often more difficult to teach than political history, which can pin its narrative both to identifiable persons and to discrete events.

The Would-Be Gentleman shows how abstract social processes shaped the experiences of an individual during a given period in the history of France. In the simulation, a student adopts the persona of such an individual and plays the "game" over the course of a semester while reading class material and participating in class discussions. The simulation begins in September 1638, shortly after the birth of the future Sun King, Louis XIV. It continues until September 1715, when Louis dies. In the intervening seventy-seven years, two generations of the Marin family attempt to raise the fortunes and status of their family. Students become intimately involved in the family's affairs and learn to cope with the long-term processes while seeking to advance as far as possible. Response to the simulation has been quite favorable: not only have students used it in conjunction with classwork to good effect, but it also won the EDUCOM/NCRIPTAL Best Humanities Software Award for 1987 and took second place in the 1987 *Wheels for the Mind* National Software Contest.

Developing the Project

When we began developing the simulation, no educational software adequately addressed these problems in the field of social history. We needed something that would complement the course syllabus and readings, making the abstract ideas and remote historical facts more immediate and accessible to students. Several years earlier, in 1978, Michael P. Carter, whose work as a historian focused on Revolutionary France, had developed an economic game, *The Old Regime*, that showed promise as a foundation for a more comprehensive simulation.

Dr. Carter, then director of systems development for Stanford University's Academic Information Resources, assisted with *The Would-Be Gentleman* and shared in the prize money along with Professor Carolyn Chappell Lougee and programmers and coordinators of the Stanford Faculty Author Development (FAD) project team.

This project team was vital to the creation of the simulation. Although FAD did not offer tangible incentives to the software developers, it did focus on removing *dis*-incentives that might have stifled ideas or frustrated initiative. Stanford's program was funded in part by a grant from Apple Computer, Inc., and operated out of the Office of the Vice-Provost for Academic Computing and Information Systems. It sought to ensure that members of the faculty received the hardware, software, design, and programming support they needed to make instructional computing projects practical. The grant from Apple was a no-strings-attached gift earmarked for support of courseware development and delivery on campus; there were no caveats that might have influenced our choices.

Based on the average costs proposed in the Introduction to this volume, our overall cost for developing *The Would-Be Gentleman* might be about $50,000. Professor Lougee was an experienced user of mainframe computers for statistical data analysis and had some experience with an IBM personal computer — used mostly as an "electronic typewriter" — but had no experience with the Macintosh computer or with higher-level programming languages. Fortunately, the professional and student programmers, designers, and team leaders of the project team were able to help in this respect. *The Would-Be Gentleman* was written in Pascal on an Apple Lisa computer for the Apple Macintosh, where it continues to live happily. The next courseware effort that the team makes will probably be different, rather than a port of the same simulation to a different computer.

We distribute *The Would-Be Gentleman* for seven dollars per copy (plus handling) through the Kinko's Academic Courseware Exchange on a royalty-free basis. As a matter of campus policy, copyright is held jointly by the author and Stanford University's Board of Trustees; the policy covers software authorship substantially supported by university resources (in this case, programmers). No warranties or liabilities are assumed with the distribution of the software.

Though it would be inaccurate to say that working on such a project *necessarily* entailed a high professional risk, it is true that few junior members of the faculty were encouraged to join the Faculty Author Development project because no assurances could be made as to how their efforts might be viewed by their colleagues in the promotion process. Professor Lougee was a senior member of the faculty and an associate dean of the school during the developmental process, so this was not a serious concern in her case. Fortunately, since the project's completion, there have been some indications that original work in the area of instructional technology is starting to receive peer recognition and favorable consideration as a measure of a scholar's standing in his or her discipline. For future projects of this sort it would be useful if Stanford could better encourage courseware development by providing faculty members with release time and with money to pay student researchers and programmers directly.

The finished product was quite polished, certainly meeting semicommercial standards, if not commercial ones, but commercial rewards were not the main reason the work was started. Professor Lougee's motivation for beginning the work was largely intangible — the desire to improve the teaching of social history, to make social history seem more relevant and vital to undergraduates. Fitting the simulation into the spectrum defined by the two extremes of textbook development and scholarly research is difficult, since it encompasses a little of both. The simulation required substantial amounts of original research to develop the content materials and extensive work on the necessary algorithms to implement historical models in a pedagogical situation. Yet the outcome, the simulation itself, is clearly an attempt to make that research and those models widely available in a format suitable for use along with classroom instruction.

Does it do what we intended? So far, the answer seems to be yes. In student reviews, as well as in testing in Professor Lougee's own classes and in those of colleagues at other schools, the simulation has gotten very favorable responses. But we have not tried to quantify such responses; the evidence of its effectiveness is anecdotal, obvious in the way that the students behave in the classes in which it is used. Since higher education seldom measures itself otherwise (witness the prevalence of student-authored course reviews, letters to promotion committees from alumni, and so forth), it seems unlikely that the community will respond with particular interest to purported quantitative measures of educational effectiveness.

How the Simulation Works

The simulation begins in 1638, with the player receiving the opening screen shown in figure 1.

The simulation confronts each player with 154 "decision points" (fall and spring of each calendar year). The player's character, Denis Marin (after 1676, his son Jean-François Marin de Mérinville), makes appropriate investment, management, and personal decisions, seeking prestige and the highest possible social standing by the simulation's end in 1715. He receives a steady stream of correspondence about economic and political opportunities, risks, windfall gains, and unexpected losses resulting from circumstances beyond his control.

> It is September 1638. The kingdom celebrates the birth of Louis le Dieudonné (the gift of God), first son of Louis XIII and Anne of Austria. Circumstances everywhere are not so joyous, however. In Normandy you, Denis Marin, have just lost your father, a bourgeois of Rouen. At age 30, you assume leadership of the Marin family, which for two generations has been moving away from its peasant origins toward the notability.
>
> From your father you inherit an office of auditeur in the Chamber of Accounts of Rouen, which is valued at £21,000. You also inherit £5054 in cash and 42 hectares of cultivable land near Chateauvallon. Use these assets to the best of your ability. If you are shrewd and manage your assets well, you may increase your family's wealth and prestige during the lifetime of Louis le Dieudonné.
>
> As you set out in the world to make your fortune, we wish you well, recalling the words penned two years ago by Pierre Corneille, friend and compatriot, for LE CID:
>
> "A vaincre sans péril, on triomphe sans gloire."
> "When there is no peril in the fight, there is no glory in the triumph."
>
> (To start the simulation, press the button on the mouse.)

Figure 1.

Marin may buy or sell land, venal offices (for 25,000 *livres* he can become honorary secretary of the king), textile shares, leases (contracts to collect indirect taxes), or *rentes* (annuities). Different investments reflect seventeenth-century economic realities and, consequently, differing probabilities for profit. For example, the potential profits from leases exceed those of land speculation, but are much riskier. Textiles, though less volatile than leases, remain vulnerable to occasional market collapses. *Rentes* perform steadily but are subject both to market fluctuations and to the vagaries of royal penury, as when the king levies an onerous surtax on them. Thus the student must know the short- and long-term potential of the various investments before deciding which makes sense at any particular time.

As a landowner, Marin has three options: to let his acreage in return for cash rents, rents in kind, or sharecropping. The weather makes the quantity of each fall's harvest uncertain, so the amount of grain received as rent and its market value fluctuate, which determines the relative profitability of each option. Profitability evens out over seventy-seven years but can differ greatly in a given year. Marin benefits or suffers accordingly from his choices. He can immediately sell grain he receives as rent in kind or as crop shares, or he can store it to sell later when scarce supplies might drive the price up. Speculation can net a handsome profit if prices rise before spoilage reduces stocks, but prices can fall too.

Marin's personal decisions include choosing a wife, having children, finding a protector, making a will, and seeking titles of nobility. The marriage "market" presents Denis, or later Jean-François, with information on the personal characteristics, family status, and dowry of from four to six available young ladies. Marin seeks a wife who can bring him fortune and connections, but he must observe the age's proprieties carefully. If he foolishly courts a woman whose status exceeds his own, her humiliating refusal will so shame him that no family will entertain his courtship proposal again for several years. Once married, Denis and Jean-François begin to have progeny, which affects both their family's future and annual living costs. The simulation reflects differing reproductive experiences between the first and second of these seventeenth-century generations. In the first generation, children begin to arrive one year after the marriage and arrive regularly at twenty-four- to thirty-month intervals. In the second generation, children arrive only if requested, since (as recent demographic studies have revealed) the French elite began practicing birth control then. In both generations, children die at Old Regime rates (25 percent in the first year, another 25 percent by the age of twenty).

A player's investments and social standing over the course of the seventy-seven years depend directly on his "protector." The protectors for the first generation are the financial/political figures who dominated the early years of Louis XIV's reign: Cornuel, Particelli, Mazarin, Fouquet, and Colbert. Marin must meet the prerequisites for acceptance into one of their clientele networks (usually success with some investment, a wealth minimum, or a certain status ranking) or face some heavy liability each year (a monetary fine, a harvest failure, or a confiscation). Once accepted, he enjoys a series of windfall profits but must bail out into another coterie if his protector seems about to fall — a tricky maneuver to accomplish, as changes of allegiance were in the seventeenth century. The second Marin generation must ally itself with one of the principal factions at court: those centering on Madame de Maintenon, the Duke of Burgundy, and the Dauphin. Each has its own prerequisites for inclusion and its own rewards of membership. As in the first generation, not belonging to one or the other coterie severely affects Marin's finances and prestige.

The objective of the simulation is to raise prestige, so seeking titles, not merely money, becomes the heart of the exercise. Successful investments did not directly translate into prestige under the Old Regime, nor do they in the simulation. Only by converting money into land and land into nobility can Marin translate his fortune into status. Status, measured in the exercise on an artificial index of 0-100, is most easily achieved by acquiring titles (*vicomte, comte, marquis*). The simulation displays two indices: wealth (expressed in *livres*) and status (expressed on the 100-point scale); wealth alone does not matter at the end of the game.

Student Responses to the Simulation

The instructor's manual that Professor Lougee wrote to accompany the program described not only the basic premise of the simulation but also her own experiences during its development and testing. The following section is adapted from Professor Lougee's manual:

Though the simulation may sound dry and technical, its whimsy makes it fun for students to play. Chateauvallon, the Marin estate, is also the name of the French television saga that imitates "Dallas." The names of the three successive heads of the Marin family progress from plain to extravagant — Denis Marin, Jean-François Marin de Mérinville, Hyacinthe-Florent Marin de Mérinville — suggesting the increasing refinement, even frivolousness, of the higher reaches of the French social hierarchy. The correspondence reproduces verbatim certain colorful letters actually sent by members of Louis XIV's court. For example:

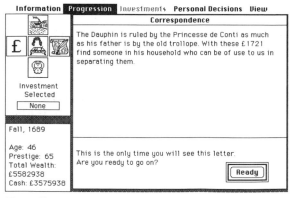

Figure 2.

In my class, part of the simulation's value was as an ice-breaker, stimulating dialogue among students independent of the professor. As I walked to the first class meeting after students had begun to work with the simulation, I could hear from down the hall excited accounts of vicarious experiences they had had in Louis XIV's France. One student arrived late because a group of his friends at the dorm had been using his Macintosh to "play the game" when he needed to print out his homework. In class discussion, someone would often interject, "Hey, I know her!" when the name of a potential bride or of a person mentioned in the letters came up. This amusing and interactive computerized exercise helped them establish a stronger personal identification with the subject than they typically would through reading alone; in a sense, it made their coursework a living historical experience.

We have tested the simulation twice in sophomore/junior-level seminars at Stanford University; it could also appropriately be used in graduate-level courses on the seventeenth century. Because it imparts substantial technical information and requires several weeks to play, it is probably inappropriate for freshman European survey courses. It has, however, been used effectively in more-focused freshman seminars. A colleague who used the simulation at a liberal arts college in a freshman seminar found it "an enormous success."

> The students couldn't stop talking about their computer experiences. Initially they commiserated with each other over their lack of success at improving their positions in the world. Then they began to share insights into the keys to success and failure in the game. This discussion led to questions about early modern society and an examination of differences in mentality between seventeenth-century France and twentieth-century America

In my ten-week sophomore/junior-level seminar on the France of Louis XIV, I distributed the simulation to students at the first meeting, with no instructions other than how to use a Macintosh. Students were expected to work on the simulation each week and turn in their best "1715 screen" — which reported their status at the simulation's end — at each class meeting. The course's readings proceeded week by week through the topics integral to the simulation: rural economics, demography, the structure of the court, royal finance, status representations, popular revolts, and so on. When students applied primary and secondary readings about each aspect of the France of Louis XIV to the simulation, they understood why the choices available had certain consequences. As they came to understand why these consequences differed from those of twentieth-century America, their scores in the simulation improved.

Indeed, understanding the difference between past and present consequences of similar actions was the overall intent of this teaching tool. When they acted from twentieth-century motivations rather than from seventeenth-century assumptions, students fell neatly into the traps set for them. A common way of losing the game was to arrive at 1715 with wealth and high status but without an heir. Students explained in these cases that they had chosen not to have any children in the second generation because "kids are so expensive!" Words to reflect on in the 1980s, surely, but not an attitude any responsible family-builder in the seventeenth century would have had.

Grasping the central lesson of the simulation — that wealth was not as directly connected to status/prestige under the Old Regime as it typically is in American society today — sometimes came slowly. In the second week of the course one especially earnest student came to my office to tell me that "there is a bug in your program." I was delighted to have his help in identifying flaws to correct. He proceeded to explain the "bug": his wealth kept going up, but his status index kept going down. This he considered "unfair." I explained to him that it might look like a bug or unfairness to twentieth-century eyes but that if he learned to think like a seventeenth-century person, he would understand why it was happening. (He had in fact been making money from leases, which were lucrative but somewhat disreputable in the seventeenth century. Each purchase of a lease therefore costs the player status points in the simulation.) Throughout the course, I required students to find patterns in the consequences of their choices and to understand and use them for interpreting a society far different from our own.

The students' immersion in twentieth-century realities had another unexpected outcome in the early weeks of the simulation's use, which we had to move swiftly to correct. Several students "broke the bank" rather early on, attaining status 99 and posts as First Gentleman of the King's Bedchamber. This was, of course, not faithful to seventeenth-century experience, so I asked them how they had done it. Simple: they knew that if they waited long enough, harvests would fail and grain prices would skyrocket, so they simply hoarded their grain until that happened — forty, fifty, sixty years if necessary. Knowing seventeenth-century conditions well, I had never thought of this strategy and so had not provided historically accurate obstacles to this outlandish outcome. We added rats (a spoilage factor that accelerates with the number of seasons one holds on to one's grain) and peasant rebellions (popular confiscations of grain hoards when harvest failure deprives the local community of sustenance). By the time students did their readings on peasant rebellions, they understood why long-term speculation on grain was impossible in the seventeenth century.

Fiction, Reductionism, and Future Challenges

Even with these adjustments, the simulation is not perfectly calibrated. Nor does it perfectly represent seventeenth-century experience. The protagonist adopts the name and some biographical details of a man, Denis Marin, who was among the clients of the financier Cornuel. Real too are the offices on sale and their prices, the individuals composing the various coteries, the events that altered fortunes or protectors' power, and the range within which agricultural production and prices oscillated. But of course the simulation itself creates a fiction: the open-ended decision making combines historically valid fragments into wholly novel situations. So is the simulation teaching history at all? Even more open to question is the central device of the simulation: the prestige index, which quantifies the unquantifiable. Estimations of prestige in any society are highly subjective and draw on many tangible and intangible elements. How can one legitimately reduce this subjectivity and complexity to a crude numerical scale?

Two considerations may speak to these questions of fiction and reductionism. What students learn by referring to the index is not the particular numerical designations that the index artificially attaches to offices and titles but rather the underlying principles of Old Regime stratification: the suspicion of new wealth, the importance of land as a bridge from wealth to social standing, the power of titles in a formally hierarchical society. Moreover, the simulation does not stand alone but is used with readings that present the actual operation of the various facets of seventeenth-century life. The simulation personalizes and brings into focus for students the historical realities they find in primary and secondary written sources.

As it stands, the simulation's "life" should be fairly long. Neither the model nor the content is likely to become dated in the foreseeable future. What seems most likely to limit its future usefulness is the rapid change in microcomputer environments. It presently uses the standard Macintosh interface, an interface that will probably cease to be acceptable to the average university student within a few generations.

So far we have distributed over a thousand copies through the Kinko's Academic Courseware Exchange. We hope eventually to have the courseware integrated into the book publishing distribution circuit, whether in modules or in complete series. Other campuses can purchase it for seven dollars per copy at any Kinko's Copy Shop, by contacting Kinko's at 800-235-6919 (in California, 800-292-6640), or by writing Kinko's at 255 West Stanley Avenue, Ventura, CA 93001. For technical information, contact Academic Information Resources at Stanford University, Stanford, CA 94305.

Next on our agenda is the job of converting this time-specific simulation into a generic template that others can adapt to various times and places by substituting the appropriate categories, data, parameters, and special features to a different historical context, without having to write *all* the algorithms and formulae from scratch. One such conversion has already been completed: *The Would-Be Dvorianin*, created for seventeenth-century Russia by Dr. Carolyn Pouncy of the Russian Research Center at Harvard University. Just as Professor Lougee's simulation rested on the shoulders of Dr. Carter's *The Old Regime*, we hope that such a generic template will allow others to stand on our shoulders and build new and different simulations to meet the complex demands of classroom teaching. Stanford's Courseware Authoring Tools (CAT) project, successor to the Faculty Author Development project, is now working with Stanford professors to develop social science simulations using a Hypercard-based tool kit (*Alias*) designed for that purpose by Brodie Lockard.

Note

Portions of this article were published previously by Professor Lougee in *History Microcomputer Review* 4, no. 1 (Spring 1988) and in *Outlook,* a publication of the Columbia Teachers College; the *Outlook* article also served as the instructor's manual sold with the software.

Chapter 7

Writing *Introduction to General Chemistry*

Stanley G. Smith
University of Illinois at Urbana-Champaign,
Ruth Chabay
Carnegie Mellon University,
and
Elizabeth Kean
University of Nebraska-Lincoln

Work on *Introduction to General Chemistry* started in 1981 as a result of discussions between Tom Sears, now president of Falcon Software, and Stan Smith. Sears, then a publisher of educational software under the COMPress label, felt there was a need for programs to help students with their first chemistry course. A seven-disk series on organic chemistry and a series on polymer chemistry for the Apple II microcomputer had just been completed, so it was reasonable to initiate a new project at that time. After much discussion between Sears and Smith about the instructional level, work on the first lesson was started.

Although one can point to the time when the first code for *Introduction to General Chemistry* was written, this does not reflect the previous work that made writing the program possible. A more realistic starting point was the fall semester of 1972, when a chemistry graduate student, Ruth Chabay, wanted to work on a nontraditional thesis project. With special approval from the department head she initiated work on programs — with her thesis advisor, Stan Smith — for teaching general chemistry by computer. This work was done on the University of Illinois PLATO system. Little was known at that time about how to write lessons that were easy to use, interesting, and instructionally effective. Educational literature provided little help in dealing with the many details of interactive tutorials. Each approach had to be tested with hundreds of students and usually revised and tested again until a working procedure was developed. The process took all of Chabay's graduate student years plus two years during which she was on the staff at Illinois. Additional programs needed to complete the course were developed later by Carolyn Moore.

The result was a general chemistry program that has run for over a decade and has been used as a required part of instruction at the University of Illinois with over ten thousand students. This research was critical to the later development of *Introduction to General Chemistry*.

Although early research on instructional design and lesson development was done mainly on large mainframe computers such as PLATO, the development of microcomputers in the late 1970s caused major changes in instructional computing. In 1979 Dave Curtin, Professor of Chemistry at the University of Illinois, argued that an Apple II had enough computing power and adequate graphics to do many things then being done on mainframe computers in the area of computer-based teaching. He finally took Smith to the local Byte Shop and said "buy this one." As Smith wrote the check, Curtin carried the computer to his car for the trip home. This Apple II+ was the computer on which much of *Introduction to General Chemistry* was written. The insistence by Dave Curtin that instructional programs of the type developed on the PLATO system could be written on a microcomputer was instrumental in starting the necessary development work.

With any new computer, the first task is to find the tools that will make it interact with students in an educationally effective way. The computer screen must be as clear or clearer than the best textbooks. Student input must be simple, easy, and intuitive, and answer judging must be flexible.

The language of chemistry uses uppercase and lowercase, superscripts and subscripts, Greek letters and other special symbols. Although the keyset on the Apple produced only uppercase, it was clear that the graphics display was capable of doing everything that was needed, given the right software. However, representatives from Apple with whom plans for writing these lessons were discussed assured us that what we felt we must do simply could not be done on their computer.

After months of searching the literature, making phone calls, and holding extensive discussions, the pieces required to create the displays were assembled. A character generator program, written by Chris Espinosa at Apple and available at the computer store for two dollars, made it possible to put characters on the graphic display screen. Computer magazines were searched page by page for clues on how to enter lowercase. Everything that looked like it had a chance was ordered and tried. The Program Line Editor, written by Neil Konzen, finally provided the solution. However, making the lowercase letters readable on the Apple editor screen required installation of a new ROM chip.

The solution to the problem of writing chemical formulas with subscripts, as in H_2O, came from a program published by John Figueras, a chemist at the research laboratories of Eastman Kodak. This program provided a grid on which formulas could be constructed; they were then converted into shapes that could be displayed on the graphics screen.

The final piece needed to start writing the programs was discovered in April 1981 when Smith gave a seminar at Valparaiso University. In discussions there it was learned that Professor Edgar Nagel had discovered how to pass equations as strings from Apple SoftBASIC to the ROM equation parser and return the numerical result. This allowed students to enter expressions in response to questions and allowed the computer to evaluate the responses.

With this odd collection of tools, the first versions of *Organic Chemistry*, *Polymer Chemistry*, and disk 1 of *Introduction to General Chemistry* were written.

As a result of writing these lessons, it was clear that additional computing tools were needed for the efficient production of interactive instructional lessons on a microcomputer. After much discussion with Al Avner, an expert on computer-based teaching on PLATO, a list of the desirable special computing features was produced. Al suggested that Paul Tenczar might be interested in writing machine-language extensions to Apple SoftBASIC to implement these ideas. Paul was the originator of the TUTOR language on PLATO and had just formed his own software company to develop tools for writing instructional programs on microcomputers. After many months of very hard work by Paul Tenczar, Al Avner, and Stan Smith, the authoring system called EnBASIC was produced. EnBASIC is an extension to BASIC that provides user-defined characters in four sizes, along with state-of-the-art answer judging. (In a debate between Tenczar and Smith about how to judge answers, Tenczar had pointed out that he knew which letters in the student's response were wrong. This resulted in the development of a unique spelling markup for misspelled words, a great help to students because it provides feedback on exactly what is wrong with answers that have simple spelling or typographical errors.)

As EnBASIC evolved, the first disks of *Introduction to General Chemistry* were rewritten to take advantage of its features. Of course, writing in a language still under development meant that each program had to be revised many times to work with the most recent version of EnBASIC. However, using EnBASIC to write real programs made it possible to test ideas and features as they were being developed.

After the first three disks were completed, Paul figured out an easy way to control the color of the text. The results of adding color were so dramatic that we started over again, doing everything in color. Since at that time displays ranged from TV sets to color monitors, authoring was done with both a black-and-white and a color monitor connected to the same computer. Each display was designed so that it was clear on both monitors.

As the authoring tools accumulated, it became clear that the next major problems were content, instructional design, and programming. The earlier work had been done on a university mainframe computer as part of a special program to promote the development of computer-based teaching programs, and permission to translate the programs to microcomputers could not be obtained; therefore, all-new lessons had to be created. Over a decade of experience with about one thousand students per semester provided the background for designing *Introduction to General Chemistry*.

Because of her earlier work, Ruth Chabay was contacted to see if she would be interested in contributing to the new programs. At that time she was working at the National Institute of Health using large computers for modeling chemical systems. To even look at what had been done required that she first buy her own Apple computer. Next, much time had to be spent on long-distance phone calls discussing how to write the programs and how to use EnBASIC, which at that point had no written instructions and was still changing on a daily basis.

For lesson development, each author took primary responsibility for specific programs. Disks were exchanged by mail nearly every week so that revisions and new material could be reviewed and consolidated onto maotor diolio, An the work progronood, the amount of mumury in the Apples was rapidly changing from 16K to 48K. We decided to use the full 48K for the lessons. Even with 48K it was sometimes necessary to leave periods off the ends of sentences to save a byte. It took a very understanding publisher to deal with these types of problems.

In June 1982 Smith presented a paper, "Teaching with a Microcomputer," at Georgetown University in Washington, D.C., at which time he met with Chabay for a few hours to talk about lesson development. Much of the available time was spent looking for a place to play video games, after which the two drafted an outline of the game *ChemMaze*, which was published a year later as disk 6 in the *Introduction to General Chemistry* series. Because of the complexities of the programming and the design, exchanging programs by mail was simply too slow to maintain continuity of ideas. Therefore, modems were set up and code was exchanged over the phone on nearly a daily basis until the design was finalized. Because of the need for speed in the game, it was necessary to learn to program the Apple in machine language and interface it with displays in BASIC.

As soon as the first disks were in usable form, Smith put an Apple in his car and drove to several schools and showed the lessons to teachers to get their input. He also felt that the work should have an independent review before publication. Therefore, Betsy Kean was contacted. As director of chemistry tutoring services at the University of Wisconsin, Kean had a good understanding of the kinds of things that cause problems for students. Her reviews were so complete that they crossed the line from review to contribution, and she became a coauthor. She went over each lesson as a professional who tutors students one-on-one. Every display was evaluated to be sure that the development of concepts was logical and clear. This assured that these lessons would indeed serve as a personal tutor to students. Kean also contributed ideas for the content of new lessons, which were subsequently developed.

Selecting the content is critical to the success of a lesson; what is omitted is often as important as what is included. Only the fundamental constructs needed to develop specific ideas were included. As a result, students often comment on how much easier it is to understand the programs than the textbook. A great deal of effort goes into finding the minimum words needed to communicate the information. Pictures and diagrams with high visual impact are used to add clarity. Although each screen has specific content, that content is often designed to play additional roles in the student learning process. Some parts of the programs are deliberately redundant to provide review. Others are included to set the stage for later work. The same question may be asked several times with different wording to ensure understanding and to promote flexibility with the language of the discipline.

The nature of the student-program interaction is one of the most difficult parts of the design process. Because the student needs to be an active participant in the learning process, the student is asked to use the presented information as soon as possible, with later review for reinforcement.

Seven years after starting work on *Introduction to General Chemistry*, ten topics have been completed. The next disk is about half done; a handwritten draft of the content of another has been produced. The total amount of time required to produce this type of work exceeds the traditional reward structure by a large amount.

The choice of the Apple microcomputer was a major concern during the development period. Much time was spent looking also at the Atari, Commodore, and TRS-80. The decision was made to stay with the Apple, until the announcement by IBM of the PCjr. On the day of the announcement, Smith picked up a PCjr at the computer store and started the process of adapting the programs. The first step, of course, was to deal with displaying chemical formulas with subscripts on the screen and with the associated problem of spacing between lines of text. Smith suggested that his glider-pilot friend Hank Krejci, who had his own software company (HFK Software) that produced the QERTY word processor, might be able to help. Krejci quickly produced a program that interfaced with IBM PC BASICA to give the desired fonts on the screen, as well as a word processor type of student input. This software was first used to convert the organic chemistry programs from Apple to the PC. When the process was well worked out, the task of applying the procedure to the general chemistry programs was given to Electronic Courseware Systems.

A great deal of work has been devoted to adapting existing programs so that they run on the current generation of microcomputers. This need to update existing materials greatly reduces the amount of new instructional material that can be written. This also requires the personal purchase of additional hardware. Unfortunately, the latest and fastest new microcomputers pose nearly the same set of problems for authors of instructional software as did the first Apple II+'s. Superscripts, subscripts, and line spacing are still a problem, made more complex by having to deal with multiple display modes such as CGA, EGA, MCGA, and VGA in addition to Apple ProDOS, Microsoft Windows, IBM OS/2...

The personal computer makes it possible for individuals to write instructional programs on their own, without institutional or governmental support. One simply buys a computer and goes to work. The only direct costs are a few floppy disks. However, if one is on the academic staff of a college or university, colleagues are not usually appreciative of this endeavor, which introduces other types of costs that vary greatly with the institution. Tenure is a prerequisite.

Although writing instructional material requires little outside support, using the completed programs does. Moderate to large class sizes require a significant investment in hardware, space, and support personnel. Major institutional support is needed. This usually means outside funding, since quality is most safely measured by the amount of money a project attracts from industrial or federal sources.

We approached the writing of these programs with over a decade of experience in designing, programming, evaluating, and using instructional lessons and with about fifty years of combined teaching experience in the field. Because every line of computer code influences the educational effectiveness, student programmers were not used. Persons with limited experience in programming and instructional design may benefit from discussion with various campus support groups to help them get started. However, if the latest technology or very new approaches are employed, institutional support groups specializing in CAI may be of little help because their structure often supports only the way things have been done in the past. For example, when *Introduction to General Chemistry* was started, many people on the staff of the Computer-Based Educational Research Laboratory at the University of Illinois advised us that only mainframes could be used for teaching and that microcomputers would never see much use in education. The director described the work as a "waste of time."

The completed programs in the *Introduction to General Chemistry* series are published by Falcon Software. The programs are used in a large number of high schools, two- and four-year colleges, and universities. In this mode, the educational institution provides the student with both the hardware and the software. Since many students can use a single copy of the software, the total number of copies of a given program required for a class is small compared to the number of textbooks needed. As the number of students using their own computers increases, then software needs to become available to individual students. Although this greatly expands the number of copies in use, the tendency to use pirated copies could reduce the number obtained from the publisher to the point that it is not possible to sustain the effort to produce, distribute, and support quality software. If a large body of complex courseware is to be created, a mechanism for distribution of software is needed that will provide adequate rewards for authors and publishers and that will safeguard the intellectual property rights of authors.

Part Two:

Curriculum Perspectives

Curriculum Perspectives

Those of us who have served on curriculum committees, whether focused on general education or on a discipline or profession, know how difficult it is to reach a consensus on educational priorities. There is some truth but little solace in Woodrow Wilson's widely quoted quip: "Changing a university is like moving a cemetery." The goals of general education continue to be broadly accepted and applauded, however, as does the related proposition that language skills are a keystone of both general and specialized education. But the national reports cited in the introductory chapter of this book reported serious cracks in this keystone and suggested an increased role for instructional technologies as a repairing mortar. Nowhere in the curriculum are the problems of academic governance more complex than in writing and foreign language programs. The educational world view of scholars in these areas, moreover, is somewhat foreign to the traditional academic computing world. These basic areas of the curriculum thus present an important challenge to the potential of interactive technologies to strengthen the undergraduate experience.

With these interesting but thorny issues of curriculum, philosophy, and technology in mind and with the goal of increasing faculty participation in the EDUCOM Software Initiative, I asked two groups of scholars — one group from a variety of writing programs and the other from foreign language programs — to examine the following questions:

- What are the discernible directions among current attempts to employ technology in your area of the curriculum?

- What are appropriate goals for the role of educational technology in your basic area of the curriculum?

- What must be done to achieve these goals, how should it be done, and who should do it?

These questions and my further remarks in this introduction were intended to provoke reflection, not to prescribe the groups' written responses.

Large enrollment figures, such as those that are a by-product of a universal writing or foreign language requirement, magnify the problems of student and faculty access to technology. Questions of access to technology in basic curricula, in turn, raise broader issues of equity, both for students and for scholars. For example, many campuses offer "developmental" writing or foreign language courses in addition to basic introductory freshman composition and language sequences. These make-up programs are sometimes separated from their antecedent academic units by arrangements that bestow little or no professional authority to participating instructors. Many of the students in these programs, moreover, have had little exposure to technology and cannot afford to own personal computers. Serious issues of student and faculty equity thus confront the educational potential of technology in such programs. These issues must be addressed if technology is not to exacerbate the extremes of undergraduate preparation, institutional economies, and faculty empowerment. We should ensure, for example, that technology will have an opportunity to contribute to developmental writing programs in economically stressed urban settings as well as to honors writing programs at affluent private colleges. We should ask how the role of technology in language learning is affected by, and might affect, the Byzantine governance arrangements that sometimes prevail among literature, linguistics, and language learning programs. A few remarks on writing programs and a few on language programs will reveal nuances on the above themes and will also introduce some other concerns addressed in the two essays defining this part of the book.

The Role of Technology in Teaching Writing

Improving students' writing skills is increasingly described as the responsibility of all academic departments — writing across the curriculum. *Writing is thinking* is a commonly heard phrase that moves writing from the realm of an independently taught skill to the collective responsibility of the entire faculty. Most faculty members, however, continue to hold their English departments or writing programs responsible for students' writing deficiencies. In most institutions the major responsibility for honing students' writing thus continues to reside in the composition or writing program, whether administered or only endorsed (but usually controlled) by the English department. On the overwhelming endorsement of word processing by those writers who have tried it, many writing programs are turning to technology to enhance their effectiveness. Developing students' writing skills thus

- is universally viewed as important,

- is usually the political domain of one academic department — English — in which the faculty's primary interest is likely to be the study and teaching of literature, and

- can be addressed by the most ubiquitous genre of personal productivity software, word-processing programs.

Although word processing can be an aid to writing, there appears to be no universal agreement about its role in teaching students to write. Still, many students have themselves bought word processors, and many campuses are attempting to give all of their students access to word processing in public microcomputing labs. An increasing number of schools, however, are going further by establishing writing labs. The idea is an old one: to give students structured assistance with their writing problems. In the new labs, however, the traditional assistance of a trained writing tutor is incorporated into a word-processing environment and is often supplemented with educational or diagnostic software writing aids. These new software packages are usually developed around a word processor. Some check grammar, even style. Others help students select a topic, organize an approach to it, and outline their ideas. The potential of these "front-end" and "back-end" writing aids appears to be so great that even commercial software developers have entered the arena with new products, and some writing labs have adopted these commercial products or have developed their own versions. The labs are sometimes extended to provide structured class experiences in which students can share their writing and teachers can select an anonymous example of student writing to display electronically for the entire class to critique and edit in a shared network environment.

These trends suggest several comments and questions:

- Although not a sufficient condition for good writing, writing practice is generally accepted as a necessary condition. Does the fact that word processing makes writing easier suffice to encourage the practice of writing?

- How can the quality of technology-based writing programs be assessed?

- Should all students have access to writing labs? If not, what selection criteria should prevail?

- Should writing labs include software writing aids beyond word processing? If so, can this be accomplished in the presence of multiple hardware/software standards among the writing labs on any one campus? Will the absence of a readily accessible campuswide standard for student writing technology disenfranchise some students?

- If all students should have access to writing labs, how can the resulting resource problems — including the inevitable space problem — be resolved? This would appear to be a particularly difficult issue if writing labs are to be used to provide structured classroom writing experience.

- What is the difference between a writing lab and a writing classroom?

The Role of Technology in Teaching Foreign Languages

Technology has long played a role in foreign language instruction. Traditional audio technology, however, is no longer the sole component of the venerable language lab. Computing technology plays an increasingly important role in language study as more computer-based materials appear — materials that take advantage of the computer's ability to integrate a variety of other media, such as the compact disk, the videodisk, and various devices for voice recognition and synthesis. The rough outlines of new interactive multimedia language labs are already discernible.

Because the study of a second language is not yet an integral part of the overall American educational experience, language programs in higher education must contend with uneven language skills in the freshman population. New technology-based curriculum projects in language study address this diversity and reflect a variety of goals. Some projects focus on translation and reading skills, some on writing skills, some on speaking skills. Some seek to integrate these goals in a cultural context. Others appear to be aimed more at the scholar of literature than at the struggling language student. The interest of business and government in language training is likely to increase the pressure on the practical aspects of basic language instruction.

Issues of governance are at least as pronounced in the basic foreign language program as in the writing program.[1] The language-literature rift disrupts the coherence of language instruction on many campuses. Responsibility for the foreign language curriculum, moreover, is often spread over several departments and is sometimes in the hands of untenured or temporary instructors. Can a proper role for instructional technology be articulated in this environment? If so, by whom?

Mathematics?

The reader may wonder why the language skills cited above as "a keystone of both general and specialized education" did not include the language of mathematics. Indeed, I initially planned to include a paper on the role of instructional technologies in mathematics education in this part of the book. A series of discussions with leaders in the field led, instead, to this brief recapitulation of some of the extensive efforts already underway within the mathematical community. These efforts include, for example, a collection of papers on the subject edited by David Smith, Jerry Porter, Carl Leinback and Ron Wenger[2], "A Mathematics Software Database" initiated by Steve Cunningham and David Smith and appearing regularly in the pages of *The College Mathematics Journal*, and a new department, "Computers and Mathematics," edited by Jon Barwise for the *Notices of the American Mathematical Society*. These and newly emerging initiatives — a collection on visualization in mathematics education to be edited by Walt Zimmerman and Steve Cunningham, for example — owe much to individual initiative and to the organized support of the Mathematical Association of America's Committee on Computers in Mathematics Education. The mathematical community and the larger scientific community have come to realize that technology can play a mitigating role in the abundantly documented national decline in students' mathematics achievement. The National Science Foundation, for example, has awarded twenty-two grants in its curriculum development program for the calculus. Many of these awards will enable technology-based curriculum development, but in my professional opinion as a mathematician, this flurry of activity masks a potential irony that deserves mention.

Mathematicians have had a long and symbiotic relationship with computing technology. They were present at the birth of the computer and of computer science but only recently have seriously engaged the challenge from Picasso that introduced this book: "Computers are useless They only give answers." First numerical computing and then symbolic computing (in the form of a growing body of computer algebra systems) contributed to the mathematical research agenda and to the education of the best undergraduates and graduate students majoring in mathematical sciences. But only now are mathematicians seriously looking to interactive technology as a resource to the basic mathematics curriculum that supports so many other curricula and that powers the nation's competitiveness. Much remains to be done if, for example, the clients of calculus are not to abandon the course before we who teach it come to grips with the implications of computer algebra systems for content and pedagogy. There are ready excuses but little consolation in the glacial speed with which industry vendors are responding to the need for better interfaces between their systems and natural mathematical language. We must forge new interdisciplinary partnerships joining the scientific and mathematical academic community and the hardware/software industry in order to seize the pedagogical opportunities for mathematics education that inhere in today's visual, symbolic, and numerical computing environments. It would indeed be ironic if one of the most powerful of human intellectual constructs, mathematics, was not enriched as an educational keystone by the empowering technology that it helped to create.

Concluding Remarks

These introductory remarks were intended to reveal how both the promises and the problems of instructional computing in key areas of the curriculum are magnified by its potential to affect all students and by the inheritance of awkward structures of faculty and curriculum governance. Throwing in the towel, however, is not an acceptable response, for any attempt to strengthen American education should not ignore the foundation on which higher learning is erected. Those who would help technol-

ogy realize its potential to contribute to teaching and learning must be
alert to organizational, political, economic, pedagogical, and social realities, as well as to technical issues. It is precisely the complexity of these
realities and issues that argues for more academic involvement in
EDUCOM and for supporting the involvement of EDUCOM in that area
of academe traditionally governed by the faculty: the curriculum.

Note

1. Peter Patrikis, ed., *The Governance of Foreign Language Teaching and Learning* (Proceedings of the Consortium for Language Teaching and Learning,
   1988).
2. Smith, D. A., Porter, G. J., Leinback, L. C., and Wenger, R. H. (Editors),
   Computers and Mathematics: The Use of Computers in Undergraduate Instruction, MAA Notes Number 9, Mathematical Association of American,
   Washington, DC (1988).

Chapter 8

Computers in Foreign Language Teaching and Research: A "New Humanism"

Nina Garrett
Carnegie Mellon University

with

James Noblitt
Cornell University

and

Frank Dominguez
University of North Carolina

Introduction

This chapter explores the present and the potential roles of the computer and its allied technologies, interactive audio and video, in foreign language education, both teaching and research. It assesses the implications of technological developments to date and draws in broad outline the shape of the endeavors already conceived for the future. Its focus is on those needs of the discipline that advanced technology can help to address, rather than on the technology itself. We suggest to both academics and nonacademics that technology can support and enhance a far broader range of the activities of foreign language teacher-scholars and language learners than is generally recognized. In so doing technology can help to integrate the efforts of scholars from diverse areas of the discipline, and this integration creates an attitude we call the "new humanism." Technology allows the humanist to pursue traditional concerns in new ways, using its power not only to enhance, extend, and expand on the values of a particular discipline, but also to establish more productive, principled connections among the disciplines of the humanities generally.

We want to address the concerns of professionals, both within and without academia, who are interested in realizing the potential of advanced technologies in foreign language education: that is, faculty, administrators, and computing support staff; hardware industries; software publishers; and the business and government sectors whose urgent need of personnel well trained in other languages lends support to academe's own interest in the humanistic value of language learning.

Although many language department faculty are interested in the computer, they often conceive of its potential only in terms of the most mechanical tasks at both ends of the continuum of disciplinary activities: in language learning it is acknowledged to be useful for drill and practice, in literary scholarship for word processing. One of the major goals of this paper is to indicate the wide range of other activities in all areas of foreign language education that the technology can enhance, and moreover to suggest that the computer can bridge traditional gaps between teaching and research, and between language and literature.

Department heads and deans concerned with the strength of academic programs, and with the research status of their faculty, acknowledge the growing demand for genuine integration of the computer into the discipline's teaching and research, but they are often unsure how that integration can be accomplished either cost-effectively or beneficially for students as well as faculty. As is also the case for other disciplines of the humanities, those concerned for the governance of foreign language education and scholarship have not yet arrived at any generally accepted criteria for recognizing and rewarding serious intellectual contributions implemented on the computer.

Academic computing administrators and campuswide computing support staff who must develop support structures for the computing activities of all disciplines face special problems in dealing with foreign language education. Language faculty are likely to be less technologically sophisticated than their colleagues in science; their teaching and research needs are qualitatively different (most obviously in that they demand the ability to process language rather than numerical systems) and they are generally less able to articulate these needs in terms that computer scientists can understand. Although the latter seldom think of their work as directly relevant to foreign language education, the need for non-roman character sets and for speech processing, to name only two obvious areas of concern, requires understanding and commitment on their part to the foreign language enterprise.

Hardware and software vendors and distributors are frustrated by the relatively smaller market opportunities in humanities education and by the fact that there is so much less agreement in these fields than in the sciences on course content, the nature of the learning process, the potential contribution of technology both to the teacher-scholar and to the learner, or the forms that contribution might take. This discussion should give hardware and software developers not only some insight into disciplinary constraints but also a better sense of the possibilities.

Business and government, though acutely interested in the outcome of language education — greater language proficiency in college graduates — have generally not yet come to understand the ways in which technology might affect that outcome. Language education, conditioned by traditional programs, still trails well behind the technological potential. It is crucially important for the academic community and its nonacademic partners to develop a common understanding of the new potential for growth that is equally advantageous to the particular needs on both sides.

The diversity and the multiplicity of computing efforts in foreign language education are such that this account cannot hope to be complete. However, even a far more comprehensive description of current initiatives would still not adequately convey the impact on the field, because every kind of computer use, no matter how specialized or limited it may seem at first glance, has implications for a number of problematic issues in the field as a whole. Our intent is to provide not a compendium of programs or projects (we mention only a few examples) but rather a principled overview of the disciplinary concerns that technology may address, and to suggest ways in which the field itself and the role of technology in it are changing.

The structure of this account is recursive rather than linear. Part 1 creates a context for understanding the field as a whole and the shifts in perspective taking place as a result of the introduction of technology. Part 2 outlines the field's three major areas of teaching and scholarship — literature, linguistics, and language — and lays out current and projected developments of technology use in the teaching and the research of each area. Part 3 focuses on a number of issues and problems that are raised by technology in humanities education generally, in foreign language education particularly, and explores them in terms of current and projected developments. Part 4 sketches out some implications, with recommendations for successful integration and balanced growth, and adds a brief conclusion.

I. New Tools, New Humanism

The concept of a "new humanism" to be explored here represents one of the most exciting developments coming out of the participation of advanced technology in education. The twentieth century has witnessed a trend, resulting from the explosion of technological progress generally, toward dissociating the humanities from the sciences, but higher education began in the 1970s to see the disadvantages of that trend. Professionals in science and engineering now realize not only that all college graduates need enough understanding of language to write cogently, but also that a study of the humanities provides the quintessential context for developing the meaning of scientific and technical advances. Professional schools of all kinds now actively recruit liberal arts graduates. At the same time, humanists recognize the need for enough literacy in scientific and technical areas to function in a world increasingly dependent on information technology. But the "new humanism" takes us significantly past these tentative rapprochements, in that it integrates technology and humanistic research and education in unprecedented ways. In conferences demonstrating the uses of technology in education, chemists and art historians, mathematicians and literary critics, psychologists and linguists, enthusiastically share educational techniques — but more important, they recognize that technology bridges disciplinary and cultural divisions by enabling teachers, researchers, and learners in every field to deal directly, and across traditional disciplinary boundaries, with the diverse and complex data of human endeavor.

The enthusiastic attention lavished on new technological tools causes some scholars to fear that the technology is undermining or distorting traditional values of humanistic study. We should not forget that for our counterparts of other eras, the printing press and the typewriter seemed

crude and and humanistic. The values of the humanities are not changed
by the adoption of new tools for scholarship and teaching. For the new
humanist, the scholar's workstation is now as appropriate to the
discipline's undertakings as the quill pen was in other days.

It is precisely the underlying values of humanistic study and education
that need to be stressed here. Some of the major ways in which technology enhances these values are already clear; they appear again and again
in a wide variety of activities across the field and will be explored in some
detail in the following sections of the chapter.

One of the most vivid and most attractive themes is *authenticity;* the
computer and interactive technologies can bring the primary and supporting data of the discipline within the grasp of the researcher and the
learner alike. Hypertext and hypermedia allow immediate access to an
extraordinary wealth and variety of information about literature and its
cultural context. Audio and video materials present authentic communicative language in as dynamic a form as can possibly be achieved outside
the country where the second language is spoken, and also provide a vital
cultural context for the understanding of literature. Language in all its
manifestations — as human communication, as literary expression, as
linguistic system — can be more directly experienced, explored, and
analyzed by learners and scholars.

Another major theme is *empowerment.* Foreign language teacher-scholars have access to vastly expanded sources of traditional information
through electronic links to distant libraries and bulletin boards. Researchers without travel support, or those in small institutions with limited
libraries, or those whose specialities are unusual or narrowly defined, can
make use of technology to break through scholarly isolation, to establish
regular contact with their intellectual colleagues, no matter how widely
scattered. But in addition to increased access to traditional data, the
technology also makes possible access to entirely new sources of authentic language data: audio and video not only allow the teacher to bring the
foreign language and culture to the classroom but also allow the scholar
to analyze and interpret new aspects of language and communication. The
technology supplies new tools for organizing those resources for both
pedagogical and scholarly purposes — for collecting, presenting, shaping,
reworking, and analyzing language not only in traditional text form but
also in aural and visual modalities. Technology thus extends and facilitates a wide range of the discipline's long-standing activities, lending new

power to continuity and tradition, but it also empowers new approaches to old problems and provides the means for undertaking new kinds of exploration and for achieving new insights. Its use does not represent any radical change in the way the study of the humanities is conceived; it extends old perspectives and opens up new ones.

A final leitmotif is *integration*. Renaissance humanism gave us the ideal of the teacher-scholar, the one inseparable from the other. But in our time teaching and scholarship are sometimes in tension, with the two being differently governed and differently rewarded. Twentieth-century thought is intensely analytical, and although analysis has generated new intellectual power, it has also caused fractures and splits. Language as a means of artistic expression (literature), language as a vehicle for communication (language), and language as an abstract system revealing the shape of human thought (linguistics) are taught, even within the same department, as separate disciplines and for separate purposes. Visionary though it may seem to many, those familiar with the technologies to which the foreign language teacher-scholar and student now have access already see the potential — still largely unrecognized and unrealized — for bringing about a synthesis of humanistic and scientific knowledge hitherto fragmented by disciplinary boundaries and limitations on the representation of knowledge. It is this synthesis we mean to evoke by our references to a "new humanism."

II. Technology and the Structure of the Discipline

Before we examine the role of technology in the various endeavors of foreign language education, the relationship among them must be understood. This section sketches out the departmental and disciplinary relationships of literature, linguistics, and language and the relationship of research and teaching within each. Without this basis, we cannot understand the constraints on, and the challenges posed by, the integration of technology into the research and teaching of the discipline.

One way of understanding the relationship of these apparently quite different enterprises within foreign language education is to see them in a hierarchy of entailment. The traditional model (at least for foreign language departments in major research universities and liberal arts colleges) establishes literary research as the primary endeavor of most faculty members. Their own research, and that of their peers in the field, then becomes the basis for the content of the courses offered in foreign language departments: research informs teaching. Research and teaching in this model may be based on explicit development of critical theory or on historical approaches to textual scholarship and editing. As in other departments of the humanities, the purpose of language departments' overall curriculum is to provide a solid overview of the structure of the discipline (i.e., the principles of literary study), of the major texts of the canon, and of a variety of critical and scholarly approaches to the interpretation of these texts. Some students from majors other than foreign language take literature courses to fulfill a general education or humanities requirement, but the undergraduate foreign language major is traditionally designed to prepare students for academic careers as literature teacher-scholars.

Promotion and tenure in such departments and institutions tend to be very largely dependent on research.[1] Undergraduate teaching is always said to be an important criterion for advancement, but its actual importance may be very slight, depending on the department and the institution. Active involvement in the research and general knowledge of the content area of one's own courses is all that is needed to qualify a teacher, and teaching ability is not seen as dependent on training; teaching methodology is not generally considered to be important in literature courses.

The traditional model of research and teaching in literature also works relatively well as an account of the linguistic enterprise of foreign language departments. The primary responsibility of language department faculty interested in linguistics is to undertake research on the linguistic aspects of the department's languages. As in the case of literature, this research may be historical, focusing on the development of the language over time, or it may be based on current theories; historical and contemporary approaches are generally perceived as having approximately equal intellectual value. Such research provides the content for the linguistics courses offered. As above, teaching methodology is not at issue; knowledge of the content is the main prerequisite for teaching. These courses are less commonly taken by undergraduates as part of general education or humanities requirements, and few language departments offer full-fledged undergraduate majors in this area.

In the logical sequence, then, the literary and linguistic research undertaken by the department's faculty informs the department's curriculum — the structure of courses and degree programs, syllabi, materials development — through which the faculty convey the literary and linguistic core content to students. The field does not normally focus on individual learners or their learning processes but rather on the texts, and the techniques for working with them, that learners are supposed to know.

The third enterprise of foreign language departments, the one devoted to language itself, stands in sharp contrast to the other two; it does not fit the traditional model and is generally perceived in most departments and in the discipline as being both intellectually and politically inferior. In some cases all faculty members are expected to participate in language teaching as a service to the department, while in others the basic language courses are handled by graduate teaching assistants supervised by faculty members. In the latter situation the department may hire a "methodologist" or "pedagogy specialist" for the supervisory position, which is often not tenure-track. Even where tenure is in principle possible, it is much harder to achieve in these positions and almost always depends on the faculty members' ability and willingness to publish on research in literature or linguistics quite independently of their language teaching or supervisory duties. Research in the area of language teaching is universally assumed to be methodological or pedagogical in nature, and such studies are never seen as equivalent in intellectual value to literary or linguistic work.

The content of language courses is therefore not considered to be informed by research proper to this part of the discipline (though the design of the syllabus is supposed to reflect current methodological research), but rather is considered to derive from traditional linguistic descriptions distilled in pedagogical grammars. In pedagogically up-to-date programs this traditional linguistic content is complemented by — or sometimes even largely replaced by — material based on contemporary work in sociolinguistics and pragmatics, areas seen as bearing more directly on communicative language use than does syntax. Most foreign language teachers, however, have had only superficial training, if any, either in linguistics or in these "communicative" extensions of linguistic study, and no training at all in undertaking research in these areas. The purpose of courses in language is generally assumed to be to prepare students for upper-level literature (occasionally linguistics) courses. Language learning is widely regarded as training rather than as education, mastery of a skill rather than of a body of knowledge, and thus is seen in terms of its usefulness either in other language or literal studies or in other fields. (Elementary courses or a minor in a language are increasingly being recommended to students in professional fields such as business, engineering, social work, etc.) In other words, the content of language courses — the description of language — is regarded as dependent on the research of another discipline (linguistics) and as serving the needs of other fields or professions. And in contrast to the model for literature and linguistics in which basic research *informs* teaching, pedagogical research *derives from* teaching.

Another major feature of the language enterprise (noted here because it will be important in discussions of the role of technology, below) is that, in contrast to literature and linguistics, the training of future teachers in language stresses teaching method far more than course content. The actual description of the language is assumed to be accessible in linguistic or pedagogical grammars, so that most of the methods training is concerned with improving teachers' understanding of the sociolinguistics and pragmatics of the language and with techniques for actively involving individual learners in language use, rather than with techniques for imparting a body of knowledge about the language.

The internal structure of foreign language departments, then, tends to reflect relatively separate concerns for teaching literature, linguistics, and language, and for research relating differently to those three enterprises. With this departmental structure as background, let us examine the role of the computer in the research and in the teaching of these three sectors of language education.

Two preliminary points should be made. First, the prerequisite for all research and teaching applications is of course the appropriate development of the technology itself — the hardware, the interfaces between devices, and the software necessary in the particular area of foreign language. The development of all these is for the most part undertaken not within the foreign language departments but by computer scientists. Included here are the development of technical features governing storage, manipulation, and retrieval of text, both in memory and on-screen, in forms amenable to humanists' uses:

- Foreign language characters (roman and non-roman) and diacritics

- Printing capabilities

- Graphics and animation

- Interfaces with audio, video, and CD/ROM

- Authoring systems

- Database management

- Networking, electronic mail, and bulletin boards

- Artificial intelligence capabilities

Language faculty themselves seldom undertake this kind of work in depth; most have no training or inclination for it. There are of course some who become experienced in and enthusiastic about the technology, but such work by faculty is usually regarded as anomalous and avocational, not as part of the serious humanist's "promotable" activities. As the technology becomes rapidly more specialized, however, decisions about the design of these features can no longer be made unilaterally either by computer scientists or by humanists. Intelligent decisions about the configuration and design of the humanist's workstation cannot be made by computer scientists who have little idea of how a scholar might employ such technology, and the humanist without insights into the potential of hardware and software will conceive of only the most pedestrian uses.

Second, a distinction must be made between the involvement of foreign language teacher-scholars in *using* technology-based materials for research or teaching and their involvement in *developing* these materials or tools for themselves or their students. As we pointed out in the section discussing the structure of the discipline, teachers of literature and linguistics tend to have little or no training in teaching methods, and their teaching materials conventionally lie ready to hand in published works. They tend, therefore, to have less experience either in using or in developing new tools or materials designed for specific research or teaching functions. By contrast, language teachers — although they certainly depend heavily on language textbooks — receive extensive training, in their methods course, in developing supplementary materials as well as tools and techniques for integrating realia and other sources of authentic language data into their classroom activities. However, we know of no foreign language teacher training program that includes a systematic presentation of current technologies, provides a discussion of their pedagogical rationale, and suggests techniques for incorporating their use. Colleges of education often offer general courses on educational technology, but these are seldom directly applicable to the particulars of language teaching. Courses on the *development* of technology-based language materials are offered at several major universities (e.g., by Robert Hart at the University of Illinois and Sue Otto at the University of Iowa).

Faculty in all disciplines are hampered in the development of teaching materials of any kind by the fact that such activity does not help them to achieve tenure or promotion. This problem is more acute for language teachers than for their colleagues in literature or linguistics because language teachers usually have heavier course loads, more contact hours with students, and more lesson preparation and because they are expected to publish in fields different from their areas of expertise.

In the following sections we will consider the applications of technology (already implemented or just being conceived) first in the research, then in the teaching, of literature and linguistics.

Literature

Most active foreign language teacher-scholars have already accepted the computer as a useful tool for writing up literary scholarship and research — that is, for word processing — but relatively few have as yet recognized it as having any intrinsic role in actually carrying out research. However, great advances have been made in the past five years in developing text databases and tools to enable humanists in English literature, history, classics, etc., to access and manipulate text. Foreign language teacher-scholars are rapidly coming to recognize that these tools and techniques are equally available and important to them. The nature of the data of literary study — the primary texts and the secondary literature — has not changed, but the speed and flexibility of the new tools for analyzing those data can make qualitative as well as quantitative changes in what can be done with them. With the complete works of a writer (or of a period, or of a genre) available on CD/ROM and addressable by text-retrieval and concordance-producing software (such as the Oxford Concordance Program or *WordCruncher*), scholars can undertake comprehensive explorations of word or phrase associations and collocations, even of grammatical information, allowing a virtually infinite range of textual, critical, and interpretive analyses. Copyright problems are acute, but publishers do make available the rights to produce electronic versions of editions, which may then be employed by scholars for their own purposes with proper citation, just as to a printed version. Texts with annotations or several variants are rapidly becoming available in a variety of languages. Scholars can even create their own electronic versions of a text that is not yet commercially available by using an optical scanner, if they have explicit permission from the publisher to do so.

The potential of these tools for enriching and extending the teaching of literature is as yet barely recognized, and teaching applications lag far behind research ones. However, wider availability of computers to students is beginning to allow significant innovation in literature teaching: students can now be given direct access to the text corpora and the text analysis software tools themselves, so that they gain, in effect, hands-on experience in behaving like active literature scholars, in dealing directly with the data, rather than being passive recipients of information about the data as mediated by the teacher. In a course on *Faust* developed by Garold Davis at Brigham Young University, for example, instructors assign papers to be written on the incidence of certain words or phrases, or the juxtaposition of key themes. The technology thus empowers the student as well as the teacher-scholar.

Another technology-based approach to teaching literature is not directly related to the actual research activities of the teacher-scholar but provides the student with direct access to all the background or contextual information that the teacher thinks is relevant to understanding a literary work. The electronic presentation of a literary work in hypertext or hypermedia form allows the student to explore both the text itself and an indefinitely large set of related materials contained in databases linked to the text and to each other. A rapid proliferation of hypermedia authoring systems is providing even computer-novice teachers with routines for linking text, audio, and video materials together for nonlinear, open-ended browsing by students. Hypermedia materials can now be created with relative speed and ease on the leading microcomputers, even by non-programmers, with software tools such as *HyperCard, LinkWay, Guide, HyperTies,* and the *Audio-Video Connection.* (Authoring systems for materials development will be discussed in more detail in the section on language teaching.) Hardware limitations still hinder the development of lesson materials with large amounts of digitized audio, but this is an area of acute interest to so many educators that we can expect significant advances soon.

For example, a demonstration lesson on Thomas Hardy's novel *Jude the*

Obscure, prepared by Randall Jones at Brigham Young, shows how the entire text or large selections of the novel can be made available for a variety of searches and analyses on-line. Databases of marginal notes, glosses of various kinds, and maps of Hardy's fictional world and of the Oxford area on which it was based are all available to the student at the click of a mouse. An expanded version could also include an interactive video exploration of a typical Hardy-esque countryside and of homes from that period, giving students who have never been to England an otherwise impossible-to-achieve sense of Hardy's world. In addition, selections of dialogue from the novel could be stored via digitized sound to allow students to hear Hardy's dialect and dialogue style "live."

One of the best-known hypermedia programs now available to humanists is *Intermedia,* developed by the IRIS working group at Brown University. *Intermedia* already supports substantial materials for a variety of Brown courses. *Intermedia* materials designed by George Landow for a survey course on English literature include a huge amount and variety of historical, social, economic, biographical, and visual material, providing a rich context for the study of major texts. *Intermedia* allows the creation of high-resolution illustrations and graphics; by the time this report appears, it may also support color, foreign language characters, audio, and video, and thus could lend itself directly to the creation of similar materials for foreign language literary texts.

Very little materials development along these lines has as yet been undertaken by foreign language literature teachers, but this is due largely to the fact that they have for the most part not become aware of the possibilities; they still tend to think of text as book, of the computer as useful only for word processing or for verb drills, and of video as constituting recreational "culture-breaks." However, even a brief demonstration of *Intermedia* or similar projects is usually enough to spark enthusiastic recognition of the pedagogical power of the spoken version of a poem, of the performance of a scene from a play, of the visual associations in a literary work with the art of the period, or of providing either unlimited or carefully controlled access to annotations such as glosses, transcriptions, contextual enrichment, graphical analyses, or grammatical, idiomatic, or sociolinguistic explanations. The rapidly increasing production of videodisks, which allow instant access to still or full-motion video material under the control of the computer, presages the possibility of providing full cultural context for any text. Even without hypermedia, hypertext allows teachers to give students all they need to find and to analyze differences in successive editions of a work and to make unmediated and immediate connections to cultural material, explanations, and allusions of all kinds at whatever level of detail is desirable, for any interesting text, regardless of whether it has been published in an annotated edition.

Linguistics

Within foreign language departments the use of the computer in research on the descriptive and historical linguistics of a particular language is still minimal. Most faculty members think of the role of the computer in linguistic research as limited to parsing (automatic analysis of grammatical structure), but major parser development projects tend to be undertaken within departments of linguistics and cognitive science because they are generally motivated by language-independent theoretical concerns and by research in computational linguistics, artificial intelligence, and cognitive science. (The development of limited foreign language parsers has been undertaken by Dana Paramskas at Guelph, the Project Athena team at MIT, David Evans at Carnegie Mellon, and Robert Hart at the University of Illinois, among others, but these projects are designed for error analysis, i.e., for language teaching, to be discussed below.) A great deal of non–language-specific work in computational linguistics is in principle adaptable to language-specific research in descriptive and historical linguistics, but for the most part these tools and techniques await discovery by foreign language professionals. However, Donald Becker at the University of Wisconsin has developed a computer program that derives diachronic changes in Germanic verbs by applying the rules of various older Germanic languages to basic roots, and another that illustrates phonological rule applications, both of them suggesting models usable in general or language-specific philological research.

The relatively recent development of the field known as corpus linguistics rests directly on the resources made available by technology; this approach has been taken further in Europe than in the United States. Instead of basing linguistic analyses on isolated or *ad hoc* examples of utterances, linguists can explore enormous electronic corpora of selections of written (or transcriptions of spoken) language via text-retrieval software like that discussed above in literary research, allowing for a wide variety of linguistic studies. Syntactic features that can be identified in terms of lexical items or in specific morphological strings can be similarly

analyzed, and this approach to syntax is particularly congenial, for exam
ple, to current linguistic work in the context of lexical-functional theory.
Such corpora are already available for several European languages, and
others are under development; European linguists are considerably more
active than most of their American colleagues in applying the corpora to
their research.

The development of machine-readable dictionaries has led to the recognition of the important role that technology-based lexicography can play
in supporting natural language understanding, text generation, and dictionary design. As yet, little of this work has been brought to bear on foreign
language education, but the potential is there.

In the teaching of descriptive and historical linguistics within language
departments, as in the teaching of literature, the use of computer materials is still rare. (There may be more activity within individual departments
than is apparent; the population of faculty and students involved in these
studies is so small that those who develop such programs have little
incentive to try to market them, and so the programs remain unknown.)
Elmer Antonsen at the University of Illinois has developed a program for
teaching the phonetic transcription of German in the International Phonetic Alphabet on PLATO, and Becker (see above) has made some experimental use of his programs in teaching. In principle there is no reason
why a wide variety of programs incorporating linguistic analysis routines
should not be integrated into this teaching. (Of course, at the simplest
level, electronic-workbook programs can be devised for Old French or
Old Norse as well as for modern French or German, but that is then
language teaching, not linguistics per se.)

To a considerable extent the same technological tools and databases
can support both literary and linguistic research and teaching, especially
where the two areas intersect at stylistic analysis and literary translation.
Compilations of large databases of texts from any period and the development of concordance programs are of enormous value both to literary
scholars and to linguists. However, traditional distinctions between parts
of the field still sometimes operate to prevent a recognition of the com-
monalities; Douglas Kibbee, professor of romance linguistics at the University of Illinois, who has given presentations on the American Research
on the Treasury of the French Language project, has found that colleagues in literature to whom the material could be most useful do not
attend the presentations because they assume the subject to be "linguis-

tic, not literary." The exploration of such databases may be further frustrated by disagreements on whether projects should be staffed by computational linguists more familiar with the technical problems of manipulating text or by literary or language scholars more concerned with the intellectual issues.

Language

In discussing the role of technology in the language enterprise, we reverse the sequence of our considerations; as we pointed out in the section on the structure of the discipline, in both literature and linguistics the research of the field directly informs its teaching, but that is not the case in language. Here it is generally taken for granted that research is based on teaching, that it is purely methodological in focus. Following this conventional perspective, we will begin by exploring the role of technology in language teaching and move thereafter to an examination of technology-based methodological research. At that point we will abandon the conventional perspective and suggest a potential role for technology in an entirely different area of research, that of second language acquisition. This section will therefore be considerably longer than the discussions of technology in the literary and linguistic enterprises, not only because many more language teachers than literature or linguistics teachers are already active in or interested in using technology and because more directly relevant materials are already commercially available, but also because this new and promising research agenda is still almost totally unfamiliar to most foreign language teachers.

Turning to the role of computers in language teaching, we still see that most commercially available materials represent a simple transposition of practice materials usually offered on paper. The content is for the most part conventional pedagogical linguistics, and the form is still largely shaped by traditional pedagogical theory. By far the largest segment of these materials is grammar and vocabulary drills; many have been commissioned by publishers to accompany language textbooks as "electronic workbooks." Although many teachers feel that drill and homework are precisely those aspects of language teaching that should not take up class time and should therefore be relegated to the computer, others feel that drilling vocabulary and grammar should play no role at all and — because they think of the computer as supporting only these activities — dismiss the entire enterprise of computer-assisted teaching. Without getting in-

volved in the general issue of whether or not grammar should be explicitly taught, we would still argue that good drills differ significantly from
bad drills in underlying pedagogical theory, in design sophistication, in
user-friendliness, and in sensitivity to individual learners' learning strategies.

Some lessons are called "tutorials," but the tutorial function is usually
limited to reworking the textbook explanation as a preliminary to drills.
Very few computer-based language materials are intended to substitute
for, or expand on, textbook presentation or explanation of language structures or functions, but those that do (e.g., Frank Dominguez' *Spanish
MicroTutor* or Martin Rice's Russian verb tutor), tend to be extremely
well received both by students who find textbook explanations inadequate
and by teachers who wish to avoid spending time filling that need.

The teaching of foreign language reading skills has as yet been addressed in very few programs, but projects under way at the University of
Minnesota (Dale Lange) and the University of Iowa (Geoffrey Hope) are
developing authoring software to allow teachers to create for their own
chosen reading texts a wide variety of helps and guided activities. The
teaching of writing has traditionally received little attention in the foreign
language curriculum, and little development of computer-based materials
has been undertaken. An exception is James Noblitt's *Système-D*, which
gives students a French word processor and on-line access to related
databases of lexical, grammatical, and usage information. However, recent years have seen the development of a number of programs and
curricular innovations in the teaching of writing in English, and many of
these are excellent models for computer-assisted support of foreign language writing. (See the chapter in this volume entitled "Computers in
Writing Instruction.")

Some programs offer simulations, games, or problem-solving activities
in the foreign language, ostensibly calling for active language production
in meaningful communicative activities, rather than language drill, which
is frequently devalued as passive, inauthentic, and decontextualized.
Some of these programs aim simply at engaging learner participation and
require no actual language production, only comprehension and subsequent response choices from screen offerings. Others call for language
input from the learner but make no attempt to control accuracy, basing
computer-student interaction on very simple pattern-matching. Any more
complex interactions with learners are likely to be based on fairly tradi-

tional answer-judging and therefore often employ narrowly defined lexical or grammatical criteria more than is immediately apparent; in other words, many such "games" or "meaningful activities" are really grammar lessons in disguise. (They also tend to control learners' moves fairly rigidly and in fact often present, or encourage learners to produce, language that is just as inauthentic as drill material, from the perspective of sociolinguistic and discourse appropriateness.) Only the most ambitious language programs currently under development, most notably Project Athena at MIT, have the resources to bring artificial intelligence and advanced parsing techniques to bear on the processing of relatively free-form learner-computer interactions, allowing both grammatically and communicatively sensitive feedback to student input.

The rapid expansion of interactive audio in digitized form is attracting strong interest, but language teachers are still frustrated by the limited availability and the high cost of the necessary massive storage capacity. Because so many institutions still have traditional audio labs, there is broad continuing interest in audio tape and thus in the development of inexpensive computer devices that can be built into such labs to control audio lessons on a more sophisticated level than that offered by a simple tape player. Again, the materials developed for this kind of interactive technology tend not to differ radically from pre-computer versions; that is, much of it is in the familiar listening-comprehension, dictation, or pronunciation drill formats.

Video is another matter. The phenomenal surge in the availability of VCRs and the proliferation of videotapes has met with immediate enthusiasm on the part of language teachers because of their recognition of the crucial importance of presenting learners with language in its cultural context. Although still beyond the means of most foreign language programs, satellite dishes, now mushrooming on foreign language buildings across the country, testify to the powerful attraction of authentic foreign language video — video broadcasts that were created for viewing by native speakers of the language, not for language pedagogy purposes, and that can be taped for immediate "fair use" classroom purposes.

The low cost and immediacy of tape makes it likely to be the preferred medium for video for some time, but it does not lend itself as well to computer-controlled interactive materials development because locating specific segments for students to work with is slow and imprecise. Videodisk technology has already attracted great interest and some major funding for foreign language teaching. The PICS project at the University of Iowa is securing copyright permission from European producers of authentic video so that teachers can receive disks together with a variety of support materials, including interactive lessons controlled by the computer. Project Athena at MIT has created French and Spanish videodisks that contain numerous variations on complex story lines to involve students in long-range interaction with characters and settings, and German videodisk materials created at Brigham Young University for the Defense Language Institute are the basis for lesson generation at the Air Force Academy. As yet, relatively little foreign language material is commercially available on videodisk, and production costs can be high, but as the technology becomes more accessible it is certain to be the fastest growing area of interest in technology-based language learning. Most academic projects in interactive video so far have aimed to teach listening comprehension; projects include the lesson formats developed by PICS, the Project Athena program *A la Rencontre de Philippe*, Edna Coffin's program in Hebrew, Ray Wakefield's work at the University of Minnesota, and the Air Force Academy materials. But video can also teach other skills: Robert Hart and Ulric Chung at the University of Illinois have developed prototype materials for vocabulary learning, and another Athena project, *No Recuerdo*, is designed to teach question and response communication skills as well as listening comprehension, with a special focus on cultural appropriateness and linguistic accuracy. Jack Abercrombie at the University of Pennsylvania has developed software for making pedagogical use of inexpensive foreign films on video disk. Nonetheless, most teachers still feel that the major benefit of video is its ability to create the cultural context rather than its potential to teach the language itself, and there is likely to be ongoing debate about the relative pedagogical value and cost-effectiveness of various uses.

The recent development of relatively simple utilities for creating hypertext and hypermedia programs has ushered in a new kind of technology-based language learning materials design, in which teachers can link together whatever information and help they think their students may need in performing some language task or exploring some body of language data. (We could call them "browsing programs.") The software, the same as that described above in discussing the teaching of literature, permits the nonlinear linking of numerous related databases through which learners can browse ad libitum. In the language-learning context this means, for example, that students can perform any of a variety of language tasks — reading or listening to a passage, possibly answering questions on it, working out grammar exercises, writing an essay, translating a text (virtually any task that does not require the computer to deal with students' spontaneous oral production) — in an electronic environment that provides instantaneous access to anything the materials developer chooses to include: a dictionary, a reference grammar, usage notes, cultural notes, literal or idiomatic equivalents, visual material in the form of graphics (animated or static) or photographs (still or video), audio material (digitized or analogue), and related material from other disciplines as well. This configuration of support for language activities allows learners to take the initiative in seeking whatever help or information they need or want. The development of such materials is certainly time-consuming, but current hypertext programs already allow relatively inexperienced teachers to structure attractive and dynamic programs.

Students' paths through such materials can be truly open and under their own control, so that the teacher has no idea what the students have seen or what they have learned, or branching options can be strictly controlled. Many promising programs of this kind have been demonstrated at teachers' conferences, but there is little discussion as yet of the pedagogical appropriateness of the various possible designs. Many seem to be based on the teacher's feeling that students ought to be delighted to have, and will be able to learn a great deal from, unlimited access to all these data rather than on a coherently planned connection between what students are likely to be able to make of the data, what the pedagogical purpose could or should be, and how one can ascertain whether that purpose has been achieved.

This brings us to the issue of authoring. Very few language teachers have the time or the incentive to learn a full-fledged programming language. Even authoring languages require a commitment beyond the realm of possibility for most teachers, and the advantage of their flexibility and power is offset by their difficulty. On the other hand, teachers who use off-the-shelf, "closed" lessons (i.e., programs that allow no input or modification by the teacher) usually become very quickly frustrated either by the inadequacies of the program or by a variety of mismatches between the content, design, or pedagogical objectives of the program on the one hand and the goals or styles of the teachers or the needs of the students on the other. The most serious inadequacies are usually seen to be in the area of error analysis and feedback. Even "templat." lessons, in which teachers can insert their own vocabulary lists or multiple-choice questions, tend to be quickly discarded by teachers who have any serious interest in the potential of the technology; their simplicity is offset by the lack of flexibility and power.

The solution lies in authoring systems, and the rapidly increasing number of commercially available authoring systems shows that vendors are aware of the demand. However, some of these systems are far more suitable for business and training than for the academic setting, and many of those designed for academic use are all-purpose or non-discipline-specific. Learning language is very different from learning other subject matters; therefore, the structure of language learning materials — and the authoring systems that enable their production — will often have to be governed by quite different design principles. The design even of authoring systems specifically by and for language teachers still has a long way to go in making the development of pedagogically sound and friendly language learning materials intuitively clear to teachers. The major hindrance to the development of good foreign language teaching software is teachers' lack of training in the principles underlying lesson design, so that even when a pedagogically experienced classroom teacher works together with a skilled programmer, the resulting materials may well be very crude by instructional design criteria.

In principle, authoring systems designed to be particularly suitable for language teachers should obviate many of the difficulties. However, the flexibility and adaptability of an authoring system is constrained by the uses to which its developer imagines it being put. Many authoring systems therefore allow — and by their existence encourage — teachers to create conventional electronic workbook exercises and not much else. Even authoring systems that support more interesting lesson designs may require or assume more sophistication than the average teacher brings to the task — and there is a direct correlation between the flexibility and open-endedness of an authoring system and the time required to learn to use it well. In principle, therefore, a really good authoring system for language learning materials will be designed on the basis of the best current language learning theories, suggesting a variety of strategies for the design of good lessons. Although this is certainly a tall order when considered in the context of language learning at all levels and for all purposes, some segments of the enterprise are being addressed by more limited authoring systems. Development teams at the Universities of Iowa and Minnesota are working on authoring systems for developing reading materials and at the University of Arizona on one for listening comprehension materials.

Research in corpus linguistics, discussed above, has the potential for contributing to language teaching, although probably for the most part indirectly. For example, teachers with access to the Pfeffer Spoken German Corpus, a transcription of about four hundred spontaneous interviews, can compare traditional textbook rules for a certain structure with the way that structure actually appears in spontaneous utterances by native speakers and can revise or expand their own explanations accordingly. Advanced students might be taught to investigate such questions themselves. Other developments in computational linguistics are becoming available to language teachers and language materials developers; for example, on-line foreign language dictionaries can be attached to foreign-language word-processing programs to facilitate composition writing. Randall Jones (Brigham Young) is currently developing a database of oral interviews with a wide variety of native speakers of German in a variety of sociolinguistic and cultural contexts; both the audio versions and the transcriptions will be usable for research and for teaching purposes.

The use of technology in teaching language is both further advanced and more controversial than its application in teaching literature or linguistics. The question of its efficacy or cost-effectiveness is still hotly debated, and urgent demands are made for research evaluating it. Unfortunately the evaluation questions are too often themselves confused; the pedagogical effectiveness of the computer cannot be assessed without a detailed exploration of the language materials delivered on it, of the ways teachers and students integrate these materials into classroom activities and the whole curriculum, and of a number of extremely important characteristics of individual language learners. Fundamentally, therefore, the controversies surrounding the use of technology derive more from lack of agreement in the field as to the nature of the language learning process than from any coherent opposition to the technology per se.

These problems and controversies should not disguise or detract from the urgent and growing demand in the profession for the realization of technology's potential. Foreign language enrollments are increasing, and the need for foreign language competence in business, industry, and government is increasing even more rapidly. Educational reform movements are putting pressure on educational institutions at every level to introduce or expand foreign language offerings at more advanced levels and in less commonly taught languages, and to produce learners who are proficient in authentic language-production situations. Meeting those demands will be flatly impossible without a massive increase in the use of technology, and that will require a concomitant increase in funding for developing materials and training teachers.

When we turn to consider the role of technology in the research effort associated with language teaching, the parallels with the role of technology in literary and linguistics research break down. We posited a logical relationship in which research in these areas forms the basis for the content of the relevant courses offered. Our exploration of the role of technology in teaching such courses suggested that one of the most significant innovations is the presentation to the learner of the authentic data of the discipline. One logical extension of this line of entailment would be research collecting data *from* the student on how literary or linguistic learning takes place in a technology-mediated environment. As yet, however, since there is no substantive materials development for foreign language literature or linguistics study, there is, perforce, no such research on how students learn this content.

As we have seen, however, there has already been considerable technology-based materials development for language study, which then allows for research on how language is learned. Even here there has been so far only scattered research, but the potential is rapidly attracting attention. This section on testing and research will therefore focus on the third of our three disciplinary endeavors, but will conclude with some indication of the potential for research on learning in the other two as well.

For the purposes of this discussion, testing refers to the assessment of the student's level of learning for the purpose of arriving at some decision about the student — grades, placement, requirement completion, certification of various kinds. Research, in contrast, refers to the assessment of the student's performance for the purpose of contributing to some theoretical enterprise. In the context of language study the term *research* is almost universally taken to refer to methodological research, based on pedagogical theory. However, classroom language acquisition research is gradually beginning to be recognized as a quite different enterprise, which is based on linguistic, sociolinguistic, and psycholinguistic theory. Both will be addressed here.

Testing

At the simplest level, computer testing can refer to administering on the computer any foreign language test that could also be given in some other medium. For example, a conventional paper-and-pencil test on grammar, reading or listening comprehension, spelling, dictation, or essay writing may be put onto the computer (listening materials will require some interfaced audio delivery) so that students type in their responses. In such testing the computer may also perform some basic error analysis on the typed-in responses, comparing them with pre-entered correct answers and collecting scores of right and wrong answers. Many commercially available computer language lessons have a test section where previously drilled material is presented without feedback or correction opportunities and scores are collected.

In contrast with traditional tests, computer-adaptive testing (CAT) is based on techniques that allow the creation of an infinite number of individualized tests, each one specifically adapted to the examinee's ability. A database contains a bank of test items strictly ranked as to difficulty, and the computer begins the test by selecting a few items at a plausible level. The student's response to these items allows the program to estimate the student's ability, and the next items are selected to test that estimate; with each response, the program adjusts its diagnosis. The theory underlying CAT is known as item- response theory, which assumes that the ability being tested in such a format is a single unified trait, and there is a good deal of ongoing controversy over the question of whether the complexity of language performance can be adequately assessed by tests based on such an assumption, of whether language ability can validly be considered a unified trait. Several language testing experts currently offer a cautious hope that some language tasks can be articulated finely enough so that tests can be designed to draw on a single dimension of language ability, at least well enough for placement testing. Computer-adaptive placement tests have already been developed by Jerry Larson at Brigham Young University for English as a Second Language and for Spanish; a French version is currently under development.

Numerous other projects are under way to implement the concept of CAT for a variety of foreign language testing purposes. American Council on the Teaching of Foreign Languages (ACTFL) is currently working on a computer-adaptive reading proficiency test as the logical sequel to the

oral proficiency interview. The Defense Language Institute has designed
a computer-adaptive reading proficiency test for Russian whose format
will be suitable for both listening and reading comprehension tests in a
variety of languages. Patricia Dunkel at Penn State and Robert Ariew at
the University of Arizona have a joint grant for developing computer-adaptive listening comprehension tests which will also be based on the implementation of the ACTFL/ETS (Educational Testing Service) proficiency
guidelines. It is clear that the near future will see the development of a
wide variety of technology-based adaptive tests, where test items may be
presented in aural, visual, or text form and the student's response given
orally, in typed form, or registered via some other device, for example by
means of a mouse or a touch-sensitive screen. The computer's analysis of
such student data may be extremely helpful in testing for course placement or in assessing certain subskills of language proficiency.

Research

The issue of what constitutes research in language education is a
complex and muddy one, even after we set aside the conservative position
that language teachers should publish research on literature or linguistics. Many in the field take it for granted that language education research
can only be methodological or pedagogical in nature, attempting to correlate the effect of some pedagogical treatment on student performance
(individual students or, more commonly, class groups) with scores —
sometimes general course grades, sometimes scores on specialized tests
designed for the research. The computer can fit into this context in two
ways. First, in principle, "computer-based methodological research" could
refer to any study that used computer-generated test scores to assess the
effect of the methodology being studied; here the computer is simply a
more efficient tool for doing conventional studies. Second, the computer
can collect and analyze data on the efficacy of the technology application
itself in language learning. Unfortunately this is the only kind of computer-assisted research that occurs to many language teachers, and —
equally unfortunately — not only teachers but also many administrators
expect this kind of research to generate definitive answers to questions
about the value and cost-effectiveness of technology-assisted language
learning.

These expectations cannot be realized, for two reasons. First, the use of
computers does not constitute a method or a methodology of language

teaching; a wide variety of methods or approaches or philosophies can be implemented in computer-based language materials. Studies on the delivery system used for materials can never be carried out independently of a serious assessment of the materials themselves. Second, it is almost impossible to devise a well-controlled methodological experiment to test whether technology helps language learning because there are too many uncontrollable variables: the individual teacher's working style, the individual learners, the design of the technology-based materials themselves, and the ways in which they are integrated into the language curriculum.

Much more promising are the smaller-scale studies in which most of these pedagogical variables can be held constant while the effects of changing one of them can be traced. For example, a number of studies have explored the correlation of features in learning style, or strategies of computer use, with success in mastering language learning tasks. Such studies can be carried out nonintrusively (i.e., without setting up any special research task for students or intervening in their language production task) by attaching a key-press tracking facility to any computer (or interactive audio or video) lesson that is assigned to language learners and analyzing each student's moves through the material. Data on the amount of time spent, the help sought and what is accomplished with it, the number or proportion or type of errors in contrast to correct performance on any part of the task, and the paths chosen through the material can all be analyzed for insights into features of materials design or curricular integration that will greatly improve the efficacy of the technology. Eventually we will have good information to answer many parts of the following query: "What kind of language learner, at what level or in what circumstances of language study, in what kind of learning task, can make best use of what kind of technology-based learning assistance?" This kind of pedagogical research should reach beyond language pedagogy to incorporate current work in cognitive and educational psychology and man-machine interaction.

In contrast to methodological research, second language acquisition (SLA) research investigates the language learning itself, not in the context of the pedagogical treatment but in relation to characteristics of the learner (for example, age, native language, or cognitive style) or to linguistic, psycholinguistic, or sociolinguistic features of the language performance context. To date, far more SLA research has been carried out on learners of English as a Second Language than on foreign language learners, and most research on the latter has examined nontutored, or immersion learning, rather than conventional foreign language classroom learning. Very little such research has involved the computer in any capacity; the following discussion therefore suggests potentially important new research directions instead of reporting on an already accepted research methodology.

Learner data in the form of scores can contribute to SLA research when the underlying theory makes predictions that can be confirmed or disconfirmed on the basis of comprehension or production responses that are either right or wrong. Here again the computer can function as a highly efficient data elicitation and collection device for research tasks also possible in other modalities. In such research the role of the computer is independent of the particular SLA theory under investigation. For example, the much-cited morpheme order acquisition studies of the 1970s attempted to confirm certain SLA hypotheses about the order of acquisition of specified English morphemes on the basis of the learner's scores on a task requiring the choice of the correct morpheme in 80 percent of its obligatory contexts. Later work raised serious questions about the validity of this research, but its data elicitation and collection task could easily be implemented on the computer for more carefully motivated theoretical purposes. Another example of SLA research that employs right-wrong scores on language tasks is the linguistic work investigating hypotheses from government and binding theory, which predicts that children's acquisition of certain syntactic structures is triggered by their recognition of the presence, in their language input, of other related structures. Such research could compile scores for grammaticality judgments on, or for actual production or comprehension of, these critical structures and their correlation with the "triggering" structures.

Scores are not the only information that computers can return about learner language. Parsing programs based on constructs of artificial intelligence, now being developed in several different research contexts, can analyze reasonably free-form language input (i.e., not just filled-in blanks) and can return a detailed syntactic and morphological specification within limited domains and thus can provide linguistic analyses of learner language extremely useful in SLA.

Recently, however, the focus of SLA research has shifted from analysis of the language learner's product, the utterance itself, to analysis of the language processing that goes on in the learner's mind. Current pedagogical concern with communicative competence and proficiency has fixed research attention on learners' ability to communicate spontaneously in the language, rather than on their degree of mastery of specified grammatical structures. The theoretical interest in this kind of research lies in its connections with other psycholinguistically motivated work on first and second language acquisition. The hypothesis underlying much of this research is that learners of any language (first or subsequent, in or out of the classroom) acquire it by trying to impose their own idiosyncratic organization on the input, trying to work out their own guesses or "rules" (usually unconscious) about how meaning and form are connected, which are the basis for their production and comprehension of the language. For the purposes of this kind of classroom SLA research, scores are not likely to be very revealing. Research attempting to support or disconfirm such processing hypotheses requires data showing how learners actually express and comprehend meaning, showing why one form is chosen over another, and showing under what circumstances an utterance is comprehended as meaning one thing rather than another.

From this perspective the fundamental goal of learner language analysis (whether that analysis will inform pedagogy or the development of SLA theory) is not just to state what the errors are but to understand why the learner makes them — not to describe the differences between the learner's language product and the native speaker's but to understand the differences in the processes of putting together the utterance. Linguistic analysis of the product, even the most sophisticated parsing, does not of itself provide insight into the process.

What kind of data, and what kind of data analysis, can provide evidence of learners' idiosyncratic ways of constructing meaning? And what role can the computer play in the undertaking? Technological constraints being what they are, we can leave out of consideration for the moment any computer analysis of the processing of spontaneous, meaningful spoken foreign language communication, but all the other language skills can be technologically explored now that the integration of audio and video with the computer can be taken for granted.

The interest here is in the computer's ability to interact with learners, while they are in the act of using the foreign language in some meaningful activity, to find out how their foreign language thinking reflects the language input. There are two related but different kinds of computer research that allow insight into the process. In the first, the computer keeps

~~first~~ ~~of~~ ~~every~~ ~~move~~ ~~a~~ ~~learner~~ ~~makes~~ ~~in~~ ~~a~~ ~~technology~~ ~~based~~ ~~language~~ ~~task~~
but does not interrupt or intrude. In the second, the computer interacts
with the learner in the course of performing the language task on-line; the
computer provides feedback on input, poses questions to assess understanding, etc. Both these kinds of studies require the designing of a
research task in which the technology (either the computer by itself or
with interactive audio or video) does not simply deliver stimulus-response
tasks but rather provides an environment within which complex meaningful language processing is required and supported. Such an environment
may include graphics, animation, culturally authentic audio or video,
simulations, and so on, but these are not a necessary part of every
meaningful language activity at every level or for every type of learner.
Research on reading comprehension or on writing strategies, for example, may need only a simple text-presentation format.

In the first kind of study, the program can set the learner a language
task, provide appropriately complex resource materials to be drawn on,
and track the learner's every move from the task through whatever helps
are sought and back to the task. For example, to study how learners
actually go about learning to read in a foreign language, reading comprehension task materials could allow the learner on-line access to glosses at
several levels of difficulty and to various kinds of assistance in top-down or
bottom-up processing — highlighting techniques or mark-up with symbols to cue certain kinds of reading. The data collected on precisely what
each student calls for, and at what point in working through the passage
and answering questions on it, could then be correlated with independently measured learner characteristics to explore various questions. Do
learners of a certain age, or at a certain level of learning, or with certain
cognitive styles, or in reading certain kinds of material, tend to employ
reading strategies of one kind or another? How consistently? With what
success?

Analogous research can easily be imagined for listening comprehension: the learner is presented with audio material under the control of the
computer and is offered multiple helps — audio replays of large or small
segments, the appearance on screen of single words or whole phrases,
grammatical analyses, glosses, etc. Research on learning to write in a
foreign language becomes possible with the introduction of programs like
Système-D, in which the learner assigned to write a composition has
access to a lexicon with usage examples, reference grammar, and idiom-

atic phrases on a range of topics and conversational functions. The program keeps a record of queries to the databases. For individual learners or groups with particular characteristics, we could ask, for example, whether they seem to be doing a lot of word-for-word translation or are trying to structure meaning directly in French, what they don't bother to look up but prefer to guess at, etc.

Since any language system consists of its vocabulary and its grammar, the learning of these two components is obviously essential to the development of the traditional four skills: speaking, listening, reading, and writing. An investigation of the processing that goes into the classroom second language acquisition of vocabulary and grammar thus has the clearest potential for linking foreign language research with work in first language acquisition and linguistic and psycholinguistic theory. Little research in foreign language education has as yet been done on vocabulary learning, but research in cognitive psychology and first language acquisition suggests the importance of a multimedia environment to allow audio, video, or graphic representation of word-meaning relationships and concepts and of multiple optional activities to help forge the connections — copying, repetition, examples, choices of native or target language definitions or paraphrases, placement in semantic networks, etc. Studies of different cognitive mechanisms, or of conscious and unconscious strategies for connecting or keeping separate the mental lexicons of first and second languages, could have far-ranging implications for the development both of pedagogical efforts and of language acquisition theory generally.

Similarly, although much current foreign language pedagogy sharply devalues grammar teaching, the development of grammatical concepts is a sine qua non of all communicative language ability. Although foreign language educators have studied, and heatedly debated the value of, learners' mastery of *grammar rules,* until recently neither our theory nor our research tools have allowed research on learners' acquisition of *grammatical concepts.* If we work from the hypothesis, implicit or explicit in many approaches to language acquisition theory, that language learners structure their own idiosyncratic "rules of thumb" for connecting meaning and form in the language being learned, we can design language tasks to require the production or comprehension of meaningful language in contexts that allow unprecedented insights into learner language processing. Exploring those individual rules, the ways they overlap with and differ from the "real" rules of the language, and the ways they confirm or challenge the predictions of linguistic and psycholinguistic theory could contribute to a radically ambitious research agenda for foreign language education — and again, the findings would be equally significant to the improvement of pedagogy and to the development of interdisciplinary theory.

The computer can play two different roles in this kind of research. First, its ability to elicit, collect, and analyze masses of data automatically, objectively, consistently, and rapidly — to track a large number of details at once and analyze the relationships among them — is crucial to the investigation of anything as complex as the underlying reasons for learners' language idiosyncrasies. One of the major hindrances to the development of this kind of psycholinguistic theory has been that the research demands so careful and thorough an analysis of the data that few substantive studies have been undertaken in depth on more than a few subjects.

Second, an even more intriguing role for the computer lies in its potential for interacting directly with the learner in the act of producing language, its ability to respond specifically to learners' input and thus to shape their subsequent utterances. The computer not only can track the processing but also can immediately analyze the product and present learners with the analysis as feedback — instantaneously, while they are still in the mind-set that produced it — and ask them to revise their processing with its help. The detailed data on these interactions provide extraordinarily interesting evidence of what the learners think their errors are and what they think they need to know to correct their errors — evidence of how they think language works.

III. Underlying Issues

Having considered the role of technology, actual and potential, in the research and teaching efforts of foreign language education, let us turn back to some of the underlying issues that must be addressed in the effort to form a context for the successful development of the "new humanism."

We spoke earlier of the ways in which technology can empower the foreign language teacher-scholar by extending and expanding the discipline's traditional activities and allowing access to unprecedented amounts and kinds of data. However, that empowerment itself raises new issues. The availability of computers varies enormously from one institution to another, as do the institutional structures controlling and supporting the implementation of the computers. Humanists who have come to understand the potential of the technology in their own work want unmediated access, but they do not necessarily want to acquire the technological skills that will make them independent. However, the support offered by centralized academic computing services is often not based on an adequate understanding of the discipline; ideally, therefore, institutions should distribute specialized computing support to related groups of disciplines. At the same time, care must be taken that those humanists who have not yet had the opportunity to consider a serious application of computers are not disenfranchised by their inability to articulate their needs in terms that computer scientists can understand.

The empowerment process is a cyclical one. Technically inexperienced teacher-scholars who are asked what they want computers to do for them will at first respond only in terms of the computer's similarity to other tools and its applicability to tasks with which they are already familiar. Only when new possibilities are demonstrated to them in the conceptual framework of their own discipline will they begin to expand their own ideas as a basis for new uses; only after several passes through this learning cycle can they take the initiative in suggesting more complex research and teaching implementations. Available hardware and software have shaped humanists' perception of technology and the discipline's sense of its appropriate purposes. We are now at the point of a major breakthrough in which the teacher-scholar's recognition of the possibilities orders the priorities of technological development, instead of the other way around. The designer of an authoring system, just as much as the designer of a workstation, structures the tasks to which the product can be put, and not until both hardware and software are developed in substantive consultation with disciplinary specialists will the new humanist be fully empowered.

Changes in empowerment will cause, as well as result from, shifts in governance, both in foreign language departments and in the university. Those who control the allocation of resources must understand that the disciplines of the humanities need technology just as much as those of the sciences. Business, industry, and government, as well as academia, recognize that the study of the humanities in a liberal arts curriculum adds

depth, flexibility and an understanding of cross-cultural human values
and makes graduates more broadly educated than does vocational training. But the significance of the new humanism lies in its potential to go
beyond adding these attributes to integrating them with scientific and
technological sophistication. The vast resources of data and data-manage-
ment power that technology can marshal expand the knowledge base to
the point where both research and teaching in foreign languages, literature, and linguistics can be truly cross-departmental, even interdisciplinary. A hypermedia exploration of a novel can include data from history,
sociology, psychology, art, music, film — just as research in history or
psychology or sociology can refer to data found in novels. The parameters
within which research projects are conceived—and the lines of funding
for those projects — will have to be redefined to allow for this broadened
understanding of humanism.

The most fundamental shift implied by the disciplinary perspective
afforded us by these technological possibilities is in the epistemology of
the discipline. Traditionally, knowledge of a foreign language consisted of
mastering a number of items or facts about the language, just as knowing
the literature consisted of knowing a body of facts about it. Although
computers can certainly still provide instruction to students in those facts,
they can also make the primary data directly available to students, give
them the opportunity to browse and explore, and structure an environment within which they can organize and interpret the data for themselves. Knowledge so acquired is not a set of items or facts but is a
process, a way of thinking or making connections, a dynamic flexible
structure of relationships. (In fact, this shift is taking place in all disciplines.)

Again, this shift in epistemology both requires and results from a shift
in the way the foreign language curriculum is conceived. Traditionally the
curriculum has been an ordered, linear sequence of items. Knowledge of
literature accumulates in a set of century or genre courses; knowledge of
linguistic structure proceeds from simple to complex, building from
sounds to sentences. Knowledge in this sense is quantifiable: "I've had
three years of Spanish" is a meaningful statement in the traditional curriculum because we know with a fair degree of accuracy what items of
knowledge have been accumulated in three years. And "traditional" software (lessons developed within that epistemology) offer the mastery of
discrete bits of knowledge to be fitted into that linear item-based curricu-

lum. With the resources made available by the technology, the foreign language curriculum can now be structured as a network of related ideas about the primary data, in which the learner is helped to develop the information-processing mode of thought that characterizes the teacher-scholar's own approach.

This shift also raises new issues. The technology allows for the entire learning enterprise to be driven by learner inquiries. Materials could be developed — indeed, some already exist — to offer the individual learner, working alone with the computer, all the data needed to develop a profound and solidly contextualized understanding of a piece of literature, with every possible path of exploration through the data made available. But how will learners make use of the data? How will they know what paths to follow, where to branch off, how to return to a main line of inquiry, how to make meaningful connections? Do we want the learner to be in complete control? How can we know what suggested or imposed structuring of the exploration will be most helpful? These questions can be developed as hypotheses for research not only into the language learning process but also into the process of interpretation and criticism. But as educational issues, they cannot be answered on the basis of hunches or traditional notions about the discipline or its students; they must be answered on the basis of a serious consideration of the epistemology of this new humanism.

The power of technology to facilitate a new kind of research — we might call it CARSLA, computer-assisted research on second language acquisition (acquisition now in its broadest sense) — suggests a larger perspective on the central role that technology can play in unifying the several endeavors of foreign language education. We suggest that technology has the potential for bridging gaps between the research on literature, linguistics, and language acquisition, gaps between the teaching of these three areas, and gaps between research and teaching generally. The development of a disciplinary agenda for realizing this potential will depend on attention to a wide variety of factors, some of them intellectual and theoretical, others political, financial, and practical.

The sine qua non of such an agenda is the idea that it is possible. Teachers who have not been trained to think about language learning from these perspectives have little basis for conceiving of such research, and disciplinary, departmental, and institutional structures do not support it. Nonetheless, the unified perspective on language learning briefly sketched out here can serve as a framework integrating the learning of communicative language, linguistics, and literature, and the research supported within each area could also develop as an integrated effort.

The kinds of research emphasized here cannot be undertaken without the computer, and the kind of computer design principles our agenda requires will be developed only by combining of the theoretical concerns of the scholar and the sophisticated input of the computer expert. In fact, a CARSLA agenda cannot be planned without an unprecedented synergism among three groups of people who do not usually talk to each other or read the same journals: those who can realize the potential of the hardware; those who develop the literary, linguistic, or language acquisition theories that structure the research or the instruction; and those who can implement those theoretical principles in the design of the software for either research or teaching.

The research agenda is thus an interdisciplinary one, with all the usual problems of interdisciplinary endeavors. Governance issues can play a major role in enabling or inhibiting CARSLA. (Many governance issues in foreign language education have already been explored in the conference on that problem held by the Consortium for Language Teaching and Language Learning, but this kind of research effort was not a topic there.) Among the major factors discouraging language faculty from undertaking CARSLA projects are problems of disciplinary recognition, promotion and tenure, which in turn are linked to questions of the relative status of literature, linguistics, and language teaching or language acquisition theory in the field of foreign language education. The status of the computer is closely linked to the status of language teaching, since faculty tend to think of instructional computing as limited to the elementary levels of language learning, which are commonly regarded as having less intellectual value.

Many universities are currently considering adding computers to their language labs or setting up computer facilities for humanities in general or language courses in particular. Unfortunately most plans for such facilities are designed without an awareness on the part of administrators, computing consultants, or even language faculty themselves of the intellectual potential of CARSLA. As a result such facilities tend to be conceived of merely as extensions of the old language lab — i.e., as service units — and are often headed by managerial and technical personnel rather than by faculty or research associates with the intellectual credentials for attracting both the inside interest and the necessary outside money to establish a serious ongoing research agenda. Junior faculty looking for "promotable" research will not be encouraged to invest time and energy in research in a lab, fearing with good reason that instructional computing or software development will hinder rather than help them in getting tenure. The irony is that psycholinguistically motivated language acquisition research is not only theoretically respectable and intellectually rigorous but also has the potential to contribute simultaneously both to the development of a significant body of theory and to the improvement of basic language education — a cause strongly espoused by a series of national recommendations for improving American education. Furthermore, as we have pointed out, work from this perspective can also help to join the student's experience in learning language and literature into a seamless whole of humanistic import greater than can be realized in the conventional dichotomy between language and literature courses.

At the same time, efforts must be made to inform granting agencies about the potential and the significance of this effort. The National Endowment for the Humanities (NEH) is interested in foreign languages only in terms of the humanities content of foreign literatures; it shies away from projects in methodological research or materials development for language teaching and has tended to be reluctant to fund computer-based projects even for literature teaching, though it has supported the development of machine-readable dictionaries and text corpora. The Department of Education supports materials development, especially for the less commonly taught languages, and supports a fair amount of research on language education. But the teachers on its review panels inevitably vary widely in theoretical sophistication, and a great many language teachers are still prejudiced against research that seems too theoretical. The National Science Foundation supports linguistic research and has begun to underwrite projects in second language acquisition, but in contrast to the Department of Education, it demands a primary focus on theory and therefore tends to reject overtly classroom-oriented projects. Whether we can convince private foundations that classroom-oriented projects can contribute significantly to the revitalization of language education is uncertain.

Conclusion

If anything has become clear from this discussion of the possibilities and the problems of integrating technology into the foreign language curriculum, it should be that the enterprise is in flux. The values and goals of humanistic research and teaching have not changed, but shifts in perspective and priorities are inextricably linked to the evolution of new tools and techniques for exploring the primary data of the discipline. This state of flux presents considerable uncertainties for all concerned. Foreign language faculty are both attracted by the potential of computers and anxious about the changes computers may bring to their work, and the new humanism is plagued by all the risks attendant on interdisciplinary work in today's academy. Department heads lack precedents or criteria for assessing ground-breaking interdisciplinary work and even for distinguishing intradisciplinary leadership and innovation from trivial bandwagon-jumping. Vendors and distributors of hardware and software value the education market but have a generally inadequate understanding of the disciplinary structures and forces that shape it; the foreign language sector is a relatively small one and its needs are difficult to understand or predict.

The risks will become less for both the academic and the nonacademic partners as academics become better able to articulate their particular needs to the vendors and to insist to their disciplinary peers and their campus administrators that using technology in research and instruction does not vitiate, but rather enhances, the fundamental values of the discipline. Until now the impetus for the integration of technology into foreign language education has been largely hardware-driven, with teacher-scholars for the most part reacting to the vendors' marketing efforts. An understanding of the intellectual issues raised by the technology will allow humanists to articulate their needs from within a stable conceptual framework, rather than from the basis of a sometimes superficial grasp of technical marvels, and that will place the cooperative development of the technology on a much sounder footing for all concerned.

But this mutual understanding will not be achieved easily or quickly. It depends on principled, long-range education of the new generation of humanists; neither the demonstration of new products nor the occasional two-hour workshop will do the trick. At present there are still few senior faculty members with enough experience and sophistication to serve as mentors for junior faculty and graduate students in developing a coherent sense of the role of technology in the discipline. We know of no foreign language departments offering courses or regular supervised hands-on experience in discipline-specific implementations of technology for either teaching or research, though language labs and resource centers are increasingly expanding their offerings in this area. Foreign language educators do not need to learn to program or engage in basic materials development, but it is to everyone's advantage — we would go so far as to claim that it is essential — for the presently emerging and the future generations of teacher-scholars to be sophisticated users of technology-based materials and technological tools in all aspects of their professional lives.

The technological tools necessary to teach or do research in literature, linguistics, and language learning are strikingly similar, that is, generating intelligent and creative applications of technology reveals the underlying unity of the enterprise. Tools devised by teacher-scholars doing research on literature may be useful to their colleagues in certain linguistic efforts and vice versa, and the way both groups implement technology in their research can be the basis for significant efforts in teaching literature and linguistics. Similarly, thinking through how such tools should be designed, and how the content they deliver should be organized for the learner, requires input from the language teacher-scholar.

We believe that the computer has the potential for effecting change at every level of teaching and research in foreign language education. Just as databases and text manipulation programs are making possible literary and textual analyses that were previously inconceivable, data elicitation and analysis capabilities can allow unprecedented insights into the multifarious workings of language in the human mind.

It has not escaped our attention that the challenges we face are remarkably similar to those faced by Renaissance humanists. The printing press gave rise to an unprecedented public dialogue among humanists and scientists, a dialogue that crossed linguistic and cultural boundaries and created a community of teacher-scholars. Those "old" humanists also employed technology to process the authentic data of their disciplines and to advance their own conception of the meaning of education. We stand at a similar historical crossroads. We foresee that the technology itself may have the power to transform foreign language education by bringing about a new synthesis of disciplinary concerns.

Notes

The original conception of this chapter was developed by James Noblitt; he also contributed to the section on linguistics. The principal author is Nina Garrett whose area of special interest is language acquisition research. Frank Dominguez is largely responsible for the section on foreign language pedagogy. Much of the information on text processing for literary and textual scholarship came from Randall Jones, Professor of German at Brigham Young University. Valuable contributions and comments were also made by Jack Abercrombie, Susan Bland, Margret Hazen, and Robert Hart.

1. In smaller and/or less research-oriented institutions or departments there is likely to be less emphasis on faculty members' independent literary research and more on their ability to teach literature courses as part of a general humanities curriculum. Faculty in such departments may have a master's degree rather than a Ph.D. in the language and may be promoted entirely on the basis of their teaching ability and their general service to the department and the institution.

Chapter 9

Computers in Writing Instruction: Blueprint for Progress

Helen J. Schwartz et al.[1]

American institutions of higher education embrace many different missions and set many different goals for the learning of their diverse student bodies. But students everywhere write, and faculty everywhere assess their students' knowledge at least in part on the basis of what they write. Writing is thus at the heart of every curriculum, and institutional planning for improvement in learning falls short whenever it fails to take into account the need to include the teaching of writing explicitly as a key element in the curriculum. Today this observation engenders little controversy. Indeed, in the last decade a careful look at the state of student prose has led to the reestablishment or invigoration of writing requirements and writing programs on many campuses. But now institutions find themselves being asked for the first time to invest not just in the teaching of writing but in the *tools of writing,* in microcomputer laboratories and classrooms, in word-processing software, and in letter-quality printing. Computing is an expensive resource for any institution, and using computer technology for writing radically democratizes the need for that resource: potentially every student in every class requires substantial access to it. Yet, proposals to accommodate such a dramatic increase in the use of computing simply to accommodate a change in the technology of writing will be treated skeptically, and with reason: such changes will require an institution to reallocate and refit existing space, retrain staff and faculty, and create new budget lines for personnel, for the acquisition of computers and for their maintenance and replacement. And for what benefit? If word processing is merely "fancy typing," as we have all too often heard, then it is an attractive convenience, nothing more. We believe, however, that the benefits of "fancy typing" — quickly produced and attractive text — are in fact among the *less* significant of the benefits that computers bring to the teaching and the practice of writing.

In this essay we make the case for the powerful educational advantage that current computer technology brings to writers: in the workplace and in academe, for both students and faculty, not only in the writing classroom but also throughout the undergraduate curriculum. We argue further that new developments are bringing about a radical change in text, calling for a redefinition of writing that will affect the nature of learning and communication both inside and outside of academe. To meet the challenges and demands we have described, institutions of higher education will need new planning and new partnerships. We offer a blueprint for progress, based on the reality and promise of computers in writing, described more fully below. We then outline the kinds of support writing faculty will need in order to realize current advantages and share in forming a changing conception of writing. Finally, after advice to academic administrators, we list our specific recommendations. Throughout, our goal is to help institutions in many different academic settings to decide the level and pace of commitment suitable for their academic mission. We address ourselves to the potential partners who must put into practice the blueprint for change presented here: faculty, academic administrators, technicians and administrators for information technology, developers and vendors of hardware and software, current and future employers of college students, as well as funding agencies in government and the private sector.

Computers Changing Writing

Three converging trends underlie the argument for bringing computers into the writing classroom.

- The habits of writers are changing.

- The character of writing instruction is changing.

- The nature of text itself is changing as it is increasingly created and stored in the electronic media.

These changes are already transforming the way writing is practiced and taught now and they hold promise of radically redefining what we mean by *text* in the foreseeable future.

1. *The habits of writers are changing.* The practices and habits of writers — from elementary school children to business people — are already being formed and transformed by word processing and other computer-delivered writing aids. Not enough is yet understood from research about the character and quality of electronically produced texts when they are compared with texts produced with a typewriter or with pencil and paper. But this much is evident: the genie is out of the bottle, and there's no putting this particular genie back. Once people begin using word processing fluently, they generally prefer it to any other medium. The only factor that seems to limit the spread of word processing as the writing technology of choice for undergraduate students is lack of access. Give students a computer laboratory — in the basement of a dorm or in a library — and they will gravitate to it immediately. What will they be doing there? For the most part, these students are writing, everything from problem sets to journals, from poster copy to musical scores, from love letters to senior theses. They write in French, Hebrew, Russian, and Chinese. They integrate graphs, charts, and mathematical symbols into their writing. They design the appearance of their writing with fonts and graphics, they "publish" it, and they send it electronically around the world. These are not fantasies of the future, but pictures of what students are already doing where facilities are available to them.

2. *The character of writing instruction is changing.* But we hear our colleagues asking, when students write on computers, they may write more and write more willingly, they may produce text more quickly and attractively, but are they writing better? Do they write more correctly, more soundly? Do they think more deeply or express their thoughts more cogently? Not necessarily. Writing is a rhetorical act: it requires an author with something to say and an audience to whom to say it. Although computers make putting words together faster and easier, they do little to raise the writer's awareness of a specific audience, nor do they compel writers to dig deeper or think harder. The inescapable conclusion is that learning to write effectively requires sound instructional support. And computers contribute significantly to the powerful and effective new strategies that writing teachers have developed. To see how technology sup-

ports pedagogy, we must summarize the pedagogical aims and methods of the field.

Over the last decade, writing instruction has been reconceptualized. In the past, much instruction called attention to the characteristics of good texts, focusing on correctness of form, content, and grammar. Increasingly, however, theorists and practitioners have focused on the rhetorical process: how authors learn what they have to say and how they communicate it through text to audiences. This process-centered pedagogy has shifted attention away from the fixed, surface features of a completed text and toward the fleeting and often invisible cognitive and rhetorical activities that produce texts. It asks students to understand writing not simply as the finished product, but rather as the entire series of activities constituting that finished product: critically reading others' texts or critically examining events, objects, experiments, or ideas; exploring one's own reactions and those of others; tentatively expressing those reactions in words; gradually structuring those words into a text; sharing the text with readers; reconsidering all aspects of this process and reformulating the text accordingly.

As the emphasis in writing instruction has shifted from products to processes, writing has increasingly been seen as a powerful learning tool not only in traditional writing courses but throughout the curriculum. When students come to see that writing encompasses both learning and communicating, they can adapt their writing strategies to a wide range of writing tasks: an essay for a freshman English class, a research paper for Archaeology 388, a position paper for student government, or a marketing analysis on the job. When faculty across the curriculum understand and exploit writing as a process, they can help students see both the cognitive and the social (that is, the contextual) dimensions of writing. Only the various faculties can explain the rhetorical dimensions of their own disciplines: How does this knowledge fit into the continuing conversation in the field? Who has said what to whom, and what is at stake with a particular answer? What are the characteristic styles of expression and argument with this "discourse community"? The process-centered pedagogy developed by writing faculty, therefore, provides a way for teachers in all disciplines to exploit student writing in their courses to enrich and improve the process of learning — whether in economics, biology, or art history.

Computer technology offers significant support for these pedagogical aims and methods. Teachers of writing who have introduced their stu dents to the simplest form of electronic writing, a stand-alone microcom puter equipped with word-processing software, have discovered that they can greatly facilitate process-oriented writing and writing instruction. The emphasis on writing process puts a premium on rethinking and reorgan izing in the course of writing, and thus on frequent rewriting. While working, the writer may create many and varied provisional texts, each of which may look quite different from the others: in the course of one task, a writer may produce jottings, lists, outlines, notes, and paragraphs, all written and eventually overwritten as the process plays itself out. Process oriented instruction challenges teachers of writing to guide this process effectively, requiring instructors to intervene as writing takes place and to show students how to manage the multitude of forms they create and the wealth of responses they receive. With the help of technology, teachers can demonstrate the writing process directly, share moments of writing experience among groups of students both in and out of class, and provide timely feedback about the content or readers' reaction to which writers can easily respond. In these ways, the technology supports both current theory and widespread practice.

Despite the comfortable fit between technology and pedagogical the ory, however, the benefits of computers in writing instruction have been difficult to study. (Reviews of research are listed in the bibliography.) So many variables appear, so much change in the writing environment oc curs when a new technology enters, that standard evaluation practices and procedures have been inadequate to describe these changes. Never theless, research shows some important benefits for students. The most measurable effects show improved attitudes toward learning in general and writing in particular. Those more positive attitudes may be in part responsible for a second observable phenomenon: higher retention and completion rates. In studies at LaGuardia Community College of the City University of New York, the University of Minnesota, and Texas Southmost College, for example, significantly more students in writing courses that employed the technology in intrinsic ways (that is, not simply to automate drill and practice but to teach writing as a complex set of processes) completed the required courses as compared with students enrolled in the same courses taught without the new technologies.

These effects suggest that using computers in writing instruction may offer the most immediate educational gain to our most marginal students, to those coming to higher education with the least preparation and with the highest failure or drop-out rates. Ironically, the institutions and programs that seem least able to provide the full and rich environment required by substantive use of technology may stand to gain the most from its use. The changes that the entire writing environment are undergoing, however, make it essential that educational institutions prepare all students for the world in which they will live and work. And that world will be increasingly dependent on the electronic word.

3. *The nature of text is changing.* At the center of every college and university is its library of texts. But what is a *text?* By *text* we have traditionally meant a collection of symbols representing words. Since the fifteenth century, the medium of these texts has generally been fixed print. But with the advent of electronic information technologies, the definition of *text* as "words in fixed print" is beginning to expand and change. Two characteristics of this new, electronic text are especially important for our discussion of teaching writing.

First, it is no longer necessary to think of texts primarily as *collections of words*. Digitized data can equally well represent words, numbers, sounds, mathematical or musical notations, and images. The writer or creator of a text can move fluidly back and forth from one to the other, choosing the representation that, at the moment, conveys meaning most effectively. This ability to represent ideas in a variety of ways that can be easily integrated makes writing an easily used and more valuable tool in the disciplines that rely heavily on symbolic notation, sound, and visual images to express meaning. The notion of a "multimedia" presentation becomes redundant as the single, electronic medium is increasingly able to convey, as an integrated "text," ideas and information in many forms.

Second, it is no longer necessary to think of texts as *fixed in print* — or as fixed in any medium, for that matter. Experimental, unfixed, electronic texts already have a name: *hypermedia.* Accessed by computer, some of the materials that constitute a hypermedia text may be print, but others may be audio or visual images of all kinds. They may be stored in several different media, but readers should be able to look at them with little or no awareness of the original medium. In addition, these materials need not be presented to readers in a fixed, linear order. Indeed, a hypermedia text may be structured so that readers are invited to devise their own orders, or to follow multiple paths through the material as their needs and interests dictate. A new rhetoric — a new relationship between author and reader   begins to emerge in the interactive environment of the electronic text. The author may take on many different roles, perhaps as partner or advisor, rather than simply as unapproachable authority.

When we see writing as rhetoric — the ways authors create and convey ideas to audiences through text — the changes wrought by computer technology force us to redefine all the terms of rhetoric. The distinction between author and audience is blurred by electronic mail and bulletin boards, where malleable text is critiqued by readers and amended by writers and where discussions reach consensus without a clear attribution of ideas being possible. The character of text changes as more and more sophisticated tools are developed for creating, storing, and manipulating those texts. In the next decades, we are going to be witnessing changes in the definition and practice of text production — of writing — itself.

We do not believe that it is possible for institutions of postsecondary learning to ignore the curricular implications of these changes in the character of writing, writing instruction, and written text. But what is an institution's best strategy for response? We believe that there are opportunities available now for using technology to take advantage of these present and impending changes, opportunities that can be tailored to meet the needs of any institution — large, small, public, private, affluent or not. In most cases an *evolving* commitment to computer technology for writing will be the most feasible and also the most effective strategy, but the impact over time will be no less than *revolutionary.*

We challenge institutions to assign a high priority to two goals:

- Improve the quality of students' writing with the wise use of current technology and therefore build the basis for improvement in learning across the curriculum.

- Prepare both the students and the institution for the dramatic changes in reading and writing, teaching and research, that are coming in the era of electronic text — both in education and the workplace.

Clearly these goals cannot be achieved solely by the good will and hard work of the faculty and staff who teach writing. They require commitment at the institutional level as well.

Assumptions for Strategic Planning

To help both departments and institutions plan effectively, we advocate that the following five assumptions be the basis for strategic planning at every institution of higher education. These assumptions are the basis for our own recommendations listed at the end of this report.

1. *Faculty can feasibly and beneficially integrate computers into the teaching of writing.* We have described three changes in the environment for teaching writing that are promoting the increased use of technology in the writing classroom. We have also argued that improving students' writing skills is not an isolated curricular goal: writing can and should play a critical role in improving students' learning throughout their undergraduate experience. Technology that integrates the multiple tools and media of the different disciplines contributes to this larger goal by dramatically enhancing the power and the purpose (as well as the ease) of writing across the curriculum. Incorporating computers as directly and explicitly as possible into introductory writing courses is a focused, and therefore feasible, way to initiate this larger process. To ensure educational benefit, faculty knowledgeable about both writing theory and computers must lead in this effort to integrate computers meaningfully into writing instruction. And having learned from colleagues the goals and objectives of other disciplines and professional groups, they can help other faculty new to this endeavor to integrate technology and the notion of process into their modes of learning. In addition, writing instructors need to form new partnerships in order to match curricular goals of the writing program with the needs of the students and with the computer facilities available and planned. To do so, these faculty leaders need access to university-wide planning and decision making.

2. *For significant change to occur, the role of the writing teacher in most institutions must be redefined, new support for the position must be provided, and new opportunities for leadership must emerge.* Since the creation and study of texts is arguably the central intellectual activity of the academy, writing programs and teachers of writing (along with the wisdom that they can offer) can contribute the internal leadership necessary to integrate computers into the curriculum wisely and effectively.

Colleges and universities will need to include support for faculty development as a continuing cost for adequate budgeting. Administrators must plan *ongoing* faculty development as an essential cost of computing as the numbers and computing needs of faculty (as well as computer capacity) change in the years ahead.

As the potential of the technology unfolds and as the definition of *text* changes under its influence, even greater changes will be necessary in writing instruction. These are changes that teachers of writing will have to confront and should help to shape. Fortunately, those who have been reflecting on writing and on the teaching of writing in recent years have accumulated a wealth of knowledge and experience about the nature both of text and text production — writing, language, and the organization of knowledge. Many experienced teachers of writing are thus in a uniquely strong position to contribute to an understanding of the impact of electronic texts and to design new strategies for teaching students to use electronic media effectively. All those faculty who teach writing have the opportunity to be pioneers, exploring to the fullest, in partnership with other scholars and with industry, the potentials and the pitfalls of technology for transforming the ways we learn and the ways we communicate with one another.

3. *Resources for information technology (whether they be housed in departments, in computing centers, or in libraries) must be planned and allocated with the institution's curricular goals for writing in mind.* No single choice of hardware and software is right for every institution or even for every department. Administrators managing resources for information technology must balance the demands from many constituencies for the resources most suited to their particular needs. Those who teach science courses, for instance, firmly specify the technology they need in their laboratories, based on what they have learned from their own research experience with lab equipment. Research experience and individual experience in writing are also beginning to suggest that some configurations of hardware and software work better for writing than others. Those who teach writing should, like their colleagues in the sciences, vigorously specify their own needs for the technical equipment that supports laboratories appropriate to their discipline. So that the best choices can be made, institutions must cultivate this newly developing expertise in hardware and software standards and capabilities among those responsible for the teaching of writing. Furthermore, institutions must begin to budget for teaching laboratories that support writing just as they budget for laboratories that introduce students to scientific experimentation.

4. *Planning the most beneficial integration of computing into the widest*

possible range of writing activities requires collaborative interaction with a range of partners within and outside the institution. Integrating computing into writing — the most ubiquitous activity in teaching and learning — will require new partnerships within an institution. Administrators from the offices of both academic affairs and information technology will play a crucial and necessarily collaborative role in coordinating the input of their faculty and in planning for the changes and funding of facilities and support structures necessary in libraries, classrooms, faculty offices, and student dormitories and of the facilities for off-campus partners (such as employers, public libraries, and home users).

We have emphasized that any change of the magnitude we are suggesting will necessarily be evolutionary. Only a very few schools will want or need to support the most advanced experimentation and development; most others will listen and learn and will adapt ideas to their own situations. Successful adaptation requires "re-inventing" an innovation for the new home site. For an evolutionary strategy to build on its own foundations effectively, there must be helpful methods in place for describing what has been learned, for sorting out successful from failed experiments, and for recommending new directions for research and implementation. In short, we advocate a thoughtful evaluation and a sharing of the results as important aspects of this new institutional collaboration.

Because of the innovative nature of any application of technology to learning, and because of the expense as well, it is particularly important for individual institutions to allocate a portion of their resources to foster both informal interinstitutional cooperation and more formal consortial arrangements. Outreach to other colleges and universities can take many forms, from faculty participation in an electronic conference to joint courseware development projects, from sharing program descriptions to sharing scarce resources and expertise.

5. *Achieving equity of access to the most significant benefits of technology for all members of the academic community must receive the highest priority.* Technology has the potential to exacerbate the inequities that already exist in the structure of postsecondary education in America. This is a problem both within and among institutions of postsecondary education. Many of the institutions that teach the largest number of our students are already resource poor, and the demand to increase the presence of technology in courses that service many students, such as writing courses, will be especially difficult to meet. As the demography of higher education

changes and the "nontraditional" student predominates, institutions will need to develop innovative strategies to ensure equal access for commuters, older students, those with family and work obligations, economically disadvantaged students, and disabled students. New coalitions will be needed for sharing — among institutions and between different sectors of the community — but new funding will be necessary as well.

We are assuming that the changes in writers' habits, in the concept of writing instruction, and in computer technology will bring about nothing less than a revolution in the central activities of scholarship, teaching, and learning. New ways of generating, storing, and sharing knowledge with the use of information technology will touch the center of every discipline. The evolution in the teaching of writing that we recommend will be shaped in the context of that accelerating revolution. But more important, as information technology changes the questions we ask and the ways we answer them in government and work, as well as in education, the way in which writing is practiced and taught can and should substantially influence both the revolution in information technology itself and the intellectual directions in which the revolution takes us.

Technology in Support of Writing Theory and Practice

Each institution must find a way to integrate computers into its curricula in a way and at a pace appropriate for its academic mission. No single prescription is possible or desirable for writing instruction. Although a process-centered pedagogy has become the prevailing paradigm in writing classes, teachers have implemented that pedagogy with computers in a great variety of ways, sometimes only modeling computer use with a projector system, other times turning the class partly or totally into a laboratory environment or using computers as a delivery system for comments and revisions. In this section, we provide a kaleidoscopic view to accent the diverse ways computers affect student writing and teaching practices with current technology and the educational impact promised by new developments.

Writing as a Cognitive Process

Obviously, word processing is an appropriate technology for a process-centered pedagogy. A curriculum emphasizing the written product might require, say, twelve papers, one per week, over the semester; a process-centered course might expect students to complete fewer essays but to submit each text two or more times. Before computers, the technology made full implementation of this pedagogy punitive: the labor of retyping and the apparent immutability of type- or handwritten text seriously interfered with the teaching strategies. Although computers themselves do not improve student writers' understanding of the complexities of their own writing processes, they do help teachers make those important lessons accessible to their students.

Here are some practical ways that individuals working with a simple word-processing configuration can usefully transform familiar and effective writing strategies. Although these techniques have been embedded in the pedagogy for decades (some would claim for centuries), they are renewed and rendered more effective, indeed more teachable, in the electronic environment.

1. When writers use computers to facilitate their work, they probably first become aware of their utility as *editing tools*, as convenient and economical ways to correct spelling, typographical, or grammatical errors and stylistic inelegances. They can easily substitute one word or phrase for another, thereby cleaning up or beautifying a surface feature of the text. Although the impact of such changes on the overall quality or cogency of the text remains small, tools like spelling checkers or style analysis programs clearly help writers polish their texts. Still, as potent as these aids may be, they provide minimal support for what writing teachers often call "real writing," or substantive revising.

2. More central to teaching writing and revising strategies are *facilities for planning* (outlining, brainstorming, nutshelling) and exploring the topics that writers choose or the audiences for which they are writing. Teachers have always urged students to use planning techniques both before and during the composing process. But when writers execute these tasks on paper, the outcome cannot be transferred to the composing space without recopying. Computers allow teachers to show the underlying relation of planning to text production because the computer makes that connection graphically clear with split screens, simultaneous access to multiple documents, and editing commands to coordinate planning activities with text production. When writers can see and change either plans or text, they can consider revising and reshaping plans as their understanding of their material grows.

With tools aplenty, and some — such as outliners, idea processors, note cards, electronic study guides or questions, and the like — writers can use structures built into specific software but still be able to open up or transfer their texts into a full-featured word-processing environment whenever they choose. Notes inscribed electronically can be pasted into an appropriate location in the author's discussion, where they can be revised to suit their role in the context. In many software packages the outline can open to add or show the fully developed text, or it can collapse to show the logical skeleton. Text crosses boundaries, from a planning purpose to a discursive one, from a preliminary thought to a fully articulated idea.

As more software tools to aid planning and structuring activities become available, and as word processors increasingly offer these features, writing teachers can stress the strategies that expert writers employ, especially those — like revising plans and goals as well as revising discursive text — that students have in the past tended to neglect or to minimize.

3. Before the advent of word processing, writers and writing teachers tended to consider revision a "stage" in the life of an essay; it was what writers did *after* they had written a "rough draft," or first approximation. As writers move from producing fixed texts to producing electronic ones, the very notion of a *draft* changes. Traditionally, a new draft is born at the moment the page becomes too messy for further productive work, prompting the writer to produce a clean copy. Writing on a computer produces text that is always "clean" and yet always provisional. It is always being composed and at the same time revised: at no point does it seem to move from one "stage" to another. Revising, then, becomes a central activity, not one postponed until later or even last. It is always deeply embedded in the composing.

Teachers have been taking advantage of the electronic text's provisional status by intervening earlier and more often in the text's journey from its beginnings to its final form. Because a text composed electronically is never "cluttered," or overwritten, it may seem more accessible to readers other than the author, always more "public" than its handwritten or hand-edited predecessor. And most teachers find that they are more willing to require students to submit work still in preliminary stages both for peer critique and for instructor feedback when they know that students have such a powerfully efficient revising tool at hand. Whether a lab has stand-alone computers or a network, this feature of word processing allows teachers to interact with students at more intervals, commenting on early versions of a text as well as on late stages and helping students realize intentions or anticipate readers' responses while the student's text is, as it were, still "wet," still open to reformulation.

Teachers can use word-processing functions to show students how structural changes, large-scale revisions, affect the whole. Searching a document for a series of key words to determine whether the writer has in fact focused the text on important concepts can help a writer recognize when global revisions might be needed. By extracting the first sentence of each paragraph and reviewing them together, without the remainder of the text (a sort of *ex post facto* outlining), writers can check the global logic of their discourse. The same technique using first and last sentences often reveals problems with coherence and cohesion. Word processing make these techniques easy to teach as well as to apply.

4. In an electronic environment, drafting, or setting down a layer of text, merges with planning on one side and with *final presentation* on the other in ways that can be helpful to writers. Teachers of technical and business writing have long been aware of the power that visually informative texts can have. Now features of desktop publishing make that power accessible to students too, with underlining, bolding, and italics. Even beginning writers can produce visually informative text, can begin to consider the ways that lists and spacing and visual cues can affect a reader's grasp of information or point of view. And just as writers can try out many formulations of a phrase, a sentence, or a paragraph, so too can they experiment with visually informative arrangements, controlling even more fully the meanings that texts can convey.

Writing as a Socially Embedded Process

Along with the cognitive aspect of writing is its rhetorical dimension — its embeddedness in social and intellectual contexts. Both as an activity and as an object, writing is inherently collaborative and dialogic: that is, it embodies an ongoing exchange among existing texts and discussions, the writer, and audience(s). Collaboration has been variously defined: it may simply mean that a writer, working privately and alone, nevertheless draws on an awareness of "others" who have helped shape the discourse to which the writer's work contributes and to whose needs and queries the writer's text must respond. It may mean that as writers talk out their ideas with colleagues and peers, they negotiate meanings that transform or define those ideas. It suggests that writers often solicit responses to works-in-progress, using the information to help them shape or reshape their texts. It may even mean that several authors have jointly constructed a single text: all contracts and treaties, for example, are in this sense "collaborative" texts. Computer technology supports collaborative pedagogy, helping to make writers aware of the social and intellectual context of writing.

1. *Sharing work-in-progress during class:* Writing teachers and their students can foreground the social contexts that powerfully shape both writing and reading. Because electronic texts are more easily duplicated and revised than those generated entirely on paper, writers can exchange texts as freely and as swiftly as they can swap disks, and even more easily in a networked environment. Peer review has of course been practiced since time out of mind, but never before with so little difficulty. As students respond to each other's work electronically, their "dialogue" can be preserved so that the writer has a record of his or her peers' suggestions and queries — which would not be possible in class discussions or simple conversations — and a record that does not deface the text or render it illegible.

A simple hardware addition, a projection system attached to a computer available during class time, allows a new kind of modeling. As with group discussion of texts on blackboards or dittoes, everyone sees and critiques the same text, but it is logistically simple to have the writer, the teacher, or several students take a hand to the keyboard for revision. And all versions can be saved and shared, with the revision process studied.

With more sophisticated electronic environments, in particular a local area network (LAN), students can routinely exchange written work and feedback, foregrounding the essential role of readers' responses in the writer's craft. EDUCOM/NCRIPTAL's 1988 award for Best Curriculum Innovation in Writing, for example, recognized just such a use of the technology. Combining word processing and networking, teachers at Lewis and Clark College used the *Electronic Dialectical Notebook* to present reading, writing, and thinking as social acts. Students read on-line texts, wrote responses to questions the instructor posed, exchanged notebooks electronically with other students from the class, and then commented on other students' responses. The dialogues generated in this way could then be submitted electronically to the instructor.

2. *Collaborating beyond the classroom, course, or college:* When the LAN is connected to other LANs or to mainframes, students can exchange work without the teacher's mediation, even when class is not in session. This technology radically redefines the concept of a class and course, extending it across space and through time and underscoring a growing awareness that writing takes place within a community of peers.

For example, in a classroom/lab facility at Cornell, students can pick up or drop off files from the class "folder," exchange drafts and responses with their peers, and submit work to or leave notes for the instructor twenty-four hours a day, seven days a week. The extension of time and space permits students to see themselves as members of a group, an entity that is no longer defined by physical and temporal contiguity.

With electronic mail facilities, the electronic environment stretches our definitions of a course and of class participation even further. At IUPUI (Indiana University-Purdue University at Indianapolis), introductory drama students share their interpretations of literary texts with students in Finland via electronic mail. Such communications expand writers' awareness of the role that culture plays in interpretive acts while it increases their sensitivity to audience as a rhetorical force that helps shape discourse.

3. *Evaluating growth through "portfolios" with multiple audiences:* The "portfolio" method of assessment cries out for storage on computers. This growing movement proposes that all students present a rounded picture of their capabilities the way that art students have traditionally demonstrated their abilities, with the best of their work for a term or even an undergraduate career assembled in a portfolio for faculty review. This method for evaluating learning allows students in all majors to amass texts that trace for themselves and that demonstrate to others their growth during the course of their education. And this variety of assessment will no doubt have even greater applicability to a wide range of fields in the future, when even students will be writing hypermedia representations of their work. The wider audience here is the diverse group of advisers, teachers, and the student himself, who will refer to the portfolio over time. Revising the portfolio can make it useful in the graduate's application for a job or advanced study.

New Technology for a New Rhetoric

To this point, we have described ways that computers support writing

instruction with well known and widely used configurations and capabili
ties. Developing technologies will extend the gains that computers bring
to writing theory and practice, providing a new authenticity and involvement in discourse, making available new forms of inquiry, experience,
and expression, and extending these opportunities to students whose
disabilities have previously excluded them from full academic participation.

1. *Authenticating the writer's work and weaving it into the ongoing discourse:* Even as networks extend a writer's reach to a wider audience, they
also expand the resources and information that students can discover,
broadening students' fields of vision and inviting them to employ sophisticated strategies for critical inquiry. Consider the typical freshman English
research paper. Ideally, students choose a topic of interest to them, find
relevant information in libraries, and write their papers. Too often, however, students base their research papers on the first three sources they
happen to encounter, rather than on an assessment of the existing corpus
of data and opinion. On-line databases, such as "BRS" and "Dialogue,"
give students quicker and surer access to more information. Moreover,
the resources begin to match those used by professional writers and
scholars. With such resources, students can more easily discover a larger
proportion of the information — in a form more current and less cumbersome than paper indexes.

As the amount of memory easily available on a home computer increases, students will have access to reference tools formerly found only
in a library: an encyclopedia, the complete works of Shakespeare, a
zipcode book, complete census data, and so forth. In fact, some of these
references are now available on the NeXT computer. And these machine-
readable works will be usable in new ways — with a search function
replacing the need for a concordance to Shakespeare or perhaps even a
compendium such as Bartlett's *Familiar Quotations.* In addition, a compact laser disk can hold one thousand video stills, two thousand diagrams,
six hours of high-quality sound, ten thousand pages of text, and space
enough to make all these elements work together. At present, compact
disks are beginning to be interactive — both supplying and storing information. But even when they only supply information, they can make
available stable texts: the *Oxford English Dictionary,* specialized dictionaries, a thesaurus, *Books in Print,* source texts (such as Shakespeare's
folios), telephone books. The results of the 1990 Decennial Census down

to the zip-code level will be available on compact disk. The ready access to essential reference sources empowers all writers, even very young and inexperienced ones.

These electronic enhancements have particular appeal where writing instruction occurs throughout the undergraduate curriculum, in writing-across-the-curriculum programs at the freshman level as well as in writing-intensive upper-level courses, especially those with significant disciplinary content. Moreover, such uses of the technology potentially narrow the gap between students attending resource-rich institutions and those attending resource-poor ones. Students with access to an extensive library have richer possibilities for writing, or gain access to information more quickly, than do students dependent on interlibrary loan. When more research is routinely available in machine-readable form, students should be able to find, read, and copy citations electronically, regardless of the hours and holdings of their libraries.

2. *New representations of knowledge:* The expansion of information goes together with expanded ways of representing a body of knowledge. Several systems for creating and reading hypertext documents now exist, and some are already in experimental use in writing-intensive courses. Students at Wooster College in Ohio, for example, studied seventeenth-century literature with a hypertext presentation of texts and background material to which student essays were added. From these new materials, new forms of discourse are already beginning to emerge, both in the business world and in the academic one. What integrated programs do for the business writer now, turning spreadsheet data into graphs that can then be embedded in the verbal text, will soon be accomplished by digitized texts from different media for new kinds of writing. Biologists will digitize standard illustrations available as "clip art" on compact disk; art historians will illustrate their analyses with digitized illustrations. To prepare students for jobs, and to meet the challenge of new scholarly work, writing teachers will need to help establish and teach new conventions — of organization, documentation, and cross-referencing, for example. In other words, in a world rich with multimedia texts, teachers will no longer be able to teach students only the academic, print-bound essay that we have up to now known as the sole representation of knowledge. They will have to expand the notion of a text and their own skills for producing such texts if they are not to be teaching horse-and-buggy techniques in the age of the automobile.

3. *New forms of inquiry:* The experience of inquiry will be transformed as students integrate critical inquiry in a more realistic context than is available except in field research or internships. For example, an interactive tutorial under development at Carnegie Mellon leads students to consider whether medical care can ethically be withheld at the request of a person who wants to die. The program opens with background on a burn victim, Dax, who has suffered horrible burns over much of his body and requires daily, painful changes of dressing to prevent infection that would kill him. Mentally alert and articulate, with little prospect of physical improvement, Dax asks that the dressings be left unchanged. As students hear and see tapes of Dax, they are asked to make ethical choices, which then trigger branching to different interviews and follow-up questions. Students have the opportunity, during the course of this experience, to write and store their responses with word processing.

As the nature of information changes and the new forms become readily available to writers while they are writing, students will be able to pose original questions and to find answers themselves. In other words, the information revolution can induct students directly into a fuller and more authentic intellectual life. The ability to digitize the artifacts of different media will only improve access to new kinds of texts. New forms of analysis are possible that blur the distinction between the student as a consumer of texts and the student as a producer of texts. The student in music appreciation class can hear and reproduce Beethoven's Fifth Symphony in a new way, studying timbre dynamically by changing it in a digitized performance of the work as well as offering a commentary on or an analysis of the musical text . Archaeology students may construct models of ancient cities from fragmentary artifacts, using computer-aided design to help show the shape and growth patterns over centuries. New, hands-on access to field data — whether in anthropology, psychology, or ornithology — alters the way educators offer texts to students for study as well as the way students represent their command of the material to their teachers and to each other. And as these examples imply, our conceptions of composing and revising a text — in short, of writing — will need to be reconstructed. Scholars in the coming age will be constructing texts that combine media, and so too will their students.

4. *Expanded access to real audiences for expression:* The texts students write may no longer find their audience only in the instructor of a particular course. Wider, more flexible access to audiences can add authenticity

and responsibility to student writing. Desktop publishing gives students new options for disseminating their work; dissemination is no longer dependent on teachers wielding overhead projectors and ditto masters. Students can better learn to consider the needs of their audience when their writing serves some genuine, rather than a purely academic, purpose. With the technologies of networks widely available, as well as easy and friendly to use, students will be able to reach authentic audiences, for example, to post information for other students on a campus electronic bulletin board, to communicate with junior-high students at an inner-city school or with master's students in France, or to collaborate with their host student from last year's Junior Year Abroad Program even when the student has returned home. When Chinese students protested for democracy in Tiananmen Square, they sent information via electronic mail to compatriots studying at American universities and received uncensored news of events in China, news unavailable from media sources on the spot. Access to new audiences transforms ivory towers into broadcast beacons.

5. *Extended opportunity for disabled students:* The computer's capacity to digitize data removes or ameliorates academic handicaps of the disabled. Optical character readers change printed matter into electronic text that can be re-presented in forms accessible to the blind. Voice synthesizers change text into sound, helping disabled speakers to communicate. In addition to helping individuals, a computer application for writing instruction helps deaf students at Gallaudet University naturally "converse" for the first time in English (as opposed to using sign language) through ENFI, a network application that allows real-time "chat." A split screen lets students compose their texts in a bottom window and send them to an ongoing dialogue visible in the top portion of the screen.

While educators see expansive new horizons for teaching and learning, those alluring vistas will remain remote unless educational institutions prepare to make them accessible. Nor can we imagine that greatly improved interfaces — to make the cutting and pasting among digitized media intuitive, for example — will of themselves reveal to novices the necessary strategies for searching, analyzing, and organizing data or the rhetorical task of shaping a hypertextual document for its intended audience. Just as writers must learn effective strategies before word processing supports more effective writing, so too will access to hypertext and hypermedia systems require guidance. Teachers — writing teachers working with librarians and joined by faculty in all disciplines — will have to collaborate to study these new forms and to teach students how to read and write them. In the following section, we describe how faculty leadership and participation is nurtured to achieve these ends.

Faculty Champions and Faculty Development

A faculty champion or a team of innovators needs to provide leadership that combines knowledge of the discipline with knowledge of computers: educationally sound, widespread use of computers does not spontaneously emerge from faculty who have computers put on their desks. In writing instruction, faculty leadership has generally sprung up spontaneously from innovative faculty or has emerged in response to administrative initiative (the dean or a vendor gifts the department with a lab). In either case, the faculty responsible for planning and implementation will probably need alliances and know-how completely new to them: ivory tower inhabitants meet silicon basement denizens; faculty used to publishers' representatives suddenly confront vendors who speak an arcane language full of strange acronyms and invoices beyond the wildest dreams of chalk wielders; humanists prepared for lonely library research find themselves involved in administrative tasks such as setting up equipment, supervising student aides, and interesting new faculty in using the technology while also keeping collegial faith with computerphobes who vote on their tenure.

Responsibilities of Faculty Champions

A faculty champion (or champions) knowledgeable about both writing and computers has the following five responsibilities:

1. *To gain expertise in computer use through release time, technical help, and access to experts (workshops, conferences, journals, collegial networks) — initially and continuously.* Effective faculty leadership starts with innovators who are knowledgeable enough to forge the technology into a tool for educational ends. Figure 1 suggests five stages of expertise typically experienced by innovators. Although faculty have now usually experienced both interest in (the first stage) and personal acquaintance with word processing (the second), the progression to classroom use is neither inevitable nor obvious. Faculty need time to learn from an increasing

set of resources within the field of rhetoric and composition (as shown in the bibliography). In addition, professional organizations now regularly include software demonstrations and panels on computer use in their programs (as described below in responsibility 3). Teaching experience with a small pilot project helps prepare faculty champions for the logistical problems that then need to be faced on a larger scale.

1. **General interest**: will read general articles and discuss computers.
2. **Personal use**: will use word processing, for example, for their own writing or for vita or test preparation.
3. **Survival skills for class use**: will know the basics of word processing and be able to implement an established framework or syllabus.
4. **Active integration and adaptation**: will adapt modules and design uses of computers in own syllabus or course.
5. **Evaluation and reflection**: will evaluate the impact and importance of writing theory and make future curricular and program changes accordingly.

Figure 1:   Stages of Expertise for Implementing Innovation

2. To coordinate planning with the departmental chair, departmental colleagues, academic computing staff, and academic administrators. Once departments, writing programs, or writing centers plan to move beyond the pilot program, faculty leaders must prepare an evolutionary plan, showing administrators their computer needs and assessing the level of institutional support necessary for the current stage. Faculty who are farsighted and honest in their projection of long-range costs will help administrators in long-range planning and evaluation. Writing is a computer-intensive activity, whether students write during class time, in a writing center, in a computer cluster, or at home. All students, regardless of income or living arrangements, will need convenient and ample access to the requisite equipment, or the teacher's educational aims inevitably will fail. Problems of compatibility must be faced: generally students in a computer-assisted writing course must all use compatible hardware and the same software. Several equity issues surface here: on a campus with multiple machine environments (a description of most campuses), requiring every student in a particular section or course to use the same equipment may disadvantage certain students — those with relatively good access to the wrong equipment as well as those without good access to any equipment. Commuter students often need more access during class time than do residential students.

3. To plan the lab and software based on program goals. Planning the layout of a lab may raise questions about curricular goals and teaching strategies. One guideline helps focus: Imagine what should go on in the classroom before it is set up. For example, some teachers run their classes as writing laboratories and will want all their class time with computers, but others will want only occasional access. Some will require collaborative work that may call for nonlinear clusters of computers.

The choice of a word processor requires hours of reading, comparing and evaluating in terms of curricular goals and institutional realities. Are teachers willing to give up formatting capabilities (hanging indentation for bibliographies, for example) to gain commenting or an on-line handbook? Does ease of use (and short training time in class) outweigh full functioning that may be suitable for upper-division classes in technical writing or more ambitious writing projects in other fields or in senior seminars? A champion needs to confer with computing administrators about campuswide site licenses that may offer savings but with a word processor that may not accord with the classroom teacher's needs or desires.

Champions will need to evaluate software beyond word processing, whether such programs are add-ons to word-processing packages (for example, outliners, spelling checkers, or idea-generating modules) or independent software that needs to have output integratable with the word-processing program. In the past, software has been difficult to locate. Book publishers, who have good access to the college market, have been more interested in generic tools with large markets than in computer-assisted instructional packages, but they are now pioneering word-processor-plus programs. Professional organizations are establishing software fairs (Conference on College Composition and Communication), including more computer-related sessions (CCCC and Modern Language Association), and are establishing review panels (MLA). The EDUCOM Software Initiative is supporting models of professionally useful reviews that can be placed in leading journals in the field. And EDUCOM is working with NCRIPTAL (the National Center for Research into Post-Secondary Teaching and Learning) to identify outstanding software packages and applications. The MLA and NCRIPTAL initiatives provide increased access to publishing for faculty-created "home grown" software. In short, professional organizations are providing services to help faculty leaders identify and find outstanding software.

4. *To train faculty, whether newly interested or newly arrived, and to keep up with new developments in the field.* Faculty turnover means introductory programs must be repeated, but the frequency will depend on who teaches writing at an institution. Although full-time tenure-track faculty often teach first-year composition at small, liberal arts colleges, the bulk of writing instructors at large universities are part-time instructors and graduate students. As more sections involve word processing, as the level of technological complexity increases (for example, from stand-alone computers to networking), and as new software and equipment are used, trained faculty will need additional help in developing sound instructional uses.

5. *To make plans for evaluation.* Whether we consider current or emerging computer capabilities, it's clear that evaluation is crucial: to improve teaching and learning, to assess impact on teaching goals and curriculum, to improve program functioning and expansion, and to provide evidence for future funding. The following are key questions:

- What are the benefits to learning of using computers in writing?

- What are the problems?

- How can the problems be ameliorated by changes in the context (short-term changes in the class or syllabus) and by changes in the technology (better design)?

- How can the benefits be increased and extended with improved or expanded facilities at the institution?

All writing programs should monitor the use of computers, not only to involve all instructors in classroom research on teaching and learning but also to gain data for planning expansion or upgrading of facilities and requests for budget or grant support. Such evaluations may include

- tallies of the numbers and times of heaviest student use (both over the course of the day and the course of the semester), and demographic information about clients;

- student questionnaires (before and after the course) about uses and attitudes, software, and instructional practice;

- logs of user problems (needed for directions as well as maintenance);

- teacher logs reflecting on effectiveness and effect;

- student logs of their writing processes;

- records of the cost of supplies and rates of use; and

- studies of long-term effects (retention, successful completion, subsequent use and performance).

Faculty are the key figures as teacher-researchers, helping to gather information, in natural classroom settings, from students and from their own experiences. Such local research is essential, since it is based on the particular needs and strengths of the institution, and should serve as the basis for continuing program development. It may also be disseminated, since practitioners should contribute to setting a research agenda: improvement of software and hardware, pedagogical practice, and the conventions of the new classroom and of information handling. However, only a small segment of the composition community, supported at a small number of institutions, may want to carry out extended, formal research. Researchers and practitioners need to work together, with aid available from professional organizations such as the Conference on College Composition and Communication, from publications in the field, and from funding agencies in government and the private sector.

The Impact of Technological Complexity

Support for faculty leaders and instructors should be geared to faculty involvement and the technological complexity of computer aids to writing. The categories and tasks listed in figure 2 are not mutually exclusive, since categories blur with multifunction word-processing packages, nor will these categories fit every institution, but they are meant to show how planning involves more technical know-how and increased scope in planning (long range and university-wide) as the technological complexity increases.

Writing Instructor's Involvement	Responsibilities
A. Little or none	May arrange for word-processing tutorial or lab time outside class (no computer responsibilities)
B. Integration of word processing into instruction	Standardizesoftwareand hardware; modify syllabus; teach some word-processing functions; arrange for lab time (departmental responsibility)
C. Using software beyond word processing	Select software (outliners, structure editors, style analyzers, idea-generating or commenting programs, hypertext access to new materials); gain mastery of software; modify syllabus to realize educational gains; manage access to lab; coordinate purchasing (departmental responsibility)
D. Using connectivity software	Learn new functions; develop assignments and syllabus; work with technical support and other faculty (campuswide planning and responsibility)

Figure 2:   Categories of Faculty Involvement and Technological Complexity.

Only when faculty use computers as an integral part of instruction (level B and above) do potential gains warrant the inclusion of computers as a part of a writing program, rather than as a responsibility of a centralized computing center.

As the level of technological complexity increases beyond word processing, the responsibilities of the faculty champion increase, and the demands on faculty rise.

The Need for Faculty Development

As pilot programs succeed, new faculty must be involved and supported. Because the transition from personal use to classroom application is neither obvious nor easy, writing programs will need to develop a comprehensive faculty development program in the use of computers to teach writing. A successful program of any size cannot be implemented without thorough and ongoing guidance, training, and updating suitable to the kind of teachers and students in the institution. The heart of writing instruction lies in students learning from their own efforts and from teachers' guidance, and therefore faculty development is just as important as the hardware and software used.

1. *Planned faculty development is necessary.* Experience at LaGuardia Community College (part of the CUNY system) illustrates that faculty leadership and support are crucial for instructors moving from personal to classroom use of computers. At LaGuardia, three faculty began the

computer/writing curriculum as a grant-funded program to teach writing to learning-disabled students and added to their number three instructors (two part-timers) as the curriculum was expanded to the general college population in six different writing courses. Despite professed interest by thirty full-time and fifty part-time faculty, none progressed beyond a personal use of word processing until a term-long faculty development program was implemented with the advent of a new computer lab. After two such development programs, supported by ongoing evaluation and innovation, virtually every full-time faculty member and a number of the part-time faculty were qualified to teach computer-writing courses, and many have already done so. The lab operates over sixty hours a week, accommodating over twenty sections per quarter.

Even with commitment, the individual teacher can find that computers change working conditions and the teacher's autonomous and independent role in unforeseen ways. As Carolyn Kirkpatrick reports:

> The greatest problem of implementation was learning to work with the human dimension. Suddenly, simply to run a class, one is involved in new interactions with peers and support staff. A bright idea of the type that could formerly be carried out on the spur of the moment becomes impossible without advance planning and coordination. Procedures that seemed highly desirable to us were sometimes vetoed by the lab supervisor, and whether or not she had reason on her side (often she did), the negotiations took a new toll on our energies.[2]

The teacher accustomed to autonomy and to privacy in the classroom is suddenly in a new and disconcertingly populous environment. These activities all take enormous amounts of time: time to write new materials, to redesign the content of courses, to work out technological kinks, to coordinate activities with others. Without wholehearted departmental support and even the assistance of the larger institution, few individuals will be able to succeed and to continue computer-using classes without risks to their careers. And these risks are especially high for the vast majority of writing teachers, most of whom are adjuncts, graduate students, or part-time staff.

2. *Institutionalizing an innovation requires different support from that needed to pioneer it.* Champions, almost by definition, are often committed

beyond what logic or prudence dictates. But faculty who teach a course semester after semester (and even old champions) will burn out or drop out if heroic efforts are continually required. Teaching with computers needs to be made routine, with training and sharing considered as part of a normal load.

The institution should carefully consider and make known its policies about revising and creating software for classroom use. Faculty developers of software have often been discouraged because of the costs in time and money required to achieve a finished product or because of the lack of institutional support in funding or credit toward tenure. Producing and revising software assures that computerized instructional materials address the whole range of student needs — from basic to advanced writers — yet institutions should carefully match the kinds of development costs involved and their level of commitment. A faculty member interested in the long and costly process of software development should know the institution's policy on funding, royalties, and professional credit. Policies should also be clear for faculty who want to modify software, as software increasingly includes ways for teachers to author new modules of a program or modify existing ones. In other cases, faculty will develop and share new applications with word-processing text files, just as they have prepared supplementary dittoes in the past. With different levels of involvement, faculty can tailor instructional materials to their computer-based classrooms.

3. *Faculty development is demographically timely.* Since 22 percent of college instructors in the humanities will have retired between 1987 and 1997,[3] it is particularly important that the present generation of graduate students receive a sound education in composition theory and computer use in the teaching of writing. Although word processing is the technology of choice for writing dissertations in the humanities, personal use does not guarantee effective instructional use. Without guidance and support, a teacher can find computers in classes to be counterproductive: de-skilling the teacher by taking time away from literacy to teach computer use and by obstructing proven methodologies for new, unintegrated "machine" methodologies. For many graduate students, computer training and teaching experience will benefit them as job candidates in the academic marketplace as word processing becomes the universally dominant medium for writing.

4. Training must be thorough to help faculty progress through the various stages of expertise (shown in figure 1).

a. *Survival Skills:* To get beyond general-interest and personal use, teachers need training for survival skills, including, as a minimum

- a working knowledge of the word-processing program that students will be using;

- an assurance that aides will clearly and efficiently introduce the software or directions for presenting that program to students, so that time is not taken from writing tasks;

- a knowledge of what problems to anticipate and how to remedy them; and

- a familiarity with the operation and potential uses of available computer-assisted instruction or peripheral programs such as spelling checkers, outliners, or style analyzers.

The course or training sessions should move beyond survival skills, embedding the technicalities of work with computers in the consideration of the major areas of composition theory (for example, looking at revision processes or collaborative learning). At the least, faculty should go into their computer-using class able to teach an established syllabus; preferably they will be ready for level 4 — active integration and adaptation — before they begin teaching with computers. Even if participants are not using computers in their current teaching, they should know which writing course they will teach with computers in the term after the faculty development program so that they can create appropriate materials.

Training can be made experiential by a number of devices: participating in teacher-student role playing; analyzing participants as they write on the computer; having participants record their developing and changing attitudes in journals; observing, and even guest teaching in, existing computer-writing courses; discussing potential problems (such as cosmetic revision and physical problems such as eye strain and back aches).

Faculty should be sure that fully trained and computer-knowledgeable assistants will always be in the lab; they should have a chance to meet and work with these personnel as part of the development program. In addition, the in-house publication of materials for computer-based courses should be supported and rewarded.

b. *Active Integration and Adaptation:* In order for faculty to "own" their own writing programs, they should be able to set and adapt their syllabi to their students and their teaching goals. How quickly faculty can regain their sense of "ownership" in computer classrooms depends to a great extent on the thoroughness of their initial training. Taking control of the medium will be easier and more effective if faculty continue to share ideas and experiences with computer-writing colleagues — whether at meetings or on an electric bulletin board or through distribution of classroom materials they have developed. If initial training has focused on minimal survival skills, later development work should introduce the major issues of pedagogy and writing theory that are raised by computer use in composition courses. At this stage, writing faculty can be especially helpful working with colleagues in other disciplines to ensure that students continue to use their computer-based strategies at the advanced level in discipline-specific courses. Writing faculty (including graduate students and part-time faculty) thus become mentors to colleagues in other disciplines.

c. *Evaluation and Reflection:* Faculty development must be ongoing to take advantage of faculty expertise in teaching and learning and in evaluation and planning.

- Faculty need to evaluate the impact of computers on writing and the social implications of computer use, both in the educational setting and beyond.

- Follow-up sessions, especially among veteran teachers in computer classrooms, are vital to present updates on new software and hardware and to gauge the success of or needed changes in the program.

- Opportunities for publication and for professional presentations should be made known to teachers, supported (for example, with travel grants), and credited.

- Expansion of the program in number of students served or level of complexity should be decided with the advice and involvement of the faculty who will lead those changes.

5. *Faculty development programs should be tailored to the needs of the participants and to the institutional setting.* Faculty development should cover a sufficient faculty population to ensure equity of access to computer-writing classes for different kinds of students, even if only a few

ᵃⁱ ᵗⁱᵒⁿˢ ᵃʳᵉ ᵒᶠᶠᵉʳᵉᵈ ⁱⁿ ᵃ ᵖⁱˡᵒᵗ ᵖʳᵒʲᵉᶜᵗ. Fᵒʳ ⁱⁿˢᵗᵃⁿᶜᵉ, ᵇᵉᶜᵃᵘˢᵉ ᵃ ˡᵃʳᵍᵉʳ percentage of evening classes are taught by part-time faculty on most campuses, such faculty must be included in the development program to allow for sufficient coverage of evening classes.

Timing of faculty development and of support for participants should be appropriate to the situation: for example, as part of a full-semester seminar in writing theory for graduate instructors; as release time for tenure-track faculty; as pay or longer contracts or preferences in teaching schedules for part-time faculty.

Such training sessions, both initially and in follow-up sessions, should be tailored to the different needs of participants — veteran vs. new teachers, tenure track vs. non–tenure track, full-time vs. part-time, graduate students vs. continuing faculty.

6. *Faculty development must be ongoing.* Changes in teaching faculty, especially among graduate students and adjunct faculty, or expansion of the program will require that faculty development be continuous and embedded in institutional routine. Upgrading facilities will call for additional training.

Developments in computer capabilities, as outlined in sections 2 and 4, will involve teachers with colleagues across the curriculum in studying and providing guidelines for effective new writing capabilities.

Faculty development is the hidden cost when integrating computers into writing instruction. Traditionally, class preparation is considered part of the teachers' responsibilities, paid for in regular salaries. Many new technologies have been easy to add both conceptually and logistically. For instance, teachers who experienced classroom use of movies when they were students easily realize how to use VCRs, provided by audio-visual departments. Computers are different. Their complexity and versatility, as well as their costs, are reflected in changed structures within academe: no one felt a need for a vice-president for information technology in the days of language labs and film rentals. Just as new structures and partnerships within higher education become necessary in computer purchase and administration, so too are new forms of support and cooperation necessary for faculty. We argue for a careful, evolutionary plan to include computers in writing across the institution, but we have started with the key element for implementation: the faculty who must work with students to convey meaning through text. In the remaining sections of this report, we address issues of hardware and software and provide guidelines for the academic administrators who must lead and coordinate evolutionary planning for the computer revolution in writing.

Hardware and Software Issues for Planning

The wise use of technology for writing instruction can significantly benefit students in writing-intensive courses — that is, virtually everywhere in the curriculum. However, since the computer is an expensive writing tool, this use requires close attention not only to curricular goals in writing instruction, but also to issues of access, functionality, and future capacity. Although teachers often use computers ingeniously to meet curricular and student needs, there is a limit below which savings are counterproductive for the present and future. Since writing is more than correctness, no savings can be expected from increased class size or from computer use exclusively for drill. The following are three key questions of access and functionality: How will computers be used (for example, will students use computers for on-line searching or peer review as well as for drafting and revising)? What are student needs (e.g., commuter students vs. dorm students)? What are the existing facilities that form the basis for expansion and upgrades?

Access

Full and convenient access to computers is the sine qua non for enriching writing instruction with technology. Whether student writers use computers inside or outside classes, when access is highly constrained the curricular goals of a writing program are constrained — limited, for example, to rudimentary drill, "fancy typing" of handwritten drafts, or proofreading activities instead of employing a process-centered approach to writing. And when individual students find access difficult, they disrupt a class and lose learning opportunities. The working mother who cannot find a free computer during the time she is on campus falls behind her peers in the class. When she appears in class without machine-readable text, the time allocated for peer review must be spent in straight typing, or in paper-and-pencil review with its cramped messiness, or in the ephemerality of verbal exchange. When the teacher circulates, giving individualized feedback, the student may find it difficult to try out a solution suggested by the teacher and certainly cannot get experience in the specifically computer based review techniques (such as word searches) that require computer use. Unless computers are available in sufficient numbers, and at times and places convenient and equitable for student use, the educational rationale for using computers in the first place will be undermined.

1. *Numbers:* Obviously, writers need significant amounts of computer time if they are to accomplish significant portions of their writing activities with the aid of computer tools. The more fully the pedagogy integrates the technology, the greater the demands for machine time. So in a writing course using an outliner or a structure editor in addition to a word processor and a style analyzer, a student needs to use the computer to plan, to draft and revise, to format and polish. At institutions like Drexel University and the U.S. Air Force Academy, this problem is met by requiring every student to purchase a particular computer. Most institutions, however, cannot or will not mandate personal ownership. Those institutions, then, must be prepared to provide the kind of access that a full implementation of computer-augmented writing instruction requires.

2. *Times and Places:* Although ensuring enough machines for all who need them goes a long way toward meeting institutional and instructional goals, it is just as important to make the machines accessible in locations and at hours that meet the needs of the student population to be served. For residential students, that may well mean opening dormitory clusters or providing safe and reliable ways to get from computer clusters to residences late at night. For commuting students, libraries and student centers may be better locations than dormitories. Limited access can be an acute problem for commuting students, since for many, the time on campus is constrained by many factors — jobs, child care or family commitments, bus schedules or ride pools. Computing facilities must be available either exclusively during class time or in clusters that have computers free for use at peak times. Otherwise, alternate forms of access must be arranged, aided by access to campus computing facilities by phone. For example, employers committed to upgrading their work force might be encouraged to designate times or equipment for employee homework, providing call-up capability to universities. Public libraries, K-12 schools, churches, and civic groups could also be instrumental in providing remote access. Even these solutions, however, will require help from the educational institution, which must remain responsible for providing easy, low-cost, user-friendly, and reliable interfaces.

For instructors, access is also a major issue. Although personal use does not necessarily lead to instructional use (see the preceding section on preparing and supporting faculty), teachers who have easy access to computers are more likely to use them for instructional purposes. In providing access, planners cannot ignore the political realities of writing instruction. For most full-time, tenure-track faculty, easy access essentially means having a machine on their own desks, so that the tool is located among the other tools and resources of routine academic work. And this goal is nearing reality in a number of institutions. Many writing instructors, however, are not full-time or tenure-track faculty. Even at institutions where writing classes or writing students already use computers intensively, writing teachers may have the least access to computers, since these faculty members are often lowest on the faculty totem pole, recruited from the ranks of part-time faculty and graduate assistants. Since they cannot teach effectively with tools they are not comfortable and familiar with, marginalized instructors are handicapped introducing this technology to their students unless they too have convenient and full access to it. Since these faculty often do not even have offices of their own, access for them may require innovative solutions such as faculty-designated sections in an open cluster or special security arrangements within a large, shared office.

3. *Equity of Access:* Ensuring access implies more than simply making some machines of some sort available to the whole range of students any one institution serves. It also means working to ensure that some institutions do not fall so far behind that their students are missing educational experiences that advance them in finding and excelling at jobs. Such inequities across institutions create economic and intellectual ghettos. The differential between institutions is already marked and its consequences serious: some recent studies disturbingly conclude that computers for economically and educationally disadvantaged students tend to be used as mechanical tutors serving up drill-and-practice software, rather than as robust pedagogical tools serving the larger aims of writing instruction. At computer-poor institutions, students will become increasingly disadvantaged if access is limited to computer-assisted drill and practice running on inexpensive hardware while their peers at computer-rich institutions gain access to powerful multimedia tools running on advanced function workstations. When disadvantaged students have lim-

lted access to computers, they tend to be further isolated from the educational and economic mainstream.

Vendor policies have often exacerbated the problem by providing the deepest discounts to very large schools and very prestigious schools, frequently leaving computer-poor institutions with higher costs. New partnerships are needed to make sure that schools serving a high proportion of economically disadvantaged students have the same pricing advantages as those extended to computer-rich colleges, whether these are partnerships between industry and academe or are new consortia of schools.

Problems of access reveal that costs — the expenses of buying and maintaining hardware, allocating space, and providing technical support — often lie at the core of institutional planning for technological innovation. Some institutions have to sacrifice less when they allocate resources for computers. These facts suggest that the technology may widen the gap between the "haves" and "have nots," seriously limiting the intellectual and economic potential of whole segments of the population. If we are not to become an even more deeply divided society, educational institutions will have to be especially concerned about their role in giving students access to the electronic information on which we are increasingly dependent and in teaching them the skills they will need to use that information. These concerns have been the traditional rationale for teaching writing in higher education in the first place: the written word has historically provided the way into a society of educated men and women, and command of it has enabled the disenfranchised to gain full citizenship. As this emerging technology transforms the way we store, retrieve, create, and communicate knowledge, education will have to induct its students, all of them, into the new forms that literacy will take.

Functionality

Because even a fairly primitive microcomputer can support some sort of text editing or word processing, institutions often choose to supply low-end, inexpensive machines for writing instruction, but lower-quality readability and less memory than is required by "state of the art" software packages limit functionality. Like engineering students learning CAD/CAM, writers need more than what a Commodore 64 will supply. If teachers are to employ the techniques outlined earlier in this section, students must be able to use a fairly powerful word processor, one capable of interfacing easily with other instructional software and of delivering features like underlining, bold facing, and graphics that are clear and editable on screen. Increasingly they will need some features associated with desktop publishing and hypermedia. These requirements mean that institutions must plan internally for hardware that is not only sufficiently robust now but also expandable as the capabilities and features of computers evolve. Externally, partnerships among academic institutions must make known to the computer industry their needs for function and pricing policy, through organizations such as EDUCOM. The following issues should be considered in both internal and external planning.

1. *High-end needs for writing:* Although the price of computing power and memory will continue to drop,[4] bringing a phenomenal increase in the computing power that is within the reach of educational institutions, some of the computer components most necessary for reading and writing applications will remain costly. In particular, large, high-resolution displays will continue to be expensive, but are needed

- to make the screen easier to read by allowing various fonts, sizes, and styles (boldface, italics);

- to support multiple tasks simultaneously (such as on-line searching of the card catalog, outlining, and writing) by allowing many "windows" of information per screen; and

- to enhance the writer's ability to edit by displaying the text on screen in the way it will appear on a printed copy.

As long as large, high-resolution screens are expensive, there will be a powerful argument for investing in quality rather than quantity, to buy more powerful computers instead of using the same amount of money to provide a greater number of less powerful computers.

2. *Need for connectivity:* Access to data and audiences requires local and long-distance networking. Even if few instructors at a particular college or university are ready to work in a networked classroom or to teach their students to use electronic mail, the machines to which students have access must be capable of supporting networking and modems so that the installed base does not prevent future uses of those pedagogical strategies that are dependent on a connected and extended machine environment.

3. *Incompatibility problems:* Incompatible hardware and software may limit the educational impact of the technology. When a professor writes a

textbook, other institutions with similar student bodies can easily adopt the text. When a professor writes a computer program, other institutions with similar student bodies may not be able to adopt it because they may have incompatible hardware. The tremendous cost of porting software from one hardware configuration to another one that is incompatible may fragment the educational market, with software publishers avoiding programs that appeal to limited markets (such as English as a second language or honors classes). Postsecondary institutions should encourage developers in industry or academe to create tools that allow software applications to run independent of hardware and operating systems. For example, the Andrew Toolkit developed at Carnegie Mellon maximizes the hardware independence of application programs. Plans are under way to make the Toolkit operating system independent as well.

4. *Need for standards:* Increasing numbers of students will be bringing their own hardware and software to campus and will be facing incompatible computer environments. As a result, schools will lose the full aid of these additional resources for educational computing, and manufacturers will have to continue supporting different and incompatible hardware and software packages. Lack of standards for text and graphical data may limit the amount of actual computer-based collaboration possible and hinder the new forms of writing we see emerging. Academics and computer industry leaders should push for document architecture standards that will allow writers to exchange text and graphics produced with different software programs without losing formatting information.

5. *Continued support for low-end hardware:* Even when technology makes it possible to lower costs, marketing decisions undercut the prospect of increased access through lowered prices. Computer manufacturers often discontinue low-end computers, and software companies cease to support programs that run on low-end hardware. Yet with lowered costs for minimal units, institutions might be more likely to meet student needs by providing expensive peripherals (such as laser writers and electronic mail capability) but requiring students to supply their own computers as terminals. In addition, tools are needed that help programmers to write and maintain software that runs on a variety of hardware configurations, from a minimal, low-end system with fewer software features to a maximal, high-end system with more features.

Computing power will continue to be a scarce resource: demand is likely to continue to outstrip supply. Most schools will need to decide internally what mix of computers will meet their institutional needs: what part of academic hardware budgets will go for cheaper and less powerful computers and what part will be spent for expensive but more powerful computers. Externally, the computer industry should be sensitive to the academic market's needs for function and pricing.

Future Capacity

As we look toward the near future, we can already foresee some of the profound changes that digitizing words, graphics, and sound will have on the writing environment and the written text. Even if enough computers are available for the present, institutions may limit educational potential and benefits if they do not plan for expansion and upgrades. For example, even currently available hypertext applications require massive memory, and multimedia capabilities call for new peripherals (CD-ROM players, optical character readers, VCRs, sound digitizers, and the like).

For the foreseeable future, some institutions may want to plan a two-tier system in which large classes use standard but currently adequate equipment while small, innovative projects extend educational gains with high-end equipment and services. Whatever steps the institution takes to implement the current technology, however, it must keep an eye on that emerging future and must retain enough flexibility to meet it when it arrives.

Administrative Planning:
Inside and Outside the Institution

Academic administrators must lead and support careful, evolutionary planning that coordinates the efforts of all the partners working to make computers an educational benefit in writing instruction. A well-integrated planning process has many practical benefits that go beyond improvement in the writing program itself. First, the process will promote cost-effectiveness in acquisition, distribution, maintenance, and support of the technology. Second, it will help to promote a team approach that encourages expanded faculty knowledge about technology and participation in institutional decision making about the sharing of these expensive resources. Finally, it will create the foundation for a well-coordinated institu-

tion-wide environment for all users of information technology. Writing is
ubiquitous in all disciplines of the institution, and along with writing come
closely connected activities such as library research and, in most disciplines, access to text data and the ability to manipulate text data. A sound
program that teaches students how to use the computer as an instrument
for writing and research in their first course will help ensure effective,
efficient use of computing tools in upper-level undergraduate education,
in graduate programs, and in all the varieties of faculty work. Moreover,
cooperation among institutions, the computer industry, and funding agencies in government and the private sector is needed to ensure that all
students have equitable access to knowledge in its new forms: failure to
do so will disenfranchise many, barring them from membership in the
community of educated men and women.

Administrators: Guidelines for Change

Without careful planning it will be virtually impossible to create an
environment in which large numbers of students will profit from access to
computing tools for writing. At some institutions today, computers have a
large but unplanned presence on campus, and from those institutions we
can observe that with no planning there are no outcomes: computers
alone don't teach better writing. Furthermore, investment in the wrong
computing resources, whether hardware, software, classroom configurations, or support personnel, can actually hinder the development of a
curriculum that will provide maximum benefits for students.

The following guidelines outline how academic administrators can plan
educational innovation and its institutionalization for computer use in
writing across the campus.

1. *Announce an evolutionary strategy that does not overpromise and that
includes long-range goals.* Since the programs that we have been advocat-
ing in this report require the coordination of many departments and staff
members, planning should allow for a deliberate and systematic process
of implementation. A realistic joint assessment of technical resources and
human resources (in particular faculty expertise, but also support personnel) can help to get a pilot program under way; early evaluation can set
future directions; other faculty can simultaneously learn to use computers
for their own work; and the institution can develop its resources. Initial
hardware configurations should keep long-range goals in mind by at least
the length of time that the hardware configuration is expected to last,

usually four to five years (or whatever is the amortized life span of the hardware in the institution's budget).

It is a mistake to promise what may not be technically possible. Such promises, unkept, are disillusioning and discouraging to the many faculty who have been working hard for change and improvement in the teaching situation.

2. *Build faculty expertise and dialogue.* Developing faculty expertise must be an early and ongoing priority because of the learning curve involved for faculty champions and the dialogue that must be built among decision makers and potential teachers. Especially important is early access by most decision-making faculty (not just the writing program administrators) to equipment and training so that they are familiar with word processing for their own personal productivity (a powerful motivator for subsequent support) and have had some opportunity to consider relevance of computer aids to the teaching of writing.

3. *Introduce all the partners for change.* Successful planning will require collaborative effort. From department chairs, from heads of writing programs and writing centers, and from writing faculty members themselves must come the design of the writing courses and environments, the teaching strategies, and the support requirements. Outside consultants can provide technical and discipline-specific advice; their visits may constitute an occasion for collaboration. Even at an early stage of internal planning, including someone who knows about the institution's computing resources — a director of academic computing or a humanities consultant, if possible — can be helpful. Those who administer the information technology resources should provide the information about hardware, software, networking, and costs for acquisition, maintenance, and support. Faculty and technical support personnel should work out a method of reporting that will allow administrators to monitor and evaluate the educational impact of computer use.

There will be both opportunities and challenges inherent in this effort to bring together groups and individuals who may not have traditionally worked together. They may have different vocabularies and different goals within the institution's structure. They may be suspicious of one another's motives. Almost certainly one will be jealous of the other's budget, and one will be jealous of the other's prestige. Overcoming these initial difficulties is well worth a special effort, however.

4. *Make use of the institutional context.* At institutions where the overall

presence of computing for instruction has been low, a cooperative planning process for bringing computers into the writing program can become a model or a local case study of institutional planning for
incorporating computing across the curriculum. On the other hand, at
institutions where computers have already established a presence in
some departments or programs, it makes sense to look for models of
implementing computer-based curricula already in place elsewhere on
campus — for example, in engineering and architecture programs that
use CAD/CAM systems in instruction; in sociology or economics departments that have been teaching the use of spreadsheets; and in science
departments that are experienced in financing and organizing undergraduate laboratories.

5. *Integrate technology and teaching.* The central task is to integrate the
technological needs of the writing program (as defined by the writing
faculty) with institutional development of information resources. This
integration at the planning stage should extend in both directions and
simultaneously influence the evolution of the writing program and the
acquisition of computing resources. On the one hand, if resources do not
serve the real needs of many faculty and students, they are ultimately a
poor investment. On the other hand, if the writing program divorces itself
from the technological environment of the institution, it will cut itself off
from possible sources of institutional support.

What needs to be discussed — from the most general policy to the most
specific aspects of planning? What are the most important planning issues? One of the first is determining what equipment a writing program
requires, then placing those needs in the context of what is fiscally and
technologically possible. There are several issues here. The sections that
follow are not meant to be exhaustive summaries of all aspects of the
planning tasks but are intended to suggest the scope of questions to be
raised.

a. *Space:* Access to computing equipment for student writers is a prerequisite for a successful writing program — usually requiring classroom
time with computers. Thus a computer laboratory devoted to the teaching
of writing is an early necessity. But finding the space and the money to
renovate for such a laboratory is almost always the hardest topic for
planning. Managing the costs of space is generally a greater problem than
managing the costs of hardware and software, and is therefore the first
problem that needs to be resolved.

Some aspects of the space problem are technical. The amount of space needed, for instance, can be calculated, but should be based on programmatic decisions such as the number of students anticipated, the number of hours the lab will be used for class time and for open access, the use for writing (with space for drafts, notes, and books), and the kinds of equipment to be installed.

Some aspects of the space problem are political. Whose space is going to be reallocated to the computer laboratory? To whom does the reallocated space then "belong"? Whose budget pays for renovation, and for subsequent maintenance of the renovated space? Academic and administrative departments will have to weigh pluses and minuses of assigning "ownership" of the writing laboratory to the writing program or to the central administration for computing facilities.

Planning should look to the future as well. Assuming a pilot project is successful, where will be the room for expansion as programs grow in scope and need for greater student access? Planning issues for future expansion include analyzing the advantages of small and decentralized clusters versus large and centralized computing facilities. For large, multi-sectioned courses such as writing, a dedicated computer classroom will almost certainly increase the efficiency of room use. If space simply cannot be found or created, other strategies can be explored, including encouraging student and faculty ownership of their own machines, creating pools of portable and loaner machines, and providing phone access in cooperation with other partners (such as employers, public libraries, and church groups).

b. *Time:* Open lab hours at times convenient for students are as crucial to the success of the writing program as scheduled hours in class, especially for schools at which laboratories are still the primary source of student access to hardware and software. The ratio of scheduled class hours to open hours should suit the curriculum and mission of the school; it cannot be determined as X number of hours per week but will vary based on

- the number and type of assignments;

- the level of use (word processing of drafts? using on-line access to an encyclopedia? electronic mail for peer review? searching of on-line databases?);

- hours and places of student access (different at residential colleges and commuter universities); and

- students' access to outside computers (at home or work).

Economically disadvantaged students, especially in commuter environments, will need more time in class and on institutionally owned computers than will computer-owning students. The timing of the open hours is also important: open evenings are generally more popular with students than early mornings or late afternoons, but staffing and security at night can pose problems. Even students with outside computer resources may need open lab time to get access to the campus network, file servers, electronic mail, printing facilities, or specialized software.

c. *Hardware and Software:* As we have argued above, faculty input on curricular goals and pedagogical practice, as well as on some realistic vision of future development (over the amortized life of the equipment), should strongly influence the hardware platform for the writing laboratory. Faculty can provide helpful input about the importance of hard copy (and hence the number of printers needed) or the value of collaborative work (and hence the relative importance of networking as opposed to exchanging disks). Faculty should have even a greater role in selecting which software is provided in the lab and which — like a textbook or a typewriter — is to be purchased by the students.

Other planning issues for hardware and software acquisition include compatibility (as discussed above), portability, and security. In general, hardware should not invite unwanted removal, although in some cases lab equipment may have to be portable enough to double as classroom demonstration equipment. Good security measures are important, not only for hardware but for software too, with campus policies that discourage software piracy. One such policy is aggressive negotiation with vendors for software licenses that allow legal portability of software by students from the lab to their dorm or home machines.

6. *Build adequate support structures.* Providing support to teachers and students is not a one-time start-up cost but must include both maintaining the facilities and helping succeeding students and teachers use them successfully, with support increased whenever a program expands or moves to a more complex technological level.

a. *Administration of the Program:* The responsibilities of day-to-day leadership of the writing program that incorporates computing should be clear to writing program administrators and computing support staff, from monitoring hard disks and supplying paper to showing students how to use software and printers, from scheduling open hours and class time to evaluating program effectiveness and direction.

b. *Support for the Teaching Faculty:* Whether they are graduate students, adjunct faculty, or full professors, all the teachers in the writing program must have solid training in word processing, access to machines for their own use, and help with the logistics of lab use, as we have discussed above. Whenever the technical level of computer use increases, the support needs to become more technical as well. The decision to commit institutional resources and faculty time to an extensive software development process should be made very carefully.

c. *Academic Recognition and Rewards:* If faculty members are given the responsibility for administering and evaluating computer labs, they should have adequate release time and recognition for their contributions. There should be more release time during the initial year or two (since starting up takes a great deal of work), but still a significant amount once things are running smoothly. Overseeing the introduction of computers into the writing curriculum should be considered a major institutional contribution, as should learning to teach within such a program. The nature and evidence for this institutional contribution should be clear, with documents stating criteria and review procedures checked and amended to include work developing computers in instruction. The identification of authorities for outside evaluation should be made known (for instance, computer committees of NCTE and CCCC, or EDUCOM/NCRIPTAL review panels, for computer applications; NCRIPTAL and the MLA review panel for software). Publishing articles on computer-based writing classes and software reviews should count in the same way that pedagogically focused articles and book reviews count.

The extent to which teaching assistants in the graduate program should be expected to take on the additional responsibilities of incorporating computers into their teaching will vary from campus to campus. The primary goal should be for graduate students who will be teaching writing in the future to gain competence in the basic theory and practice of composition before being asked to step into a computer classroom. Later, graduate students may want experience and access to computer tools for their own productivity, for versatility in teaching experience, and for an introduction to the literacy issues raised by new computer technology such as conferencing and hypermedia.

The same issues of preparation and motivation affect part-time faculty who normally have little incentive for incorporating computers into their writing classes. Training sessions may involve babysitting costs, for instance, that make extra time unattractive without subsidies or increased pay. For many part-time faculty, extended contracts for those who teach with computers may be an attractive reward that also cuts the institution's need for additional training sessions.

d. *Support for Students:* It is appropriate to assume that students too will need training, even those with previous experience in word processing, as users master the particular hardware and software as well as the institutional network in order to undertake the writing curriculum. Although writing faculty should not be responsible for basic introduction to the lab and the machines, training to use word processing and special software for writing can often be successfully integrated into instructional time. Help and information should be available from consultants in open lab hours, from good print documentation (posters work better than manuals for the essentials), or on-line. Where possible, computer lab assistants should be skillful writers, if not tutors, themselves.

The question will also rise whether the technology itself can deliver remedial instruction and thus justify an increase in the student-faculty ratio. There may be some exercises for teaching writing that are self-paced and appropriate for students to use on an individual basis. Electronic "hot-lines" on isolated points of grammar may be useful occasionally. More often, however, faculty should be looking for the technology to increase interaction and opportunities for support among the members and instructors of the writing classes. It follows, then, that the activities we have recommended now and in the future are both faculty-rich and computer-intensive.

7. *Be realistic about assigning the costs for a computer-based writing program.* Equipment and support services must have well-identified places in the appropriate departments' budgets, but it is especially important to get the more invisible costs negotiated early. Whose budget covers the costs for maintenance and replacement of equipment, for institutionally purchased word-processing software, for the instructional software, for training faculty, tutors, and students? Our experience suggests that

some of the costs for the writing program are apparently much more affordable than others.

a. *Easy:* basic hardware, though not always the useful peripherals such as adequate numbers of printers, hard disks, file servers; basic software — operating systems and word processing, though not always the software that is most functionally appropriate for the writing course. It also seems relatively easy to replace equipment because outside funding is often obtainable and because the investment is visible, yielding quick and positive returns from the faculty and students who benefit. But careful planners will insist — correctly — on getting amortization lines into the budget to allow for the future replacement of the initial equipment.

b. *Moderately Difficult:* technical support for the computer lab (though actually the problem may be more one of retaining good help than of budgeting for it); furniture (nobody is willing to believe that chairs cost so much!); supplies (especially paper); maintenance of older but still functional equipment; additional software. The greater difficulty here is that these expenses are ongoing and have to find a spot in the annual budgets of several departments, and some of these expenses, especially for supplies, seem to escalate at alarming rates.

c. *Difficult though Necessary:* release time for the faculty developing the writing program or overseeing the computer lab; training for faculty (because traditionally considered part of salary); software development or adaptation. Sometimes it is possible to raise grant funds to help out with software development, although institutional contributions to support and continue the grant program may be very hard commitments for an institution to make.

The funding for a computer-based writing program thus may have very uneven patterns of support, unless planners can be convinced that *all* of the components are equally necessary for the program's success. Uneven funding (e.g., enough equipment but inadequate training) will lead to uneven success in implementation.

8. *Evaluate the success of the program.* As effective as we believe it to be, the strategy of introducing computers into the center of a writing curriculum remains an experiment with many different implementations addressing many different learning needs. It is therefore prudent for an institution to put part of its investment into thorough and ongoing evaluation of the outcomes of its program for both faculty and students, as we have argued above. A program for evaluation that asks departments to

report on their progress will encourage faculty to learn about what is going on at other institutions and will enable them to share their own results more effectively with others. Internal dissemination of results — for example, to inform the deans of all schools — can win interest and support for administrative reallocation of funds to writing as an act of enlightened self-interest.

Interinstitutional Policy: Equity and Access

New technologies, with their strangeness, complexity, and high cost, tend to create new problems of equity in education, as we have discussed above. Within institutions, rich resources in the sciences, engineering, and business may result in unequal access because of traditional choices of major by gender, race, and ethnic identity. Between institutions, a hidden handicap exists (aside from budget differences), since effectively integrating computers into classrooms should be faculty-driven. In the community colleges, the institutions of higher learning that show the greatest minority enrollment and have lower tuitions, the teaching load is higher than in four-year institutions. A Peat-Marwick study shows that even at the leading computer-using colleges and universities surveyed, the least part of their computing budgets goes for faculty development, so we can deduce that most community college teachers will have even less support, since they have little discretionary time to learn effective ways to use the computer in classes.

Planning to improve this situation will require intervention from state and national agencies in their patterns of funding educational innovations. A number of states, aware of the economic advantages of computer-literate citizens, have funding available competitively or according to a plan for all institutions of higher education. The federal government has set policy directions and sponsored pilot programs with promise of significant replication. In addition to funding initiatives at particular institutions, however, student access might also expand through well-defined financial aid arrangements, in which personal computers come to be widely justifiable as tools for learning, in the same category as books or a calculator.

Although issues of access vary widely from institution to institution, in the long run there will be a need for cooperative planning among institutions and support of consortial arrangements. Examples of the kinds of interinstitutional cooperation that we envision include the following:

1. *Consortia and buddy systems:* Institutions serving different student

populations can collaborate in important ways. For example, the ENFI group (an Annenberg/CPB project) has developed and evaluated ways to include real-time networked writing in instruction at five very different campuses (Gallaudet University, New York Institute of Technology, Northern Virginia Community College, the University of Minnesota, and Carnegie Mellon University) so that other campuses can judge the value of project benefits for their own campuses more accurately than with reports from only one kind of school. This report's authors, a collaboration of people from a range of institutions, learned about the diversity of practices and problems across many kinds of campus. In Michigan, the Meadowbrook Conference at Oakland University brought together teachers from institutions of higher education throughout the state and led to collaboration between researchers at NCRIPTAL (the National Center for Research into Post-Secondary Teaching and Learning) at the University of Michigan and classroom teachers and their students at other schools such as Wayne County Community College. An important channel for faculty to meet and collaborate is electronic mail, allowing faculty to access bulletin boards on BITNET or public computer networks.

2. *Regional or peer-group organizations:* Faculty with common interests at several institutions can develop a network for exchanging information and advice. For example, the League for Innovation in the Community College, a group of twenty community colleges, has a major computer project, including vendor participation, that features a national conference and the development of guidelines related to computing at the various institutions. Such organizations can also serve as an effective grapevine, helping to disseminate information on potential funding sources as well as providing peer support for implementing programs in computer-writing classes. Electronic conferences on BITNET can also be important agents for the dissemination of information. For example, the ENFI consortium of schools grew in part out of writing teachers who met each other electronically on an Exxon-funded computer conference at the New York Institute of Technology.

3. *Planning and grant-writing workshops:* Held under the auspices of EDUCOM or some other organization, these workshops might help institutional personnel might learn to plan better or write more competitive grant applications to support planning and to get hardware for effective computer-based writing initiatives.

4. *Conference involvement:* To ensure that the needs of disadvantaged

students are articulated by those who work with them, conferences about computers should plan to increase involvement by minority faculty and by institutions that predominantly serve disadvantaged students. Such involvement might include special mailings to invite attendance (for example, mailings to the institutions of the United Negro College Fund), inclusion on the selection committees that accept paper proposals, and scholarship funds for attendance. Electronic mail can be an important channel to follow up on meetings at conferences and foster collaborative research or planning.

5. *Cooperation with vendors:* We would like to see some of the consortial or inter-institutional groups described above work together to involve vendors in discount programs to help "have not" institutions as much as, if not more than, the computer-rich institutions the vendors have so generously supported to date.

6. *Advocacy programs:* Professional organizations at the state and federal level should explore ways of financing and equipping writing labs in higher education in an equitable manner. To ensure that "have not" institutions have their own voice, professional organizations should continue efforts to include, especially on committees, participants from a representative array of institutions and to seek involvement by minority faculty.

Recommendations

Faculty Leadership and Budgeting

1. For institutions to integrate computers into writing instruction, leadership must come from faculty knowledgeable about both writing theory and computers.

a. Leaders in the writing program need to work with others in the institution who can provide needed technical support, information, and administrative models.

b. Faculty leaders need appropriate incentives (such as release time) to learn about computers and plentiful assistance with the technical issues that each level of technological complexity presents. They need support to discover and evaluate existing and forthcoming materials, for example, with hands-on exploration, workshops, software fairs, and samplers) and to subscribe to relevant journals.

c. Faculty leaders have the responsibility to coordinate with departmental colleagues as well as others involved in writing across the curriculum, especially faculty who will sponsor advanced student work on discipline-specific topics. Other important partners include librarians and writing center staff (often a part of the writing program or the English department). Such cooperation will be especially important as technology brings new rhetorical possibilities to text reading and writing.

2. Faculty leaders must have a major say in software and hardware adoption and regular input and access to campuswide planning about

a. hardware acquisition, upgrades, and reconfigurations;

b. software (site licenses of essential elements like word processors); and

c. access and scheduling policies.

Since writing classes are likely to be the single largest provider of classroom computer use, writing faculty should serve on faculty advisor committees to academic computing centers.

3. Institutions need to provide students with sufficient computer access, based on the number and type of assignments, the level of use in the writing curriculum, hours and places of student access, and the level of access students have to computers outside the institution.

4. Adequate budgeting (as well as reevaluation of budgets) is essential for successful implementation and should include

a. solid technical assistance (by staff and student aides) in computer labs, and especially in networked classrooms, for starting, maintaining, and expanding the program in size or capability;

b. equipment maintenance and supplies;

c. ongoing faculty development and support; and

d. increases whenever the program increases the number of students served or involves more complex technology.

5. Every large-scale program using computers in writing should have a thorough, ongoing program for faculty development, based on writing theory

a. to prepare new instructors for teaching;

b. to help teachers develop and share new approaches and reflect on implications for theory and development;

c. to keep instructors informed as the technology and pedagogy changes; and

d. to provide different development support for faculty at different stages of expertise.

6. Adequate support must be provided for all involved in computer-based writing instruction, as appropriate to teaching status.

a. Release time or credit toward tenure and promotions for tenure-track faculty

b. Pay or longer-term contracts for part-timers

c. Institutionally viable incentives for graduate assistants

d. Agreed-on duties and rewards for faculty leaders

Institutions should spell out (in reappointment and promotion procedures and criteria) what credit the faculty will receive for creating computer-based materials, whether the materials are text files, modifications of existing software, or new programs.

7. All instructors in the computer-based program, including graduate students and part-time instructors, need a computer or a guarantee of easy access to one. Such access is also important for recruiting new faculty participants.

8. Evaluation should be part of planning, even with pilot studies, to assess impact on educational goals and academic culture and to guide long-range planning for budgeting, expansion, and ongoing faculty development.

9. A campuswide evolutionary strategy should extend as long as the current hardware is expected to last, usually four to five years.

Issues Related to Software and Hardware Providers

10. Hardware vendors not only should market high-end computers but also should continue to offer low-end machines at lowered prices. (Universities need to choose or mix purchases based on their institutional priorities.)

11. Efforts to improve compatibility, portability of software, and standard user-interfaces should be supported by developing

a. tools that allow software applications to run independent of hardware and operating systems;

b. tools that help programmers write and maintain software that runs on a variety of hardware configurations (from a minimal, low-end system to a maximal, high-end system), including networked versions; and

c. document architecture standards that will allow writers to exchange text and graphics produced with different software programs without losing formatting information.

12. Close links are needed between software developers and audience to foster

a. formative evaluation of new software tools in classroom settings;

b. attention to the needs of different student populations at a range of institutions; and

c. funding for research into the effectiveness of computer-based tools for writing.

13. Although most faculty will not be involved in software design, faculty need to collaborate with vendors and publishers as well as grant agencies (both internal and external) to develop, test, and distribute pedagogical materials that reflect different student needs at a range of institutions, needs such as

a. support materials;

b. applications for tool software; and

c. new software.

Cooperation beyond the Institution

14. Many players have a role in assuring equity of access for all students in higher education.

   a. Computer-rich institutions should cooperate with less privileged institutions in setting up consortia for faculty development, dissemination of information, and evaluation.

   b. Teams of "have" and "have not" institutions should work with vendors to extend vendors' high discounts to institutions with economically disadvantaged students.

   c. Planning and grant-writing workshops can help and can team up "have" and "have-not" institutions.

   d. Professional associations can involve minority faculty and those who serve economically disadvantaged students by including them in software fairs and panels on classroom use or on committees dealing with computer-related issues.

15. Vendors should be asked to support on-campus faculty development for training with and evaluation of their software and equipment.

16. Computer organizations such as EDUCOM and professional organizations (such as the Conference on College Composition and Communication and the Modern Language Association) should provide help, such as

   a. lists of consultants on faculty development and program planning;

   b. consulting programs for site visits;

   c. support for convention workshops; and

   d. programs to assess software and teaching methods.

17. Statewide collaboration should keep state government apprised of the condition of computer use in higher education, along with current and long-range needs.

18. Professional organizations should develop federal advocacy programs, for example to have computers defined as necessary educational tools for tax credits.

Notes

1. Report from an EDUCOM Software Initiative Committee: Helen J. Schwartz, chair (Indiana University-Purdue University at Indianapolis); Diane P. Balestri (Princeton University); Brian Gallagher (LaGuardia Community College, City University of New York); Nancy Kaplan (Cornell University); Christine M. Neuwirth (Carnegie Mellon University); Tori Haring-Smith (Brown University).
2. Carolyn Kirkpatrick, "Implementing Computer-Mediated Writing: Some Early Lessons," *Machine-Mediated Learning* 2, nos. 1-2 (1987): 37.
3. C. J. Mooney, "Expected End of Mandatory Retirement in 1990's Unlikely to Cause Glut of Profs, Study Finds," *Chronicle of Higher Education,* December 16, 1987, A1, 11.
4. R. Reddy, "Technologies for Learning," in A. M. Lesgold and F. Reif (chairmen), *Computers in Education: Realizing the Potential* (Washington, D.C.: U.S. Department of Education, Office of Educational Research and Improvement, 1983).

Bibliography

Overviews

Burns, Hugh. (1987). Computers and composition. *Teaching Composition.* Rev. and enl. ed. Ed. Gary Tate. Fort Worth: Texas Christian University Press, pp. 378-400.

Schwartz, Helen J., and Lillian S. Bridwell. (1984). A selected bibliography on computers in composition. *College Composition and Communication* 35 (2): 71-77.

Schwartz, Helen J., and Lillian S. Bridwell-Bowles. (1987). A selected bibliography on computers in composition: An update. *College Composition and Communication* 38 (4): 453-57.

Reviews of Research

Barker, Thomas T. (1987). Studies in word processing and writing. *Computers in the Schools* 4 (1): 78-87.

Bridwell, Lillian, Paula Reed Nancarrow, and Donald Ross. (1984). The writing process and the writing machine: Current research on word processors relevant to the teaching of composition. In *New Directions in Composition Research,* ed. Richard Beach and Lillian Bridwell, 381-98. New York: Guilford Press.

Hawisher, Gail. (1986). Studies in word processing. *Computers and Composition* 4 (1): 6-31.

———. (1988). Research update: Writing and word processing. *Computers and Composition* 5 (2): 7-27.

Ross, Donald, Jr., and Lillian S. Bridwell. (1985). Computer-aided composing: Gaps in the software. In *Computer-Aided Instruction in the Humanities,* ed. Solveig Olsen. New York: Modern Language Association, pp. 103-15.

Schwartz, Helen J., Thea van der Geest, and Marlies L. Smit-Kreuzen. (forthcoming). Computers in writing instruction. *International Journal of Educational Research.*

Research and Reflection about Writing and Computer-Based Writing Instruction

Arkin, M., and Gallagher, B. (1984). Word processing and the basic writer. *Connecticut English Journal* 15 (2): 60-66. The advantages in using computers with basic writers.

Balestri, D. P. (1988). Softcopy and hard: Wordprocessing and writing process. *Academic Computing* (Feb.), 14-17, 41-45. Describes ways to teach the process of writing with word processing that takes advantage of the constructable, fluid, malleable nature of electronic text.

Batson, T. (1988). The ENFI project: A networked classroom approach to writing instruction. *Academic Computing* (Feb.), 32-33, 55-56. Real-time "chat" for deaf students at Gallaudet.

Bereiter, C., and Scardamalia, M. (1981). From conversation to composition: The role of instruction in a developmental process. In *Advances in Instructional Psychology, II,* ed. R. Glaser. Hillsdale, N.J.: Lawrence Erlbaum. Outlines seven principles for instructional intervention to help young writers' cognitive development.

Beserra, W. C. (1986). Effects of word processing upon the writing process of basic writers. (Ph.D. diss., New Mexico State University). Dissertation Abstracts International, 48, 34-A. Benefits shown for basic writers.

Bridwell, Lillian, Geoffrey Sirc, and Robert Brooke. (1985). Revising and computing: Case studies of student writers. In *The Acquisition of Written Language: Revision and Response,* ed. Sarah W. Freedman, 172-94. Norwood, N.J.: Ablex. How students adapt their writing style to word processing.

Bridwell-Bowles, Lillian, Parker Johnson, and Steven Brehe. (1987). Composing and computers: Case studies of experienced writers. In *Writing in Real Time:*

Modelling Production Processes, ed. A. Matsuhashi. Norwood, N.J.: Ablex, pp. 81-107. Mature writers adapt word processing to their individual writing strategies.

Bruffee, Kenneth A. (1984). Collaborative learning and the "Conversation of mankind." *College English* 46:635-52. Theory on the social context of writing.

Burns, Hugh, and George H. Culp. (1980). Stimulating invention in English composition through computer-assisted instruction. *Educational Technology* 20:5-10. Student use of idea-generating software aids.

Case, D. (1985). Processing professional words: Personal computers and the writing habits of university professors. *College Composition and Communication* 36 (3): 317-22. Benefits and perceived problems of word-processing addicts.

Chignell, Mark H., and Lacy, Richard M. (1988). Project Jefferson: Integrating research and instruction. *Academic Computing* 2 (8): 12-17, 40-45. Hypermedia in first-year students' writing research at University of Southern California.

Collins, Terence, Nancy Engen-Wedin, and William Margolis. (1988). Persistence and course completion. *Computers and Composition* 6 (1): 27-32. Computer-based writing classes at the University of Minnesota show higher rates of retention and course completion than do regular classes.

Costanzo, W. V. (1989). *The Electronic Text: Learning to Write, Read, and Reason with Computers.* Englewood Cliffs, N.J.: Educational Technology. An overview of the impact computers can have on learning language skills.

Covey, P. K., S. Roberts, S. Bond, and R. Cavalier. (1989). A right to die? A videodisk: The case of Dax Cowart [videodisc, version 0.0]. CDEC Report #89-07. Pittsburgh: Carnegie Mellon University, Center for Design of Educational Computing. Interactive software with videodisk on medical ethics.

Daiute, Colette. (1985). *Writing and Computers.* Reading, Mass.: Addison Wesley. Speculations on the physical, social, and cognitive impact of word processing on student writers.

Elbow, Peter. (1973). *Writing without Teachers.* London: Oxford. Theory on the writing process.

Elbow, P., and P. Belanoff. (1986). Portfolios as a substitute for proficiency examinations. *College Composition and Communication* 37 (3): 336-39. Describes the rationale and procedure for using students' writing portfolios instead of proficiency writing exams to determine placement of students at SUNY Stony Brook.

Feldman, Paula R., and Buford Norman. (1987). *The Wordworthy Computer.* New York: Random House. A good introduction to computing, especially in literature.

Flower, Linda S., and John R. Hayes. (1980). The cognition of discovery: Defining a rhetorical problem. *College Composition and Communication* 31, pp. 21-32. How experienced writers envision the central elements of the writing act compared with those of inexperienced writers.

Flower, Linda, and John R. Hayes. (1981). A cognitive process theory of writing. *College Composition and Communication* 32, pp. 365-87. Theory on the writing process.

Flower, Linda, John R. Hayes, Linda Carey, Karen Schriver, and James Stratman. (1986). Detection, diagnosis, and the strategies of revision. *College Composition and Communication* 37 (2): 16-55. How student writers revise, with and without success.

Friedlander, Larry. (1988). The Shakespeare project: Experiments in multimedia education. *Academic Computing* 2 (7): 26-29+. Hypermedia for Shakespeare study at Stanford.

Gallagher, Brian. (1985). *Microcomputers and Word Processing Programs: An Evaluation and Critique.* Research Monograph Series Report No. 9. New York: City University of New York, Instructional Resource Center. What to look for in word-processing programs, how the functions relate to teaching writing, and speculations on how computers are reshaping notions of *text*.

Grow, Gerald. (1988). Lessons from the computer writing problems of professionals. *College Composition and Communication* 39 (2): 217-20. How to teach technical writing students to prepare for writing on the job.

Haas, C. (1989). How the writing medium shapes the writing process: Effects of word processing on planning. *Research in the Teaching of English* 23 (2): 181-207. Both experts and novices showed less initial and conceptual planning with word processing than with paper and pencil.

Havholm, Peter L., and Larry L. Stewart. (1988). Using OWL International Inc.'s GUIDE to teach critical thinking. (Manuscript, College of Wooster in Ohio). Hypertext in a 17th-century literature class.

Hawisher, Gail, and Cynthia L. Selfe, ed., *Critical Perspectives on Computers and Computer Instruction.* New York: Teachers College Press, 1989.

Hillocks, George. (1986). *Research in Writing Composition.* Urbana, Ill.: National Council of Teachers of English. A summary of research about writing.

Holdstein, Deborah, ed. (1987). *On Composition and Computers.* New York: Modern Language Association.

Hull, Glynda, Carolyn Ball, James L. Fox, Lori Levin, and Deborah McCutchen. (1987). Computer detection of errors in natural language texts: Research on pattern-matching. *Computers and the Humanities* 21, pp. 103-18.

Kaplan, N. (1987). The technologies of teaching. (Paper presented at the Penn State Conference on Rhetoric and Composition, State College, Penn.). Discusses the influence of technologies like the book and blackboard, as well as computers, on how composition is taught.

King, B., J. Birnbaum, and J. Wageman. (1984). Word processing and the basic college writer. In *The Written Word and the Word Processor,* ed. T. Martinez. Philadelphia, Penn.: Delaware Valley Writing Council. Retention rates are higher in classes using computers for writing.

Kinkead, Joyce. (1987). Computer conversations: E-mail and writing instruction. *College Composition and Communication* 38, pp. 337-41. Uses for electronic mail at Utah State University.

Kirkpatrick, C. (1987). Implementing computer-mediated writing: Some early lessons. *Machine-Mediated Learning* 2 (1-2): 35-45. Discusses use of word processing in basic writing classes at York College in New York City: problems encountered with evaluation, assessment, and revising the concept of writing processes.

Landow, George P. (1988). The rhetoric and stylistics of hypertext: The experience of the Brown University Intermedia System. (Paper presented at the Modern Language Association Conference, New Orleans, La.). Hypermedia in literature and across the curriculum.

Lanham, R. A. (1989). The electronic word. *New Literary History* 20 (2): 265-90. Speculates on changes in literary analysis, writing, and publication because of electronic text.

McAllister, Carole, and Richard Louth. (1988). The effect of word processing on the quality of basic writers' revisions. *Research in the Teaching of English* 22, pp. 417-27. Benefits for basic writers.

McDaniel, E. (1987). Bibliography of text-analysis and writing-instruction software. *Journal of Advanced Composition* 7 (1-2): 139-69. Descriptions of programs.

Moulouly, Mary Sue. (1988). Commenting on student writing: Some effects of computer assisted delivery. (Ph.D. diss., Carnegie Mellon University). The effect of on-line handbooks looks promising.

Mooney, C. J. (Dec. 16, 1987). Expected end of mandatory retirement in 1990's unlikely to cause glut of profs, study finds. *Chronicle of Higher Education*, A 1, 11. Professors reaching age sixty-five between 1987 and 1997 may cause shortages.

Moore, Wayne. (1985). Word processing in first-year comp. *Computers and Composition* 3 (1): 55-60. Improved retention rates with computers in writing.

Perl, Sondra. (1979). The composing processes of unskilled college writers. *Research in the Teaching of English* 13, pp. 317-36. Research shows basic writers adhere to rigid rules of writing.

Pijls, Fieny, Walter Daelemans, and Gerard Kampen. (1987). Artificial intelligence tools for grammar and spelling instruction. *Instructional Science*, 319-36. Artificial intelligence software for grammar and spelling in Dutch.

Rodrigues, Dawn. (1985). Computers and basic writers. *College Composition and Communication* 36, pp. 336-39. Useful ways of using word processing with basic writers.

Rodrigues, Dawn, and Raymond J. Rodrigues. (1986). *Teaching Writing with a Word Processor, Grades 7-13*. Theory and Research into Practice. Urbana, Ill.: National Council of Teachers of English. Theory-based guidance in creating teaching text files with a word processor.

Schwartz, Mimi. (1982). Computers and the teaching of writing. *Educational Technology* 22, pp. 27-29. A general introduction to the impact computers can have in writing instruction.

Selfe, Cynthia. (1985). *Computer-Assisted Instruction in Composition: Create Your Own!* Urbana, Ill.: National Council of Teachers of English. Delineates the requirements and process for software development.

Selfe, C. L., and Billie J. Wahlstrom. (1986). An emerging rhetoric of collaboration: Computers, collaboration, and the composing process. *Collegiate Microcomputer* 4, pp. 289-96. Study of the culture of the writing lab and computer-based writing classroom.

Shermis, Michael. *Word Processing and Writing Instruction for Students with Special Needs,* FAST Bibliography #11. Bloomington, Ind.: ERIC Clearinghouse on

Reading and Communication Skills, 1989. Annotated bibliography on basic-writing students, ESL, and learning disabled.

Stine, L. J. (1989). Computers and commuters: A computer-intensive writing program for adults. *Computers and Composition* 6 (2): 23-32. Loaners used with minorities and older students at Lincoln University; frank assessment of needs, benefits, and changes in teaching required.

Sudol, Ronald A. (1985). Applied word processing: Notes on authority, responsibility, and revision in a workshop model. *College Composition and Communication* 36, pp. 331-39. Ways to use computers in classes designed as writing workshops.

Vygotsky, L. (1986). *Thought and Language*. Ed. A. Kozulin. Cambridge, Mass.: MIT Press. A socially generated approach to language learning.

Welsch, Lawrence A. (1982). Using electronic mail as a teaching tool. *Communications of the ACM* 25, pp. 105-8. An engineering professor uses E-mail to critique students' drafts.

Wresch, William, ed. (1984). *The Computer in Composition Instruction: A Writer's Tool*. Urbana, Ill.: National Council of Teachers of English. Theory and description of word-processing and instructional software for writing.

Textbooks Integrating Word Processing into College-Level Instruction

Barth, M. E. (1988). *Strategies for Writing with a Computer*. New York: McGraw-Hill.

Edwards, B. L., Jr. (1987). *Processing Words*. Englewood Cliffs, N.J.: Prentice-Hall.

Elder, J., B. Bowen, J. Schwartz, and D. Goswami. (1988). *Word Processing in a Community of Writers*. New York: Garland.

Gerrard, Lisa. (1987). *Writing with HBJ Writer*. San Diego: Harcourt.

Schwartz, Helen J. (1985). *Interactive Writing*. New York: Holt.

Sudol, Ronald A. (1987). *Textfiles*. San Diego: Harcourt.

Wresch, William, Donald Pattow, and James Gifford. (1988). *Writing for the Twenty-First Century*. New York: McGraw-Hill.

Hardware and Software Issues

Brand, S. (1987). *The Media Lab: Inventing the Future at M.I.T.* New York: Penguin. How new media will affect human communication.

Card, Stuart K., Thomas P. Moran, and Allen Newell (1983). *The Psychology of Human-Computer Interaction*. Hillsdale, N.J.: Lawrence Erlbaum Associates. Provides a scientific foundation for an applied psychology concerned with the human users of interactive computer systems.

Char, C., D. Newman, and W. Tally. (1987). Interactive videodiscs for children's learning. In *Mirrors of Minds,* ed. R. D. Pea and K. Sheingold. Norwood, N.J.: Ablex, pp. 223-41. Classroom study of the uses of videodisk technology: how well different models of videodisks fit traditional models of learning; as alternatives to traditional media; and role of teachers.

Haas, C., and J. R. Hayes. (1986). What did I just say? Reading problems in writing with the machine. *Research in the Teaching of English* 20 (1): 22-35. Visual/spatial factors in reading text from computers influence recall of information and place-in-text as well as appropriate reordering of text.

Hansen, Wilfred J., and Christina Haas. (1988). Reading and writing with computers: A framework for explaining differences in performance. *Communications of the ACM* 31, pp. 1080-89. Sets up categories for describing differences between writing with pen-and-paper and computers.

Ledgard, H., A. Singer, and J. Whiteside. (1981). *Directions in Human Factors for Interactive Systems.* New York: Springer-Verlag. Discusses human factors issues in the design of interactive systems as well as experimental designs for use in testing the validity of an interactive system design.

Palay, A. J., W. J. Hansen, M. L. Kazar, M. Sherman, M. G. Wadlow, T. P. Neundorffer, Z. Stern, M. Bader, and T. Peters. (1988). The Andrew toolkit: An overview. In *Proceedings of the USENIX Technical Conference.* Dallas, Tex.

Reddy, R. (1983). Technologies for learning. In *Computers in Education: Realizing the Potential,* report of a research conference, A. M. Lesgold and F. Reif, chairmen. Washington, D.C.: U.S. Department of Education, Office of Educational Research and Improvement, pp. 49-60. Explores trends in computer technologies and their implications for learning and education in the future.

Schmandt, C. (1985). Voice communication with computers. In *Advances in Human-Computer Interaction,* ed. H. R. Hartson. Norwood, N.J.: Ablex, 1:133-60. Presents a design philosophy for a voice-interactive interface, based on intelligence and conversational ability.

Implementation in Academe and Societal Issues

Balestri, Diane Pelkus et al. (1988). *Ivory Towers, Silicon Basements: Learner-Cen-*

tered Computing in Postsecondary Education. McKinney, Tex: EDUCOM/Academic Computing. Experiences of innovative uses of technology in higher education.

Collis, Betty. (1988). Manipulating critical variables: A framework for improving the impact of computers in the school environment. (Conference presentation, EURIT88, Lausanne, Switzerland). Ideas about implementation, especially the effect of computers on teachers' attitudes toward teaching.

Fullan, Michael. (1982). *The Meaning of Educational Change.* New York: Teachers College Press. Theories of innovation and its institutionalization in education.

Gilbert, Steven W., and Kenneth C. Green. (1986). New computing in higher education. *Change* 18 (3): 33-50. Current educational trends and implications for institutional planning and for developers and vendors.

Heermann, Barry. (1988). *Teaching and Learning with Computers: A Guide for College Faculty and Administrators.* San Francisco: Jossey-Bass. Why and how-to.

Holdstein, Deborah H. (1987). The politics of CAI and word processing: Some issues for faculty and administrators. In *Writing at Century's End,* ed. Lisa Gerrard. New York: Random House.

Johnston, Jerome, and Robert B. Kozma. (1988). The 1988 EDUCOM/NCRIP-TAL competition. *Academic Computing* (Nov.), 30-36. Description of competition procedures and of winning software and curricular use.

Leslie, Judith W. (1987). Computing in a multi-cultural environment. *EDUCOM Bulletin* 22 (4): 20-28. Concerns for setting up a multipurpose lab for a diverse student body.

National Task Force on Education Technology. (1986). Transforming American education: Reducing the risk to the nation. (A report to the secretary of education, U.S. Department of Education). *T.H.E. Journal* 14 (1): 58-67. Recommendations include teaching computer literacy in academic (not separate) classes.

Ohmann, Richard. (1985). Literacy, technology, and monopoly capital. *College English* 47, pp. 675-89. Possible social and economic impacts of computing.

Peat Marwick. (1987). *Microcomputer Use in Higher Education.* (Executive summary of a survey conducted by EDUCOM and Peat Marwick in cooperation with the *Chronicle of Higher Education*). Trends and patterns of implementation at leading computer-using schools.

Weizenbaum, Joseph (1976) *Computer Power and Human Reason*. San Francisco: W. H. Freeman. Reflections on the societal impact and misuse of computers.

Part Three:

Institutional Perspectives

Institutional Perspectives

The preceding two articles offer evidence of the ways in which the building blocks of a higher education not only are being repackaged, but are being fundamentally altered by interactive technologies. Both articles call for stronger connections between curriculum/faculty development and the development of institutional support services for information technologies. Does the responsibility for establishing these connections fall to an institution's academic officer(s) or to its chief information officer (CIO) or to its computing support leadership? For example, a corollary to the widely admired, if not practiced, belief that writing should be an across-the-curriculum responsibility is that the technological tools of writing should be available to all students and that the technological pedagogy developed by the writing program should be known to all faculty. How can this be accomplished, and on whose desk does this buck stop? To help us understand the variety of ways that campuses are addressing these kinds of issues, I have included in this part of the book nine institutional case studies from a cross section of colleges and universities. As the following thumbnail sketches reveal, these contributions cover a broad spectrum of institutional types and institutional experiences with instructional technologies.

- Cornell has enjoyed strong leadership from its CIO position overseeing a highly distributed and very complex computing environment—from micros to supercomputers. Several vendors have contributed to Cornell's instructional computing programs. The major organized thrust, Project Ezra, was enabled by the largest single contribution, from IBM. Cornell's faculty responded to such opportunities with enthusiasm and distinction, winning four EDUCOM/NCRIPTAL awards to date.

- The phrase *research college* describes Dartmouth College and its dual emphases on research and teaching. Instructional computing has been a focus there since the early 1960s when BASIC was created on campus. The college was one of the first to "encourage" incoming students in the 1980s to own a particular personal computer, the Apple Macintosh, and systematically to place the same computer on the desks of faculty members. Presidential leadership in the 1960s established a highly centralized environment that has evolved into today's distributed approach. Dartmouth has consistently produced results (including two EDUCOM/NCRIPTAL awards). Its recent leading-edge thrust has revealed the benefits of ongoing vision, as well as the scope of upgrading costs and other costs associated with such vision.

- Drake is a private university that in the mid-1980s made a commitment to a strategic "Computer Enriched Curriculum Project." With faculty input and strong leadership, this university also keyed on the Macintosh and is supporting its faculty's efforts to develop and to use software in the curriculum. One of Drake's most interesting strategies was to target departments that appeared to be "ready."

- Iona is another private college that made a strategic commitment to a computing-intensive "chosen future." With leadership from its CIO position and with a significant part of its budget committed to computing, this campus selected the IBM line and forged a partnership with IBM based on ConnectPac, Iona's own approach to an integrated and affordable scholar's workstation.

- Miami Dade is recognized as a community college that seizes every opportunity to add quality to its programs. It is not surprising, then, that information technologies are extensively employed in the infrastructure that supports teaching and advising at the college. This case study should stir the interest of community college leaders and encourage them to examine the case studies included, along with this one from Miami-Dade, in another book in the EDUCOM Strategies Series on Information Technology: *Transforming Teaching with Technology: Perspectives from Two-Year Colleges* (edited by Dr. Kamala Anandam).

- Stevens Institute of Technology was the first institution (in 1982) to require that students own a computer (from Digital). Leadership currently comes not only from a CIO but also from an external Advisory Panel and from a campus committee that draws its membership from other academic committees. Stevens has a multivendor network and has secured its position as a technical institution that takes full advantage of interactive technology.

- The University of Illinois has a rich history of instructional computing that includes the development of PLATO in the 1960s and a host of other innovations. The computing environment on campus is highly decentralized, and the scope of instructional computing covers micros to supercomputers. Illinois has chosen not to create a CIO position but has created other mechanisms to ensure the development, the piloting, and the implementation of worthy projects. Sponsored projects are consistently evaluated, computers are widely available in student dorms, and Illinois faculty members have won four EDUCOM/NCRIPTAL awards.

- Engineering is not present on the University of North Carolina campus, and early leadership for instructional computing came from the medical school. More recent thrusts have included an across-the-curriculum project funded in part by IBM and guided by a strong campus commitment to general education. Participating faculty have won three EDUCOM/NCRIPTAL awards. Drawing on the experience of this project and taking new direction from a leadership position for academic computing, the university created a microcomputing support structure in parallel to the traditional academic computing center and continues to provide leadership for instructional computing in a distributed environment.

- Western Washington is a comprehensive university with a history of involvement in instructional computing. It is the home of the Association for the Development of Computer-Based Instructional Systems (ADCIS) and the team that developed PC-PILOT and other instructional tools, such as the hypermedia program, LinkWay. Western faculty members have won two EDUCOM/NCRIPTAL awards.

Each of these case studies, whether individually or collectively written, reflects both academic and computing service viewpoints. I used the phrase *provost's perspective* in describing to the authors my hope that their contributions would move beyond the now common descriptive listings of hardware/software and support services toward deeper issues of institutional change. I posed questions about how technology is transforming academic programs and governance structures on campus. For example:

- What could a committee of faculty, department chairs, deans, and computing service leaders on a campus similar to yours learn from you and your colleagues about integrating computing into the curriculum?

- Has your campus structured support services and faculty development programs to catalyze technology-based curriculum development and to discover its proper role in the dynamics among your faculty colleagues, their disciplines, and your institution?

- What has your campus done? How has it done it? What has worked? What has not? What are the directions for the future?

These questions were refined by a longer list, included here as appendix B, which guided the development of the case studies that follow.

Chapter 10

Cornell University: An Institutional Perspective on Using Information Technologies to Add Value to Teaching and Learning

Gordon L. Galloway

Introduction

This paper summarizes selected aspects of several years of intense efforts to weave information technologies into the fabric of teaching and learning. It attempts to address some of what we might call the "big" questions about how information technology is transforming the academic culture at the university and to what extent that technology has been strengthened or encumbered by the governing structures on the campus.

Although we acknowledge that mainframe computing, including supercomputing, has been a critical component of the transformations that have taken place, the focus of this document is on microcomputing. By reporting on our experiences, we hope to provide helpful information to others confronting the vexing problems of how best to incorporate information technologies into the curriculum.

About Cornell University

Cornell University, founded in 1868, is both a private university and the land-grant college of the state of New York. Composed of thirteen schools and colleges, Cornell has an enrollment of over eighteen thousand students, and employs nearly twenty-two hundred faculty. As a focus for excellence in both teaching and research, Cornell is supported by a large network of information systems and services, including one of the five facilities in the United States designated as a national center for super-computing.

Background of Information Technologies at Cornell

Beginnings

The cry for enhancing the "computer literacy" began in the late 1970s, when timesharing was still the conventional route to computing power. However, serious attempts to incorporate information technologies into the curriculum have taken place largely since the early 1980s, when microcomputers began to be ubiquitously available in schools and colleges.

In 1980, Cornell University selected Kenneth King as its first Vice-Provost for Computing. In the seven years of his leadership, the university dramatically expanded its use of information technologies, including the installation, in 1986, of the first IBM 3090 supercomputer as part of the Cornell National Supercomputer Facility (CNSF).

Early support for (mainframe) computing in the curriculum was driven strongly by the needs of the College of Engineering and the Department of Computer Science, although all of the other colleges, particularly the College of Agriculture and Life Sciences and the College of Human Ecology, were actively involved in enhancing what was then referred to as the "computer literacy" of their students.

Before 1984, most of the instructional computing resources provided by Cornell Computer Services (CCS), now known as Cornell Information Technologies (CIT), were public-access facilities equipped with asynchronous terminals connected to mainframes — except for fifty Terak micro-

computers that had been purchased to support all of the introductory
courses in computer science.

In 1984

Early in 1984, King and the College of Engineering embraced the
technology of the newly introduced Apple Macintosh microcomputers,
and CCS funded a large laboratory of Macs to replace the Teraks. Suddenly, all introductory computer science courses migrated from using
PL/C on the Teraks to using Macintosh Pascal running on Macs under
Macintosh/OS.

Later in 1984, IBM awarded Cornell an eight-million-dollar grant of
hardware and software known as Project Ezra — one of the Advanced
Education Projects (AEPs) funded by IBM at nineteen major universities
— for the purpose of allowing faculty to develop innovative curricular
software to run on IBM microcomputers. As a small part of that grant, the
College of Engineering was provided with its own IBM 4341 mainframe to
support studies in Computer-Aided Design/Computer-Aided Manufacturing (CAD/CAM). But most of Project Ezra's funds were used to provide
638 IBM microcomputers (PCs, XTs, ATs, and RTs) to 329 faculty aspiring to develop innovative educational software under IBM's MS-DOS
operating system.

The coincidental combination of rapid and steady growth in the popularity of the Macintosh microcomputer since its introduction in 1984 and
the continual influx of microcomputing resources provided by IBM during the four years of Project Ezra created an environment from which we
were able to learn a substantial amount about microcomputers in the
curriculum. Much of what we learned is reported in this document.

Transition

In 1988, King was succeeded by M. Stuart Lynn as Vice-President for
Information Technologies. Since Lynn's appointment, the university has
redoubled its efforts to provide the best environment possible to support
the use of information technologies by its students, faculty, and administrators.

In the fall of 1988, Cornell was able to install its second IBM 3090,
doubling the computing resources of its national supercomputer facility.
In 1989, Lynn and the College of Engineering, again embracing a leading

edge of microcomputing technology (as King and the College of Engineering had done in 1984), cooperated to create a laboratory of twenty-five NeXT computer systems for use in computer science and engineering. Once more, the stage has been set for new horizons, but this time under the UNIX operating system.

Cornell's Present Computing Environment

At Cornell, computers are used by students and faculty members in every discipline. Cornell Information Technologies provides and maintains computing hardware, operating systems, and general and specialized software to meet a broad spectrum of needs.

To make these resources readily accessible, CIT operates public terminal and microcomputing facilities, provides generous free consulting, produces informative documentation, and offers a variety of workshops and other training programs. CIT also manages a software lending library and self-training facility, provides some software for use in staffed public sites, and negotiates with software vendors to obtain substantial discounts for students, faculty, and staff. In additional support of instruction and research, CIT operates a sales unit known as Microcomputers and Office Systems (MOS), offering computing and office equipment to eligible members of the Cornell community.

Cornell's mainframe and minicomputers available for instruction and research consist of an IBM 4381-13, an IBM 3090-200, a DEC VAX 8530, two VAX 11/750s, and two MicroVAX IIs. Additionally, public or semi-public facilities providing access to more than 650 microcomputers are located in twenty-four different areas on and off campus. Students and faculty are provided with a weekly allowance of mainframe computing time and unlimited access to all of the public microcomputers; facilities are available for purchasing high-quality laser printing at modest prices.

A substantial number of computing systems and related equipment — from supercomputers to microcomputers — have been donated to Cornell by various major computer vendors in support of instruction and research. The Cornell National Supercomputer Facility provides access to two IBM 3090-600E computing systems, with vector facilities.

Cornell subscribes to Telenet, allowing access to Cornell's mainframes via a local telephone call from all fifty states, Mexico, Canada, and Europe. Besides being a charter member of EDUCOM, Cornell is also a member

of BITNET, providing two-way electronic mail service between Cornell
and other colleges and universities worldwide.

Standardization of Hardware and Software

Although any assertions about standardization are only best estimates,
it is perhaps worth noting that most, but certainly not all, of the computing hardware used at Cornell has been manufactured by seven vendors
Apple, DEC, Hewlett-Packard, IBM, Sun, Xerox, and, most recently,
NeXT. Presently, students buy more Apple hardware than any other kind;
faculty in computer science use mostly hardware made by Sun and Apple
(or Xerox), though the newest CS lab contains twenty-five NeXT workstations; most other faculty use either IBM or Apple hardware. The
College of Engineering has a large commitment to hardware made by
DEC, Sun, and Apple, while the Johnson Graduate School of Management
and the Laboratory of Computer Graphics have substantial amounts of
hardware from both DEC and Hewlett-Packard.

There are only a few discernible standards in microcomputing software. The most popular languages are FORTRAN, Pascal, C, Objective C,
and (still some) BASIC. *Lotus* and *Excel* are the most commonly used
spreadsheets; *Word*, *WordPerfect*, and *WriteNow* are the most popularly
used packages for word processing, accompanied by *PageMaker* and
Illustrator for desktop publishing. The early embrace of *MacWrite* and
MacPaint has been largely superceded by third-party software, although
the use of *MacDraw* is still extensive. The two most popular database
managements systems seem to be *Foxbase* running under MS-DOS and
Filemaker running under Mac/OS.

Technology in the Classroom

Though there has been both central and distributed support for developing curricular uses of information technologies, thus far we have not
been nearly as successful in moving these technologies directly into the
classroom. As noted earlier, there are many clusters of publicly available
microcomputers outside the classrooms; there are also many laboratories
equipped with microcomputers available for both instruction and re-

search. But there is still a dearth of adequate projection facilities for using computers routinely as part of the lecture.

Costs are at the root of this shortage, but the added labor is also a factor. Besides needing projection equipment that is still quite expensive, such facilities, especially when used by many different professors, need constant "care and feeding," routine preventive maintenance, proper security, and often additional personnel to plan or assist with presentations. Yet without more lecture halls equipped for moving technology directly into the classroom, the difficulty of integrating the technologies into the curriculum continues.

Critical Factors in the Curricular Uses of Information Technologies

Most of what now composes Cornell's technology-based curriculum materials has resulted from, and been greatly influenced by, the following critical factors:

- The extensive and immediate acceptance, especially among students, of the easy-to-use and easy-to-learn Apple Macintosh computer and its successors, the SE and the Macintosh II.

- Project Ezra, IBM's eight-million-dollar grant of hardware and software, awarded to Cornell to support faculty proposing to create innovative software for use in instruction and research.

- The "creative tension" resulting from students' widespread use of the Macintosh as a counterpoint to the use of IBM microcomputers by most of the faculty who have developed curricular software.

- The eagerness of Cornell's individual schools and colleges to support information technologies on their own, by providing computing equipment, space, funds, and other resources for their faculty — in addition to their willingness to contribute to the funding of central services.

- The establishment of the Cornell Theory Center by the Nobel physicist Kenneth Wilson, which led to the partnership — among NSF, IBM, the state of New York, and Cornell University — known as the Cornell National Supercomputing Facility.

- The vision and commitment of a resource center for information technologies designed to provide the infrastructure needed to support and sustain uses of technology-based curriculum materials.

- The willingness of both the university and the individual colleges to accept the challenge and costs of supplying and supporting suitable networking resources to ensure needed connectivity among the many nodes and local area networks on the campus.

- The ability of students, faculty, staff, and departments to purchase attractively priced microcomputers and peripherals from an internal sales organization and to obtain software at reduced prices through site licenses with major software vendors.

The Microcomputer's Impact on Faculty Teaching

The impact of microcomputers on teaching at Cornell has been both dramatic and subtle. Although the explosive interest in the Apple Macintosh has been important, the more significant component of that impact over the last four years has been Project Ezra.

Ever since Cornell's faculty discovered the microcomputer — a tool they generally believe costs little when compared with the rates paid for mainframe timesharing — there has been an explosion of attempts to develop software applications for the classroom and laboratory. Most of the curricular software that emerged from these attempts resulted from work done on the family of IBM PCs granted through Project Ezra between 1984 and 1988. Some curricular software has also resulted from parallel efforts by a significantly smaller but no less dedicated group of faculty who developed software for the Apple Macintosh.

With its promise of "free" hardware and software for use by all interested and qualified faculty, Project Ezra quickly provided a strong and pervasive stimulus for discovering how to incorporate microcomputers into classrooms and laboratories. By indirectly promoting the simultaneous and rapid development of expanded infrastructures, the project also provided Cornell with a more comprehensive understanding of the potential and the limits of microcomputing applied to instruction and research.

In fact, Project Ezra succeeded in tantalizing the interest and hastening the willingness of the entire campus to experiment with using information technologies for instruction and, in doing so, captured the imagination and the enthusiasm of many faculty and their students. It enhanced collaboration among faculty from diverse disciplines, motivated professional societies to include more focus on instruction and technology, and strengthened national collaborations through conferences, electronic mail, and the use of appropriate networks.

The "campus embrace" of microcomputing technologies has fostered traditional pedagogical concerns for improving teaching. It has motivated faculty to reflect on the content of their courses and on the style of their teaching; it has stimulated faculty to be creative and original as they sought to produce innovative software; it has elicited reviews and subsequent modifications of some aspects of the curriculum in many of the colleges. It has also highlighted the need for faculty to confront the issue of whether or not instructional computing is essential to their curricula or to the mission of the university and, if so, the issue of its acceptable costs.

All of this interest in instructional microcomputing helped us see beyond — beyond computer literacy, beyond computing only for the "scientific types," beyond the boredom of noninteractive software and the tether of mainframes, and beyond the notion of "high priests" of computing. In a sense, it helped to move Cornell beyond what *was* toward what *might be,* a progression that is very valuable for a university.

Leadership and Direction

Computing technologies have become increasingly integrated into the university's curriculum, and at Cornell there are a great many resources available to those wishing to use these technologies. As noted, there are also a variety of infrastructures to support the use of computing technolo-

gion, including a University Computing Board (composed of faculty and administrators) that advises the provost, and the office of a vice-president for information technologies.

There are no formal legislative structures within the faculty for determining how, or to what extent, or with what speed, information technologies should be integrated into the curriculum. Accordingly, the integration that does exist has come about principally through the determined efforts of individual faculty members, often supported by a visionary dean.

Thus, leadership and direction for incorporating information technologies into Cornell's curriculum is presently concentrated at the level of the individual colleges. Some colleges employ "computing coordinators" who have close working relationships with CIT, and in some cases CIT has created public facilities designed to serve a particular college's needs. Although CIT provides various kinds of global support, including advice on networking strategies and other standards, any college's embrace of technology is still fundamentally a "local" decision. The autonomy of the individual deans, coupled with the diversity of collegial needs, has fostered a substantial amount of technology-based instruction. But thus far it has not led to any institutional planning process for the systematic inclusion of computing in the curriculum.

Participation

Cornell faculty at all ranks and across many disciplines use information technologies to complement their teaching and research. However, most departments with strong programs of technology-based instruction also contain one or more faculty who have become "champions" of the technologies and who serve as both catalyst and inspiration for their colleagues. Usually, these champions are full professors, and frequently their enthusiasm for instructional computing was initially stimulated by the use of computing in their research.

Not surprisingly, faculty in the physical and social sciences are much more likely to use computers in their teaching than those faculty broadly classified as representing the arts. Although the slope of the learning curve for mastering information technologies has diminished significantly in recent years, it is still rather steep for many novices, and in some cases, faculty who do not understand computers are simply unwilling to devote time and energy to learning what they feel they do not need.

In many ways, today's hardware and software are still too difficult to master quickly, still changing too rapidly, and still too complex to be attractive to all faculty. It is interesting to note that about 20 percent of Cornell's faculty participated in Project Ezra, dedicated to creating software. But presently we have no significant data on how many faculty are actually using software to complement instruction.

Issues Associated with Software Development

Intellectual Property, Incentives, and Rewards

Software developed by Cornell faculty is presently governed by copyright law and therefore is treated fundamentally the same as books, rather than as patents. Although the university has been moving toward a comprehensive policy that explicitly addresses issues of software ownership, that document is incomplete at this time.

Though unspecified, the reward system for software development appears to be minimal. Since the time needed for developing good software is invariably great, the risks of undertaking such projects are usually unattractive to assistant and associate professors. It is therefore not surprising that most of the best software developed by faculty (either "from scratch" or by modifying existing software) has been created by those at the professorial rank. Even for professors who create excellent software, the burden of doing so is enormous; the costs of maintenance and distribution are large, and in most cases, the potential for any financial gain is uncertain at best.

Costs, Quality, and Longevity

One cannot estimate the hours needed to develop a "typical" faculty software product because the quality and the sophistication of software vary widely. However, assuming that a "typical" project results in a robust multiprocedure application with strong teaching usefulness, we estimate that its creation alone (without allowing for later support and improvements) would require about 500 hours of faculty time and about 750 hours of support personnel. At $40 per hour for faculty and $25 per hour for support, this is equivalent to $30,750. Put another way, a typically good product (with minimal documentation and usually a long way from commercial grade) probably costs between $25,000 and $50,000 to produce.

Based on our familiarity, most — but certainly not all — of the software developed by Cornell faculty is developed to noncommercial standards. A small amount might be classified semicommercial; a very few (perhaps ten to fifteen packages at most) are commercial or close to commercial grade.

There appears to be no average "useful life" for faculty-developed software. Some packages will be useful for several years without much attention. (In other words, they will outlive hardware!) For others, the initiative to meet the costs of continued maintenance must come from the faculty author — whose time and attention are the prime movers for any revision or improvement. Our experience is that software that stops being used or refined is immediately moribund.

Targeting Software

Presently there are no specific campus plans or procedures for targeting software development to entire courses or curricula. Faculty who have developed software have naturally incorporated their packages comprehensively into their own courses, but presently there is no policy for implementing "courseware" through systematic planning and procedures. Accordingly, the relationship of a typical software project to the courses it is intended to serve is a personal one, depending almost exclusively on the faculty member involved.

Evaluation

No faculty committee is charged with examining the effectiveness of technology-based curriculum materials or with recommending how these materials should be used to strengthen teaching and learning — and the unremitting pace of technology is partially responsible. Given the present reward system, by the time faculty find or create good software, learn to use it on constantly changing hardware, and incorporate it into their courses, many are ready to resist taking additional time to rigorously evaluate its effectiveness.

This does not mean that faculty using curricular software do not evaluate its efficacy. It merely means that their assessments are much more subjective than objective and much more individual than collaborative. Unlike static textbooks, software is dynamic and often unpredictable. So while a faculty member can often spot errors in a textbook relatively easily, the pre-adoption examination of software is much more complex and its post-adoption effectiveness much less amenable to evaluation.

Distribution

There is no uniform mechanism for obtaining software developed at Cornell. On campus, distribution has usually been the result of a conversation or a demonstration. People from other campuses interested in obtaining Cornell software are usually routed to CIT — and then are directed to either Ezra or MacEd channels for additional assistance.

As a result of Project Ezra and the other eighteen AEP projects, IBM currently sponsors the software collection known as Wisc-Ware, distributed by the University of Wisconsin. A number of Cornell faculty have contributed software to that collection, but some unresolved issues related to software ownership have precluded Cornell from functioning as a fully participating member in that distribution network.

Sometimes, good Cornell software is discovered through the national databases, such as ISAAC; on other occasions, faculty in the same discipline find each other from one campus to another. Since CIT is not usually involved in these transactions, we are unable to report the extent to which such software is used systematically or extensively at other campuses. The terms and costs of these arrangements are determined by each faculty member and are generally not reported to us.

There are many unsolved problems in software distribution, principally, "Whose job is it?" followed by "And who will pay the costs?" A number of faculty who have distributed software through private arrangements have been willing to make that software available — at cost — to anyone on campus desiring to use it.

Support for Technology-Based Instructional Materials

The Need for Assistance and Support

The common need of these faculty developers (as well as faculty who seek to incorporate commercial, rather than "home-grown," software into their command) is the need for assistance and support, and the range of needs is great. Examples include the need for assistance with designing software, with locating and being able to pay for good programmers, with finding enough time not only to create but also to test and refine work, with writing suitable documentation, with distributing accomplishments to others, with obtaining enough space to house hardware, with obtaining adequate technical support from a university resource center devoted to information technologies, and, sometimes, with eliciting encouragement and approbation from colleagues.

Structures for Integration and Support

The principal structures for integrating and supporting technology-based curriculum materials at Cornell were outgrowths of Project Ezra (although they also served faculty who were developing software for the Macintosh).

One integrating structure was provided by the "Ezra Coordinators," whose task became to serve as policy makers and as managers for the development of their localized academic computing. Sometimes acting alone within their colleges, and sometimes in cooperation with other coordinators, members of this group provided a campuswide infrastructure for distributing information, for selecting projects to be equipped and supported by Project Ezra, and, coincidentally, for providing support for the few faculty who were developing for the Macintosh.

Another form of support for software development was an expansion and intensification of services already provided by CCS through its unit known as Academic Computing: a specially trained group of technical consultants was created; a research and development specialist with a Ph.D. in education and experience in videodisc applications was added to the staff; and a room equipped with configurations of hardware and software common to Project Ezra served as the location for special consulting hours offered to faculty participating in the project.

The Ezra technical specialists concentrated on the "leading-edge" software and hardware provided to faculty as part of the grant, and the academic computing staff from user services, technical services, and decentralized computing services dealt with questions having a more campuswide focus. The primary goal of this matrix of specialists was to provide training and assistance for Ezra participants. But the secondary goal was to enhance the collective technical expertise of all support staff, increasing their value as consultants and subsequently strengthening the organization that would remain at the conclusion of Project Ezra.

A brown-bag seminar series, Lunchtime Bytes, was initiated in 1985, and for four years, this forum provided a weekly opportunity for Cornell faculty to share their work in instructional computing. Faculty discovered that they often knew more about what faculty in their disciplines at other colleges were doing than they did about what their Cornell colleagues in different disciplines were doing in Ithaca. For example, Lunchtime Bytes gave Cornell biologists working on the simulation of human vision a chance to talk with Cornell engineers working on image processing.

While Bytes provided a good forum for an exchange of ideas, computer "fairs" also proved a way to expose faculty work to a wider audience. Two fairs held on campus in 1986 and 1987 featured parallel sessions of talks and demonstrations of software by more than ninety faculty developers. Attendance both years was excellent, and enthusiasm was pervasive.

The MacEd Center, established in 1987 by a generous donation from Apple Computer, has been an exceedingly important component of our infrastructural academic support. The purpose of the center — an example of the "creative tension" between vendors mentioned earlier — has been to offer faculty who aspired to develop software running under Mac/OS (rather than under MS-DOS, as participants in Project Ezra) a chance to borrow certain items of Apple hardware and software for an extended duration and also to obtain limited but free Macintosh programming assistance from CIT. In our opinion, the special value of this project has been our ability to expose a relatively large number of people to a vendor's products without significant internal expense. In many cases, borrowers became buyers, and in all cases, borrowers were grateful for the chance to make that decision at no cost.

A final form of support and integration, one of the most important for many faculty, was the willingness of a group of anonymous donors to provide funds (for two years) that faculty could use to hire programmers. Approximately $195,000 of the donated funds was leveraged into $290,000 of programming assistance by requiring matching funds (two for one) from the colleges. Over two years, approximately sixty faculty were aided by annual grants of from $4,000 to $6,000, greatly enhancing software productivity. Since the donors also requested that programmers be selected from the student body wherever possible, these funds helped many Cornell students as well.

A portion of each year's funding was used for administrative costs encountered by CCS, including the provision of a full-time programmer/analyst available at all times as a coordinator and consultant for faculty programmers.

Aside from the leveraged funding for programming assistance, the functional equivalents of these infrastructures still remain. Although CIT continues to be dedicated to providing advice and assistance to all clients, including faculty developers, it is fair to say that with the closing of Project Ezra late in 1988, software development is once again more heavily focused within the individual schools and colleges.

The Microcomputer's Impact on Student Learning

Since Project Ezra's main objective was to have faculty develop innovative software and incorporate it into their instruction or research, the students of these faculty were bound to be affected by their professors trying to be "software developers." But while Project Ezra was evolving, students were also buying thousands of Macintosh microcomputers — for which only a very few faculty were developing software — and the way in which students used those microcomputers also had a profound effect on the learning process. As a result of this harmonious but parallel set of circumstances, we have witnessed some very important changes in how students use computing as part of the curriculum.

For example, many undergraduates now regard as "essential" computing tools such as word processors; spreadsheets; electronic mail and bulletin boards; statistical packages with graphics; systems for acquiring, managing, analyzing, and displaying data; and tools for bibliographic searching. The impact on graduate students and other more advanced scholars has been even greater, for they have been exposed to new microcomputing techniques: more sophisticated models of data acquisition; technical text processing with exotic notations and symbols; tools for desktop publishing; software for design, modeling, and simulation; and the potential of emerging technologies such as object-oriented programming, uses of sound, imaging, hypermedia, etc.

The combination of hardware and software that emerged during this recent period also enhanced the learning process in a variety of ways, including the following:

- Enabling students to master more difficult concepts earlier, sometimes due to

    – the intuition that comes with much thoughtful repetition of examples;

    – the enhanced ease of performing routine tasks, such as repeated computations or bibliographic searching;

    – the use of simulations and multiple inputs of data to visualize various results of changing data; or

    – the use of color as an aid to pattern recognition in disciplines such as mathematics, engineering, architecture, and design.

- Providing sufficient desktop computation power for students to calculate real answers to real problems.

- Permitting students to learn how to operate a laboratory instrument on a simulated image of that instrument, with access to all its functions.

- Capturing the potential of large databases as aids to the mastery of subjects such as foreign languages.

- Facilitating the ability of students to focus on organizing ideas and concepts rather than on completing assignments.

As a side effect, many students have also been able to develop a more mature understanding of computing technologies in general. Among their expanded insights are some knowledge of the principles and methodologies of computing, including systems analysis; the ability to recognize potential computing applications from broad exposure to many others; a familiarity with computer simulation in many contexts; and some feeling for the social consequences of the computing revolution.

Two Important Lessons Learned

On Software Development

In the last five years, hundreds of Cornell faculty have worked on developing software to run on either IBM or Apple microcomputers. A number of faculty have been developing for the Macintosh. However, since the principal objective of Project Ezra was to have faculty create "innovative instructional software in support of teaching and research," most of the software produced by faculty has been for the IBM family of microcomputers.

Cornell was fortunate in having Project Ezra provide the impetus and opportunity for an early understanding of what is required for faculty to develop curricular software. When the grant was first formulated, there was a unanimous and pervasive optimism — on the part of both IBM and Cornell — about the likelihood that faculty would be both willing and able to develop the kinds of software needed for curricular improvement. What was not understood, however, was just how difficult that would prove to be.

Some extraordinarily fine software was developed by faculty members (almost exclusively tenured) able to find the *time, energy, resources,* and *technologies* needed for producing excellent packages. But many other development efforts were not nearly as fruitful because of lack of adequate amounts of one or more of these four elements crucial for success.

Interest in the use of information technologies continues to grow, and many faculty are still searching for ways to incorporate those technologies into their laboratories and classrooms. But what we have learned in the last five years about the realities of software development — the lessons listed below — will have a lasting and positive impact on all of the faculty who participated in such efforts.

- Developing high-quality software is very difficult and exceedingly time-consuming.

- Most faculty cannot afford the time to develop original software, and the tenure system offers no or few rewards for doing so.

- Developers often have unrealistic goals and may be easily frustrated when confronted by the constraints of time, resources, or technology.

- Sufficient tools for developing reliable software quickly and painlessly were not — and still are not — available.

  – Although existing microcomputing "tools" appear

deceptively easy to use, the learning curve is still
reasonably steep for the novice.

- Faculty in the physical and social sciences are more likely to
be successful in incorporating computing into their curricula.

- Incorporating original software into the curriculum is much
more likely if it has origins in the research interests of the
developer.

- Using standard commercial packages to create curricular
applications often produces good results with minimal
problems.

- Software with a common user interface is much more
attractive for curricular use than software characterized by
multiple user interfaces.

- With appropriate planning and suitable design, good software
will be

  - simple and comfortable;

  - complementary and powerful;

  - interactive and robust;

  - visual and adaptable; and

  - used with an interface that is standard, consistent, and
  intuitive.

- Much software developed by faculty is

  - inadequately tested and debugged;

  - often highly idiosyncratic;

  - rarely sufficiently robust;

  - usually inadequately documented;

  - apparently always incomplete, even to its developer;

  - often short-lived, unless updates and improvements are
  provided.

On the Costs of Technology

We have also learned, as we might have guessed, that most efforts to incorporate computing into the curriculum do not suffer from a lack of imagination or creativity, but rather from a lack of adequate resources. Having the opportunity to investigate computing in the curriculum under the umbrella of Project Ezra strengthened the willingness of both the faculty and the administration to accept some simple truths about resources.

- The use of computer modules leads to increased instructional costs.

- The cost of hardware is trivial compared with the cost of suitable support.

- To support information technologies adequately, we will need understandable models for distributing and sharing resources and costs.

  – Central organizations providing services and support for information technologies cannot continue to be the sole providers of needed resources.

  – Neither does it seem likely that central organizations will be able to continue to provide expanded resources and support without at least some fees for service.

- The definition of *adequate resources* is always altered by the pace of technology and by the "appetite" of users for more and better hardware.

- There is no abatement of interest in using information technologies in education.

  – Desire for increased function increases costs.

  – Vendors develop technology with an eye to selling more hardware, and the ensuing obsolescence presents a continuous challenge.

  – Complexity is nearly always more expensive than simplicity.

Conclusion

The Recent Past

Over approximately the last five years, the serendipitous convergence of especially great interest in the microcomputing hardware of two major vendors — IBM Corporation and Apple Computer — has provided a splendid opportunity to engage a new set of "tools for learning," in many cases, offering enfranchisement to students, faculty, and administrators who never before had thought about using microcomputers. The experience taught us about complexity and the need for standards and about how different software is from textbooks. It provided a common denominator of interest among many faculty and rapidly changed the campus approach to processing words and ideas, though that would have happened anyway. It taught us much about planning and about the frustrations of trying to accomplish more in a given time with limited resources than could possibly be accomplished even with adequate resources.

Whereas IBM Corporation created Project Ezra specifically to permit faculty to develop curricular software, Apple Computer focused on creating innovative hardware and software that would immediately attract students. Cornell's participation in the convergence of these two different forces has been dramatically important — and positive. Many faculty now understand, at least in the first approximation, the assets and the liabilities of incorporating information technologies into the curriculum, and many students have benefited from the variety of ways computing has become an integral part of their learning.

The Present: Planning for Success

One of the important lessons we have learned in our attempts to provide a fertile environment for technology-based curriculum materials and tools is the need to differentiate, and to provide leadership and support in four major ways: facilitating the use and, where appropriate, the development of technologies; providing and nurturing services needed to apply those technologies; supporting the uses of such technologies and services where central support is most effective; and coordinating the definition and support of appropriate policies, plans, standards, and control mechanisms needed for the integrated use of information technologies throughout the university.

A principal characteristic of the transition from Cornell Computer Services to Cornell Information Technologies has been to create a new organizational structure designed to provide these four components of leadership and support.

The Immediate Future

Cornell is presently poised at a critical juncture in the evolution of its instructional microcomputing. Despite the numerous and relatively rapid accomplishments in the acceptance of technology-based learning materials, despite the virtual ubiquity of mainframes, minicomputers, and microcomputers of all kinds, and despite the dramatic enhancements in hardware and software that have taken place in the last five years, Cornell is still confronted by many of the problems outlined above. Where will the money come from to pay for the hardware, software, and maintenance necessary for greater integration of technology-based materials into the curriculum — especially now that everyone's appetite has been whetted? Which faculty members can best afford the time it takes to direct such ambitious undertakings? (And are they the best choices?) Which professionals will monitor the educational value of using instructional software? The answers to these questions are complex, but we remain cautiously optimistic about our ability to solve these problems.

The general interest and enthusiasm of students and faculty for economical and effective technology-based learning seems largely unabated. CIT believes it is now organized to constructively manage and promote that interest and enthusiasm, in a planned and collaborative approach with all of Cornell's schools and colleges. Furthermore, we expect to do so in the context of a future that will offer possibilities for using information technologies for teaching and learning in ways not yet imagined.

Chapter 11

Dartmouth College: The Evolution of Instructional Computing — Survival of the Fittest

George L. Wolford,
Lawrence M. Levine,
and
Thomas E. Byrne,

Dartmouth College actively and intensively attempts to integrate the computer into the educational process and has done so for two and a half decades. Some of the efforts have had a lasting effect, some have had surprising and unplanned effects, and some have fizzled. We like to think that we have some insights into fostering positive change, but our planning is still very much a stochastic process.

In this chapter, we suggest some ideas for making an impact on education in a positive way. We first review the history of instructional computing at Dartmouth, then describe the current environment and discuss current efforts in the development of instructional computing.

Before beginning, we offer a definition of *instructional computing*. Instructional computing often refers to the development, use, and evaluation of software designed for particular courses. In this chapter, we intend to take a broader view of instructional computing. Word processing, electronic mail, computer games, electronic card catalogues, etc. have often had as much of an effect as specifically designed courseware, and we believe that future development may lie on both fronts.

History of Computing at Dartmouth

Ancient History (1964 to 1984)

Dartmouth was one of the pioneers in making the computer accessible to the academic community. In 1964, John Kemeny and Thomas Kurtz, working with a group of undergraduates, developed one of the first timesharing systems. At the same time, they developed the programming language BASIC. Both timesharing and the language BASIC were important ingredients in Dartmouth's success in incorporating computing into the educational process. Timesharing allowed large numbers of students and faculty easy access to computing power with minimum turnaround time. BASIC was easier to comprehend than existing languages, allowing the average student to write simple programs with far less training.

Computer literacy was high; somewhere between 75 and 80 percent of all undergraduates wrote computer programs during their four years. Although computer use was highest in the sciences, there was significant use in the humanities and social sciences.

At its peak, the Dartmouth College TimeSharing System (DCTS) was housed on two Honeywell computers and accessed by several hundred terminals. Most of the terminals were housed in one of several clusters around campus. These clusters were vibrant places twenty-four hours a day, crowded with students working, showing off their expertise, and helping one another.

Dartmouth's philosophy on computer use might have been as important as timesharing and BASIC in promoting instructional use of computing. Dartmouth explicitly adopted a "library model" of computing. Students and faculty were able to use computing resources without charge. In fact, they were encouraged to use the system as much as they wanted. (There was some attempt to keep extremely large users in check, but this affected fewer than 1 percent of the faculty and students.)

During this time the emphasis in computing was on usability, stability, and availability rather than on raw computing power. At many other universities, often with large, research-driven graduate departments, the operating systems and compilers were perhaps less stable over time and oriented to provide more power. Most other universities charged for computing and had several layers of priority. Heavily funded researchers generally got sufficient and timely computing power, but other users fared less well. Instructional computing often fell into the latter category.

The opposite was true at Dartmouth. The operating system and language remained stable over long periods of time, and considerable effort was expended to insure compatibility when a change was made. Computing was free, and everybody had the same priority and access to resources. It was easier to engage in instructional computing here than most places, but it was somewhere between difficult and impossible to do high-powered research computing.

For eleven years during this period, John Kemeny was president of the college. That was in many ways a signal of the importance of computing at Dartmouth. There was a pioneering tradition and a general air of support for instructional computing.

Specific Courseware

Considerable courseware development took place during this period. This development was aided by timesharing, by the ease of using BASIC, and by the philosophy of free access. It was also aided by the large pool of skilled programmers among the undergraduates who were available to work with faculty in the development process. The language and the operating system were relatively stable throughout this period, so that programs that were developed for a course did not rapidly become obsolete.

Several instructional programs developed during that period were quite successful. In the social sciences, the largest application was "Project *IMPRESS*." The goal of this project was to provide students with access to social science databases and with software for analyzing relations among the variables within those databases. Project *IMPRESS* was used by students in economics, government, history, and sociology. More than ninety such databases were available to undergraduates by 1971. These ranged from data gathered in election surveys to data from opinion polls on coeducation at Dartmouth. Based on use statistics over a ten-month period, the data sets were analyzed nearly nine thousand times, predominantly by undergraduates. Another program, *RICEGROW*, introduced geography students to the perils and problems of raising rice in the

Philippines, using a simple simulation. A library of statistical programs was developed.

In the humanities, there were drill-and-practice programs for Spanish, French, Esperanto, German, Greek, and Latin, as well as a general-purpose vocabulary drill program that could be adapted to any language. A popular program, *BERTIE*, was used by students to evaluate logical proofs and was nationally distributed by CONDUIT.

In the sciences, there were dozens of sublibraries containing tools that aided in solving quantitative problems. Students could explore strange distributions, do Fourier analyses, and carry out numerical approximations. There was a set of programs that allowed introductory physics students to transfer digitized files of analog signals to the timesharing system for detailed analysis. Many science courses had numerous specific programming assignments.

Nonspecific Instructional Computing

In addition to software that was written specifically for particular courses, there were numerous ways that the timesharing system had an impact on education. There was a variety of commercial packages that were freely available to students and faculty. These packages included a number of statistical programs, including SPSS and MINITAB. The timesharing system supported early versions of word processing, line editors, calendars, and bulletin boards. There was also a wide variety of computer games, ranging from "football" to "hangman." Many students were seduced into computing via long hours of playing these games. Significantly, Dartmouth developed its own screen-editing terminal, the Dartmouth Avatar, which had a small amount of local memory to hold information that could then be edited in powerful ways with functions built in to the terminal. Avatar terminals transparently communicated with DCTS in order to refresh local memory and to update the file being edited.

Organizational Structure and Support for Instructional Computing

During these two decades, computing resources were highly centralized. The vast majority of the purchasing was done by the computing center. The center was managed by the director of computing, who reported directly to the provost. There was a Council on Computing, consisting of a number of faculty and administrators, which served an advisory function. The major decisions during that era focused primarily on upgrading and purchasing new mainframes, often costing several million dollars. Those costs were often amortized over time periods as long as a decade.

The support for instructional computing was diffuse. During the second of the two decades there was a director of academic computing who reported to the director of computing, but the role of the former office was somewhat ambiguous. Faculty did not have access to professional programmers to develop or implement plans for new courseware. Faculty members who wished to develop such software either had to write it themselves or find students to do so. The latter was fairly easy, since there was a large supply of students who were familiar with the system and BASIC. The computing center did employ a number of consultants, both students and professionals, who were available to provide assistance.

Rewards for instructional computing were diverse. The attitude toward faculty who developed instructional software varied across departments. Some departments viewed such development quite favorably and included it as positive information in tenure decisions. Most departments, however, did not accept such development in lieu of traditional disciplinary accomplishments. There were some well-discussed examples of computer visionaries who did not get tenure, not because they worked with computers per se but because they failed to publish in traditional ways.

The timesharing system and BASIC were sufficiently robust that the use of the system is still significant twenty five years after its inception and despite the personal computer revolution. There are still a variety of tasks that are easier to accomplish on the timesharing system. Nevertheless, there was a growing sense about a half a dozen years ago that Dartmouth was resting on its laurels in computing. Many other universities had implemented timesharing, and many now had more sophisticated and powerful computers and operating systems. It was time to move in new directions if the college wanted to maintain its reputation as a pioneer in instructional computing.

Recent History (1984 to 1986)

In February 1984, the decision was made to become part of the personal computer revolution. The college decided to *encourage* all entering freshman to purchase Macintoshes. Several aspects of that decision were important in shaping subsequent developments. The decision to move toward personal computers was made with relatively minimal faculty involvement, at first being declared merely a hardware decision. Some faculty soon realized that the decision would have a huge impact on education at Dartmouth and urged consideration and study by the faculty. The faculty eventually voted on the decision, but some felt that the administration allowed too little time to study the issues. Since much of the groundwork on vendors and machine models was done by the administration, some faculty felt that they had had too little input on issues such as the decision to choose a single vendor or on the choice of the vendor.

It is interesting to reflect on the amount of faculty input. There is a strong belief among the faculty at Dartmouth that they should have the primary say about all things that affect the educational process. The problem is that nearly everything, from building maintenance to athletic scheduling, affects education. On the one hand, if the faculty had been more involved in the decision, there might have been more early interest and involvement in the implementation of the decision and in the integration of the computers into the curriculum. On the other hand, it would probably have delayed the implementation for a year or more. We might not have been charter members of the Apple University Consortium and we might have lost significant support from Apple and other foundations.

At the time the decision was made, the Macintosh had not been officially released, but the Apple Lisa had been around for a couple of years. Essentially no one on campus had any real experience with the Macintosh, but representatives from Apple had demonstrated prototypes on campus on several occasions.

One of the biggest concerns was what the students would be doing with these machines. Since we were asking students to purchase these machines, it seemed important that these machines be integrated into the curriculum. There was very little software available at the time. A few basic applications were available from Apple, including *MacWrite* and *MacPaint*. There eventually were also a few isolated applications available from third-party vendors such as Microsoft. The applications from Apple were never intended as production software but merely as demonstrations of the capabilities of the Macintosh and of the kind of software that Apple envisioned.

It was decided that we would not require all freshmen to buy a Macintosh but would strongly encourage them to do so, beginning with the freshman class that arrived in the fall of 1984. The freshman package, a

128k Macintosh and a small amount of software, was priced at $1,250. (The price for the base package has remained relatively constant ever since, but the contents have changed substantially.) Upperclassmen were permitted to buy the machines at the same price. For students receiving financial aid, the package was included in the calculation of the amount of aid.

Approximately 80 percent of the freshman class purchased Macintoshes, and about half of those purchased printers. Of the upperclassmen, 20 percent purchased Macintoshes during that first fall. In subsequent years, freshman have continued to buy Macintoshes at nearly the same rate, but the purchase of printers has declined markedly.

At the same time that we decided to encourage students to buy Macintoshes, we decided to hardwire the campus. At that time people didn't talk about networks much, but we envisioned the hardwiring as a way of giving the students access to the timesharing system that was still the dominant form of computing on campus. Every dorm room and nearly every faculty office and lab was connected to the central network. The decision was a bit risky at the time, since Appletalk did not exist, and we — in conjunction with Apple — had to develop a workable system of connecting twenty-five hundred Macintoshes to the central system in the six months from the time of the decision to the arrival of the freshman class. In many ways the decision to hardwire the campus may have been as important as the decision to have students buy computers. We will discuss the network later.

To stimulate Macintosh expertise on campus, the college made available to the faculty during the spring of 1984 approximately 140 Macintoshes and 20 Lisas. About a third of the machines were provided by Apple; the rest came from the operating budget. Since there were about three hundred faculty members in arts and sciences, there were enough machines for only half of the faculty. The dean's office announced the availability of the computers and asked faculty to submit a request if they were interested in obtaining a machine and to specify how they would use the computer in their teaching. Surprisingly, there were far fewer requests than computers. Many faculty apparently wanted a Macintosh but had no definite idea how they would use the computer in their teaching. When the faculty realized that few of their peers had any idea either, the number of requests increased substantially, eventually surpassing the number of available machines. Provisions were made for all future faculty to receive a Macintosh when they were hired.

Courseware Development

In a further attempt to insure that students would have something useful to do with their machines, the college obtained a grant from the Alfred P. Sloan Foundation for the development of courseware. The faculty were invited to submit proposals for computer applications that would facilitate their courses. About ten proposals were accepted, and the "Sloan group" was formed.

The Sloan group adopted a team approach because it appeared that Macintosh applications would be far more difficult and time-consuming to develop than previous software. The faculty were responsible for the overall design of the application and for the intellectual content; professional programmers were hired to implement the design; and students were hired to write some of the code under the direction of the professional programmers.

We encountered numerous difficulties in using this approach to develop courseware. Since the Macintosh was a new machine with a new operating system, it was impossible to hire programmers or find students with relevant experience. The development of Macintosh applications proved to be much more difficult than anyone had imagined. The style of programming (which in the beginning had to be done on a Lisa and then transferred to a Macintosh, in language that looked like an atavistic throwback to assembly language), the enormous and esoteric ROM toolbox filled with procedures, and the insistence on a standardized and "modeless" interface were unlike anything that people had previously encountered. It was estimated that it would require a three-to-six-month learning period before a programmer could begin to produce reasonable application code. Even after a programmer became familiar with the Macintosh, it took much longer to produce applications than we had anticipated.

These difficulties had a number of unfortunate consequences. One was the problem of using undergraduates. We had a long tradition of involving students in the development of courseware. It was good experience for the students and good for the final product. With the Macintosh, however, by the time that the students became proficient, they either graduated or left for an off-campus program. A second problem was that we were able to handle only a few time of the requests for applications. In some cases it took more than two years from the time a proposal was accepted to the time the application was completed. Even in an academic world, this was too slow. After two years the professor might have left, stopped teaching the relevant course, or changed his or her mind about the need for the application. A third problem was that faculty often lost control of applications. They were too far removed from the product and had to rely on the professionals for advice about what could be accomplished and what couldn't be accomplished. Finally, because the applications took a long time to produce and because there was a long queue of applications waiting to be developed, maintenance and improvement of existing applications became difficult.

In spite of these difficulties, several high-quality applications were developed, and many of those continue to receive heavy use in the classroom. Most of the applications developed in the Sloan project were in the humanities and social sciences. In 1986, we received additional funding from the Keck Foundation for developing applications in the sciences. We mention a few examples, but a complete description can be obtained by sending for a courseware catalog. *Appletones* and *Mozart* were developed for a course on music and technology to allow students without musical expertise to gain an appreciation of music composition. *Atlas* was a generic tool for displaying hierarchical information, with the ability to zoom in on specific areas of a larger entity. *MindLab* was developed to allow students in psychology courses to carry out experiments, particularly those involving the presentation of pictorial stimuli. *Venn* allowed students in logic to practice with syllogisms. *WormStat* was an easy-to-use statistical package for students in introductory courses. *WormStat* was the only application from the original projects that was programmed, as well as designed, by the faculty member.

Dartmouth made the decision that any software produced by its courseware group would be distributed at minimal cost. Most of the packages were distributed by Kinkos at costs ranging from four to ten dollars. Members of the Dartmouth community may obtain any of the courseware applications from a public file server available over the network.

Rewards for Courseware Development

The costs and benefits for faculty who develop courseware were and are somewhat ambiguous. Presumably the copyright or ownership of the software belongs to the person who writes the code. Since the code was written by professional programmers hired by the college, the programs belonged to the college. For software developed by a faculty member on his or her own, the college's policy is to receive a portion, up to 50 percent, of any royalties, but the arrangement can be negotiated. Many of the faculty did receive summer salary from one of the foundation grants for their work on the development and testing of the applications.

Personally, we believe that concern over the distribution of royalties from courseware is not as important as some consider it to be. The vast majority of courseware does not generate significant income. Faculty should rarely develop courseware with the idea of making money. In our case, the summer salary was generally far in excess of any royalties that would have been generated.

The significant benefit issue is the role of courseware development in promotion. Is it safe for junior faculty to spend time developing courseware? There are certainly stories of faculty members at Dartmouth who were pioneers in the use of computing in instruction but were denied tenure by their departments. At least two such individuals have gone on to important jobs in educational computing. The problem is that the department has the initial and primary input into the tenure process, and though courseware development may benefit the reputation of the college, it may not benefit the status of a department. Departments gain status through scholarly publications, grants, and excellent courses. Courseware development can prove somewhat orthogonal to these measures, and can exhaust the time required to achieve the others.

In an ideal environment with easy authoring tools and generous support from the institution in the way of programming assistance, it would be possible to implement good ideas for courseware at a minimal cost to the faculty member. We have not yet achieved that situation. Tenured faculty are in a better position. Raises are determined by the deans, not by the departments, and the administration does appear to assign some value to good courseware development.

Timesharing Versus the Early Years of Personal Computers

Some comparisons concerning the development and use of courseware during the two decades of timesharing and the first two years of Macintoshes are instructive. Courseware was easy to develop using

BASIC on the timesharing system. There was a large pool of students who could be recruited to help. The system was stable over long periods of time, so that courseware developed one year would be available and would work several years later. It was simple to make the software available to the students, and as far as faculty and students were concerned, computing was free. Maintaining and modifying software was relatively easy, again because essentially all of the software was written in a common language on a common system. For the same reason, instruction and consulting in computing were similarly straightforward.

Software that was developed on the Dartmouth timesharing system was generally not portable to other institutions, since the operating system was unique to Dartmouth. The process of installing and maintaining commercial packages was difficult, since these packages had to be converted to our operating system. By today's standards, the courseware was fairly primitive and unexciting. Graphics were at a minimum and *user-friendly* was not yet a word.

During the first few years of Macintoshes on campus, software for the Macintosh was extremely difficult to develop; students were not involved to any large extent; and faculty were somewhat removed from the development process. Acquiring commercial software was a nightmare. Unlike the timesharing system, where you could buy a single copy and give everyone access to it, personal computers required that someone buy a copy for every student who needed the software. Instead of a central facility buying the software and hardware; students, faculty, and departments were forced to buy the equipment. Students were spending over one million dollars on hardware each fall. Within a few years there were several different models of Macintoshes on campus and hundreds of different software applications. Providing instruction and advice became difficult, since no one could be expected to have expertise with the variety of hardware and software that students and faculty had access to. The clusters, which had been vital places, began to disappear as students increasingly had computers in their dorm rooms. Using the Macintosh in the classroom was still a problem because adequate projection was difficult and expensive.

The software that was developed was quite good, and that software was now portable to any other campus or to any person who had access to a Macintosh. There was a sense of tremendous promise, but promise that hadn't yet been realized.

Current Status of Computing at Dartmouth

The current state of computing has evolved considerably from the first two years of having Macintoshes. We are now in our fifth class of students who were encouraged to buy Macintoshes, and about 80 percent of each class did so. Virtually every faculty member has a Macintosh, and some have three. Most of the staff also work on Macs. There are approximately six thousand Macintoshes on campus.

Faculty and students have accumulated considerable expertise with Macintoshes. The projection and use of Macs in classrooms has become fairly routine. Software, both internally and externally created, abounds.

The network has grown considerably in size, power, and function. Faculty and students can now access, via the network, any one of several mainframes, including DCTS (implemented on two Honeywell mainframes), one of several VAXes (some devoted to VMS and some to UNIX), an IBM 4381, and a Convex supercomputer. Use of any of the mainframes is free, but faculty and students do have to apply for accounts for everything but DCTS.

Network services also include an on-line catalogue of the library's holdings, access to various reference sources, public file servers, an events calendar, spooling of free public laser printing, and a wonderful mail system that permits file transfer as well. Professors and students communicate with one another over the mail system, professors leave lecture notes and assignments on the public file server, and public laser printing is sufficiently efficient that students have stopped buying printers.

A student sitting in his or her room can currently find which books in the library (or on order) are relevant to a paper on epicycles for orbit correction; see if the books are out; look up the biography of Kepler, a leading astronomer, on the on-line encyclopedia; watch a simulation of epicycles using a *HyperCard* stack developed by students; and, if really ambitious, carry out a sophisticated simulation of the effect of epicycles, using the Convex supercomputer.

Important Recent Developments

There are several developments that have recently taken place or are about to take place that we believe have important implications for instructional computing at Dartmouth. These include courseware development using *HyperCard*, the decentralization of computing support and resources, a project for making far more information available over the network, and a project for integrating high-powered workstations into the instructional process. We discuss each of these in turn.

HyperTeam

As described earlier, courseware development for the Macintosh was difficult and slow. It was hard to involve students, and faculty were too removed from the process. We had been looking for new authoring tools that would allow us to preserve the look and feel of Macintosh applications, without such difficulties.

In 1986, Dartmouth, with support from Apple, formed a group of faculty, students, administrators, and programmers to develop courseware, expertise, and training programs for *HyperCard*. Apple made a prerelease version of the application available, along with some financial support. That effort was and is quite successful. In the two years with *HyperCard*, we have increased courseware development by a factor of two or three times that developed in the five years of working on stand-alone applications.

That *HyperCard* courseware combines many of the best features of timesharing and of the Macintosh. Students and faculty did much of the actual programming and development, relying on professional programmers for assistance; the software can be maintained and revised by students at reasonable cost; and the courseware retains the friendly user interface and heavy reliance on graphics common to standard Macintosh applications. *HyperCard* essentially takes care of the user interface and lets faculty and students concentrate on the content and pedagogy.

Decentralization of Support

Until 1984, the vast majority of the computing resources, as well as the support for those resources, was centralized at the computing center. That made sense in an era when the computers had to be housed and maintained in a central location. With the advent of personal computers all over campus, and as the number of research computing users in the social sciences grew, we decided to provide some of the support in a distributed fashion. The college created the offices of Social Science Computing and Humanities Computing. Computer experts with doctoral degrees in appropriate disciplines were hired to direct these offices. Both offices were placed under the purview of the dean of faculty, who at the time reported directly to the president; the main computing center reports to the provost. (With the coming of a new president, the dean of faculty now reports to the provost.)

The faculty have been very positive about the divisional computing centers. When the Macintosh was introduced on campus, the faculty who were already sophisticated computer users were quick to see its potential. Other faculty with little or no background in computing suddenly had computers in their offices. They felt that the computers might be useful in their teaching but were not quite sure how, or even how to find out. They were reluctant to approach the main computing center for advice partly because they were afraid to reveal their ignorance in computing, particularly to computer professionals and undergraduates skilled in computing.

The divisional computer centers seem less forbidding. The directors are academics who have research and teaching experience, the primary job of the centers is to assist faculty with the use of computers in their teaching and research, the centers are located close to faculty offices, and the directors make a point of seeking out faculty to learn about their needs and interests. These centers have been instrumental in obtaining grant funds for initiatives in instructional computing in their respective divisions. Two examples are a FIPSE grant for developing a front end for analyzing large social science databases and various grants for developing language courseware. The divisional computing centers continue to be valuable resources on campus and have stimulated considerable growth in instructional computing.

The main computing center has reorganized its support services in a way that nicely complements the divisional centers. The central facility provides services that are common to all of the groups within the college. Those services include general consulting, hardware maintenance, network services, repair and recovery of damaged disks, virus fighting, providing expertise for the various mainframes, and providing expert programming help for the various systems and languages. The central facility also seeks funding for initiatives in computing that affect the entire campus, for example the Dartmouth College Information System, discussed next.

Dartmouth College Information System (DCIS)

We have learned that one of the most important things to provide over the network is information. The amount of information of interest to academia seems to be growing exponentially; more and more of that information is available electronically (in digital format); and computer database software has matured considerably. Much of the information is the purview of the library, while much of the electronic expertise is the purview of the computing center. The two joined forces to create DCIS. The goal of the project is to make as much information available over the network as possible and to provide a convenient and consistent interface for accessing that information. Several databases are already available: to date, 850,000 books and 19,000 serials from the library have been cataloged electronically. *Groliers Encyclopedia,* New Hampshire newspapers, a medical database, and a theater database containing twenty thousand playbills, theater programs, reviews, etc. are also available.

Plans include the addition of a major dictionary, a thesaurus, and databases representing the various academic disciplines such as *PSYCINFO*. As desirable journals are made available in electronic format they will be included. These additions are subject to availability and licensing agreements. Numerous internal databases are planned for inclusion on DCIS, including class lists, the college directory, records of majors, an events calendar, etc. Read and write services, such as textbook ordering for faculty, a used book exchange, and various bulletin boards, are also planned.

Students and faculty will have access to incredible amounts of information at their desktops. A professor in the psychology department was bemoaning the fact that it used to be a mark of considerable academic prowess to be able to retrieve relevant, occasionally obscure, citations. "Now any yo-yo with a computer terminal can do the same."

The DCIS is an example of a project that naturally draws campuswide computing organizations cooperatively together. The library is the main purveyor of scholarly information. The computing center provides general user support and a technical group responsible for the network and system programming. Divisional centers, support persons in the professional schools, decentralized computing projects, and individuals, including representatives of administrative and management data, are drawn to

DCIS as an efficient means of support for making information available over a network in ways that are attractive to users.

Project NorthStar

Although the Macintosh has proven adequate for most people, some groups on campus felt the need for more powerful workstations. The Thayer School of Engineering developed a list of workstation specifications for a vendor-independent project. All of the workstations would run a common version of UNIX and at least one common window-based file system and would be connected to central servers via Ethernet. The project received considerable support from IBM and also support from other vendors; there are currently about one hundred workstations (mostly IBM RTs and 6152s) located primarily in clusters and in faculty laboratories. Based on the success of the project in the engineering school curriculum, NorthStar is being incorporated into the Science Division and other departments such as psychology. The workstations are ideal for applications like simulations, computationally intensive color graphics, computer-aided design, and artificial intelligence, in addition to providing a sophisticated and distributed UNIX environment for students. In general, NorthStar represents one approach to developing a "high-end" instructional computing environment at Dartmouth.

Some Remaining Problems

In spite of a generally positive situation in instructional computing, significant problems remain. One of the primary problems concerns the profusion of different models of Macintoshes on campus and the constant need to upgrade existing equipment. Apple introduces new models almost annually, often eliminating older ones. Our recommended package for freshmen arriving in 1984 was a 128k Macintosh. Subsequent classes have purchased 512k machines (fat macs), 512ke machines, and Mac Pluses. This coming year, freshman are being advised to purchase at least a Mac Plus with a hard disk. We have created the reverse of the traditional hierarchy, in that younger classes have better hardware than older classes and students often have better hardware than faculty (large numbers of faculty still have 512ke Macintoshes).

The problem is not merely one of status. As more powerful machines become available, software developers take advantage of the additional power. Much of the new and exciting academic software won't run on older machines. Several statistical packages require at least one mega-byte of memory; *HyperCard* requires one megabyte of memory and, for all practical purposes, a hard disk; *Mathematica* requires at least three megabytes of memory on a Macintosh and really requires, to fully realize its typically most desirable features, a machine that provides sufficient CPU power and color (in the Macintosh world, a Mac IIcx). Faculty and upperclassmen are occasionally unable to use courseware developed at Dartmouth, due to machine limitations, and seniors graduate with machines that are nearly obsolete. The cost of upgrading the machines can be nearly as large as the original purchase price. Computing is no longer quite free at Dartmouth. The question of who bears these costs has also caused some consternation. Sources of funding for faculty include the individual (both personal and grant funds), the department (departmental and grant funds), the division, the divisional computing centers, the college, and the central computing services. There is continuing debate both on whether and on how to create an ongoing mechanism to provide faculty with computers and, if so, on how to fund that mechanism. Students are left mostly to their own devices for upgrade funding, and few do upgrade. Financial aid for upgrades is becoming more of an alternative. (Administrative departments, who at Dartmouth are also standardized on the Macintosh, make purchases at the departmental level.)

As mentioned earlier, the majority of the faculty machines were provided by the college and remain the property of the college. The faculty believe that their machines should be maintained at least at the level of the recommended freshman package, but this would require a substantial annual expenditure by the administration. We would also like to see a policy of reasonably priced upgrades so that upperclassmen and faculty who purchase their own machines could upgrade them when necessary.

Software purchase and licensing continues to be somewhat of a problem. Part of the problem is the abundance of good software. It is hard to keep track of and to evaluate, and it is expensive to buy. It is generally not possible to assume that students have access to a particular spreadsheet or statistical package, for example, and those applications are often too expensive to ask students to buy for a single course. It is, of course, difficult to keep pace with Apple's changing system software. The public file servers have made the distribution easy, when legal, but communicating the information is not as easy. We are hopeful about a number of network schemes to distribute commercial software over the network on an "as needed" basis.

Subtle Effects on Instruction

We believe that some of the important effects of computing on instruction were not planned. Nearly everyone on campus uses his or her computer for word processing. We don't see this as bad; word processing has taken over without much encouragement from us. Papers are easier and more pleasant to read. Faculty prepare their course syllabi on computers and are far more likely to have them ready on time and to revise them when it seems appropriate. In previous years, a faculty member might feel that a small change in the syllabus would benefit the course, but the change might not be made because of the considerable effort required to retype the syllabus. Faculty are more likely to prepare readable class outlines and to make them available to students. It is possible that the subtle effects of our computing environment, perhaps through more current and more organized courses, have a more positive effect on instruction than our organized initiatives for courseware development.

Important Decisions

In thinking back over the recent history, we feel that some of our decisions have been important in shaping the course of instructional computing at Dartmouth. One was the decision to focus primarily on a single personal computer, the Macintosh. This has had significant economies in arranging purchase agreements, in maintenance, and in providing training and user services. It has meant that for the most part faculty know that their courseware development should be targeted to the Macintosh. It has also meant that other personal computers have not prospered at Dartmouth, either in numbers or support.

A second important decision was to strongly encourage students to purchase Macintoshes as entering freshmen. About 80 percent of each entering class has purchased a Macintosh, so faculty who wish to use the Macintosh in a course can assume that every student either owns a Macintosh or has easy access to one.

A third important decision was to enter the personal computer revolution early in its history. If you want to be a pioneer, you have to be there at the beginning. It is also much easier to arrange attractive deals with vendors early in the process and to procure funding for ventures if you are perceived to be a pioneer.

A fourth important decision was to hardwire the entire campus and develop a powerful and vital network. That decision distinguished us from a number of campuses that entered the personal computer revolution at about the same time, and it may in the long run be one of our most important decisions. Easy access to information may become the cornerstone of the next decade of computing.

A final important decision, actually not a deliberate decision, was to support numerous initiatives in the development of instructional computing. Dartmouth has been a pioneer in instructional computing and would like to continue being one. It is extremely hard to foresee what will be effective in computing. The technology changes so rapidly that it is difficult to predict the success of any particular venture. If one wants to be a pioneer, the secret may be to encourage lots of ventures and to provide an atmosphere of support. Some of our ventures have failed. Others, the fittest, have survived and have generated considerable attention. Hopefully some of our future initiatives will continue to shape the world of instructional computing.

Chapter 12

Drake University: Instructional Computing —An Academic Perspective

Robert W. Lutz,
Michael R. Cheney,
and
Lawrence P. Staunton

Drake University is a private, independent university founded in 1881 and located on a campus in an urban setting. Approximately sixty-seven hundred students are enrolled in each of the two semesters in the six colleges and schools of the university: the Colleges of Arts and Sciences, Business and Public Administration, and Pharmacy and Health Sciences; the Schools of Education, Journalism and Mass Communication, and Law.

Drake University offers postgraduate study in the following programs: master's degrees in business administration, public administration, education, fine arts, journalism and mass communication, and in the liberal arts and sciences; the two-year Specialist in Education degree; and the Doctor of Education degree. The study of law at the Drake University Law School is postgraduate.

Drake University has been on the approved list of the North Central Association of Colleges and Secondary Schools since the association was established in 1913. The various colleges are also accredited by their professional accrediting agencies.

The Computer Intensive University Program

Computing activities at Drake University provide support for instruction, research, and administration. The computing environment is composed of both central computing facilities and distributed microcomputers. The staff of the computer center is charged with aiding all computer users regardless of the systems used to provide the computing.

Prior to the initiation of the Computer Intensive University Program, support and development of microcomputing activities were centered in the individual colleges and schools. Laboratories had been established in four of the colleges, and selected faculty members had acquired microcomputers with departmental or college funds. At the central facility, the academic computing system was badly overloaded. Campus terminals, printers, and microcomputers were connected to the main academic computer via "hardwire" lines that had been installed two decades earlier. No port switching equipment was in use.

During the summer of 1984, a major strategic planning effort was initiated on the campus. This activity pulled together faculty members, administrators, and trustees of the university to establish a planning effort to help the university chart its course for the future. A Strategic Planning Commission began work and by the end of the fall semester had developed a new mission statement for Drake. A key element of the mission statement noted, "Drake seeks to be a leader in the application of technology throughout its operation, especially in educational innovation." Based on this emphasis in the mission statement, a proposal was developed to make Drake a "Computer Intensive University." This proposal took into account the efforts in the various colleges and schools to introduce computing into the curriculum and set forth a series of initiatives in a number of areas.

The Computer Intensive University Program was composed of six elements:

1. Provision of a personal computer on the desk of every faculty member who would agree to work toward integrating computing into the curriculum.

2. Provision of personal computers to students through the establishment of additional laboratories and the development

of a purchase program that would enable students to buy
their own personal computers at deep discounts, with loan
funds available to aid the process.

3. A major upgrade of central academic computing facilities
to provide a more powerful processor and additional disk
storage.

4. Transfer of the old academic computer to administrative
computing and purchase of a commercial software package
to rapidly advance the level of service to administrative users.

5. Installation of a voice/data PBX to provide enhanced
telephone service to campus and to provide data access to
the desk of each faculty member and administrator and to
each residence hall room.

6. Implementation of office automation to improve clerical
support to the whole campus community.

The personal computer components of the proposal were examined,
modified, and extended by a seventeen-member faculty committee representing all colleges and schools and supported by the computer center
staff. The committee's report was delivered to the vice-president for
academic affairs at the end of April 1985. The president then requested
that the four vice-presidents, the planning director, one dean, and one
faculty member, along with the computer center staff, should examine the
complete six-part program and also incorporate the results of the faculty
study.

During the process, the university successfully completed a search for
a new president to replace the retiring president. The senior management
committee presented a complete report to the new president in late
October 1985. Following a period of study and negotiation, the project was
announced in stages. In February 1986, Drake announced a Computer
Enriched Curriculum Program, which encompassed the two personal
computer components of the program. The Apple Macintosh was chosen
as the personal computer to be supplied to all participating undergraduate
faculty, labs were established, and training began. In June 1986, approval
was given to upgrade the central academic and administrative computing
facilities; in November we contracted for the installation of a new

voice/data PBX and contracted for the purchase of a complete administrative software system.

The Computer Enriched Curriculum Program was based on the Apple Macintosh computer and a standard software set consisting of Microsoft *Word*, *File*, and *Excel* to provide word processing, data management, spreadsheeting, and graphics. The Kermit terminal emulator was chosen to provide mainframe access from Macintoshes. Our goal was to bundle this software set with each Macintosh to provide a standard "base" environment for focused training and curriculum activities.

Support for Curriculum Development

On initiation of the Computer Intensive University Program, a Faculty Resource Center was established as an extension of the academic computing division within the computer center. The mission of this unit is two-fold.

First, the Faculty Resource Center is responsible for training faculty and staff in the use of the Macintosh computer. The training programs were initially aimed at acquainting faculty with the computers they had received as a result of filing a simple application form and promising to work toward integrating computing into the curriculum. Courses were offered in unpacking and initial setup, booting the system, and the desktop paradigm. Since the predominant use of microcomputers on all campuses is word processing, numerous courses on using Microsoft *Word* were offered. Next, courses were offered in *File* and *Excel*, and additional word-processing courses were added to introduce users to advanced features of *Word*. Current offerings include four distinct courses on word processing, two on spreadsheet usage, one on data management, and two on various aspects of *HyperCard*.

Second, the Faculty Resource Center is to serve as a source of advice and examples for faculty who are interested in curriculum development activities. A software library was established and continues to grow. This library contains selected offerings of the Academic Courseware Exchange, a variety of public domain and shareware software, and a constantly growing number of *HyperCard* stacks. Commercial software publishers are solicited for donations of either real or demonstration versions of their products for faculty review. Many have responded favorably The Faculty Resource Center is open daily for faculty to examine and experiment with these software offerings.

To further encourage faculty to integrate computing into the curriculum, the university established a series of faculty development grants. The initial grants began in the summer of 1986. Only modest funds were available ($50,000), and thirty-seven faculty members received grants as salary supplements to develop projects for use in classes the next fall. The grants covered every college and school. The program was enthusiastically received in many areas. Within the School of Journalism and Mass Communication, for example, *every* faculty member applied for and received a grant. This program has continued each year with increased funding. After the initial offering, the grants were used primarily to purchase hardware or software that would contribute to a development activity. Most projects throughout the three years of support have involved using the tools provided by the standard software set (with the addition of *HyperCard*) to develop activities to be done by students.

Examples of Activities Involving Curricular Change

School of Journalism and Mass Communication

Computers have transformed the world of journalism and mass communication. From the revolution in newspapers and magazines brought about by desktop publishing to the sophisticated media planning models of advertising agencies to the automation of radio and television stations, computers have become the focal technology for all phases of journalism and mass communication. Educational programs in journalism and mass communication across the country have sought to take advantage of the computerization in the field by utilizing various microcomputer systems and software packages.

At Drake, the School of Journalism and Mass Communication made its first steps in computerization by installing a laboratory of Zenith microcomputers and by acquiring an easily taught word processor. As the faculty and students worked with the available software and hardware, the opportunities to enrich the curriculum with additional software and hardware became increasingly apparent.

With the introduction of the Macintosh to the Drake campus, the School found that the Macintosh offered the right kind of technology and the right kind of software for the faculty to build on its prior experiences and to begin to explore those opportunities that they felt not only would enhance the instruction of journalism and mass communication, but also would bring the computer more fully into the curriculum.

To consider these opportunities, the faculty in the school held a series of seminars and meetings. The outcome of these deliberations was the decision to pursue a two-pronged approach to using computers in the school. First, computers in the classroom would be used as a tool in the field of journalism and mass communication to produce news stories, magazine stories, advertising layouts, television storyboards, etc. Second, the faculty would develop courseware to enhance the classroom experience. To pursue both of these objectives, the faculty in the school applied for and received funding to develop a range of activities.

In the use of the computer as a tool, the faculty built on the earlier word-processing experience and developed special classes for both students and other faculty in desktop publishing. During the summer and into the fall, the school's magazine, *DM Magazine,* as well as two student publications, *Drake Magazine* and the *Times-Delphic,* converted to using the Macintosh for desktop publishing. As the technology of laser printing and the various desktop publishing software packages improved, the use of the Macintosh for publication-related work increased.

Advertising and public relations students also began using the computer for various activities. Particularly useful were the various paint and draw programs that could be used to develop advertising and special publications layouts. As evidence of the way the Macintosh improved the cost and presentation of professional materials, one of the first uses of the Macintosh was by a group for an advertising campaigns class, which made a presentation to a community client. The group not only won the account but also underspent the competition by about 45 percent in its presentational materials.

The school's second goal — developing software materials for the classroom — also proceeded rapidly. Faculty developed CAI modules for a range of activities: headline writing, public relations goals and objectives, television lighting, magazine layout and design, broadcast news writing, and advertising layout. In these pre-*HyperCard* days, the software development packages were a bit clumsy but nevertheless were able to provide a way of presenting much needed information to the student in a creative way. The use of computers in the practice and instruction of journalism and mass communication in now commonplace in the School of Journalism and Mass Communication.

The use of computers as a tool has worked remarkably well. In giving more control over the final product to the students and less to an outside production shop, the school has seen its various student publications win numerous awards for both writing and design. The school's magazine, *DM Magazine,* recently won first-, second-, and third-place awards in a number of categories in a prestigious national competition, while the student newspaper was recently honored as the best non-daily student newspaper in the Midwest.

The courseware development efforts have also worked well. Students are able to use, view, and review the basic information and materials for a range of classes. Several current projects, including a series on advertising campaign planning and strategy and a multidisk set on media history, were demonstrated at the national conference for journalism educators. Drake University's School of Journalism and Mass Communication has been and continues to be a major player in using computers to better educate the future journalism and mass communication practitioners of tomorrow.

The Department of Physics and Astronomy

Computers were of course invented by physicists, and they have been among the earliest and most prolific users. Yet, the use of the computer has only recently become accessible to those without NSF grants. Accordingly, computation as a regular tool of the profession has emerged only recently. Drake University has been committed to quality undergraduate instruction from its founding, and the Department of Physics and Astronomy has undertaken to incorporate computational techniques into its undergraduate curriculum for many years past. Of course, with access limited to the campus mainframe, assignments in computational techniques were limited to advanced junior and senior students using batch-mode FORTRAN submissions.

The advent of the Computer Enriched Curriculum Program for the university as a whole afforded the Department of Physics and Astronomy an unprecedented opportunity to revolutionize its undergraduate curriculum. During the initial phase of the project, one member of the department applied for and received a faculty development award to spend a summer becoming completely familiar with the Macintosh's capabilities and its many nuances. One of the outcomes of that effort was the development of a number of CAI modules for use in the introductory curriculum. These eventually included purely demonstration simulations for the introductory astronomy service course, graphical interactive student drill modules for the introductory physics sequence, and several sophisticated student-driven investigation packages for higher-level courses. These have been reviewed in *Wheels for the Mind* and have otherwise been made available to the profession at large.

As the university initiative progressed, the promise of easily accessible computers for all undergraduates prompted certain members of the department to suggest a complete review of the undergraduate course structure for physics majors. They suggested seeking to incorporate computational techniques and investigations into the very first physics course. Several curriculum meetings followed, and the members of the department soon divided into two camps: those with great enthusiasm for the prospect, and those, largely of the older generation, who expressed considerable doubt as to the merits of such a project.

To make the story very short, and overly simplistic as well, a routine election for chair of the department became a referendum on reform of many aspects of the department's administration, and in no small measure on the modernization of the curriculum. A new administration, committed to the Computer Intensive University Program, was installed, and the new chairman was the faculty member who had been active in CAI development. Shortly thereafter, due to the resignations of faculty bound for higher positions at other institutions, the new chairman had the opportunity to hire two young faculty members who, as part of their job descriptions, were dedicated to the implementation of a computationally intensive curriculum throughout the undergraduate years.

The new chairman submitted a proposal to the project committee to fund a Macintosh computational laboratory to be housed within the department. Its subsequent funding led to a pedagogical leap. The introductory two-semesters-with-calculus physics sequence for majors was replaced with a three-semester sequence in which computational techniques represented about half of the expanded course content. (The balance was made up of topics usually omitted from the standard sequence.) The change was instituted abruptly, with the course structure and accompanying laboratory being designed in the summer preceding implementation.

The first semester began with a two-week introduction to the spreadsheet *Excel*. Thereafter, all laboratory experiments were conducted in the Macintosh laboratory, and data reduction and graphical analysis on the computers were required. About one class in five met in the same Macintosh laboratory for additional instruction in numerical investigative techniques. The outcome was that the students became familiar with the computer as a tool that allowed both analysis and investigation of analytically intractable problems.

In the second semester of the new course sequence, elements of Microsoft BASIC were introduced. Students were given working source codes devoted to the numerical and graphical analysis of some problem they were studying in the lectures. They were then required to modify the small central portion of the codes to investigate a different technique or a related physical problem. The point was never to present the students, many of whom had not yet completed a formal course in programming, with a blank screen and a problem to program. Always, the extant code was explained and the possible modifications discussed. The screen, menu, and mouse manipulations were always included as standard general subroutines that did not vary from application to application. In other words, the source codes were modular in construction; students did not need to delve into those parts that were not central to the problem at hand. Of course, a certain, frankly large, fraction of the students were familiar with programming before matriculation and did indeed delve into the Macintosh capabilities; however, even those with no prior experience managed to benefit from the assignments. Undue exasperation was *not* reported.

The second semester included a lengthy computer-based take-home portion of the final examination, which all of the continuing students completed with some degree of originality. (Only about 30 percent of those beginning the sequence finished in good standing. However, this attrition rate is not unusual historically for the introductory sequence for physics majors. Drake University admits students according to an ACT–Class Rank scenario without regard to intended major.) At the end of the first year, the instructor received a university award for curricular innovation.

The major impact of the revamped curriculum is expected to be felt in subsequent years, when truly computer-literate students percolate throughout the higher-level undergraduate courses in the physics and astronomy curricula. Already, the "give them working code and ask for modifications or investigation of related phenomena" paradigm has been implemented in many of the upper-division courses with success. The new young faculty have embraced the project with enthusiasm and, with guidance and coding assistance from faculty experienced on the Macintosh, have contributed their fresher insights into physical phenomena.

Of course, the final judgment as to the success of the effort awaits the performance evaluations of the current crop of undergraduates in the graduate schools in which they will eventually enroll. We have, however, great confidence, as well as preliminary data that justify a most sanguine attitude for the present. Indeed, even those among the older faculty who originally were opposed to the curricular reforms have recently expressed an attitude of acceptance and a willingness to cooperate to the extent of their abilities. The modular paradigm promises to allow their involvement to a greater extent in the future than perhaps might have been anticipated at the outset.

The Department of Physics and Astronomy has undergone considerable organizational and attitudinal changes over the past three years. No small portion of that metamorphosis has been due to the impact of the commitment by the university to the implementation of a computer-intensive curriculum. Our recruiting is now based on delivery of that curriculum, and has proven successful. We look forward in the next several years to the enjoyment of interacting with students whose computer sophistication will challenge us to effectively challenge them.

Thoughts and Comments

Faculty Reward Structures

No curricular change will occur in an institution unless the faculty members determine that change is needed. Even if a faculty member determines that change is desirable, a decision must still be made to actually engage in such an activity. Given the number of competing forces that pull at faculty — forces such as teaching, research, advising, committee service, and consulting — a faculty member must perceive that some benefit will accrue as a result of choosing to invest time in a major curriculum development activity.

The benefits that might accrue include (1) professional satisfaction in knowing that students have profited from the curriculum development activity, (2) recognition by peers, (3) consideration of the activity in salary, promotion, and tenure decisions, and (4) other rewards that the university might choose to offer.

Items 3 and 4 offer some promise for promoters of computing in the curriculum. Certainly, an administrative decision can be made to offer "other rewards" for faculty who are involved in curriculum development activities. At Drake, faculty who need computer equipment or software to engage in a development project get to keep the equipment and software on completion of the project. The university hopes that this mechanism provides tools for future development projects and will spur the faculty member to recognize the value of engaging in such activities. Many Drake faculty members have received equipment that builds on prior development grant hardware and software for new projects.

It is much more difficult to modify salary, promotion, and tenure procedures by administrative measures, since these procedures are the purview of the faculty itself. Nevertheless, with faculty "champions" arguing for the consideration of curriculum development, along with teaching, research, and service, it is possible to make modest changes in the procedures.

It is clear that if faculty perceive that engaging in curriculum development is a detriment to career advancement, no curriculum development will take place.

Specifics of Instructional Development Grant Performance

At Drake, funds are set aside each year for curriculum development projects. Faculty proposals are solicited three times a year. The typical proposal requests hardware and/or software to develop courseware to be used in a specific class. The faculty member outlines the courseware to be developed and the tools necessary to accomplish the task and describes how the students will benefit from the activity. A Peer Review Committee, composed of faculty, a dean, computer center personnel, and a senior administrator, judges the proposal and awards the grants. Academic computing staff provide support for the investigator and administer the funds. Project results are archived in the Faculty Resource Center and are available to all faculty as examples of successful projects. Results tracking is handled by the deans of the various colleges and schools via faculty activity reports that are used in annual salary reviews.

The explicit and implicit rewards offered via this mechanism have been very successful, in that many more requests for funds are received than there are available monies. It remains to be seen how promotion and tenure decisions will be affected as a result of these activities. Preliminary results suggest that there is great reluctance to attribute scholarly merit to software development activities that cannot be peer reviewed via normal publication mechanisms. That is to say, if the software or courseware development activity can be published in a reviewed journal, then the activity is viewed as scholarly. If the software development activity is not formally published, the activity is viewed as "counting" toward the teaching component rather than the research and scholarly activity component in review processes.

The Generation Gap

Of major concern at Drake has been the question of a "generation gap." Would we find that senior faculty display no interest in using technology to improve both teaching and research? Although no formal analysis has been done, there is no apparent lack of interest on the part of senior faculty. The choice of a "user-friendly" computing platform seems to have overcome the barrier of fear of technology.

Department or College/School Leadership

In the two examples (journalism and physics) described above, leadership by a "champion" was a necessary and sufficient condition for success. In each case, the leadership was provided by a faculty member who subsequently assumed an administrative role. In areas where a "champion" did not emerge, the progress has been much slower. The lesson is that potential champions have to be identified, nurtured, and encouraged to assume a leadership position.

Computer Skills Threshold Problem

To engage in curriculum development activities, a faculty member must acquire enough facility in using a computer to recognize where it is appropriately used in the curriculum. Thus, an extensive program of training must be offered in a manner convenient to the faculty member. At Drake, at least three different classes are offered each week during both the academic year and in the summer on a variety of topics. Courses

routinely offered include "Introduction to Macintosh," Introduction to
Word, "Intermediate Word — Course A," "Intermediate *Word* — Course
B," "Personalized Form Letters/Creating Tables," "Introduction to *Excel*,"
"Intermediate *Excel*," "Introduction to *HyperCard*," "Intermediate *HyperC-
ard*," and classes on using VAXMail and BITNET. These classes have
been of critical importance in overcoming the threshold problem.

Assessments of Learning Outcomes

At some point, the evaluation of curriculum development activities
must move beyond the anecdotal evidence and begin to include other
measures. We are considering monitoring Graduate Record Exam results, job placement, and salary statistics and surveying graduates. No
studies have been conducted to date.

For the Future

At Drake University, as at many other institutions, there is a rapidly
growing demand for additional functionality in linking one computer to
another to share files, texts, pictures, and electronic mail. Though these
capabilities exist at present in crude form, faculty and students used to the
desktop paradigm wish to move information over a network using this
paradigm. This task is enormously complicated for an urban university
such as Drake, where three-fourths of the students do not live on campus.
Many students commute large distances to attend classes. Efforts in the
future will be directed toward addressing this issue in a manner that will
provide full functionality for the off-campus student.

As is well known, the development of quality courseware requires a
very large amount of effort. To aid in the process, the university needs to
enhance the support provided to faculty. The primary vehicle will likely be
an addition of skilled Macintosh programmers to take on custom programming under faculty direction. We are presently seeking funding to
provide this level of support.

Finally, the rapid advance of computing technology, both hardware and
software, will necessitate upgrading the level of technology on campus. It
certainly appears that technology will advance more rapidly than the
university's ability to fund upgrades. A mechanism must be found to
provide for a smooth transition from one level of technology to the next on

an economically sound basis. For this problem, we offer no advice. We can offer only the consolation that we all have this same problem.

Chapter 13

Iona College: Instructional Computing from the Institutional Perspective

Antony S. Halaris
and
Lynda W. Sloan

Introduction

Iona College is a medium-sized, comprehensive liberal arts college that endeavors to develop informed, critical, and responsible individuals, equipped to participate actively in culture and society. The college has grown into a complex institution of two major campuses and two branch locations. It serves a diverse student body enrolled in associate through postgraduate degree programs, continuing education, and professional development seminars. Its curricula encompass more than thirty degree programs in the arts, sciences, and business. It has also enriched the traditional liberal arts curriculum with components in problem solving, science and technology, and information technologies.

The use of information technologies throughout the academic community has been a long-standing strategic goal. From 1981 to 1985, the college actively promoted the use of computing by faculty, students, administrators, and staff. In 1985, with the formulation of Iona's "Chosen Future," the college reaffirmed its desire to "permeate information processing technology into every area of the curriculum and in academic and administrative offices."

Iona College installed its first computing system in 1966. Since then, computing resources have grown from one mainframe to a network of mainframes, midrange systems, advanced workstations, and several hundred microcomputers. Computing and information technologies were once synonymous. Now, information technologies encompass computing, electronic information services, and data communications.

Developments in information technologies have been the catalyst that has changed the campus and significantly affected instruction and learning. Over the last ten years, the campus has made computing and information technologies an integral part of the educational process. To do this, Iona had to make a case for a computing-literate college, prepare the campus for change, encourage faculty to adopt computing as an instructional tool, and provide for the effective delivery of computing resources. Iona is now a computing-intensive campus. The college is currently developing its next generation of information systems to create the "information technology–immersed" liberal arts college.

The Information Technologies Evolution on Campus (1979–86)

The Science, Technology, and Computing Literacy Program

In 1979, Iona College began to explore a "New Liberal Arts" for today's society. Iona had long engaged students to study questions that affected their daily lives. Understanding that today's society was scientifically and technologically more sophisticated, Iona felt that it had a responsibility to prepare its students to live and work in an information-based society.

Iona wanted to create an environment in which all aspects of campus life would embrace the ethical, imaginative, and effective use of computing. In 1979, Iona made a commitment to convey the importance of computing, science, and technology to its students. The college began the Scientific and Technological Literacy (STL) Program, creating two task forces. The Computing Literacy Task Force was established to develop a computing literacy curriculum. The Science and Technology Task Force was created to develop a curriculum for scientific and technological literacy.

The Computing Literacy Program had two objectives. The first was to promote an understanding of the computer's role in today's society. The second was to provide the knowledge and skills to use computing as a problem-solving tool. Both goals were essential if the college was to develop a computing-literate academic community. The Computing Literacy Task Force defined the goals of a computing literacy program and developed a computing literacy curriculum. From 1981 to 1983, Iona worked with its students, faculty, and administrators to pilot test the program.

Integrating Computing across the Curriculum

Before computing could be integrated into coursework, the faculty had to become computer literate and understand the role that computing could play in enhancing instruction. Iona promoted faculty development through faculty enrichment grants, advancement incentives, and computing support services. Faculty enrichment grants provided release time for education and for research and financial support for professional development and the acquisition of personally owned systems. Faculty participated in seminars, graduate education, and the Iona Information Technology Fellows Program. The college subsidized the costs of graduate education and professional development. It provided hardware and software and subsidized the costs for faculty who wished to purchase their own systems.

In 1983, Iona College revised its core curriculum to include components in computing literacy and science and technology literacy with an emphasis on problem-solving skills. The new core curriculum required undergraduates to complete a three-credit course in computing literacy during the first semester of their freshman year. This course formed the core of the computing literacy curriculum. It included fundamental computing concepts and computer-based problem-solving tools. It helped students develop the skills to use computing directly for problem solving. Business students were required to complete an additional three-credit course, "Computing Applications for the Business Setting." Arts, humanities, and science students could complete comparable courses for their areas of study.

During 1983–85, the majority of the faculty became knowledgeable computer users. They began to integrate computing into their individual disciplines. Some faculty acquired software developed at other institutions. For others, the absence of available software provided the incentive to develop their own materials. The college provided financial support and release time to encourage faculty to develop instructional software. During that period, it also accepted software development as one of the criteria for promotion and tenure.

The Computing-Intensive Campus

By 1985, the campus had become computer literate. Computing was a basic instructional tool. General-purpose software and subject-specific software were readily available. There was widespread use of computing across the curriculum.

The new core curriculum created a computer-literate student body. Students had the knowledge and the skills to use word processing, electronic spreadsheets, graphics and presentation systems, and electronic communication tools. Since the students were proficient in computing, the faculty could focus on discipline-specific applications. Faculty could use instructional computing to help develop students' critical thinking and problem-solving skills. The following examples illustrate how curricula and instruction have changed.

Accounting

The accounting department understood the computer's role in the accounting profession and was concerned that it was not reflected in the curriculum. In 1983, it decided to make computing a fundamental component of the accounting program.

The accounting department was able to adapt one of the commercially available accounting systems as an instructional tool. However, there were no student materials to accompany the textbooks. The faculty development program awarded sabbaticals to two faculty to develop software and instructional materials for the introductory accounting courses.

Computing became an integral part of the introductory accounting, cost accounting, and taxation curricula. The benefits to students are increased productivity, experience with up-to-date accounting practices, and better preprofessional training.

Communication Arts

Professional associations for journalism observed a lag in introducing technology into journalism education. The communication arts department wanted to help create professional writers, editors, and publishers with strong journalistic skills and a command of the technology used in journalism. It has introduced information technology components into its current curricula. Following approval by the New York State Department of Education, the next step is an M.S. program in journalism with concentrations in magazine journalism and electronic publishing. The new M.S. program is planned for Fall 1989. The curriculum is designed to create "a new generation of journalists who will practice their profession without the handicaps of many of their predecessors who found technology an occupational hazard."

Computing will play a role throughout the curriculum. Advanced journalistic writing will incorporate the use of the on-line *Associated Press Stylebook*. Editing coursework will include on-line copy editing. Electronic publishing will use desktop publishing and computer graphics. Coursework also will include the use of electronic databases such as CompuServe, CD/ROM, and WORM for information gathering and investigative journalism. Students will explore the use of modern technologies such as videotext, teletext, teleconferencing, and computer conferencing.

History

As part of its curriculum, the history department introduced students to the process of historical research. To make the experience more realistic, the history department sought to create a "real life" database that could be used with computer-assisted research technologies. A joint project with St. Paul's Church, in Pelham, New York, made this goal a reality.

St. Paul's Church, a historical site under the U.S. Department of the Interior, has a collection of pre-revolutionary documents. The materials contain a wealth of historical, medical, and sociological data for this period. Because of the age and condition of the documents, the collection had not been widely available to faculty and students. The history department worked with St. Paul's Church to create a machine-readable version of the collection. Faculty and students may now conduct research using the database. Faculty use the database in teaching historical research.

The St. Paul's Church database gives students the opportunity to see historical research in action. It also provides the history department with opportunities to apply quantitative problem-solving tools in a traditional liberal arts discipline.

Marketing

As part of its goal of preprofessional training, the marketing department wanted to provide its students with experience in "real life" marketing applications. Its goal was to better prepare students to function as effective marketing professionals.

The marketing department integrated computing throughout the curriculum. Marketing simulations are used in marketing research, strategic marketing, and new product marketing courses. In the principles of marketing course, students use case analysis and marketing decision-making software. In consumer behavior, students use software to help them describe market segments both demographically and psychographically. In new product marketing, students use *Lotus 1-2-3* and other software to help them design a new product and formulate a marketing plan for the product. In international marketing, students have access to an international database that enables them to analyze the economic, political, and behavioral characteristics of international markets.

Mathematics

In mathematics, some students have difficulty understanding abstract mathematical concepts. To address this need, the mathematics department acquired and developed software for work in general mathematics, precalculus, calculus, and complex variables. In addition to courseware, some mathematics instruction was modified to include a formal computing laboratory.

The "Calculator and Computer PreCalculus Project" (Ohio State University), True BASIC, *Epic*, *Calcaide Calculus*, *Master Grapher*, and *3D Grapher* are some of the tools used in the program. Software is used as a classroom demonstration tool to supplement lecture material. Outside of the classroom, students may use the software for drill and practice, experimentation, and independent study. The different applications of instructional software have allowed students to visualize and understand abstract mathematical concepts.

Scientific And Technological Literacy (STL)

The STL Program focuses on societal themes of energy, environment, and health. In addition to developing scientific and technological literacy, the program also develops a "systems point of view" for students, to emphasize the processing of information.

The STL Program builds on the skills developed in the computing literacy program. Students use word processing, electronic spreadsheets, and database management packages as part of their coursework. Through extensive writing assignments, students develop their written communication skills. Through modeling and quantitative methods, students develop critical thinking and problem-solving skills that can be transferred to other areas and disciplines.

The techniques of the STL Program have recently been extended to computer music. A new course, STL 200 — Scientific and Technological Literacy: Computer Music — is designed to develop a foundation for science and technology literacy through the study of MIDI and computer music. The development of increasingly complicated MIDI applications requires more technological and scientific understanding. This spiral method of learning leads to discussions of algebra, trigonometry, graphical analysis, binary notation, and coding. The intrinsic interest that most students have in modern music provides the excitement and motivation for learning.

The STL Program has been extended to the outside community. Iona's participation in the Science and Technology Entry Program (STEP), currently in its third year, is funded by a grant from the New York State Education Department. The program is intended to increase minority student interest and participation in science, technology, and health care careers. Along with laboratory-based science activities, counseling, field trips, and academic enrichment, a major component of the STEP summer program is intensive instruction in the use of microcomputers. The students in the summer program learn to use the information technology tools just as do the students enrolled in the STL core courses.

An Institutional Infrastructure for a Computing-Intensive Campus

Planning for Information Technologies

As the academic community became increasingly mature in its use of computing, the college realized that the successful use of instructional computing depended on both the availability of software and the effective delivery of computing resources to faculty and students. In 1985, Iona focused on the infrastructure needed to support a computing-intensive campus.

The Information Technology Sub-Group of the Strategic Planning Task Force identified issues of organizational structure, professional development, and curriculum development that needed resolution. The task force concluded that the college's organizational structure was not consistent with its strategic goals for information technologies. It also concluded that the computing environment should be expanded. It specifically addressed issues concerning the computing facilities, the mechanisms by which computing resources were delivered, and the program for the individual acquisition of computing systems. The Committee on Computing continued the work of the task force and proposed a computing infrastructure. The current environment reflects the work of these two groups.

Organizational Structure

In 1986, Iona established the position of Vice-President for Computing and Information Services. As the "chief information officer," the vice-president reports to the executive vice-president and serves as a member of the president's cabinet. This individual is expected to address and to balance the information technology needs of the academic community. His responsibilities include the following:

- Integrate and coordinate the information technology activities of the college.

- Provide guidance, coordination, and planning for technology-based programs.

- Develop new directions for increasing the quality of existing technology-based services.

- Oversee the integration and coordination of information technology in the curriculum

- Oversee the development of educational software and support its technology.

- Encourage the imaginative use of the technology by faculty and staff.

- Develop a strategic plan for integrating the technology-related functions of the college.

- Coordinate the financial and personnel resources allocated to information technologies.

- Promote Iona College's strengths in information technologies.

The Computing Center reports to the vice-president for computing and information services. Previously structured by service group as a combined academic and administrative center, the Computing Center was reorganized by function. It now consists of the Software Development Center and the Data and Information Centers. The Software Development Center supports the development of both academic and administrative systems. The Information Center provides user services to students, faculty, and administrators. The Data Center supports the hardware, data communications, and systems operations for both academic and administrative computing. The divisions of data communications, office systems (secretarial services, duplicating, and graphics arts), and institutional research, as well as the Institute for Computer Studies, also report to the vice-president for computing and information services, who has "dotted line" relationships with academic programs in computing and information technologies.

Development of Institutional Strategies

Computing Philosophy. To make computing a fundamental problem-solving tool, Iona envisions computing as

- a utility that is readily available and transparent to use;

- an integrated set of services, spanning a variety of computing platforms and operating systems environments; and

- a resource to be provided by the institution.

A Strategy for Funding Computing. The dynamic nature of the field and the rapid rate at which new developments are introduced make this an area that requires continuous infusion of new funding to remain current. To position an institution at the cutting edge of technology implies an even higher level of funding.

Iona's funding strategy allows the college to achieve its desired level of funding and to optimize the benefits received from the funding. Formulating this strategy meant answering the following questions:

- How much funding is needed to support information technologies?

- What are the sources of the funds?

- How can these funds be maximized?

Iona's funding strategy calls for internal and external funding. Although internal funding (operating budget and capital budget) is the primary source of funds, Iona decided to supplement funding through grants, vendor relationships, research-and-development projects, and the licensing of Iona-developed software.

Iona's strategy provides for increasing its technology base by building on previous years' purchases. Purchasing power can be increased with educational allowances and volume discounts.

The academic community's preference in microcomputers was influenced by software availability. Preferences often changed according to the current state of instructional software. The existence of a microcomputer strategy was essential to take advantage of volume purchases and maximum allowable discounts.

Iona formulated a long-term workstation strategy. It used several criteria to select a workstation standard. The manufacturer of the workstation had to be well established, with a proven record in computing. It had to support a family of workstation products that could provide growth and upward mobility. In addition, the company's philosophy had to support an evolutionary product line.

Basing a workstation standard on these criteria has provided the college with many benefits. It allows Iona to support its users' growth, maximize the purchasing power of its computing budget, upgrade technology at minimal cost, and incrementally enlarge the technology base.

Computing Policies and Procedures

The computing policies support the institutional strategies. They define access to computing, supported computing environments, acquisition of personal systems, computing fees, and funding for computing.

Access to Computing. All members of the academic community may use mainframe and personal computing services. Students automatically receive a computing account. Student computing resources are determined by course registrations. Faculty and administrator accounts are created from personnel and payroll data.

Computing services and facilities are available twenty-four hours a day. These resources are accessible from any location on campus and remotely through telephone connections. Iona's philosophy also requires that computing services be easy to use, require minimal training, and reflect a "walk-up-and-use" approach.

Supported Computing Environments. The policies for supported environments recognize the dynamic nature of computing equipment, operating systems, data communications, and networking. Following an open environment philosophy, the policies support a range of computing platforms: microcomputers, advanced workstations, midsized systems, and mainframes. The policies also mandate that application tools, information systems, and information services be available for different environments. Data communications policies support currently available multiple media (twisted pair, coaxial cable, and fiber-optic cable), as well as provide the flexibility to take advantage of future technologies.

The college centrally manages and controls computing resources to provide an effective operation. This includes the acquisition, installation, and maintenance of workstations. Technical support and user services are also centrally managed but physically distributed.

Acquisition of Personal Systems. The college's policy on the personal acquisition of computers reflects the philosophy of computing as an institutional responsibility. Iona does not require its students to purchase personal computers. On the other hand, it makes it financially attractive for individuals to acquire personal computers. In 1982, the college established the PC Acquisitions Program to promote the acquisition of computing systems by faculty and administrators. In 1983, the program was extended to students. Still in place today, the program provides consulting services on purchases; provides discounted purchasing of new hardware, software, and data communications resources and system upgrades; and supports equipment maintenance.

Computing Fees. Iona's policy on computing fees follows the library model and reflects the philosophy of a computing utility. Fees are not charged for the use of the library. Similarly, there should be no charge for the use of information technologies. Computing fees have been removed from most of the courses that once carried them. Other than a few exceptions, Iona does not have a specific fee for information technologies usage.

Funding for Computing. The college uses the operating budget and capital budget to fund the acquisition of hardware, software, and data communications resources. This is the source of funds for physical facilities such as computing laboratories. Iona allocates 5 percent of its operating budget for computing. This is above the reported national average of 2 to 4 percent. Without this higher level of funding, the college's computing activities would be seriously constrained.

Nevertheless, Iona realizes that its ambitious program in information technologies cannot be achieved with only internal funding. The college actively seeks and receives external funding for new and innovative applications of information technologies as well as for curriculum development. It also raises funds from the licensing of Iona-developed software to other colleges, universities, and commercial organizations.

Information Technologies Resources

Centralized Computing. Mainframe systems for academic and administrative computing include an IBM 4381-P23, an IBM 4381-P02, and an IBM 9370-M60. VM/SP is the host operating system. MUSIC/SP, VM/CMS, and ConnectPac support academic computing. VSE/SP supports administrative computing. The processors are loosely coupled into a systems network through channel-to-channel adapters. Physical connectivity of the workstations to the processors is provided through IBM 7171s, IBM 37x5s, IBM 3x74s, and IBM Token Ring Networks.

Workstations. Iona selected the IBM PC family as its standard workstation. Most systems are IBM PCs (PC, XT, AT) and IBM PS/2s. Some Apple II and Macintosh systems support special applications. Advanced workstation support is provided by Sun 3/50 and IBM RT/PC workstations.

Iona established its first microcomputer laboratory of 25 IBM PCs in

1991. This marked the last time that Iona purchased terminals. Over the last eight years, the college has made a significant investment in workstations. Most terminals have been replaced with personal computers. Currently there are 750 personal computers on campus, most with terminal emulation hardware and software.

Physical connectivity of workstations is supported in several ways. Depending on physical location, workstations may be connected directly (coaxial or four-wire), through telephone lines, or through work groups (i.e., token ring networks and a fiber-optic backbone). Local area networks (LANs) are installed in selected computing laboratories and academic and administrative departments.

Workstation clusters exist in computing laboratories and in faculty and administrative offices. Computing laboratories are available on all campuses. There is at least one laboratory in each major building. The Computing Center manages the majority of the student facilities. Some departments have established special-purpose laboratories to support new directions in instruction and new educational programs.

Other Instructional Computing Resources. Faculty have access to computing through the use of campus systems or personal systems purchased through the PC Acquisitions Program. There is also a loan-out program, which allows faculty members to check out microcomputers, software, and data communications equipment, much like checking out a book from the library.

Faculty may also use computing laboratories for class meetings. Each faculty member may reserve a computing laboratory for class use for a maximum of 25 percent of the class contact hours. Some laboratories are equipped with large-screen projection systems. Most laboratories can support a one-to-one ratio of students to workstations for "hands-on" use. Lately, there has been a trend toward departmental acquisition of portable computers and lightweight, overhead data-projection systems (e.g., Kodak DataShow or Apollo DataShow). These facilities supplement the institutional large-screen projections systems available in selected classrooms. Laboratory assistants are available to work with faculty during class presentations and hands-on exercises.

User services include training and education, publications, consulting services, and software development. The Institute for Computer Studies offers a wide range of seminars and courses for the academic community as well as the outside community. The Information Center develops seminars to meet specific departmental needs. Consulting services are available to faculty through the Information Center and to students through the computing laboratory assistants. The Computing Center also publishes user guides, technical bulletins, and a monthly newsletter.

Delivering Instructional Computing to the Campus

Issues of Technology Management and Campus Connectivity

Iona, like most of higher education, experienced a microcomputer revolution on campus in the early 1980s. The increased interest in microcomputers led the college to explore the role of the personal computer in instruction. As the development of PC-based software accelerated, instructional computing shifted from mainframes to microcomputers. At first, some on campus thought that personal computers would eliminate the need for mainframes. Now Iona, like most universities, recognizes that different systems are needed to support a full range of computing activities.

Computing changed from a single environment to a set of independent and overlapping environments. Selected services such as office automation, graphics services, and library systems are supported on the mainframe and on the microcomputer. Users routinely have to access multiple systems. They want their personal computer to be the center of the computing universe. From a single workstation, users want easy access to all processors, peripherals, application systems, and on-campus and external information services.

The convergence of computing, communication, and information services made it possible to move data between services and platforms. The academic community demanded the creation of an "information archipelago" from previously separate "islands of technology." This "information archipelago" presented users with a more powerful problem-solving environment. It also presented users with a more complex environment, which they were responsible for managing. Users found themselves asking the following questions:

- What services and facilities are available?

- Where can I find these services and facilities?

• How can I use them?

From an information technology manager's perspective, these questions became the following:

- What computing resources (data, software, processors, and peripherals) are to be delivered to users?

- How are services mapped to computing platforms and operating systems environments?

- How does the user learn to use services from different environments?

- How is the user affected by the differences between the user interfaces and by the inconsistencies between environments?

Most of these questions were associated with the growing fragmentation of the computing environment. There was a need for a user-friendly network navigator to help create an integrated, connected environment.

Problems in Delivering Instructional Computing to the Campus

The impact of instructional computing was also affected by the problems the college faced in delivering PC-based computing. While some issues were specific to the microcomputer, others resulted from the existence of multiple environments. Responsible for implementing the College's computing philosophy and policies, the Computing Center had new concerns.

Authorization and Access. PC-based computing did not provide for the automated validation of user authorization. What procedures should be used to ensure that only members of the academic community were using the computing facilities?

As a computing utility, the facilities and services were to be available twenty-four hours a day. Since microcomputer software was manually distributed, the availability of microcomputer laboratories hours was limited by available staffing. How could microcomputer services be extended to comply with computing policy?

The access policies called for easy-to-use computing. The absence of an integrated computing environment required extensive user training and support. How could training time be reduced? How could access procedures, user interfaces, and keyboard standards be made more consistent?

Support of Microcomputer Software. The academic community had an insatiable demand for new and upgraded software and a need for increased numbers of available software licenses. How could the base of PC software be increased while remaining within a software budget? What should be the criteria for purchasing site licenses and multiple licenses? How should multiple licenses be allocated among the different computing laboratories?

Software is regularly upgraded by the developers. How could software upgrades be distributed effectively to computing laboratories and user departments?

The college had a formal policy regarding the proper and ethical use of microcomputer software. How could the problems of unauthorized copying of licensed software be avoided?

Supporting the User's Data. There was a shift in technology from the use of 5.25-inch disk media to 3.5-inch disk media. How could the college take advantage of the new technology while protecting its existing investment in equipment? How could the incompatibilities between the two media be overcome?

Most users were unfamiliar with, or did not regularly use, procedures for backing up their data. How could the users be protected against the potential loss of their data?

Most users needed to produce their reports in printed form. How many printers were required to support this demand? What type and mixture should be chosen?

Iona College's Solution

Between 1981 and 1985, Iona College sought a solution to these problems. Unable to find an existing solution, the college decided to develop a system to provide more effective delivery of information technologies. The development of the ConnectPac system began in early 1986. The system became available in September 1987.

While seeking a solution to its connectivity problems, the college was interested in preserving its investment in information technologies. It decided to take advantage of existing computing and communications facilities. This decision was influenced by the requirements for network performance, reliability, ease of use, and ability to support a wide range of microcomputer software. It also considered the dynamic nature of net-

working technology, networking costs, and constraints on Iona's resources.

ConnectPac uses mainframe computing facilities as network servers,
file servers, print servers, and environment manager. The system provides a transparent interface to all computing and information services. It
integrates local microcomputer services with the mainframe and with
external computing services and creates a single system image. Users
can access all services from a single workstation through a series of
menus. Users need not know the computing platform associated with a
service. This transparency allows the Computing Center to change the
physical environment without affecting service to its users. With
ConnectPac in place, the computing activities more accurately reflect the
college's computing philosophy and policies.

Authorization and Access. Users receive a single computing account for
all systems and services, regardless of platform or environment. The
system validates that the user is a member of the academic community.
The user profile determines which environments and services an individual might access.

All facilities and services are available twenty-four hours a day. Computing laboratories do not need to be staffed to remain open. The equipment
is physically secured, and software distribution is controlled by Connect-
Pac.

The user interface is consistent across the different computing environments. Both keyboard usage and user procedures are standardized. Computing is much easier to use. The intuitive nature of the user interface and
the extensive on-line help facilities significantly reduce training requirements.

Support of Microcomputer Software. Centralizing the majority of the
available microcomputer software licenses increases the effectiveness of
the software budget. It is no longer necessary to a allocate specific number of licenses among the different facilities. The ready availability of
ConnectPac-managed software minimizes the demand for site licenses.
Since the system monitors software usage, the college can determine
when additional licenses of specific packages are needed.

Software upgrades do not need to be distributed to each facility or
department. Only the ConnectPac server copy must be upgraded. Users
receive notification when software has been upgraded and can directly
upgrade any local software copies.

The system prevents the unauthorized copying of software. Vendors have given the college permission to use ConnectPac as the network file server for distribution. This applies to both single-user and network versions of software.

Supporting the User's Data. Users can create virtual PC disks on the mainframe. By removing the dependency on physical drives, the college can purchase new systems with new devices while continuing to use its older systems. The Computing Center routinely backs-up mainframe data, which includes ConnectPac disks, thus protecting the user against the potential loss of data.

Mainframe and microcomputer printers are integrated into a mainframe-managed network of printers. Users can select any printer on the network, regardless of location. Access to specific devices can be restricted through password protection. The ConnectPac printer network resolves many of the questions regarding the number, type, and mixture of available printers.

Funding the Development of Information Technologies

The college allocates a significant percentage of its budget to computing and information technologies. However healthy the budget, it cannot support all the demands of the academic community for new and expanded services and facilities.

The college has discovered that other colleges and universities are interested in Iona's software. Because of this, it has been able to establish vendor relationships with IBM to further develop and promote the software. The college uses this income to advance on-campus computing services and facilities.

Joint Study with IBM. In May 1988, Iona College announced the establishment of a joint study project with IBM in the area of campus computer connectivity. The eighteen-month joint study is enhancing and extending ConnectPac to support additional computing environments (workstations and operating systems). IBM is providing computing equipment and licensed software valued at approximately a half a million dollars. The results of the joint study will be made available to other colleges and universities.

Iona as a "Cooperative Software Supplier." Cooperative Software Suppliers are one part of an IBM Business Partner program that was initiated to meet the needs of IBM's customers by providing specific information

systems and specified marketing assistance. Other partnership arrangements are IBM Authorized Remarketers (IR), IBM Authorized Application Specialists (AS), IBM Authorized Industry Application Specialists
(IAS), and IBM Authorized Agents (Agents).

In May 1989, IBM named Iona College an IBM Business Partner —
Cooperative Software Supplier (CSS). As a CSS, Iona has agreed to allow
IBM to market ConnectPac to higher education institutions. This will
allow Iona software to be marketed nationally by IBM and will provide
funding for further software development and research.

Toward a "Scholar's Workstation"

Technologists in higher education have described the "scholar's workstation" as a workstation from which faculty and students can access
information technologies needed for teaching, learning, and research. At
Iona, this is becoming a reality.

Through ConnectPac, Iona is providing an environment in which faculty and students can electronically communicate and exchange materials. Faculty can create syllabi, notes, assignments, and examinations.
Students can receive these materials, complete coursework requirements, and submit materials to their instructors. Faculty can comment
and grade materials and electronically return them to students. "Electronic office hours" allow an exchange between faculty and students at
any time either is working.

Library services are also available. Bibliographic research can be done
at any time. Researchers are not limited by the library hours or by having
to come to the library. By November 1989, expanded library services will
include on-line assistance and person-to-person communication between
a researcher and an on-line reference librarian.

New technologies are extending the way library research is conducted.
Users can access off-campus bibliographic databases for reference and
research at other campuses or libraries. The reproduction of documents,
in full text form, on compact disks makes it possible to store the issues for
several journals for one year on a single compact disk. In the "electronic
library," a user can access the library catalog, locate references to be
researched, read articles at the workstation, and create electronic notes
that can be merged with other documents or materials.

From a single workstation, a user can access appropriate computing equipment, software, data, information systems, or information services. The academic community can access electronic communication for both campus and external use. Mail services include electronic mail and facsimile (FAX) services. Document services allow authors, coauthors, and reviewers to cooperatively produce publications and research. Value-added processing allows the office systems group to produce the document in its final form. Information services include access to library systems, on-campus databases, and external information services. A project is under development to make centralized CD/ROM services available to all workstations on the ConnectPac network.

The college plans to extend the services available to the user. It would like to include voice mail as part of mail services. It would like to extend information services to include full-text information services and laser disks. It would like to support video and videotext services, not on specialized equipment but on the general-purpose workstation. Experimentation with LinkWay (an IBM program product) and ConnectPac is producing exciting results in the delivery of video images and voice services through the ConnectPac network.

Summary

Ten years ago, Iona College established a goal and a direction to achieve a leadership position in information technologies. Since that time, there have been challenges to meet and obstacles to overcome. Many times the College found itself working in areas where there was no established body of experience or expertise. The college has undergone many changes and has developed a strategy for managing these changes.

Iona has learned and grown from these experiences. It has developed its resources in information technologies. It has developed its human resources — faculty, administrators, and technologists. It has learned how to use computing to improve instruction and learning. Iona is in a stronger position to move to the next plateau.

The increasing power of the workstation will make it possible to implement applications not feasible with today's technology. Forecasted communication speeds will make it possible to deliver information in different forms and media. Delivery of graphics, voice, video, and videotext will become commonplace. New, advanced and diverse forms of instructional software will provide faculty with opportunities for teaching and learning.

The next decade will be as challenging as the last one. Technologists must learn more about the new technologies — how to use them and how to make them readily available and easily used. Faculty must understand more about how individuals learn and which tools facilitate learning. Until now, most measures of the effectiveness of instructional computing have been subjective. It will be important to learn how to measure the impact of these technologies on learning.

The elements are here or just on the horizon. It will be possible to immerse all areas of the college in information technologies. As the power of computing has been brought to the user's desktop, so can the power of information technologies be brought to the classroom and the student's desktop. The next challenge for higher education is to learn how to harness the power of information technologies to produce a more exciting and effective teaching and learning environment.

Acknowledgments

The views expressed here are those of the authors. However, the authors would like to thank colleagues who contributed materials for this paper. Especially helpful were Dr. Harry Dunkak (history), Dr. Larry Goldstein (marketing), Mrs. Clover Hall (Computing Center), Professor Robert Lavelle (mathematics), Professor Edward Martin (accounting), Dr. Warren Rosenberg (biology), Dr. Victor Stanionis (physics), and Dr. George Thottam (communication arts)

Miami-Dade Community College: Pragmatism and Futurism

Kamala Anandam

Introduction

> There is a scent of flowers amid banks of palms. There is a
> sense of splendor, like no other, in the flashing color of
> academic regalia, and a fine level of dignity. Graduation…

So began a journalist's report (May 1987) about the graduation of ten thousand students across booming urban South Florida. Eighteen hundred of these graduated from Miami-Dade Community College. The commencement ceremonies, capturing the proud spirit of the college and the community, were conducted in English, Spanish, Creole, and sign language. Remarkable accomplishments rarely fail to catch the fancy of the reporters: a woman in her forties with five children returning to college and graduating at the end of four years; a mother and a daughter graduating at the same time; a seventy-year-old man graduating; and the first young man in a Cuban family to receive a college degree.

From its humble beginnings in farmyard shelters that inspired such pet names as Chicken Coop College and Pig Pen U, Miami-Dade has grown into a sprawling entity with thirty-two permanent buildings divided among four campuses (a fifth is getting under way) and numerous extension centers. The college opened its doors to 1,428 students in 1960; today it enrolls more than 69,000 credit and 48,000 noncredit students annually. Since 1960, over 115,000 degrees and certificates have been awarded to graduates. Miami-Dade's twenty-fifth anniversary was in 1985, the same year the college enrolled its 500,000th credit student and also became the first community college in the United States to have graduated 100,000 students. In explaining Miami-Dade's exploding growth during its infancy, Dr. Peter Masiko (then the college's president) said, "We were at the right time at the right place with at least some of the right answers."

In their book *Access and Excellence*, John Roueche and George Baker have designated Miami-Dade Community College the number-one community college in the nation according to nominations by national leaders in higher education.

> Excellence resides where there is commitment and support,
> whether in large or small schools, in urban or rural schools,
> or in schools with high or low socio-economic status.
> Probably no other community college in the world faces the
> student diversity that Miami-Dade does. ...Hence, if "input"
> is considered, no college has a more difficult chore in terms
> of attempting to meet the needs and to identify and correct
> the academic deficiencies of its learners than does
> Miami-Dade. Yet, this college has made an overwhelming
> difference, demonstrating that access and excellence can be
> achieved.[1]

The authors attribute the college's success to the culture that has evolved around a common core of assumptions, beliefs, and ambitions in responding to external circumstances and at the same time maintaining internal integrity. Needless to say, this culture could not have emerged without the faculty, staff, and administrators who worked together toward a common goal under a great leader, Robert McCabe. In his article "The Miami-Dade Story," Steven Zwerling concludes, "If the number one community college (and I say that now more as convert than critic) could continue to model modes of institutional self-transformation to colleague community colleges, directing their attention not to the systems (the software) but to the process (the people), Miami-Dade would continue to write history."[2] That is a legacy Miami-Dade is proud of and will be eager to continue.

What has helped Miami-Dade to be innovative is that the college is both pragmatic and futuristic. It is pragmatic in using whatever technology is available to support *all* its faculty and *all* its students. Several of the technological innovations in education at Miami-Dade have survived be-

cause of their utility and scope, and in time they have become institutionalized. The college is seldom fascinated with the razzle-dazzle aspects of
technology. Indeed, it appears to prefer a "workhorse" type of technology
to reach out to its thousands of students. That is the practical side. On the
futuristic side, the college has paid attention to the institutional infrastructure that facilitates uses of technology. For instance, it created the Division of Educational Technologies to support the faculty; it created a
Media Production Center (MPC) to produce telecourses for college use
as well as for marketing to other institutions; it established a Product
Development and Distribution (PD&D) office to market institutionally
produced educational materials; and it adopted an Incentive Revenue
Sharing Policy that will allow faculty to market the software they develop
through the PD&D office. More recently, the college has undertaken a
five-year project on "Teaching and Learning" that seeks to provide,
among other things, a purpose and context for integrating technology
with teaching practices and learning activities.

Organization and Governance

In its three decades, the college has structured and restructured itself
many times to meet the needs of its changing clientele and its employees
who have to meet the challenge. Miami-Dade is a multicampus institution
with each of its campuses created to respond to the growing needs of the
local community. The college's president, Dr. Robert H. McCabe, is supported by a district (centralized) organization that includes five vice-presidents — Administrative Services, Business Affairs, Education,
Institutional Advancement, and Program Advancement. Reporting to the
district vice-president for education is the associate dean of educational
technologies; under the vice-president for administrative services are the
dean of management information systems and the directors of the Media
Production Center and of telecommunications; and under the vice-president for business affairs is the director of auxiliary services, which includes the PD&D office.

Each of the campuses is administered by a vice-president who reports
directly to the college's president. The campuses are basically organized
with four deans supporting each vice-president — deans for Academic
Affairs, Student Services, Administrative Support Services, and Community Services. The Medical Center Campus, the smallest of the campuses,
has a dean for Allied Health Technologies and one for Nursing Education

in the place of a dean for Academic Affairs. Each campus also has a full-time or part-time person designated to support the faculty in the use of technology for teaching and learning.

Two observations on this organization deserve attention. Over the college's thirty-year history, several top-level administrators have stayed on and have developed preferences for the areas they would like to administer. Consequently, certain offices report to certain vice-presidents by preference rather than by logic. By and large, this strategy seemed to have worked well until recently, when the need for technological support for faculty came to the forefront. As of this writing, the college is considering a thorough study using external consultants to determine how best to organize itself to facilitate the integration of teaching and technology.

The second observation about the organization centers on the age-old issue of centralization versus decentralization. The autonomy of the vice-presidents to administer their respective campuses as they see fit has certainly helped each campus to meet the needs of its unique clientele. This autonomy, unfortunately, makes it rather difficult to coordinate activities from an institutional perspective and to achieve an institutional thrust for academic computing. From the perspective of this writer (who has been with the college since 1974), it seems that the fulcrum for future directions alternates between centralization and decentralization as tensions mount on one or the other side. This is because the college believes that autonomy results in greater creativity and that centralization helps to consolidate the outcomes of that creativity.

In terms of local and state governance, the college's president is responsible to the local District Board of Trustees, which in turn is responsible to the State Board of Community Colleges (within the State Board of Education) and to the State Commissioner of Education. The State Board of Community Colleges is empowered to oversee and coordinate the individually governed public community colleges. It directs the activities of the Board of Education's Division of Community Colleges and is composed of the commissioner of education, one student, and eleven lay citizens appointed by the governor, approved by four members of the State Board of Education, and confirmed by the Senate in its regular session. The lay citizens are appointed for varying terms of two to five years and the student for one year. The State Board of Community Colleges is responsible for establishing the rules and policies that will ensure the coordinated, efficient, and effective operation of the state system of community colleges.

At the local level, community college district boards of trustees are composed of five members when the jurisdiction is confined to one school board district, as it is at Miami-Dade. Trustees are appointed by the governor, approved by four members of the State Board of Education, and confirmed by the Senate in its regular session. The community college's president is the executive officer and corporate secretary of the board of trustees. Each community college district is authorized by law and by the Department of Education to be an independent legal entity created for the operation of a community college.

Fiscal Status

Miami-Dade's budget for the year 1988–89 was $134.5 million. Of this amount, $126.5 million was classified as the "General Current Fund," the fund recurring from one year to another. The remaining $8 million belongs in the category of "Restricted Current Fund," which is not guaranteed by the state from one year to another. The sources for the general fund are state appropriation ($83,246,000), student fees ($30,508,000), and other income such as interest and overhead recovery ($5,055,000), Florida Lottery ($5,604,000), and special items ($2,087,000). Historically, 55 percent of the budget is spent on instruction. Institutional support receives 20 percent, academic support receives 17 percent, and the rest is spent on other activities. The full cost of instruction for 1986–87 was $3,188 per Full-Time Equivalent (FTE) student. Even though this figure has more than doubled in the last ten years, there is no real increase after adjusting for inflation. Community colleges in general have not received their fair share of the state funding for higher education, although almost half of all undergraduate students are enrolled in community colleges. Not only that, the allocations range anywhere from 15 to 31 percent of the total appropriations for higher education. The per capita expenditure for community college students in Florida is less than that for high school or university students.

On the positive side, one of Florida's statutes mandates that 2 percent of the prior year's state appropriation be allocated by the institution to Staff and Program Development (SPD). For 1988–89, this amount was $1,562,000. The SPD funds have been highly useful in providing the appropriate training in relevant strategies and technologies to enhance teaching, facilitate learning, and support the faculty on a timely basis in adopting and adapting those strategies and technologies. Some of the money has been awarded as small competitive grants for faculty to pursue self-initiated projects to improve their teaching.

The Faculty

Full- and part-time faculty numbered 835 and 1,403 respectively in 1988–89. Even though the number of part-time faculty is almost twice the number of full-time faculty, the college adheres to its long-standing principle that no more than 20 percent of the credits offered will be taught by part-time faculty. Despite this principle, the college administration is now concerned about the number of part-time faculty who may not have cultivated an empathy for or commitment to the mission of the college and its goals.

Seventy-three percent of the faculty is white, 15 percent Hispanic, 10 percent black, and 2 percent other nationalities. Two and one-half percent of the faculty is twenty-one to thirty years of age; 21.4 percent, thirty-one to forty years; 39.2 percent, forty-one to fifty years; 24.7 percent, fifty-one to sixty years; and 12.2 percent, sixty-one years or older. Obviously, retirement is right around the corner for an appreciable number of faculty, a fact that prompted the college's president to launch the Teaching/Learning Project, which will be discussed later in this chapter. "It is far easier to influence the new faculty than to change those who have been with the college for several years" is the adage applied here, and with 30 percent of the faculty expected to retire in the next five years, the influence is likely to be substantial.

The mean compensation, including fringe benefits, for faculty at Miami-Dade was $32,669 in 1988–89. The workload for all faculty is computed by a point system, with a basic college-year contract of 198 days equating to 144 total points and a college-year contract of 226 days equating to 168 points. (Teaching a three-credit course is equated to 12 points.) The workload totals approximately thirty-five hours per week, which typically includes fifteen hours for teaching, five hours for research or preparation, five office hours for student conferences, three to five hours for student academic advisement or related duties, and the remainder for professional duties such as committee assignments, course development, in-service training, and sponsorship of an organization. Criteria for promotion in academic rank have been classified in five categories: (1) performance as a member of the faculty, (2) experience and length of service, (3) educational preparation, (4) professional standing and growth, and (5) community service. As will be discussed later in this chapter, the college is revamping these criteria.

The faculty at Miami-Dade Community College enjoys a high degree of participatory governance through the Governance Constitution of the Faculty Senates.[3] The current constitution ensures faculty a full voice in college governance with a separate faculty senate for each campus and with the Faculty Senate Consortium to deal with collegewide faculty concerns. The constitution's preamble states:

> Recognizing a common membership in a community of scholars dedicated to the enlightenment of the human spirit and the preservation of the best in American education, both faculty and administration affirm and accept a proper share of responsibility to promote the harmonious functioning of all parts of this association.

What is interesting about this commitment to a shared responsibility is that it resulted after two unsuccessful attempts by the faculty to become unionized. Both campaigns lost by only a few votes, and the narrow margins pushed the administrators toward the concept of shared responsibility. Under the constitution's jurisdiction, section one details the faculty senates responsibilities as follows:

> The Faculty Senates shall be primarily concerned with the initiation, review, monitoring, and evaluation of College-wide Policies and Procedures and campus governance dealing with: a) matters of educational policy, including curriculum, instruction, degree programs, and registration; and b) matters of faculty interest, including personnel policies, evaluation, promotion, academic freedom, salary, fringe benefits, conditions of employment, campus reorganization, budgetary processes, student affairs, faculty appeals and grievances.

The Students

The ethnic composition of Miami-Dade's student body has evolved similarly to that of the Dade County population that the college serves.

Between 1976 (the first year for which these annual data are available) and 1988, Hispanic students became the majority (from 26 percent to 51 percent), while white non-Hispanics decreased by more than one-third (from 50 percent to 30 percent) and black non-Hispanics decreased a little (from 19 percent to 16 percent). Miami-Dade has the largest Hispanic enrollment of any college or university in the United States with an enrollment over twenty thousand; among these same schools, Miami-Dade has the fifth-largest black student enrollment. The college also enrolls more foreign students (approximately twenty-three thousand, of whom 88 percent have the status of immigrant/refugee/asylum, from all over the world) than does any other college or university in the country.

A few other trends in the college's student population, based on comparisons of 1976 and 1988 figures, are worth noting here also. The average age of students is shifting upward; 42 percent are over twenty-five years of age, and of these, 41 percent are over thirty-five and 24 percent over forty. Consistently through the years, most students at Miami-Dade (48 percent) are continuing on from the previous semester, while 24 percent are new (first-time-in-college) students, 18 percent are former students returning, and 10 percent are transferring midyear from other schools. Since 1970, the proportion of students attending part-time has increased considerably, from 40 percent to 64 percent.

Miami's international connections have given the city opportunities to develop an economy based on international banking, finance, trade, and tourism. Within this context, Miami-Dade offers educational programs to train a large number of its service-oriented and other employees, provides transfer students with two-year (associate) degrees to prepare them for continued studies in a four-year institution, meets the personal interests and lifelong-learning goals of its citizens, helps underprepared students come up to the college's Standards of Academic Progress (SOAP), challenges outstanding students with its "Emphasis on Excellence" program, and supports the foreign students with bilingual studies and ESL/ENS (English as a Second Language/English for Non-Native Speakers) curricula.[4]

College Priorities in a Historical Perspective

Distance Learning

As early as 1970, the increasing number of part-time students enrolling at the college led to the introduction of telecourses to allow students to study at home. Students view television programs or listen to radio programs along with reading textbooks and study guides. This mode of delivery has permitted a large number of students, sometimes thousands, to enroll in a single course.

When faculty members do not see students on a regular basis and when students tend to complete their work at different times, course management is neither simple nor easy. The college developed a mainframe-based authoring system, *RSVP* (Response System with Variable Prescriptions), which is used by the faculty to manage courses, score students' tests, provide detailed and individualized feedback in the form of printed letters, and generate grades. Time after time, *RSVP* is the winner in student evaluations.

Student Support Services

In the late seventies, the college made an institutional commitment to provide computerized support to faculty and advisors by testing and placing students in appropriate courses, monitoring students' progress term by term and cumulatively, alerting students at midterm about their progress, consistently applying the Standards of Academic Progress (SOAP), channeling students to the appropriate courses through computerized advice, and graduating the students by computerized audit. This infrastructure for placement, registration, advisement, and SOAP not only conveyed an unequivocal message to the faculty that the administration cared, but also put in place a vehicle to consistently administer a program of equity and excellence.

Under the SOAP policy, if students do not maintain a "C" grade-point average (GPA), they are progressively warned, placed on probation, suspended for a term, and finally dismissed. From 1981 to 1986, well over seventeen thousand students were suspended or dismissed. The Standards of Academic Progress conveyed to the community that the college is sincere in fulfilling its mission of "access and excellence." This made all the difference in getting the community to rally behind the college's cause.

If students were to be held accountable under SOAP, the institution was obligated to monitor and inform them of their progress in a timely fashion. The college used *RSVP* to develop a mechanism for informing students about the status of their academic progress and attendance midway into the term. Faculty provide two pieces of information — about attendance and academic progress — and *RSVP* does some complex evaluations of each student's record (credit load, previous performance, native language, basic skills, and the like) to generate a personalized one-page letter of advice.

The first and most obvious benefit of this monitoring system is that it intervenes early enough to alert students and to tell them what they can do if they are having problems with any classes. The system also yields information that enables the college to better manage its student support services — for example, advisors who help students select appropriate courses, and campus personnel who need to plan ahead for students likely to be referred to labs and special courses for improvement. In a self-study conducted by the college in 1980, a majority of the students interviewed (91 percent) and faculty members returning questionnaires (68 percent) perceived the system as positive and recommended that it be continued.

The Advisement and Graduate Information System (AGIS), developed by Miami-Dade using Title III resources, was instituted to provide students with consistent academic advisement about graduation requirements, as well as correct and up-to-date information about transfer requirements to colleges and universities in Florida. Whenever a student drops or adds courses, the student's graduation status changes and a new report is available from the Advisement and Registration Office on any of the campuses. A subsystem of the AGIS notifies students if they register for a course that is not needed for their major or their transfer, or if they drop a course that would affect their graduation status; they are requested to visit an advisor to review their schedule and determine whether they have made the best academic decision, based on their goals.

Each component of this support system addresses all the students; frees up the faculty and staff from mundane tasks such as registering students, proctoring tests, and checking transcripts for graduation; and makes available more staff time for students. Overall, the college has succeeded in creating an institutional environment that carries the mes-

sage, "We mean business... we care." If the college had waited to get
state-of-the-art hardware and on-line communication access for students,
reaching the forty thousand students might have remained a dream even
to this day. By using *RSVP* for conveying individualized information, the
college transformed the dream into an institutional operation in a matter
of three months.

A General-Education Requirement

When Miami-Dade Community College revisited the general-education
curriculum in the late seventies, it included a health/fitness course in its
core curriculum. This particular offering has been extended to industries,
school employees, hospital patients, and noncredit students. As the
course begins, students assess their current status by taking measures
(under supervision, of course) of resting heart-rate, systolic blood pressure, diastolic blood pressure, height, weight, number of sit-ups and
push-ups, and much more. A scanner, a PC, and a printer are used to
process the student data and to produce an individualized assessment
report for each student. *Camelot*, an authoring system developed at
Miami-Dade, is the driving force behind this application. The processing
is repeated at the end of the term, with the addition of comparative
analyses of the pre- and post-class measures. Both times, faculty get a
class report for each of their sections. Although only a couple of faculty
members developed this *Camelot* application, the program is being used
by eighteen faculty members for about two thousand students, term after
term. Incidentally, each faculty member is free to customize the feedback
to suit his or her own needs.

Entry and Exit Examinations

In 1978, the Florida legislature mandated that all freshmen, whether
entering a college or a university, should be tested for basic skills and
properly placed. With administrators, faculty, and staff growing increasingly discontented over paper-and-pencil methods of testing, the college
decided to use computerized adaptive testing programs marketed by the
College Board. This form of testing is based on item-response theory
research and allows students to take a basic skills test in approximately
one-half the time required for paper-and-pencil tests. It does so by selecting each question based on the student's answer to the previous question

and determining the student's placement level within sixteen to eighteen questions. Since the test is on a microcomputer, it is available any time during the day that a student wishes to be tested. Students using this mode of testing do not have to be bunched into large-group testing sessions.

Through the League for Innovation, Miami-Dade formed a partnership with IBM Corporation and the College Board. IBM agreed to provide fifty microcomputers, and the College Board agreed to provide its computerized adaptive testing program as part of a one-year pilot on the South Campus of the college. The pilot proved so successful that it has been expanded to other campuses of the college.

At the exit level, the state of Florida created the College-Level Academic Skills Test (CLAST) in 1979 and made it a requirement by law for the award of an Associate of Arts degree in Florida and for admission to upper-division status in state universities in Florida. The test was first administered in October 1982. Students must achieve passing scores on four subtests: writing, reading, computation, and essay. Miami-Dade developed practice tests for the first three parts, as well as an evaluation form for faculty to use for the essay part, and programmed RSVP to provide individualized reports to students. In 1986, the RSVP application was converted to run under the *Camelot* system.

For each of the three main areas — writing, reading, and computation — several versions of practice tests have been developed. These are used in special CLAST workshops for students or as pre- and post-tests given at the beginning and end of a course of study. Either way, the tests evaluate a student's level of competence in the basic skills expected of a junior in college. *Camelot* or *RSVP* then produces a detailed, individualized analysis of the student's strengths and weaknesses in these skill areas. This project highlights for Miami-Dade the sizable front-end investment of time in planning and designing that needs to be made by content specialists and the concomitant investment of money in people's time that needs to be made by the college.

Teaching/Learning Project[5]

Launching the Teaching/Learning Project in 1985, the college's president, Dr. Robert H. McCabe, said, "The focus of our efforts must now be directed toward faculty development in order to strengthen teaching and learning." The project is organized so that student learning will become an institutional goal; administration, faculty, and support personnel will attempt to work as a team toward achieving this goal; all will learn to recognize that faculty members are the key players in this effort; technological strategies will be utilized to attain the institutional goal; and administrative practices and organizational arrangements will be altered to meet teaching and learning needs.

The Teaching/Learning Project is yet another example of tackling a problem at its roots. The outcomes of this project will begin to show in the 1990s. If track records have any bearing at all, Miami-Dade Community College is well on its way to showing that equity and excellence can comfortably coexist in an educational environment and that technology has a useful role to play in the process.

The results of this project so far are as follows:

1. The "Values Statement" is included in all college publications, including catalogues and staff manuals.

2. Beginning in the fall of 1988, orientation for new faculty has been different (with pre-service as well as in-service experiences, including mentors in the first year).

3. A graduate-level course in "Learning to Learn" and one in "Classroom Feedback" were offered as pilots by the University of Miami in the fall and winter terms of 1988–89, thereafter to be offered on a regular basis. New faculty will be required to take both courses during their probationary years; tenured faculty will be encouraged to take them.

4. Teaching and learning concerns will be emphasized more prominently in budget decisions and in setting priorities for completing work orders.

5. Two videotapes — one exploring classroom feedback, the other cultural differences in learning styles — will become available for faculty use.

6. At a luncheon on June 7, 1988, funding for the first twenty-four of one hundred Endowed Teaching Chairs was announced. Although no chair will be filled until committee-recommended criteria and procedures are

established, this ground-breaking concept is assured of becoming a reality.

The "Learning to Learn" course has recently been retitled as "Effective Teaching and Learning in the Community College" and includes the following topics:

1. Teacher Characteristics and Teaching Styles.

2. Discovering Relevance: MDCC Students, Demographic and Attitudinal Characteristics.

3. Learner Characteristics and Learning Styles.

4. Motivating Students.

5. Planning Courses and Lessons.

6. Applying Institutional Resources to Classroom Teaching and Learning.

The topic of institutional resources is designed to emphasize technological resources such as CAI, CMI, test banking, interactive video, audio-visual services, and computer labs.

The "Classroom Feedback" course has also been retitled — as "Analysis and Appraisal of Learning Processes" — and includes the following topics:

1. Analysis of the Learning Process: Formative Assessment.

    a. Tools for teacher-controlled classroom process analysis.

    b. Implementing the analysis of classroom processes.

    c. Interpreting data from classroom process analysis.

    d. Attaching meaning to the results of classroom process analysis.

2. Tools for the Evaluations of Teaching Effectiveness: Summative Assessment.

    a. Testing.

    b. Using test results to improve teaching and learning.

c. Technological support for evaluating students
learning.

d. Application of assessment principles to individual
disciplines.

A critical component of the Teaching/Learning Project is a new set of
proposals for faculty advancement that ties Miami-Dade's reward system
to professional performance as it relates to the criteria set forth in the
project's Faculty Excellence Document. These criteria center on the faculty member's motivation, interpersonal skills, knowledge base, and application of the knowledge base. The set of proposals is intended to establish
consistency in college policies and procedures for performance evaluation, for continuing contracts, for promotions, and for Endowed Teaching
Chairs. By-products should include greater participation by faculty in
decision making, clarification of the role of administrators in this process,
emphasis on performance in day-to-day activities, and assurance that a
variety of sources will be used in the evaluation process. The faculty
evaluation, which will examine primary professional responsibilities (e.g.,
classroom teaching, student conferences, academic advisement, departmental activities such as curriculum development and committee work)
and supporting responsibilities (e.g., professional growth and development, service to the college outside the department, community service),
will require student review, self-review (performance portfolio), and
chairperson review and will make peer review optional.

The Steering Committee for the Teaching/Learning project consists of
eighteen faculty members and seven administrators. Working under the
guidelines of this committee are eight subcommittees — Values, Teaching/Learning Environment, New Faculty, Faculty Excellence, Classroom
Feedback, Learning to Learn, Faculty Advancement, and Institutional
Support — each chaired by a faculty member. Approximately sixty faculty
members and sixteen administrators have participated in these subcommittees. Two additional committees have begun their work on Part-time
Faculty and Faculty Support.

Collegewide Technological Support

Division of Educational Technologies

The Division of Computer-Based Instructional Development and Research was created in 1977 to support faculty and staff who wanted to integrate technology into their curricula. In its twelve years of operation, the division has simultaneously shortened its name to Educational Technologies and expanded its scope to include an ever evolving matrix of human considerations and technological tools in teaching and learning. The evidence of this expansion exists throughout the college.

Instructional Support

The staff for instructional support includes systems developers, who design and implement systems to meet the college's needs for educational technology support; systems analysts, who are responsible for instructional design, the management of systems applications, hardware/software operations, the supervision of programming staff, and the evaluation of the technological products in teaching/learning situations; technical staff, who provide programming support; and an editor, who writes and/or refines the instructional materials prepared for students, instructional reports prepared for faculty and administrators, and other materials intended for public consumption.

The division has always promoted collaborative effort. The advantages of the team approach are that systems developers are involved with faculty and thus establish a broader educational perspective for the products they design; content specialists are exposed to the systematic approaches required by technological tools and thus refine their educational practices; and both groups listen to the instructional designers and thus become sensitive to the wisdom offered by cognitive psychology. Accordingly, the division has sought technological tools that are flexible, open-ended, and transportable. A significant answer has been authoring tools. The division develops them, examines ones that others have developed, and integrates both into Miami-Dade's technology-based projects. From areas as diverse as chemistry, writing, data processing, health and physical education, psychology, nursing, library services, English as a second language, human anatomy and physiology, accounting and business, history, humanities, and student support services, to name only some, faculty members have sought the division's support to help them meet their needs for individualizing feedback to students.

The Division of Educational Technologies' projects have been funded in a variety of ways. Sometimes faculty members have been granted release time or monetary compensation for a campus- or college-sponsored priority; other times they have worked on a voluntary basis on a project for a single class. On either basis, the division has confirmed the importance of both a strong sense of personal commitment to the possibilities that technology offers to education and the administrative support in the form of time or money that is necessary to maintain motivation and drive to complete a project.

With Miami-Dade's current focus on ways to improve the teaching/learning environment will come further incentives, in the form of in-house credit, salary increments, and so on, as a way of recognizing innovative projects. Additionally, the division has been instrumental in establishing a collegewide Incentive Revenue Policy to reward those who develop marketable-quality software. For large projects involving yearly salaries and major equipment, Miami-Dade has entered into partnerships with other institutions, making its own matching contributions and sometimes receiving additional funding — as a show of support for existing commitments — from agencies such as the Exxon Education Foundation, the League for Innovation in the Community College, and IBM Corporation. The division has also helped faculty to compete for and win the Wolfson Foundation grants administered by the college.

Training Support

Under the auspices of the League for Innovation, Miami-Dade Community College is one of six institutions selected by IBM in 1988 to serve as technology-transfer centers for educational software. At Miami-Dade, this center is called the Instructional Technology Center and operates under the Division of Educational Technologies. IBM equipped the center with fifteen PS/2 Model 25s networked to a PS/2 Model 80 as a file server, and it donated educational software for demonstration purposes. The college is supporting two full-time staff members (one professional and one technical assistant) to run the center. Training support offered by the ITC includes seminars on the use of the IBM PS/2 Model 25, workshops on a variety of software packages — word processing, database, spreadsheet, *Camelot*, and *Banque* — and small group sessions for reviewing software.

Initially, the workshops emphasized computer literacy; plans are under way to focus on instructional applications.

Starting with the academic year 1989–90, the college established a Teaching/Learning Resource Center, on each of the four campuses, to be staffed by two professionals, one of whom will support faculty with ideas for using technology for teaching and learning. Approximately one million dollars has been allocated for these centers for the first year of their operation. IBM has come forward to support this endeavor by providing some hardware (eight PS/2 Model 50s, four PostScript laser printers, and four *InfoWindow* stations) to be used by faculty in the Teaching/Learning Resource Centers.

Informational Support

To facilitate communication among faculty about all the technological support available at the institution, the division has established an Ed Tech bulletin board in the electronic mail system developed by the MIS division at the college. Although personnel are not yet in place to maintain this bulletin board, the division plans to include the following sections:

1. Introduction and Hints for Use

2. "Dear ET": Comments, Questions, and Answers.

3. ET News/Calendar and ITC Schedule.

4. MDCC Projects (Software Development and Research).

5. MDCC Projects (Software Implementation).

In the print mode, the division publishes a biannual newsletter, *TIES* (Technological Innovations in Educational Settings), which has an international readership. *TIES* provides a forum for faculty to describe technological applications for teaching and learning and presents information concerning emerging technologies and their relevance to teaching and learning at Miami-Dade Community College.

Media Production Center

The Media Production Center (MPC) was established in 1964 and has produced video materials for instructional as well as informational purposes. In 1988, twenty-three of the seventy-two requests for video produc-

tion were in support of instruction, forty-nine for information. The center
also provides service for art and photograph production.

In the seventies, the center was heavily involved in full-scale video
production for television courses. Generally, these telecourses consist of
twenty-four to twenty-eight half-hour television programs that can be used
for a semester of sixteen weeks. The television series produced at Miami-
Dade are marketed throughout the world by the PD&D office. Having
tried both high-cost/on-location and low-cost/in-studio productions, the
college is leaning toward the latter. An example at the high end is the "Art
of Being Human"; at the other end is "Survival Spanish."

The role of the MPC staff varies with each project. In the case of Star
Service (a telephone registration system), involvement was intense. The
script was written entirely by an MPC producer, based on interviews with
the client and on print materials provided by the client. Each draft of the
script was reviewed by the client, with changes reflected in the next draft.
The MPC feels that this approach is the most satisfactory for materials
that are largely in the affective domain.

In contrast, the MPC's involvement in scripting for interactive videotapes and videodisks, which have been largely in the cognitive domain,
has been minimal. As a result, its role has been to serve as a technical
resource, working to create visualization based on the script and adapting
video editing and dubbing to meet the needs of interactivity.

Due to the relative infancy of interactive video, the MPC has faced
unique problems such as (1) the use of more than one type of reference
code, (2) the placement of the reference code on the appropriate audio
track, and (3) the assurance that the reference code begins at the head of
the tape. Each of these has required close communication between the
assigned producer and the requester (client).

There is at times an issue regarding "ownership" of the product. Some
clients feel it is their baby; others are surprised to learn that the MPC
requires their participation in developing the materials. The MPC's view
is that the product is more valuable (has more attention-holding power,
delivers a clearer message, and is more comparable to commercially
developed products) when "ownership" is jointly held. When the academi-
cian and the media producer are working in tandem, the chance of obtaining a successful product is increased.

Campuswide Technological Support

There are four main campuses, each headed by a vice-president who in turn is supported by four deans, one each for Instruction, Administration, Student Support Services, and Community and Business Relations. A fifth campus, Homestead, is in the making and is expected to have a similar organizational structure. The names of the campuses in the order of the oldest to the newest are North, South, Mitchell Wolfson New World Center, and Medical. The start date and current annual enrollment of each of the four campuses are as follows:

North Campus	1960	20,861
South Campus	1967	29,507
MW New World Center Campus	1970	13,597
Medical Campus	1977	5,557

At the North Campus, a tri-ethnic mix of students includes 26 percent white non-Hispanic, 31 percent black non-Hispanic, and 40 percent Hispanic. Among the more than 750 chapters of the Phi Theta Kappa scholastic honorary society, the North Campus chapter has been rated number one, contributing a national president, a national vice-president, and two state presidents over the last five years. The campus has a satellite dish with downlink, and it is used for cocurricular programs in social science, science, political science, and criminal justice. In the remedial programs, interactive videotapes and videodisks are being used for math and reading respectively. The accounting department has set up three computer labs for students to work on their own and for faculty to instruct students with hands-on experience. An interesting development is the establishment of a generic graphics lab that is being used by the departments of engineering, architecture, and fashion design. More recently, the music and art departments have begun to set up their own computer labs. An advisory committee made up of all the department heads and reporting to the dean for instruction meets regularly to discuss and decide future directions for the campus. One idea that is being seriously considered is to move all the computer labs into one building to permit the sharing of equipment and lab staff among the various departments.

At the South Campus, the ethnic mix of students is 38 percent white non-Hispanic, 0 percent black non-Hispanic, and 34 percent Hispanic. The campus has consistently emphasized faculty and staff development, including computer literacy. Judging from the number of workshops offered, this campus is likely to have a higher percentage of computer-literate faculty. There are three computer labs for student use — Apple/MAC, IBM, and AT&T. These are set up as generic labs for use by several different departments. Students are charged a lab fee, in addition to tuition, to cover the cost of maintenance and support personnel. In remedial programs, interactive videodisks and CAI materials are used for math and writing. The music department is preparing to upgrade and enhance its computer use. Faculty enthusiasm for instructional software development is blossoming in various departments. Authoring expert systems such as the *I CLASS FUSION*, coupled with in-house expertise, seems to kindle this enthusiasm and keep it alive.

At the Mitchell Wolfson New World Center Campus, the ethnic mix of students is 18 percent white non-Hispanic, 12 percent black non-Hispanic, and 69 percent Hispanic. The campus is located in the heart of downtown Miami and is the only urban campus in the Greater Miami area. Students at the campus represent almost 45 different languages and 120 different countries, giving it an international flavor. This campus runs the Open College, which offers radio and telecourses to students at a distance. Approximately fourteen courses are offered each semester in this mode, with an average enrollment of one hundred each. The IBM computer lab for Business and Technology is heavily used to offer courses for students and for industries in the community. The ESL (English as a Second Language) department uses off-the-shelf "drill-and-practice" computerized modules. Of much interest to the campus is the locally developed *Reading to Learn* computer program in social science. The program consists of a series of quizzes administered by the computer to provide students with an unlimited number of trials, which are not graded. A comparative study conducted by the campus has shown that students who used this program did better on the final examination.

At the Medical Center Campus, the ethnic mix of students is of 38 percent white non-Hispanic, 26 percent black non-Hispanic, and 33 percent Hispanic. The campus is located within a large medical complex including the University of Miami School of Medicine, the county-operated Jackson Memorial Hospital, the Veterans Administration Hospital, and the Bascom-Palmer Eye Institute. The campus is a heavy user of computers for banking questions and for generating tests for various courses. A four-station computer area has been established for faculty use. The peer tutoring and discussions that take place in this area are quite impressive in quantity and quality. The campus is currently exploring the use of interactive videodisks in nursing and allied health courses.

On all four campuses, a number of "champions" have emerged whose expertise, enthusiasm, and commitment have attracted a following among their colleagues. Even though there is a danger in multiple leadership (sometimes referred to as "guruvial drifts"), the danger of not being active and of not aspiring is worse. Fortunately for Miami-Dade Community College, the Teaching/Learning Project provides an ongoing context for improving teaching and learning. Technology will be used and tested under this umbrella, since each campus established a Teaching/Learning Resource Center (TLRC) in the fall of 1989 and staffed it with two professionals, one of whom is experienced in instructional design and in the use of the computers. By establishing these campus centers at a cost of almost a million dollars, the college plans to make support available and accessible to the faculty more locally and to make the district division of Educational Technologies a resource to the TLRCs.

The Impact

As at many other institutions, microcomputer labs have sprung up on Miami-Dade campuses in the last five years, with accelerated growth in recent years. Much of this is attributable to faculty initiative and administrative support. While the college has made large-scale investments for institutional priorities, it has also facilitated and supported faculty initiatives. Consequently, technological support for students shows up in various forms and is observable in highly visible places as well as in quiet corners.

There has been no grand scheme for the use of technology in teaching and learning activities. In other words, there is no academic computing plan for the college. Instead there is an institutional environment that responds to needs and that stimulates solutions. Miami-Dade Community College is in tune with George Keller's ideas on strategic planning — participatory, tolerant of controversy, taking calculated risks, constantly modifying, and concentrating on the fate of the institution above every-thing else.

The college has enjoyed a stability of leadership for its thirty-year existence — the first president for one and one-half years, the second for twenty years, and the present president, who was also the executive vice-president under the second president. Of course, the continuity in philosophy and the commitment to the college's mission have helped the college move forward with its programs. The priorities of the college have always been made clear to the employees.

The college is aggressive in obtaining funds for its innovations. An able staff assists the college in submitting proposals for external grants. The staff of the college foundation is on the go all the time to raise money to support college activities, including the one hundred Endowed Teaching Chairs to honor excellence in teaching among the faculty. Now and then, luck comes Miami-Dade's way, and it came in a big way with an endow-ment of $3.2 million, popularly referred to as the Wolfson Grant, given by the first chairman of the Board of Trustees. The income from this and other endowments (approximately half a million) is used annually to fund competitive proposals submitted by faculty and administrators. A greater proportion is granted to the faculty. The Florida legislature's mandate to allocate 2 percent of the operating budget for faculty and staff develop-ment continues to support the training of people and the development of projects.

The college is also careful about its public image and accountability. The two offices that are primarily responsible for this aspect are Public Relations and Institutional Research. Both have been expanded in person-nel to address the needs adequately. The college's goal is to let the public know what the problems are and what Miami-Dade is doing about them.

What do all these observations mean for the integration of technology and teaching? For one thing, top-down and grass-roots innovations have coexisted and helped move the college along the direction it has charted for progress. The direction is governed by principles rather than specif-ics. The major principles include the following: 1) preserving the open-door admission; (2) providing access to information for people to do a better job; (3) keeping track of students at all times and directing them appropriately; (4) justifying the cost of innovations by the unique services they provide, so that the greater the number served and the greater the individualization, the easier it is to justify the cost; (5) focusing on underprepared and minority students as a critical goal to fulfill the college's mission; (6) attacking a problem at its roots and not merely on the surface; and (7) not getting too comfortable with how things work, since they are likely to change.

Because of the size of the college and because a number of large projects have been undertaken by the college, a collaborative working arrangement has developed among faculty, administrators, and staff. This tendency is noticeable when faculty seek the assistance of the technical staff to design, develop, or adapt educational software. Getting one's writing reviewed, critiqued, or edited has become second nature to most faculty working with the staff of the Educational Technologies division. Working together with the instructional designer and an editor improves the products of faculty members.

Most faculty members and most academic administrators agree that individualizing instruction is critical in helping students to succeed in college and, thereby, in preserving the open-door admission policy. While technology is accepted as a vehicle for individualizing instruction, it is also seen as a support vehicle rather than as the primary vehicle. The "human touch" provided by the faculty is regarded very highly by students and administrators.

When the college instituted the Standards of Academic Progress (SOAP) and put its resources into developing a computerized system for tracking students' progress, it witnessed a turning point in faculty attitude about teaching at Miami-Dade Community College. Did we predict this phenomenon? Not really. But it happened, and it made all the difference. Through a series of computerized student-support programs such as SOAP, AAA (Academic Alert and Advisement, which is the midterm alert), and AGIS (Advisement and Graduation Information System), the college established a student information system and made that database available to faculty, advisors, researchers, and administrators in order to enable them to fulfill their responsibilities more completely, more accurately, and in a more timely fashion. These systems have reduced manual labor in several areas (cost savings), have helped the college identify students who need additional or specialized help, and have strengthened educational programs accordingly. The application of technology in student support services has had a great impact on the educational program. Moreover, with this infrastructure in place, the college is in an advantageous position to explore new frontiers in educational technology.

The Teaching/Learning Project is expected to provide the infrastructure for the exploration and implementation of educational technologies. When the improvement of teaching and of student learning is built into the criteria for faculty promotion, when the college recruits new faculty based on their familiarity with information technology, when the college arranges for two graduate-level courses to be offered, one on learning and another on educational research, when the college expects to raise faculty salaries to the highest level in the state, and when the college is committed to establishing one hundred Endowed Teaching Chairs, a clear signal emerges that teaching at Miami-Dade is an honorable activity. Miami-Dade is consistently attempting to attract the best and to help them become even better. If technology does not find its place in this teaching/learning environment, where else can it find its niche? "Finding its place" here means sensible, broad-based, and long-lasting applications.

Meanwhile, a number of activities on Miami-Dade's campuses are preparing faculty for further experimentation with technology as an aid to teaching and learning. The faculty may be "workshopped out" on computer literacy. The Wolfson Grants have supported the development and implementation of technology-based instructional programs. The establishment of computer labs has stimulated the faculty to conduct classes in labs with large-screen projection equipment hooked up to a computer. The competition between faculty wanting to hold classes in these labs and students wishing to do their homework assignments in them is increasingly keen, and the campuses have begun to make available mobile units for classroom instruction. In several departments, a technological "guru" has emerged and is prodding the department to clamor for support to do its thing. It is no small task to let experimentation flourish and at the same time to channel new energies into a system of cohesive endeavors. In applying technology to the teaching/learning process, Miami-Dade has not made earthshaking technological breakthroughs. Yet neither has it stood still. Day by day, month by month, and year by year, the college is fostering the integration of teaching and technology, is developing the people who can make that happen, and is shaping the environment in which it can happen.

Notes

The author wishes to acknowledge the assistance of Kristi Lozano and Lorne Kotler in preparing this chapter.

1. John E. Roueche and George A. Baker, *Access and Excellence: The Open-Door College* (Washington, D.C.: Community College Press, 1987), 187.
2. L. Steven Zwerling, "The Miami-Dade Story," *Change* (January/February 1988), 10-23.
3. Miami-Dade Community College, "Governance Constitution of the Faculty Senates," *Manual of Policy*, I-80.
4. The topics on fiscal status, faculty, and students are derived from Miami-Dade Community College, "Factbook, 1989" (unpublished). Statistics about the college are taken from this report.
5. Miami-Dade Community College, "Teaching/Learning Communiques." Information related to the Teaching/Learning Project is drawn from several communiques from the project director's office.

Chapter 15

Stevens Institute of Technology: Integrating Information Technology into the Curriculum

Joseph J. Moeller, Jr.

Introduction

The incorporation of computing and information technologies in higher education has the potential to fundamentally affect the nature of the teaching and learning process as we know it today. From ubiquitous workstations that combine data, video, and voice systems, students and faculty will communicate more effectively. In addition, they will call on resources distributed throughout campus and beyond. Yet, there are many challenges to be addressed as this integrated academic environment takes shape.

Significant technological issues must be addressed and in some cases have yet to be defined. Even more important, the use of technology in the curriculum will require educators to deal with important pedagogical issues. How do students learn more effectively in a technologically rich environment? What instructional approaches stimulate creativity and inquisitiveness? How can access to extensive information resources facilitate the development of integrative thinking? What creates the desire to continue to learn?

Faculty, staff, and, in many cases, students at Stevens Institute of Technology have been considering these issues for more than a decade. Because the integration of computing into education is still in its infancy, much of the attention to date has been on individual courses. Always in mind, though, has been the broader and longer term impact on the total curriculum. There are often similarities in approaches and common instructional tools among courses. However, there is also a uniqueness associated with each course, a uniqueness that offers expanded horizons for the use of technology. A key challenge at Stevens, and for higher education in general, is the assessment of these projects and the incorporation of successful components into a knowledge database that will contribute to improved instructional activity.

Stevens has focused on three essential issues. First, our students must be prepared to accept the computer and related technologies as partners in the educational process and in professional practice. Second, our faculty members must be presented with incentives to experiment with information technologies and to reexamine their pedagogical approaches. Finally, our institution must provide the technological and organizational infrastructure necessary to support a creative and effective teaching/learning environment.

The Stevens Environment

A fundamental goal at Stevens has always been to prepare students for successful careers in a rapidly advancing technological world and for lifelong learning. More than a decade ago the faculty concluded that capable and effective professionals would need to be "computer fluent," and we embarked on a plan to convey to undergraduate students the attributes associated with computer fluency. The educational goal of this program is to develop in all students a level of computer fluency necessary to assume a leadership role in the utilization of computers and communications technology in all aspects of their professional life. Fluency, as Stevens defines it, is manifest through the following attributes:

1. A willingness and propensity to turn to the computer as an educational aid and tool for professional practice.

2. The ability to engage in dialogue with the computer and to utilize related technologies in a comfortable manner.

3. A knowledge of the capabilities and limitations of available computational facilities.

4. The ability to develop and use computer programs written in a high-level language and to apply them in solving significant problems.

5. A specific knowledge of and experience with numerical methods; modeling, simulation, and design; problem formulation for efficient computer-based solutions; available software packages and their applications; and computer-based instrumentation, data acquisition, and processing.

The development and the implementation of computer-based educational experiences require frequent and easy access to computing resources. As an early step in the creation of a computer-integrated educational environment, Stevens was the first college in the country to require undergraduates to own a personal computer. Currently, each Stevens undergraduate owns or leases a sophisticated personal computer system (an AT-compatible computer running the MS-DOS operating system), and hundreds of additional computer systems are in the hands of faculty and administrators and in public-access laboratories on campus. With the personal desktop computer as a focal point, faculty members at Stevens have identified or produced courseware and computer applications in every academic discipline offered at the institute. These materials range from computer-assisted instruction and tutorial modules and simulations for core courses to professional-quality analysis and design programs for engineering practice in upper-level electives.

Yet even with a capable personal computer on each desktop there are limitations in both computational power and information resources. This has led to the creation of a wide variety of departmental computing laboratories for educational and research activities. These laboratories contain PCs, workstations, and minicomputers that serve specific disciplinary courses such as computer-aided design, simulation and modeling, computer graphics, languages and operating systems, and automated manufacturing systems. Commercial, public domain, and in-house software applications are featured in these departmental facilities.

The latest phase of information technology development at Stevens has focused on resources for collegewide access. Through a series of external grants and contributions totaling almost seven million dollars, we significantly expanded the central systems in our computer center. A cluster of computational servers, a series of file/database servers, a computer conferencing server, an information server, and a communications server have all been installed, hosting a wide variety of systems, utilities, and applications software. In addition, the most important component of this recent project is the establishment of a state-of-the-art, campuswide Ethernet and fiber-optic network linking virtually every academic and residence hall location and almost every computing system on the campus. This initiative, which we call the CREATE Project (Computing in Research and Education for an Advanced Technology Environment), has resulted in the infrastructure needed to support fully distributed, multi-vendor computing and communications. From their desktops, students, faculty, and staff have access to an increasing variety of information resources on campus and to a growing number of external networks (such as BITNET) and computing resources (such as the John von Neumann Supercomputing Center).

Organizational Impact

The organizational structure at Stevens has changed substantially to accommodate the increasing emphasis on computing and information technologies. Initial efforts were nurtured with then existing structures, such as the Educational Development Office and the Undergraduate Curriculum Committee. It soon became apparent that modified or new entities were required. We initially established two *ad hoc* faculty-administration committees, on computer planning and computer operations, that reported directly to the chief academic officer. Faculty members have been involved in the planning and decision-making processes related to campus computing from the very beginning, and their participation, in turn, has been outstanding.

As new opportunities evolved, so did the organization responsible for computing and networking. A vice-president for information systems now provides a point of coordination and planning for all academic computing, communications, and information-related initiatives and support. The directors of computing and communications resources, the computer service center, management information systems, and the library report within this group. In addition, a thirteen-member Committee on Academic Computing, which has succeeded the two *ad hoc* committees and is composed primarily of faculty, is chaired by the vice president. This committee meets on a regular basis to consider strategic directions for CRE-ATE and for the personal computer program. It is responsible for providing guidelines and recommendations for the continuing development of academic computing initiatives and is concerned with instructional computing activities, research computing, computer planning and operations, assessment activities, and information dissemination. The members of this group are also members of other Stevens committees (e.g., those dealing with the undergraduate curriculum, graduate study, and academic standards). As a result, strong linkages are established for incorporating computing initiatives in the total institutional structure.

The computing and communications resources staff is responsible for all major computing systems based in our computer center, as well as for distributed computing including timesharing, local area networking, and external data communications. This professional staff has provided technical support as part of the personal computer evaluation and selection process and network development, and ongoing user support and consultation. A key element here has been the involvement of the staff, along with faculty, in planning and decision making. The computer service center has evolved from an initial focus solely on personal computer logistics, distribution, and maintenance to a full-service operation attending to personal computers, peripherals, terminals, workstations, and data communications equipment throughout the campus. We have found such support to be both essential and cost-effective in an intensive computing environment. Based on fees for service and cost avoidance (e.g., on external maintenance contracts), the center now operates on a break-even or surplus basis. The library, our largest information system on campus, has recently installed an automated system for its operations. Through this system, and through additional student-developed software and interfaces, all members of our community can have direct access through the network to an electronic catalog, a suite of information services, and a variety of database servers providing both abstract and full-text search capabilities.

Faculty Initiatives

Faculty members are, of course, the key to a successful implementation of computing in the curriculum. We have found that faculty development and incentive activities are essential in this regard. At the departmental level, it has been important to distribute workstations to faculty members to promote a familiarity with the machines and their potential uses. We have also provided hardware, software, peripherals, and network interfaces for faculty-student development teams and for laboratory applications.

Shortly after the introduction of a personal computer requirement, Stevens established a special initiative called the Personal Computer Incentive Program. Through it, two-thirds of our full-time faculty members purchased their own computer systems to use at home, with a significant subsidy from the school. These systems are used for courseware, applications development, and professional activities at home, thereby supplementing computer facilities available in each academic department. Many faculty report that they have also used this "home environment" to further develop their computer fluency. Faculty members producing courseware have conducted workshops dealing with approaches to curriculum enhancement and course materials development. Speakers have been invited to discuss computer integration in various disciplines, and hands-on faculty seminars have been held.

A hallmark of our approach to a computer-intensive campus has been the focus on curriculum development. This approach has been possible largely because of significant support (in the form of summer compensation, academic-year release time, programming assistants, and professional staff consultants) for faculty-led development initiatives. Such support has come from a wide cross section of corporate, foundation, and government grants. It has enabled faculty to target their course topics and concepts that can be more effectively presented and understood through computer-based activity. The distribution of courseware development funds is coordinated by the Committee on Academic Computing, in response to internal proposals submitted by faculty members. With the availability of higher-quality applications and utilities software from commercial and other external sources, development projects have increasingly incorporated the use of such products in courses.

Many of the software development projects have been oriented to personal computer applications that students can execute on their own systems. These range from tutorials on engineering mechanics to simulations of biology laboratory experiments. Other projects have targeted workstation platforms in departmental laboratories for activities such as computer-aided design and modeling. The following are examples of several projects currently being implemented:

- The development of tutorial software for the statics and dynamics courses, to facilitate problem-solving skills and mechanics concepts.

- The incorporation of the use of integrated software (e.g., spreadsheet-graphics-report writer) in the engineering experimentation laboratory. These software tools are supplemented by computer-based data acquisition and control of experimental apparatus.

- The simulation of the procedures that a student would use to breed fruit flies for genetic analysis in introductory biology courses. Initially, the program is used by students to assist with the experimental design to correlate types of genetics associated with fly traits. For the advanced student, this *SITfly* program facilitates gene-mapping experiments.

- The introduction of computer-based tools in freshman calculus courses to facilitate an understanding of course concepts and to enhance problem-solving skills and experiments.

- The network-based access to and distribution of course materials for the personalized system of instruction (PSI) courses in physics. The electronic format of these materials will permit individual, self-paced progress in course activities.

- The synthesis and development of a two-dimensional mesh generator for finite element analysis, to be used by students in several mechanical engineering courses. This generator includes an expert system and several knowledge bases. It is part of a pilot project in the development of a Mechanical Systems Modeling Center.

- The creation of a network-based text analysis facility to supplement student writing skills throughout the curricula.

More sophisticated development efforts incorporate multiple distributed systems in network-based applications. For example, a three-year grant from the U.S. Department of Education's Fund for the Improvement of Post-Secondary Education supports an interdisciplinary team of faculty and programmers to integrate network-based simulations of real, complex systems (e.g., chemical reactors) in a multicomputer (PC, workstation, mainframe, and supercomputer) setting. Students working at their desktop computers transparently utilize the processing and data management resources of all of these systems to solve engineering and scientific problems presented by the instructor. As a result, they gain greater insight and a more fundamental understanding of the dimensions and interdependencies involved in such problems. We are confident in stating this because a significant evaluation component is included in the project. The project team, composed of a faculty member with assessment expertise, a graduate assistant, and two external evaluation consultants, has established several measurement techniques and approaches to assess educational impact. By all measures, improvements have been noted and quantified.

Efforts to assess the effect of computer integration and computing resources on the educational process have been ongoing at Stevens since the personal computer requirement was established in 1982. An Evaluation Group headed by a faculty member coordinates these activities. In addition to focused assessment efforts, such as that described above, student surveys administered each year provide information on computer utilization, including percentage of coursework requiring use of information systems, the type of applications employed, and satisfaction with hardware, software, and support services. This information has been used to guide curriculum and faculty development efforts. Alumni are surveyed one year following graduation to determine the effect of undergraduate computing experiences on their professional work. They also provide information on computing technologies currently used in business and industry. The experimental nature of the campuswide network and its potential for providing distributed applications in an academic setting are equally important. Therefore, evaluation of the CREATE Project has been broadened to include data that document the extent to which network implementation and instructional objectives have been achieved.

To conduct the design and evaluation of the educational innovations that take place in new networked environments, Stevens is being guided by a distinguished Advisory Panel on Computers and Learning, com-

posed of educational leaders of international distinction. This group of six
individuals meets on a regular basis to consider the impact of computing
at Stevens, the implications of a "wired campus," and the relationship
between the institute's activities and those occurring at other colleges and
universities.

The Advisory Panel established five primary themes as topic areas for
review and discussion:

- Evaluation — the impact of the CREATE Project and
  networking on attitudes, professional development, student
  and faculty recruiting, etc., is considered.

- Institutional Framework — the interactions and
  organizational structures that are developing through the
  CREATE Project, and the effect of networking on these, are
  studied. Faculty incentives, impact on professional
  development, and support of network activity are discussed.

- Economics — the cost (initial and incremental) of the
  CREATE Project and cost-benefit implications are studied,
  and comparisons to alternative approaches are considered.

- Interinstitutional Cooperation — the interactions through
  informal contacts (visits, seminars, presentations) and through
  more formal arrangements among colleges and with
  corporations are reviewed.

- Technical Implications — the effects of hardware and software
  decisions on the attainment of educational objectives are
  investigated.

The outcomes of the Advisory Panel's discussions are recommendations and guidance that can benefit both Stevens and the larger academic
community.

Development projects concentrating on computing and networking in
curricula vary widely in scope. Some require minimal support — perhaps
only a loan of a personal computer to a faculty member. Others are much
broader, such as the federally funded project described previously, which
is supported at over $100,000 per year. The typical project includes a
faculty member (whose time is valued at $40 per hour), an assistant/pro-
grammer (valued at $25 per hour), and the technology (hardware, soft-

ware, network interface, etc.), resulting in a total average cost of $21,500 per project.

Early software development projects at Stevens were somewhat idiosyncratic in that the focus was often on a narrowly defined product targeted to a specific topic in a course or discipline, and the development team (faculty and assistant) often worked in relative isolation from other project teams. While recognizing the benefits of focused attention to a particular product, we also moved to broaden the impact of such efforts on other development projects and to avoid the trap of "reinventing the technological wheel" with each individual project. Development seminars to demonstrate products and share technical experiences have been held, and a software library has been established.

During the past two years, a Stevens Software Development Support Group (SSDSG) was formed to centralize some of this activity. The group, guided by a faculty member and consisting of a full-time technical developer and several graduate and undergraduate students, was charged with assisting faculty with courseware production. The SSDSG staff is intended as a campuswide resource to aid in software documentation and in the transfer of technology and skills among projects. It also evaluates existing commercial and public-domain software and provides reviews of such products. Particular attention has been directed to assessing authoring systems and recommending campus standards for such tools. However, the requests from faculty for SSDSG services have been limited to date. With a few notable exceptions, developers seem to feel most comfortable when directly involved in the software production and its subsequent use in courses. On the one hand, this is a positive factor, since it generally leads to a more thorough introduction of technology in the course. On the other hand, when the faculty member moves on to other course assignments, what he or she leaves behind is often not standardized or generic enough to be easily accepted and used by other faculty. For the technology gurus and champions, immersion in a software development project is usually exhilarating enough to warrant the expenditure of time and effort. But the more casual computer user often views such an effort as an extra burden when compared with other professional demands and consequently does not feel as compelled to participate in computer integration projects.

Fortunately, a high percentage of the faculty at Stevens is oriented to computing and related technologies. As a result, dozens of software productu hu.. lu . .. .l. ..lu.u.l u. uulu.lud fu. uuu.ucwu.lt. A few of the faculty-developed instructional software products have evolved to commercial standards, and discussions with publishers are ongoing regarding publication and distribution.

Stevens has established an institutional copyright policy for computer software developed internally. When software development is funded by Stevens, or when institute-owned equipment is used, the rights of ownership and authorship in any resulting computer program or documentation belong to the school, subject to Stevens' obligations to external sponsors. If Stevens elects not to exercise the copyright of any material, it can assign the copyright to the author(s), subject to shop rights for internal use. The policy regarding royalties for computer software developed through a Stevens-supported project provides the majority share to the developer. In fact, 100 percent of the first twenty-five thousand dollars of net royalties goes to the author. One-third of the royalties in excess of twenty-five thousand dollars also accrues to the author. Educational development initiatives by faculty are recognized as important at Stevens. Decisions on promotion and tenure take into account these activities, but strong emphasis is placed on grants, linkages to research endeavors, professional journal papers, and other forms of scholarly recognition that are outcomes of a faculty member's involvement in computing and the curriculum.

External Support

The technological infrastructure at Stevens would have been very difficult to implement without active participation by vendors in the form of hardware and software donations and allowances as well as contributions of technical expertise. We have established strong partnerships with Digital Equipment Corporation and AT&T on a campuswide basis. As one of only thirteen colleges and universities to participate in Digital's Campus-Wide Grant program, Stevens benefited from DEC's significant support as we configured the campuswide network and major computing facilities. Close interactions with Digital's staff have helped us to closely monitor technology directions and standards. Similarly, our partnership with AT&T has permitted the cost-effective acquisition of hundreds of personal computers for students, faculty, and staff and has facilitated strong relationships between faculty at Stevens and researchers at AT&T. The company's equipment donations program has also added a variety of hardware, software, and networking products to the institute's laboratories and the campus network.

In addition, companies such as Sun Microsystems, Apple Computer, and Ardent Computer have worked closely with several departments to meet discipline-specific computing and networking needs. On the software side, educational agreements with Microsoft, Borland International, and Boston Business Computing, among others, have permitted a comprehensive distribution of software products to the entire campus population.

As previously mentioned, a large number of courses have been identified for the incorporation of computing activities. Many of these require dedicated time for planning and software development, often funded through grants from corporations, foundations, and government in support of Stevens' computers in education initiatives. The state of New Jersey has aggressively pursued the introduction of computing and networking activities in higher education by establishing several competitive grant programs for public and private colleges. Stevens has been the beneficiary of this support through a series of awards for both single-course and campuswide projects. Major contributors to the computing in curriculum effort include:

- Alden Trust

- Allied/Bendix Corporation

- Apple Computer, Inc.

- AT&T

- Bell Communications Research

- Bell Telephone Laboratories

- L. K. Comstock Company

- Digital Equipment Corporation

- Dreyfuss Foundation

- E. I. DuPont de Nemours

- Exxon Corporation

- Exxon Education Foundation
- General Electric Foundation
- Grumman Corporation
- Hewlett-Packard Company
- Intel Corporation
- New Jersey Bell
- New Jersey Commission on Science and Technology
- New Jersey Department of Higher Education
- Northrop Corporation
- Sun Microsystems
- U.S. Department of Education
- Westinghouse Educational Foundation

Student Impact

Students involved in computer-based educational activities such as those at Stevens have opportunities to improve their abilities to understand (1) basic concepts and theories through increased examples and firsthand problem solving made possible by computer-based dialogues and simulations, and (2) practical, real-life situations in which complex, open-ended problems must be defined and analyzed in order to find the best-possible solutions. In addition, students have the opportunity for more immediate, unimpeded access to knowledge bases, in the form of both data and other individuals. Perhaps the most demanding challenge is to broaden students' perceptions of the computer from a word processor or programming machine to a partner in learning and professional practice.

Through the CREATE Project, we have established several support activities designed to help students assimilate into a computer-intensive setting. These programs begin in the summer before the freshmen year and continue throughout the undergraduate experience. In an effort to ease the transition of freshmen into a new school with a new computer, we have initiated two summer activities. The first is a series of hands-on personal computer workshops offered on campus for all new students. The workshops are conducted by upperclassmen (under faculty guidance) who have expertise in using the personal computer. They provide an introduction to the hardware and software, as well as to the use of the utilities (e.g., word processing, spreadsheets, graphics) distributed with the system. Freshman response to the sessions has been enthusiastic. Through the second activity, freshmen may pick up and take home their personal computer systems for the summer before entering Stevens. They are also provided with a faculty-designed instruction manual highlighting the use and applications of the computer.

Once first-semester coursework begins, Stevens operates a Personal Computer Assistance Program (PCAP), in which a group of knowledgeable undergraduate student computer users, under faculty direction, serve as "computer tutors." PCAP members visit dormitories in the evenings and are available during the day to consult with commuting students about system use and curriculum assignments. They also staff hot-line phones in microcomputer rooms and provide consultation via electronic mail to answer questions from users and to resolve problems on-line. In addition, the PCAP members, as well as other students, faculty, and staff, conduct seminars on specific computing-related topics (e.g., language compilers, network resources and functionality, applications packages). These seminars, open to all members of the community, promote interaction on both instructional topics and professional interests.

Even with increasingly sophisticated academic software for teaching and learning, its acceptance is not easily guaranteed. Students, at least those at Stevens, generally expect to use their computers primarily for word processing and programming (this is evident from attitude questionnaires given to incoming freshmen each year). Since programming assignments in courses usually count for credit, there is a built-in incentive for this use. In contrast, instructional software has often been provided by faculty to supplement course activities, and in many cases its use carries no credit toward a course grade. A heavy course load, coupled with lack of direct incentive for using instructional software, has at times led to minimal use of such software. Part of the problem lies in the lack of a simple, common software interface. In addition, much commercially available educational software, and even that developed for courses by faculty, often takes more time to learn than the student is able or willing to devote. We have noticed that the instructional products developed to commercial standards are more readily accepted and used by students. This situation argues for a more intensive look at how true computer integration in courses and curriculum should be approached; this issue is under consideration by our Committee on Academic Computing and by many colleagues in higher education.

On campus, many students are participating more directly in the educational development process. Their computing abilities have resulted in involvement in courseware development, tutoring, and consulting, areas that were previously the province of graduate students. Faculty-student and student-student interactions in these areas have also increased dramatically.

Challenges for the Future

Since its inception, our approach to establishing an environment rich in information technologies has involved a significant amount of experimentation — with new ideas, new technologies, and new instructional activities. We have been fortunate to benefit from these efforts through positive effects on teaching, learning, research, and scholarship. Yet, there are many challenges and opportunities ahead. Our strategic plans to meet the academic information systems challenges of the future include the following:

- Focusing on incorporating learner-centered computing tools and instructional approaches in the curriculum. Although dozens of software applications have been developed at Stevens, we are far from achieving a true integration of computing and networking in education. In this regard, the Committee on Academic Computing is assessing current activities and needs. Appropriate and meaningful applications in learner environments highlight the curriculum needs. A group of fifteen faculty members with responsibility for freshman/sophomore core courses is meeting to discuss an interdisciplinary approach to computing integration in the curriculum.

- Continuing the transition from a computer-intensive
  to a computing-intensive environment and from a
  network-intensive to a networking-intensive environment.
  The Stevens community must determine how best to fully
  apply the technologies that exist in instruction, research,
  and administration.

- Assessing the opportunities for software development and
  marketing as an enterprise at Stevens. Faculty, staff, and
  students involved in software production are meeting to
  define standard platforms for developing applications,
  user interfaces, graphics, communications, and data
  manipulation tools.

- Identifying focused initiatives that are critically dependent
  on information systems. Several of the interdisciplinary
  applied-research areas at Stevens are planned to build on
  an expanding state-of-the-art distributed computing and
  communications environment. The outcomes of these
  research activities should provide direct benefits to our
  software development and instructional computing initiatives.

- Considering the integration of data, voice, and video
  technologies on campus to establish a sophisticated
  infrastructure for learning and working. Students and faculty
  will increasingly need access to information-processing
  resources in which interactive technologies are easily
  accessed and applied.

We are convinced that using computing and information systems strategically at Stevens can enhance our abilities to work effectively and efficiently while also sharpening the professional preparation of students and the scholarly endeavors of faculty.

Acknowledgments

Planning, review, and recommendations for this chapter came from a number of individuals at Stevens. I am pleased to acknowledge the thoughtful contributions of Francis T. Boesch, M. Peter Jurkat, William Mullins, Roger Pinkham, Bernard Rosen, and Donald Sebastian.

Chapter 16

The University of Illinois at Urbana-Champaign: Computing and Instructional Innovation

Richard F. Wilson

and

George F. Badger

The most meaningful way to conceive of the organizational structure used to support instructional computing at the University of Illinois at Urbana-Champaign is as a "loosely coupled" system. On a campus of over one hundred departments, three thousand faculty members, and thirty-five thousand students, very few things are organized — if by *organized* is meant some central unit or person is in control. Initiative is taken in multiple locations in response to the needs and expectations of a diverse constituency. This does not mean that anarchy reigns; it does mean that both initiative and support services are decentralized in many cases and that coordinating mechanisms have been established to encourage the sharing of information and to reduce unnecessary duplication.

This chapter begins with an overview of those computing services at Illinois that are central to instructional innovation and moves to a discussion of key issues that we have faced and resolved or that continue to need attention. The focus is on what we have learned about using computers in instruction that might be of interest to those at other institutions and on what challenges remain.

Computing Support Services

Computer-Based Education Research Laboratory (CERL)

The first interactive timesharing computer-based educational system was developed at Illinois in 1960 and was named PLATO (Programmed Logic for Automatic Teaching Operations).[1] In 1967 the Computer-Based Education Research Laboratory (CERL) was established to house the PLATO system and to provide a base for other instructional development activities. The PLATO system has always been considered both a research and development system and an educational delivery system.

Besides the original development of a large-scale computer-controlled instructional system, CERL is recognized for the invention of the plasma panel display. From its early years, the system has supported a wide variety of instructional styles and simulations. System capabilities, authoring utilities, and user options have evolved in response to user needs. In addition to the interactive graphic display capabilities, PLATO users have experimented with various peripheral devices, including touch-sensitive display, random-access recorded audio, speech, and music synthesis, and color slide projection superimposed on the computer display. By 1975 the first PLATO microprocessor terminal was in use, and by 1980 an accredited course was taught in a PLATO microcomputer classroom.

Today, the CERL computer-based education systems serve over twenty-two hundred graphics terminals throughout the United States, with over six hundred of those terminals at UIUC. Major campus classroom sites are housed in five departments. The systems support a library of approximately ten thousand instructional programs in over one hundred subject matter areas, from accounting through zoology. They deliver over one million user-service hours per year. Current CERL research efforts include such diverse areas as computer-generated music, computer-adaptive testing and measurement, and voice recognition.

The most recent advance of computer-based education technology, called NovaNET , has been operative since 1987.[2] NovaNET uses satellite communications to connect a growing network of graphics terminals around the country to the central processor and memory at UIUC. Although the NovaNET environment is brand new particularly in its hardware components but also in the expanded capacity of its system software — the best system features and software products resulting from CERL's twenty-five years of experience serving nonspecialist users have been incorporated into the NovaNET environment.

Computing Services Office (CSO)

The Computing Services Office (CSO) is the traditional academic service unit of the campus. The office operates eight mainframe systems, manages eight microcomputer laboratories, and provides a collection of computer access and user services for both instruction and research. It was organized as a separate department in the early 1970s but had been in existence before that time as a program within the computer science department.

For most of its life, the Computing Services Office has focused on centralized, large-scale computers as the means of delivering service. Beginning in the late 1970s CSO began to follow a strategy of using small, special-purpose machines for individual clienteles, sometimes locating the machine within the space assigned to a discipline. By the early 1980s CSO had begun to use microcomputers as a means of delivering service. At the present time, there is more service delivered through microcomputers than through mainframe systems.

CSO provides one-half of the instructional computing on campus and 20 percent of the research computing. The remainder is provided through departmental facilities, PLATO (for instructional work), and the National Center for Supercomputing Applications (for research computing). The tradition of the campus has been very strongly toward distributed computing for research. The movement toward distributed computing for instruction has been a relatively recent phenomenon, based almost entirely on the evolution of the microcomputer.

In addition to providing computing services, CSO serves as the focal point for coordinating computing efforts on the campus. In this role, it has been instrumental in campuswide networking. Funding for both research and instructional computing has occurred through direct appropriations from the campus, complemented by some income from grants and contracts. This has allowed the office to work on all types of computing without letting economic considerations drive decisions.

National Center for Supercomputing Applications (NCSA)

The National Center for Supercomputing Applications (NCSA) is a university-based supercomputing facility and research center designed to serve the national research community. The center is one of the National Science Foundation's supercomputing centers and receives additional funding from the state of Illinois, Industrial Partner Corporations, strategic vendors, and the campus. NCSA operates two supercomputers (Cray-2 and Cray X/MP-48), two Alliant FX/8s, and numerous workstations. Over 2,500 researchers at 150 institutions across the country are supported by NCSA. The center has a strong program in local and remote training for the research community. NCSA is involved in developing technology-based curriculum materials and tools through its staff, campus faculty, the center's adjunct faculty, and faculty at other institutions. For example, a team of UIUC faculty has established a "Renaissance Experimental Laboratory" containing twenty Silicon Graphics 4D/20 Personal Iris workstations to support curriculum development around high-end graphics workstations. The team has designed courses that incorporate computer graphics into the curriculum. These courses will serve as models that other schools may follow. The classroom is being used by faculty in art and design, computational chemistry, biophysics, computational geometry, and mathematics.

NCSA has developed software for use in many educational contexts. The educational effectiveness of software is evaluated by the faculty and students involved. NCSA has a staff to assist faculty members in assessing their software needs and in developing and assessing support materials for graduate and undergraduate courses that integrate computational science and supercomputing concepts.

The center is a heavily networked environment and serves as a demonstration site for the campus. NCSA also has developed a national leadership position in computer graphics and scientific visualization. The center has produced considerable software for the workstation environment to enable supercomputers to be used to analyze results graphically. This software has been released into the public domain. NCSA produces a newsletter, science highlights, and information of interest to the computational science and engineering communities. The center's Visitors Program allows researchers to spend time on campus interacting with NCSA staff and scientists in an interdisciplinary environment.

Instructional and Management Ocrvices (IMO)

One of the missions of this campuswide unit is to assist faculty members in the design of courses and the evaluation of instructional effectiveness. An important part of this mission in recent years has been providing assistance in the development and delivery of computer-based instruction (CBI). Such assistance may take the form of determining the feasibility of an idea or selecting an authoring system. In addition, IMS provides assistance in evaluating the impact of computer use on the instructional process and student outcomes. Trained evaluators discuss instructional computing projects with instructors and propose alternative evaluation designs and strategies.

IMS also produces a monthly newsletter and sponsors faculty seminars and workshops on instructional computing. The newsletter features descriptions of faculty instructional computing projects; discusses CBI development tools; announces hardware grants and awards; identifies sources of commercial and clearinghouse courseware; and provides a calendar of CBI events on campus. The seminars provide an opportunity for faculty members to demonstrate their software to colleagues on campus. Participants often discover ways to adapt the ideas discussed to their own fields of interest.

IMS also operates a "hands on" graphics center for faculty members and their assistants to use in evaluating the usefulness of microcomputers in producing inexpensive instructional media (e.g., overhead transparencies, slides, and handouts). During the center's first semester, more than two hundred faculty members from sixty-three departments used computers to produce instructional media.

The desire to integrate computers and videodisk technology in an effective learning environment precipitated the development of the Electronic Storyboarding System. IMS developed a "windowing" procedure that enables computer and video elements to be viewed for precision and continuity matching during original video production. For the first time, it became easy to compose a videotape while maintaining compatibility with the author's computer graphics. The result was a reduction in support staff video production time of 29 percent and in faculty video production time of 35 percent, a significant savings considering the labor intensity of videodisk production.

Computers in Residence Halls

College students do most of their studying wherever they happen to live. Residence halls provide facilities for offering computing services to large numbers of students twenty-four hours a day, seven days a week. At Illinois, freshmen predominate in residence halls. Consequently, the provision of residence hall computer sites, along with computer education at those sites, contributes to efforts to introduce new students to computers and computing services on campus.

The housing division operates its own office of Student Computer Services (SCS), and most of the funding used to support residence hall computer facilities and services is derived from room and board payments. The housing division also has received a substantial amount of hardware and software as gifts or at greatly reduced prices in conjunction with research projects involving computers in residence halls.

Three of the residence hall computer sites (which are monitored by student employees and are open from noon to midnight) are supported by the university's Computing Services Office. Ten additional sites installed during the past two years are not monitored and are open from twelve to twenty-four hours per day.

Central Stores

Historically, the sale of microcomputers to departments has been the responsibility of Central Stores, a unit within the university that keeps frequently used products on inventory for immediate delivery to departments. Central Stores created a computer center within its operation to handle microcomputer sales and services. Like many other institutions, the university decided to sell microcomputers to faculty, staff, and students in the mid 1980s because of the growing significance of microcomputers to the work of these individuals and because of the special discounts being provided by computer companies. These individual sales initially were the responsibility of the campus bookstore but eventually were made a part of the mission of the Central Stores computer center.

In conjunction with its responsibility for individual sales, the Central Stores computer center opened a micro order center (MOC) in the student union. The MOC is adjacent to a student computer laboratory and a micro resource center (a software library) run by the Computing Services Office. At the MOC, students, faculty, and staff can use demonstradon equipment, seek purchasing advice, have eligibility determined, and place orders. The MOC's proximity to the laboratory and particularly to the resource center provides additional opportunities for consultation and for equipment use.

Departmental sales and service operations have evolved since 1985 as well. At first, the computer center was involved only in sales activities. Within a short time, departmental demand for maintenance service prompted the center to expand. Placing these functions together in the Central Stores computer center has had a number of advantages: customers have the same point of contact for both sales and service; technical staff who service machines can give better sales-related consultation; costs are kept to a minimum by using staff in both areas; equipment that goes down soon after departmental purchase can be replaced immediately from sales inventory so that the department does not have a delay waiting for warranty repair; costs of services are partially subsidized through sales revenues; and beneficial maintenance arrangements can be negotiated with computer companies.

Instructional Issues

Campus-Level Leadership in Instructional Innovation

Several times in recent years the campus administration has debated whether to appoint a "computer czar" to provide campus-level leadership in computing. Each time, the idea has been rejected because of concerns about centralizing computer planning and creating a new administrative structure. To attract the kind of person needed and to be successful in coordinating a broad range of activities, the university would have to give the appointed person authority at the level of a vice-chancellor. There was some reluctance to make this move because of the belief that computing should remain a service function within the academic and administrative structure of the campus rather than a line function competing directly with these units for resources. Nevertheless, some coordination and planning was needed, a fact that led the vice-chancellor for academic affairs to appoint an Educational Technologies Board and a Network Planning Committee in 1988.

The primary responsibility of the Educational Technologies Board is to advise the vice-chancellor on present and future needs and directions in the use of computers and other new technologies in instruction. The charge is extremely broad, comprising a variety of ways in which instructional computing might be advanced on the UIUC campus.

- Introducing faculty to new tools for the development of instructional materials.

- Developing plans for dedicated classrooms and lecture halls, with computer equipment on site.

- Using local area (and eventually campuswide) networks for instructional purposes.

- Making recommendations to the vice-chancellor on the annual allocation of funds for equipment.

Although instructional computing is quite appropriately considered a part of the larger educational mission of the university, it must also be understood within the context of faculty responsibilities to do scholarly and scientific research. Despite the current budgetary crisis, when a faculty member at the UIUC begins a research project, he or she expects and receives substantial institutional support. The university's library is among the best in the world, with massive collections and a fully computerized, on-line catalogue. The research services office provides excellent assistance in the pursuit of public and private grants. The Research Board of the Graduate College responds directly to faculty proposals each month, minimizing the obstacles to the early advancement of any project, and supports faculty travel through its Scholar's Travel Fund. Still more exotic resources are provided at the NCSA and elsewhere. These, of course, are the perquisites of a major research university, one that expects its faculty members to be the leading authorities in their fields.

At such a university, faculty members will become actively involved in instructional innovation only insofar as similar institutional support is offered. Faculty members should not be asked to choose between being innovative scholars and being innovative teachers — first because, in virtually every case, the choice will be in favor of research; and second because it is inconsistent with the overall mission of the university to ask such a question in the first place. In the future, it must be as easy to introduce complex technologies into undergraduate instruction as it is to begin a research project, for example, to write a grant proposal, begin research on a new article or book, or conduct a scientific experiment. Only then can faculty be expected to do both.

The problem of introducing innovative technology into undergraduate education, therefore, is not simply one of rewarding good teaching as well as research (although we can certainly do a better job at this). More particularly, it is a problem of providing support, including information, equipment, release time, salary, technical assistance, and expert evaluation and measurement. When a faculty member has a worthy proposal, these things must be provided immediately, generously, and continuously — in short, they must be provided in the same spirit that we currently provide support for research.

Faculty Perceptions About Involvement in CAI

An important issue at Illinois and elsewhere around the country is whether faculty members are rewarded for participating in departmental efforts to computerize the curriculum and for spending time developing software. Several programs at the campus level attempt to support faculty members in the development of computer-supported teaching materials and course modules. The Undergraduate Instructional Awards program provides grants to faculty members to support the development of new coursework or major revision of ongoing courses. In recent years many of the projects that have received funding involved the development of materials that make use of computers. The recently appointed Educational Technologies Board also provides funding for the application of computer technologies to instruction. Instruction is an important dimension of promotion and tenure decisions, and a careful evaluation of instructional contributions is required. Each case must include a list of all courses taught, enrollments, and grade distributions; a self-review of instructional activities, including any exceptional contributions to course or curriculum development; results of student evaluation questionnaires; and evidence from peers of "significant contributions to instructional programs of other instructors." Thus, the development of courseware is recognized in terms of benefit both to an instructor's own courses and to the courses of colleagues, at Illinois and elsewhere.

One effort to assess awards for software development was undertaken by Robert L. Davis, an IBM consulting scholar and the dean of the School of Engineering at the University of Missouri-Rolla. His study, conducted in 1988, focused on identifying which faculty members were developing courseware, what their motivations were, and whether or not such activity was institutionally rewarded. To answer these questions he sent a survey to nineteen research institutions awarded IBM Advanced Education Project grants. The grants funded significant CAI development at each school.

At Illinois a copy of the questionnaire was forwarded to the principal investigator of each project funded through our grant. Ninety-one questionnaires were mailed; forty-three were completed and returned. The respondents included twenty-two professors, nine associate professors, seven assistant professors, and five academic staff members. For this group, half of the CAI development was being done by professors, a group not pressured by promotion and tenure concerns.

Respondents were asked how they had fared compared with other faculty in regard to promotion and tenure. A follow-up question asked how they expected successful development of courseware to affect faculty members in the future. The responses of the sixteen assistant and associate professors are summarized below and show that very few faculty members below the rank of professor expect work on CAI to help them win promotion or tenure.

	Software Development			
	Impact on Promotion		Impact on Tenure	
	Recent experience	Future experience	Future experience	Recent experience
Positive	14%	19%	14%	14%
Negative	29%	38%	5%	14%
No effect	57%	43%	81%	71%

Similar questions were asked about the effect of current and future involvement in CAI development on salary. As the data below indicate, only a quarter of the respondents expect to be rewarded monetarily for their work. Nearly as many expect to be penalized.

	Software Development	
	Recent experience	Future experience
Positive	28%	28%
Negative	21%	19%
No effect	51%	53%

With such low expectations for reward of any kind, and some expectation of penalty, it is surprising to note that 65 percent of the respondents reported that they plan to continue developing courseware.

Another 23 percent reported that they planned to continue but at some future date. Respondents were asked what had led them to the decision to continue (or not continue) courseware development. The following are some sample responses of those planning to continue:

"I believe it is important to introduce innovative teaching methods. Recognition and acceptance will probably come only later, if at all."

"There are wonderfully hard problems in trying to produce exercises which are not just rote."

"Because I care about the students. They are enthused about it and I know they benefit."

"The courseware is closely linked to my research needs, so research programs typically spin off into courseware."

It is clear that faculty members are engaging in courseware development for the benefit of their students or for personal satisfaction. Only one respondent provided an explanation for his decision not to continue courseware development. It consisted of a single word: "Time."

Respondents were asked what incentives would encourage further courseware development. They identified release time, student/staff support, and hardware availability as by far the most important. Salary and promotion/tenure rewards followed. Peer approval, royalty payments, and courseware ownership were ranked lowest. Responses to a question about how the campus could have helped further with recent projects, and comments about problems encountered, were consistent with these rankings. Release time, student/staff support, and money were most important. The questionnaire also asked if institutions should limit courseware development to full professors or nonregular faculty. Eighty-nine percent of those who responded to the question do not feel that software development activities should be restricted.

Impact of Computing on Teaching and Learning

Given all the time, effort, and money devoted to computing over the last five years, it is not surprising that we receive frequent inquiries asking for an assessment of impact. At Illinois, faculty are very interested in this question, and an evaluation component has been built into every campus-wide effort to support the use of computers or software development. Recent projects of this type include Project EXCEL, a three-year equipment grant from IBM; Seedlings, a three-year matching grant from Apple Computer; and projects funded through a student computer fee that was instituted in 1987. Results of EXCEL project evaluations illustrate what we have learned. The principal objective of the grant was to support instructional innovation through uses of advanced computing technologies. Projects receiving funding through this grant were required to conduct an evaluation, giving special attention to how student learning was enhanced, how computers were used, what instructional changes occurred, and how the curriculum was modified. A few results of these evaluations are described below.

Comparative Studies

Several projects compared students who used computers with students in the same class who did not use computers in order to determine the effects of computer use on teaching and learning. A good illustration is the evaluation conducted for a project on the use of interactive videodisks for teaching general chemistry. In Chemistry 100, the videodisks were used as laboratory replacement equipment. Students were randomly selected for the computerized and noncomputerized test groups. A written, seven-point quiz was used as a basis of comparison between the two groups. The twenty-five students who used the videodisk equipment earned a mean score of 4.76, significantly higher than the mean of 3.89 earned by the twenty-seven students who completed the laboratory experiments using traditional methods. Similar results were obtained for another course.

Assessing the impact of computer use was not restricted to academic performance. A faculty member in the School of Architecture developed a computerized design studio and an architectural information system to aid students in architectural design. Based on studio observations by architectural faculty from outside the project, students using the computerized studios scored significantly higher than their noncomputerized counterparts in such areas as attendance, participation, discussion/interaction work done in the studio, morale/esprit de corps, and organization.

Surveys

Attitude surveys were another common means of project evaluation. Many project leaders surveyed students to determine attitudinal changes resulting from the use of computers. For example, a faculty member in nuclear engineering developed an evaluation plan for his project on the use of computers in courses on radiation measurement and laboratory instrumentation. He administered surveys to students in the semester immediately before and the semester immediately after computerization. Students answered questions on a scale of 1 to 10, with 10 being the most positive response. According to the students, the addition of computers into these courses made the experiments slightly better educational experiences, slightly more applicable to their careers, slightly more complex, and slightly more enjoyable. Significant improvements were seen in the quality of equipment and the usefulness of microcomputers. In addition, students spent twice as long doing laboratory write-ups before the addition of computers as they did after computers were used.

In a similar survey administered to students using a new laboratory for electronic imaging for artists and designers, a faculty member in art and design found that 68 percent of the students thought they learned topics more quickly using the computer and 72 percent felt their design capabilities had improved due to computer use. Of the 107 students surveyed, 98 percent thought the computer experience would increase their potential for employment and 94 percent wanted more class offerings using the computers.

Finally, a faculty member in music and in electrical and computer engineering used a survey to determine the effectiveness of his project, which used an IBM PC-AT for the demonstration and instruction of musical acoustics phenomena. An attitudinal survey was administered to the students taking the course. A significant number of students felt the computer demonstrations made it easier for them to grasp the concepts illustrated and increased the depth of their understanding of these concepts. Most students said they would use the computer if it were available for hands-on use outside the class.

Effects of Instructional Computing on Course Content

Instructional computing affects not only the way in which material is taught but also the range of material that can be covered in the classroom. A faculty member in environmental engineering incorporated personal computers into a course on the design and planning of civil engineering systems. He found that the amount of material that could be covered in the course expanded significantly. The computer allowed the instructor to devote less time to theoretical topics and to include more problem-solving aspects. Based on examination scores, students suffered no loss in comprehension of theoretical concepts; gains in problem-solving ability were made at no expense to theoretical background.

Though not conclusive, the results of these evaluations are encouraging and suggest that microcomputers are having a positive effect on both the cognitive and affective aspects of teaching and learning. The campus views the EXCEL evaluations as preliminary indicators of impact and has built similar evaluation expectations into other courses with computing projects, including an instructional development grant from Apple Computer and projects funded through a campus computer fee.

Software Ownership

The University of Illinois completely revised its copyright policy in 1983. The resulting policy continues to be fine-tuned but in general seems to work well, serving the needs of the faculty and staff and the university. The revision changed the entire thrust of the policy, adopting an approach that generally declines institutional ownership of copyrightable works except when a direct and demonstrable institutional interest in such ownership exists. The policy makes no differentiation between software and other copyrightable works except to the extent that software may be patentable, in which case the provisions of the institutional patent policy would be applicable.

The approach has been to minimize the university's involvement with copyrightable works to the extent possible, for both philosophical and practical reasons. Philosophically, the university wishes to encourage and reward creativity, promote the dissemination of copyrightable works developed in the course of university activities, and restrict its role in the absence of a direct university interest. Practically, the university has neither the desire to exploit copyrightable works nor the expertise to handle their publication and marketing on a large scale. Generally speaking, it seemed inequitable and unrealistic to ask authors to relinquish rights to us when we would not be able to handle them well. We rejected a course in which the university would have devoted resources to a marketing and development program large enough to compete with other outlets for such materials. The university adopted the traditional academic attitude toward the production of books and articles, in which the institution does not claim ownership rights as the foundation of its policy and extended it to other categories of copyrightable works in all media.

Under university policy, the ownership of copyrightable works belongs to the authors except in the following three circumstances, in which the university claims such rights of ownership as it may require:

- Where the terms of an external contract require the university to hold or transfer ownership.

- When the work was expressly commissioned by the university.

- Where the work was created as a specific requirement of employment or as an assigned university duty.

If works owned by the university generate income, the university's normal practice is to share with the authors 50 percent of the net income received.

In circumstances where university resources over and above those "usually and customarily provided" (office space, library facilities, regular salary) are used in the creation of the work, the university requires, as a minimum, that a nonexclusive, royalty-free license be granted to the university for use in the university's internally administered programs of teaching, research, and public service. It is in this circumstance that the largest policy issues remain.

First, and of the least concern, are the circumstances in which the university retains or requests more than the minimum license. Despite early misgivings, this has not been an especially troublesome area, since consensus as to the equitable handling of such situations has been achieved with little difficulty in most cases.

Of more concern, and an issue that has not yet been resolved, is the fact that currently all use of the university's computing resources is considered to fall into the category of resources "over and above those usually and customarily provided." This is likely to remain the case for our mainframes and supercomputers. However, microcomputers, as they become ubiquitous for faculty members, will at some point become "usually and customarily provided." We have not yet grappled with how that determination will be made, nor with who will make it. However it may come about, when it does, we may well need to consider revising our copyright policy in order to claim a nonexclusive, royalty-free license to use software developed on university microcomputers. To differentiate between more traditional copyrightable works and software will be a big step for us, one we have been unwilling to make before. On the other hand, though comfortable with our current philosophical approach to copyright ownership, in all likelihood we *will* want to retain the right for software developed on university computers to be used in classes and research programs without royalty obligations.

Ownership of Facilities

Current planning for facilities ranging from microcomputers to large-scale systems shows an emphasis in three areas. An active program encouraging the ownership by individual students of basic systems will provide a substantial portion of computing for students within the next few years. At the present time, approximately 28 percent of the incoming students bring a computer of some kind with them. The campus has encouraged the purchase of such equipment for several years and has provided various microcomputer software and hardware support activities, including a very active program of making available commonly used and public-domain software. The problem of incorporating these systems into the network is under consideration both through the residence hall program, for those who live in dormitories, and through the local community telephone systems and cable television.

The second element is centralized campus ownership. This occurs both through the machines purchased in the residence hall system and in the Computing Services Office. In both cases, a large number of relatively general computing systems are made available. The Computing Services Office also offers some workstations and a large variety of mainframe-based services.

The third element of ownership is in departments and colleges, and this is the fastest growing of the three areas. The pattern that will probably arise is that the departmental machines will be the more expensive and more discipline-specific equipment, whereas the generic equipment will be provided through campuswide organizations.

Overall, the campus has set a planning target of fifteen hours of contact per week per student in the busy part of the semester, with approximately 80 percent of this occurring on relatively generic systems and 20 percent on more advanced and, therefore, more expensive systems. This implies approximately one university-owned machine for every six students at a point when 50 percent of the students have their own machines as well.

In addition to ownership, several other aspects of operating computing facilities show evolving responsibility patterns. Our expectation is that economy of scale will be a driving force toward the centralization of support for hardware maintenance, software distribution, site licensing, and communications. Less economy of scale exists as the machines become more specialized, and certainly discipline-specific software and faculty-developed software will reside nearest those who are interested. As the network becomes more pervasive and capable, we expect that students will not travel to equipment unless the equipment is so specialized that it cannot be distributed. Thus, facilities must be provided at the point of convenience to the end user, a determining factor in defining patterns of responsibility.

Use of Residence Hall Computer Sites

The location and hours of operation of residence hall computer sites have been important issues for the campus. Studies conducted over the past four years show that sites located closest to the normal traffic flow of students are used most. For women, in particular, it appears that a computer site located in a convenient and public area is more attractive, especially at night, than a site located in a more remote area (e.g., in a basement area). Public area sites across from, adjacent to, or close to a hall's main office where on-duty staff can be found at all times have proven to be the most secure from thefts and damages and consequently remain open without incident (even though unmonitored) twenty-four hours a day.

In many ways, residence hall computing complements other campus resources. For example, as activity begins to decline on the central campus in the late afternoon, activity in the residence halls begins to increase. A study conducted during the fall semester of 1988 showed that as campus computer sites were preparing to close at midnight, more students could be found using computers in residence hall sites than at any other hour of the day.

Students entering residence halls will have different needs or desires to use computer facilities and different levels of knowledge of computing. Several studies at Illinois have shown that women and minority students (particularly blacks and Hispanics) have not had equivalent access to or experience with computers before they entered college. Women, in general, have significantly higher levels of computer anxiety than do men when they confront an academic environment requiring some skill in using computers. The housing division attempts to address these problems in several ways.

In addition to on-paper and on-line information, Housing's SCS staff provides an ongoing program of computer education in residence halls. Many noncredit workshops are offered in the residence hall sites. Most are directed specifically at novice users and involve topics ranging from a general introduction to what is provided at a given site to how to use specific software packages.

SCS staff also offer, in conjunction with the Department of Educational Psychology, a two-credit course that trains peer tutors. This course provides instruction not only on how to use hardware and software but also on how to teach others (particularly computer-anxious novices) to use these resources. After completing this course, students may apply for paid positions as peer tutors. These peer tutors maintain a schedule of times they will be available in various residence hall sites. While they provide a great deal of assistance to other students, the very presence of peer tutors appears to be somewhat comforting to novice users, who fear that they will make mistakes or that something will go wrong and they will not know how to resolve the problem. As a result, many novices use the sites at times when they know peer tutors will be available to provide assistance.

Students also learn to use computers in residence halls by enrolling in courses that faculty teach in the sites. The housing division has offered the use of some sites as classrooms during the morning and early afternoon, when general use is lowest. Most freshmen on this campus must take a rhetoric course, and several sections that teach students to write with the assistance of word processing have been offered in residence hall computer sites.

Some residence hall sites provide terminal access to the PLATO system and to mainframes operated by the Computing Services Office. Plans for the future include linking what are now local area networks with each other and with campus mainframes. Also proposed are telecommunications systems that would allow access from a student's room to the residence hall networks.

Networking

The campus made major strides in networking in the late 1970s when terminals were connected to mainframe computers through a coaxial cable system. This system was extended to most of the buildings on campus very early, and the concept of providing access through minor charges to the customer was established and institutionalized.

In the early 1980s a task force worked out the basic strategy for replacing the purchased telephone services with a campus proprietary telephone switch. The task force then made several key decisions that led to the present networking structure. These included decisions (1) to install optical fiber near all major buildings and immediately to extend that fiber into a number of buildings (2) to run relatively short, unshielded twisted-pair circuits between telephone closets and every telephone outlet, and (3) to build networking around a structure that was independent of the telephone system itself. As an adjunct to this, the campus recognized that the external wiring and fiber plant would probably need to be changed over time as media standards emerged and as the amount of media increased. For this reason, there is as much empty conduit between buildings as there is conduit with media in it.

The advent of the supercomputing center gave us the opportunity to do high-speed networking even before this new fiber plant was put into place. A relatively small fiber-optic network was built connecting the supercomputing services to a number of major client departments. The first generation of Proteon token ring products was used, and that experience led to the use of Proteon products throughout the campus backbone. Between 1987 and 1989 a further development of the networking strategy has led to a policy of connecting all buildings to the backbone and connecting each user to local area networks and to a building gateway to the campus network. The basic structure of this network is based on the

TCP/IP Internet set of protocols, although other protocols are carried between peer systems.

After a long debate, the campus decided that providing a base level of networking services to every member of the community was a sufficiently high priority to fund centrally and has gone ahead with such a funding plan. Additionally, emphasis has been given to making major services, such as the library, academic computing, administrative computing, and supercomputing, easily available and to actively participating in the advancement of the regional and national networks and their associated services.

One of the first steps taken in this direction was to consolidate, in a single design office, representatives of the separate offices for telecommunications, administrative computing, and academic computing services. CSO has responsibility for the construction of the network backbone and many of the academic departmental networks.

Microcomputer Sales and Service

The principal issue involving microcomputers sales has been whether the individual sales program could be structured in a way that would meet institutional objectives without antagonizing local retailers. There have been three phases to the university's resale activity. In the first phase, the university purchased equipment and resold the machines through the campus bookstore. Local computer stores objected to this arrangement and filed suit. At about the same time, the state legislature passed a law that prohibited the university from engaging in sales activities that were "in significant competition" with local retailers. The suit is still pending, and the applicability of the state law to computer sales has not been resolved.

Nevertheless, the university revised its resale program in a way that would involve the retailers while still providing substantial discounts to individuals on campus. In this new program, the university's Central Stores computer center, which previously had sold equipment just to departments, purchased inventory for resale from contracted manufacturers. The equipment was then transferred to contracted local retailers for sale to eligible faculty, staff, and students. Individuals went to those retailers for pre-sale consultation, eligibility determination, and purchase. Checks were made out to the university; the purchase price included an overhead cost for the university and a commission that the university paid to the local retailer.

While this arrangement provided discounts and involved local retailers, it had a number of disadvantages. The university was responsible for ordering and managing the inventory, handling all the financial transactions, and negotiating contracts with the retailers; it was still in the sales "loop." In addition, students were at a particular disadvantage because all of the retail locations are somewhat distant from campus; it was not convenient for students to access demonstration equipment or obtain information. The university has been able to address these problems through another change in its resale program.

The new contracts with computer manufacturers permit students, faculty, and staff to order their computers directly from the manufacturers. The customer makes a check out to a contracted manufacturer, which delivers equipment to a retailer of the customer's choice for pickup. A separate check for fifty dollars to cover handling costs is written to the university. Under this arrangement, the manufacturer contracts with the retailer for support services; the university's relationships with local retailers are cooperative but not contractual. In addition, the campus is no longer responsible for individual sales inventory or financial transactions. Our role is to negotiate the lowest possible price from manufacturers and to facilitate sales.

Another important issue for the campus is equipment maintenance and repair. The best maintenance arrangements involve designating the computer center as a service center for both warranty and post-warranty repair. Technicians are trained and authorized, with additional support available when needed. The manufacturer pays the university for doing warranty repairs, and parts for post-warranty repairs can be purchased at a discount. This arrangement is in place for several manufacturers.

Not all maintenance is handled as conveniently for the university. In some cases, post-warranty parts cannot be purchased at a discount. Partial solutions include purchasing parts as finished goods at discounted prices and purchasing rebuilt parts from third parties. Older machines present different problems and require a number of strategies: purchasing inexpensive third-party parts and stocking such items as floppy drives, hard drives, and replacement motherboards, which frequently fail. The least desirable situation, from a departmental perspective, is to send equipment off-site for repair. Perhaps the major organizational problem in the service area is the need to maintain staff morale when customer demand for immediate attention is high.

Vendor Relationships

The campus has had research and development relationships with computer companies for many years, and a set of policies and procedures has been developed for handling grants and contracts. Generally, these relationships have been between individual faculty members, research teams, or departments. The advent of the microcomputer brought a new challenge because of broadly based needs and opportunities relating to the institution's instructional mission.

Over the last five years, the campus has participated in a number of gift and grant programs where the primary focus, at least from an institutional standpoint, was to improve the instructional process. Initially, we scrambled to find ways to respond to the burgeoning demand for microcomputers and tried to respond to the opportunities made available by the computer companies. Minimal attention was given to the longer-range role that these companies might play in our instructional program. Our objective was to get computers into the hands of faculty and students; the companies' objective was to stimulate sales. Although satisfying demand continues to be a problem, the campus has become much more intentional about its relationship with computer companies and has a better vision about the role that these companies might play. For instruction, the campus has defined three types of relationships: development projects, pilot studies, and implementation projects. The roles of the campus and the computer companies vary with each of these activities.

Development Projects are initiated by individual faculty members who wish to create software or use existing software or hardware in unique ways to enhance instruction. The need is for a modest amount of equipment (one to three machines) and funds to see whether the idea will work. Results of the project are usually tested with a small number of students. This is a logical area for computer companies to become involved in. The university provides the expertise, and a company helps with equipment. The investment is modest and yet critical to developing new applications and improving instruction.

Once the development stage has been completed and evaluated, the results are ready for *Pilot Studies*. At this stage, the project moves out of the "laboratory" and into the classroom, perhaps to a section of a course.

Computer companies have a role to play in this stage because of the obvious benefits to accrue from the successful testing of a project that appears to have potential for wide use. The institutional responsibility also increases. Whereas a development project may be initiated on the strength of an individual faculty member's interest, a pilot study should have departmental support. This support should be financial as well as moral.

Assuming the pilot test is successful, the project moves to *Implementation*. The technology is tested in an entire course or curriculum. At this stage, the balance between institutional and computer company support shifts toward the institution. Although a company may wish to participate in some fashion, for example, by providing larger than normal discounts for quantity purchases, the primary obligation is with the institution to implement a project.

The issue faced at Illinois was how to accommodate these three stages of development. Initially, the pilot studies and development projects were supported through gift and grant programs made available by computer companies and *ad hoc* institutional commitments of funds and other resources. One of the major problems was that a new organizational structure had to be created each time a broadly based grant program was initiated. Furthermore, much of the momentum dissipated once the grant ended. To address these problems, the campus administration appointed the Educational Technology Board, which, among other things, serves as a point of coordination for pilot studies and development projects. The specific programs vary by company, but all focus on *instructional* innovation.

Once projects reach the implementation stage, funding is handled in standard ways, for example, seeking new state funds or reallocating existing funds. In addition, two years ago the campus instituted a computer fee of twenty dollars per semester to enhance student access to computing technologies. The fee is administered by a committee of seven faculty members and seven students and focuses on supporting projects that will maximize student access, that is, implementation projects. During the first year, the funds were used to support both public-access sites and sites that·were located in departments and that were made available to students in the department.

This year the fee was increased to twenty-eight dollars per semester and was merged into tuition. This merger took place because students

objected to income generated by the fee being used to support the departments that had restricted-access sites. Students argued that fee income
should be used to support public sites that were "general utilities"; to the
extent that sites were restricted to students in particular curricula, and
were directly tied to instructional objectives, the students felt funding
should be provided by tuition. By moving the fee into tuition, the campus
avoids this conflict and is able to fund both public and departmental sites.
In any case, this income is an important source of support for implementation projects. Such funding is inadequate, but it provides a way to meet
some of the important implementation needs.

Final Observations

The University of Illinois has a long history of using computing technologies to support instructional innovation, but over the past five years both
the number of faculty members involved and the range of disciplines
affected have increased dramatically. This growth has placed tremendous
strains on existing support structures and has caused a reassessment of
the institution's historic preference for decentralized computing decisions. In addition, efforts to stimulate faculty involvement in computer-
based instruction have led to some tentative conclusions about practices
that seem to work reasonably well — and some that appear dys-
functioned. A few of the more important conclusions are listed below.

1. There are always scarce resources and a long list of apparently
meritorious projects. In evaluating the potential for success, we have
found key indicators to be faculty enthusiasm, departmental support in
the form of money and release time, and information on what students will
see or do that will be different.

2. There is considerable demand for computer use in instruction, as
well as lofty statements about the impact of computing on the instructional process. There is a dearth of information on the impact of computing technologies on teaching and learning.

3. As a general rule, the use of computers does not reduce the cost of
instruction. The computer does not replace traditional forms of instruction; it simply makes it easier to cover some material and provides a way
to cover other material that was either difficult or impossible before.

4. There is minimal evidence that departments recognize the impor-

tance of course work development in salary, promotion, and tenure decisions. Nevertheless, faculty enthusiasm for developing computer-based instructional materials is thriving and could be stimulated significantly if salary and promotion criteria gave greater weight to the creative and scholarly aspects of using computers in instruction.

5. It is important to develop a policy on software ownership and royalties, both to remove impediments to faculty in software development and to eliminate the endless discussions that accompany settling disputes on an *ad hoc* basis.

6. It is relatively easy to find funding and support for small-scale development projects and pilot studies and equally easy to frustrate faculty members who have proven the value of a project but have no way to implement that project more broadly. A campus plan for innovative uses of technology must address the funding required both for development and for implementation projects.

7. Two major ways to fund computing needs are through corporate gifts and student ownership. Gifts typically include only the hardware and require start-up costs of about 70 percent of the value of the gift and recurring costs of 40 percent. Student ownership passes most of this burden to students and provides them with a much more effective service. It is important to establish an expectation for student ownership (currently 50 percent at Illinois) and a campus commitment for the remainder.

8. There is an increasing acceptance that a universally available network is an essential service, is a matter of equity and competitiveness, and should be provided as part of the normal working environment.

9. The distributed computing model works well in most instances, but it does allow major incompatible, or at least uncoordinated, service mechanisms to arise. This problem may become acute for units outside of the normal academic structure, where different goals and funding mechanisms pertain.

Notes

1. PLATO is a registered trademark of Control Data Corporation; the PLATO system is a development of the University of Illinois.
2. NovaNET is a development of the University of Illinois and is a registered Service Mark of University Communications, Inc.

The University of North Carolina at Chapel Hill: Instructional Computing

Margret Hazen
and
Anne Parker

The UNC-CH Environment

The tradition and character of the University of North Carolina at Chapel Hill have shaped the history and will continue to shape the future of instructional computing. UNC-CH is the nation's oldest state-supported university. It opened in 1795 with a curriculum in classics and, in addition to research activities, has placed a high priority on a liberal education throughout its history. This tradition continues today, with over one-half of its twenty-three thousand students enrolled in the College of Arts and Sciences.

UNC-CH is one of two research universities in a state-supported, sixteen-campus university system. Approximately 40 percent of its funding comes from state appropriations, 25 percent from grants and contracts, and the remainder from tuition, gifts, investments, and other income. Of the two academic divisions of the university, the Health Affairs division, consisting of the schools of Dentistry, Medicine, Nursing, Pharmacy, and Public Health, is responsible for a majority of the grant funding.

State support affects the way UNC-CH conducts its computing business, resulting, for example, in a strong multivendor environment. State support also means that UNC-CH will very likely never require undergraduate students to purchase a computer. A requirement of the university's charter is to provide education at the lowest possible cost, and computer purchase would be equivalent to paying an extra year of in-state tuition.

Unlike most other universities of its size and stature, UNC-CH has no school of engineering, which on other campuses often provides computing technology leadership. The absence of an engineering school has not, however, prevented UNC-CH from developing a strong tradition in academic computing. Instead, computing has grown in "nontraditional" disciplines such as English and classics, as well as in the sciences.

Like most large research universities, and consistent with national trends, UNC-CH is highly decentralized, particularly with regard to research and instructional decision making. Consequently, there are a number of centers and agencies that provide instructional computing support. The central computing agencies — Academic Computing Services, the Microcomputing Support Center, and Administrative Data Processing — cannot dictate hardware and software selections, since this would be inappropriate in a research environment. Computing support responsibilities, particularly for instruction, are therefore shared and coordinated among central agencies, divisions, departments, and schools. The popularity of computing is evidenced by the approximately four thousand university-owned microcomputers on campus. In spite of this popularity, the distribution is uneven, and many faculty do not have ready access to a computer.

An innovative research orientation, public funding, a focus on humanities, a strong tradition of quality undergraduate instruction, and a decentralized, entrepreneurial culture create an instructional computing environment that is exciting and dynamic. There are, however, difficulties. Decentralization, coupled with growth, has strained the informal communication systems on which faculty and administrators rely. Planning is difficult; there is often an unwillingness to adopt ideas from outside sources; and a wide variety of hardware and software is in use. Perhaps the most important obstacle to instructional development is the lack of institutional incentives for undertaking instructional activities. Research, not instruction, is weighed most heavily for faculty promotion and tenure at UNC-CH.

Instructional Computing at UNC-CII: Late 1960s through Early 1980s

Instructional computing has a long history at UNC-CH, first based on mainframe instructional computing in the late 1960s and evolving into microcomputer instructional computing in the early 1980s. The many differences between the characteristics of instructional applications on mainframes and of microcomputers are mostly due to the capabilities of each machine, including software written for it, and to the time and resources required to develop instructional applications on each.

Mainframe Use: Late 1960s, and 1970s

Beginning in the late 1960s and continuing into the next decade, mainframe academic computing (on the IBM 360/370/4300 series) has included a small, but significant and consistent, portion of instructional applications even beyond computer science courses. Several examples of instructional computing existed centrally, and one instance of instructional computing software development continues at a decentralized (Medical School) level.

Central academic computing resources provided instructional mainframe software ranging from business simulations (e.g., *General Purpose Simulation System V [GPSS]*, *Tempomatic*, the *Executive*, *Emory*, and *Pizaz Games*, *DYNAMO*, *Finansim*, *EXPERSIM*), and drill-and-practice modules to concordance analysis (e.g., the *Oxford Concordance Program*), and statistical analyses (e.g., *SAS*, *SPSS*, etc.), and geographical mapping (e.g., *SYMAP*, *CAMIVA*, *SURFACE*, and *SYMVU*). Among these, the application most solidly integrated into instruction has been statistical computing. In all instances, however, faculty members used preexisting or purchased instructional computing software — the development of instructional software was not supported by central academic computing.

At a decentralized level, the UNC-CH School of Medicine, at the initiative of William D. Huffines, M.D., formed an instructional software development team in the Medical Sciences Teaching Laboratories in the early 1970s. Authoring systems were evaluated and Coursewriter was chosen, in part because several existing medical applications could be imported from Ohio State and the University of Chicago. Using IBM's *Coursewriter* residing on UNC-CH's mainframe, several histology modules, still in use by students today, were developed during the late 1970s. Some of the *Coursewriter* materials are now being converted to a compatible mainframe and microcomputer authoring system, *Phoenix*, by Goal Systems. New courseware is currently being written to be used both jointly and separately by mainframe and microcomputer presentation systems. Since the *Phoenix* system has the capability, migration toward interactive videodisc courseware is anticipated.

Faculty involved in instructional computing projects during the early years were typically "computer literate." In most instances, faculty members initiated projects and served as their own support teams. Support from main academic computing agencies was generic — assisting with mainframe software installation, resolving basic problems, providing funding and terminals for student access to the mainframe instructional software, and occasionally providing instruction on the use of generic software in a faculty member's class. Only the School of Medicine provided programming support for the development of instructional software, both in the form of a full-time professional and medical student summer employees.

Most centralized mainframe instructional applications were either tools, simulations, or multiple-choice drill-and-practice modules — all text based. The CDC PLATO system with its graphics capabilities has not been available at UNC-CH except on a limited basis through a research project, the Carolina Population Center. Many instructional software applications also overlapped with faculty members' research activities. Instructional computing in the late 1960s and early 1970s can generally be characterized as oriented to mainframes and texts (versus graphics), with a heavy emphasis on tools and predeveloped software that in many instances overlapped with research functions. All of the software was centrally housed, and student access via terminals was offered in various locations on campus. Within schools and departments, a few were beginning to experiment with minicomputer hardware.

Microcomputer Use: Early 1980s

As the instructional potential of the microcomputer became apparent, a few faculty members independently experimented first with the TRS-80 microcomputer, then the Apple II and the IBM PC. Several projects undertaken at UNC-CH illustrate these experiments. One was a successful application of existing software, two were single development projects,

and was won a multiple project development effort. While the UNC CH
mainframe academic computing unit was wrestling with the issue of cost
recovery, many faculty took advantage of UNC Educational Computing
Services, which provided support services to all sixteen campuses in the
UNC system.

Psychology Apple II Lab

Professors David Eckerman, Mark Waller, and Richard King of the
psychology department have taught a course in laboratory and general
psychology every semester since 1981, primarily using several instructional software packages from CONDUIT. Approximately 250 students
per year conduct laboratory research using networked Apple II+ computers located in the psychology department. The lab was originally funded
with an NSF undergraduate instructional equipment grant, which the
university matched. Software was granted through IRSS (the Institute for
Research in Social Sciences). Departmental teaching assistants and one
full-time departmental staff member supported the project.

The course was designed to permit psychology majors the experience
of gathering and analyzing behavioral data to increase their understanding of the strengths and limits of behavioral science. Throughout the
semester, students participate in a dozen exercises and write six lab
reports. Some of these exercises employ CONDUIT software, for example:

- The method of constant stimuli used to assess the
  Muller-Lyer Illusion

- Feature detection (Neisser procedure)

- Retrieval from short-term memory (Sternberg procedure)

- Short-term forgetting (Brown-Peterson procedure)

- Comparison of recall, cued recall, and recognition

- Simulation of the effects of crowding

The first four exercises use the *Laboratory in Cognition and Perception*,
the fifth exercise uses the *Computer Lab in Memory and Cognition*, and
the last uses *FIRM: Florida InteRactive Modeler*.

School of Law Projects

In October 1982, Thomas Hazen, a law professor, applied for and received an Apple Foundation Grant to develop a corporate law simulation using Apple *SuperPilot*. The *Corporate Acquisitions* software simulates a planning session between a senior partner and an associate in a law firm representing a company faced with a hostile takeover. The simulated discussion involves applications of relevant state corporate law and federal securities law provisions. Having no prior computing experience, Professor Hazen developed the simulation with the help of a summer research assistant who was also a law school student.[1] The simulation was completed during the summer of 1983 and was used in the fall 1984 semester for the second-year basic corporations course. Students used the *Corporate Acquisitions* simulation on an optional basis on one Apple microcomputer.

In 1987 the *Corporate Acquisitions* simulation was converted to *Hyper-Card* on the Macintosh as part of a university Loaner Program and will be published by the Center for Computer Assisted Legal Instruction (CALI). The simulation is now used in the Law School computer lab, as is a second *HyperCard* program, *Small Issues Exemptions*, a rudimentary expert system module with hypertext features. This program will take a fact pattern presented by the student and respond with appropriate Securities Exchange Commission rules and regulations. With its hypertext explanatory features, students can learn the interrelationships of various exemptions from registration under the federal securities law.

Biology/Ecology Lab

In October 1981, a biology professor, Alan Stiven, with several colleagues received an NSF grant that purchased Apple IIs for their research. By 1982, these faculty were moving to IBM PC microcomputers, and the Apple IIs were allocated to a new general-purpose instructional computing lab, which also featured a networked IBM PC section. Since then, over 140 students per semester have taken the core ecology and population biology course and use several instructional software applications to learn population biology concepts and to model species population growth, competition, and trophic levels. These programs include the following:

- COMPress' *Biobits — Growth and Interactions, PopGen, Mendelian Genetics, Population Growth*

- Oakleaf Systems' *Population Genetics, Key Stat, Ecological Analysis Programs*

- Several faculty-developed software applications including Professor Stiven's *Population Ecology Tutorial*

School of Medicine Simulation Project

The Office of Research and Development for Education in the Health Professions (ORDEHP) was established in 1970 to improve instructional programs in the School of Medicine. In 1980, Professor Charles Friedman began his first development project on the Apple II. He developed an interactive testing program for pediatric residents with support from the American Board of Pediatrics and the Spencer Foundation. Professor Friedman also began a second application — a natural language interface clinical simulation codeveloped with Professor Douglas Drossman and a visiting scholar. This led to the development of a complete simulation authoring system, with workshops to help others learn to use the system. An authoring manual and templates were produced to facilitate the system's use. By 1984 the *Mrs. Jones* case was being used by medical students at UNC-CH, but by 1985 the hardware situation had changed significantly, and a decision was made to port the simulation to the Macintosh. In the interim, the Apple II system was used by Professor Friedman to pursue research interests relating to instructional computing. A study comparing simulation interfaces was completed, and conversion to the Macintosh environment continues today. The *Mrs. Jones* simulation has had part-time programming and instructional design support throughout its development.

Arts and Sciences UNC/IBM Courseware Development Project

In 1983 Professor William Graves, then the associate dean for General Education, negotiated a contract with the newly formed IBM group ACIS (Academic Information Services). His plan included ten faculty members — two in mathematics, three in English, two in classics, three in romance languages — who agreed to participate in the development of instructional software for large-enrollment, introductory undergraduate courses. The contract with IBM provided faculty members with hardware, hardware maintenance, software, and graphics development and programming support. Training, instructional design, and project management skills were contributed by the university. Consequently each faculty member had a complete set of support services available for the development effort.

An additional nineteen Arts and Sciences faculty projects were added on a proposal basis in February 1984, and a second contract arranged in May 1985 provided for ten new projects in the Schools of Business and Education. Some project faculty had familiarity with mainframe computing, and a few had microcomputing experience.

The Courseware Development Project organized towards its development commitments during the spring of 1984. Faculty members received training and were assigned student programmers. These student programmers were carefully selected, trained, and supervised by full-time project personnel. The project grew in scope and purposes, adding several annual seminars and workshops and doubling the number of projects, so that additional staff members were hired and trained. In addition to supporting instructional software development and offering national seminars, the personnel of the Courseware Development Project provided a general-purpose microcomputing support service for project faculty.

Several instructional software packages have been accepted for publication by Harcourt Brace Jovanovich, including the following:

- Professor John Semonche's simulations in American history: *1865 — Should the Southern States Be Readmitted to the Union?* and *June-December 1894 — What Action Should the President Take Concerning the Pullman Strike of 1894 and Its Aftermath?*

- Professor Frank Dominguez's first-year Spanish tutorial: *Spanish MicroTutor*

- Professor Joseph Lowman's clinical interview simulation: *SuperShrink I*

- Professors Cynthia Dessen and Maria Abricka's Latin etymology tutorial: *LexiTect*

- Professors Joseph Wittig, Erica Lindemann, and Laurence Avery's pre-writing tool: *The Writing Tutor*

- Professor Richard Rust's literary terminology tutorial: *LitTerms*

- Professor Andrew Scott's third world political simulation: *Castellon*

- Professor Ladnor Geissinger's mathematical tool: *Exploring Small Groups*

- Professor William H. Graves' introductory mathematics modules: *MathPac*

- Professor Clare Tufts' introductory French modules: *Micro French*

- Professor Mark Applebaum's set of statistical tools: *Statistician's Toolbox*

Another two (*Stage Lighting* by Professor R. Graves and *Glossa* by Professor Jay Bolter) have been placed for distribution with WiscWare, a Calculus tutorial (*CalcLab* by Professor Karl Petersen) is to be distributed by Harper and Row, and a chemistry tutorial (*Spectroscopic Analysis* by Professor Thomas Sorrell) has been placed with University Science Books. Three projects received NCRIPTAL software awards: Professor Geissinger's *Exploring Small Groups*, Professor Semonche's third simulation, *1912 — Can You Get Your State To Approve a Woman's Suffrage Amendment?* and Professor Dominguez' *Spanish MicroTutor*. These three instructional software programs are described in further detail below.

American History: Simulations. Professor Jack Semonche, of the history department, developed, with Jordan M. Smith, three simulations. Students taking American history supplement their classroom time with simulations that they access from a network menu in a campus lab.

The first simulation, *1865 — Should the Southern States Be Readmitted to the Union?* places students in the role of a U.S. senator in December 1865 and asks them to interact with six historical senators to determine whether to admit representatives of the former Confederate states to the legislative body. Next, students encounter *June-December 1894 — What Action Should the President Take Concerning the Pullman Strike of 1894 and Its Aftermath?* in which they play the role of the president of the United States, who confronts the Pullman Strike of 1894 and who then seeks to devise a federal policy on labor-management relations for enactment by the Congress. Finally, a third simulation, *1912 — Can You Get Your State To Approve a Woman's Suffrage Amendment?* asks the student to play the role of a politically active citizen trying to enact, through the initiative procedure, a state constitutional amendment extending the franchise to women in 1912.[2]

All three simulations were programmed in Pascal with full support from the Courseware Development Project: hardware, software, student programmers, programmer analyst, instructional designer, and graphics artist over a period of five years. The first two simulations have been published by Harcourt Brace Jovanovich, and the third is being distributed by the author.

Mathematics: Exploring Small Groups. Professor Ladnor Geissinger of the mathematics department developed *Exploring Small Groups*, a program that helps faculty teach, and students learn, about properties of small groups and other binary operations. It is used by Professor Geissinger in his elements of modern algebra class and is available for student use on a campus lab network. *Exploring Small Groups* was programmed in BASIC with Courseware Development Project support: hardware, software, student programmers, and instructional designers over a period of three years.

Spanish: MicroTutor. Frank Dominguez, a professor of romance languages, developed a Spanish tutorial for beginning Spanish students that is used at UNC-CH for Spanish 1, 2, and 3. Students access these tutorials primarily in the Foreign Language Laboratory. Professor Dominguez and other instructors use these tutorials to permit students to learn grammar using the software and thereby to increase the amount of classroom time available to the instructor for other activities like oral performance skills. Each lesson consists of four main units: a pre-test, a tutorial, tutorial exercises with feedback, and a post-test. *Spanish MicroTutor* was programmed in Pascal, Assembler, and *PC PILOT* with Courseware Development Project support: hardware, software, student programmers, and instructional designers over a period of five years. *Spanish MicroTutor* was also by funded by the U.S. Department of Education and the Lindau Foundation.[3]

Before participating in the Courseware Development Project, most project faculty members were not familiar with the hardware — the IBM PC — that was provided for them. It was difficult to understand the potential of a new tool without familiarity, and most faculty members therefore followed a sequence of first familiarizing themselves with the microcomputer's word-processing capabilities before attempting to develop an instructional application. After becoming aware of the new capabilities microcomputers offered, most faculty members focused specifically on aspects of their teaching experience that they thought could be improved using this new tool. Most faculty members received significant project support in the way of training, administration, programming, extensive student programming supervision, graphics design, and instructional design. Many faculty members have expressed that they felt they could not have produced their software without such support.

The software produced by the Courseware Development Project introduced some innovations to instructional computing: color, animation, and graphics techniques were employed, as well as a wide range of well-developed instructional strategies: drill and practice, simulation, tutorials, and problem-solving tools. One of the strengths of this university — the humanities faculty — was a major contributor to instructional computing efforts. These development projects contributed significantly to the increased use of instructional computing software at UNC-CH, but without external support, development was not an option for other, non-project, faculty members.

Summary

Two patterns emerge out of the twenty years of mainframe and early microcomputer instructional computing. First, instructional software development was largely supported by external funding, with instructional software access largely supported by internal resources. Second, the time it takes to develop instructional software plus the time it takes an instructor to integrate it into the curriculum is typically a greater amount of time than the university's incentive structure, with its emphasis on research, permits. It is understandable, then, that software addressing both a faculty member's research and instructional goals (as does statistical computing, for example) was more frequently used on a continuing and broad basis. However, in spite of problems with institutional incentives and the need to acquire external funding, each new hardware advance has encouraged additional faculty members to attempt to use the technology to creatively address teaching needs. The number of faculty members using instructional computing is increasing with hardware and software improvements and has more than tripled across the mainframe to microcomputer transitions.

Responses to the Growth of Microcomputing in the Early 1980s

The widely publicized instructional computing events of the early 1980s increased campuswide awareness of computing and its potential application as an instructional and research tool. A great flurry of activity occurred, with microcomputing becoming a priority focus of academic life.

The proliferation of microcomputers, along with the increasing involvement of computing in instruction, raised a number of issues: Who would provide the needed public labs and classroom equipment? Who would help faculty, administrators, and students with computing problems? Who would train the uninitiated. In other words, the expectations of the early 1980s led to a widespread recognition of both access and support needs, with support incurring expenses far greater than the cost of the original hardware. The university responded to these needs by creating a new organization, the Microcomputing Support Center, and by adapting an existing unit, the Media Center, which became the Center for Teaching and Learning and the Classroom Technologies Service Center.

The Courseware Development Project as a Support Model

The UNC/IBM Courseware Development Project not only was an example of development and use of instructional computing, but also provided an early microcosmic example of how faculty members adapted to microcomputers; concurrently, it provided a model for the services required to support the use of microcomputers by faculty.

The Courseware Development Project faculty, like faculty elsewhere, focused first on the microcomputer's ability to facilitate the writing process with word-processing software, rather than its ability to aid the teaching process with instructional computing software. This was found to be a necessary step to familiarize faculty, even those familiar with mainframe computing, with the potential of such microcomputer features as color display and windows. Instructional software development is not and cannot be expected to be an instructor's first computing task.

The Courseware Development Project provided many support services to faculty members: training in word-processing and authoring software, repair services, phone-in or walk-in help with the hardware and software, a student lab, and projection equipment for software presentations. These support services were provided first to the project faculty and subsequently became a model of services that could become available to others. In contrast, the academic computing center, with a largely receipts-supported budget, did not, for the most part, offer microcomputing services. The necessity of basic support did not, however, escape the attention of those non-project faculty members who were struggling to adopt the new technology without the benefit of these services. In August 1985, in recognition of that need, Professor and Associate Provost John H. Harrison IV formed the Microcomputing Support Center to address campuswide needs for basic microcomputing support services.

Institutional Responses: Access, Incentives, Information

As external support for instructional software development projects declined locally (as well as nationally), the institutional strategy for instructional computing had to shift. High-cost, labor-intensive services were replaced by low-cost services that served larger numbers of faculty, staff, and students and by services that encouraged self-sufficiency. For example, instead of custom programming, attempts were made to locate and acquire appropriate software tools. Institutional instructional computing support began to focus on three primary areas: access to technology in the student labs and in the classrooms, improving local and institutional incentives, and information gathering and dissemination.

Access to Technology

Access to technology for instructional purposes requires two different locations, one in a computer lab for students using software to master content materials and another in the classroom for instructors teaching with technology.

At UNC-CH, public microcomputer laboratories began with one established by the UNC/IBM Courseware Development Project in 1984. It was clear that students would need access to personal computers to use whatever software was developed by the project. With the formation of the Microcomputing Support Center, the number of laboratories grew rapidly, to ten campuswide microcomputer labs and fourteen small residence hall clusters. All are open to the university community but are primarily used by students. In addition to these public facilities, a number of departments and schools now operate laboratories for the exclusive use of their undergraduate majors and graduate students.

The strategy used to establish and manage these labs is one of collaboration. The Microcomputing Support Center provides basic services, and the collaborating department provides content-specific support. The degree of collaboration and the specific division of responsibilities (student wages, maintenance, supplies, management, etc.) vary for each situation. The Microcomputing Support Center supplies a basic collection of software including word-processing, operating system, and utility software. Academic departments provide software used for instructional purposes.

All the microcomputer laboratories except for residence hall clusters are staffed by student assistants with at least sufficient knowledge to begin and end each of the software packages available in the lab. Faculty members provide additional support in the form of a teaching assistant in the lab for a few hours a week if the complexity of instructional software or the assignments warrants it.

Students are free to use the laboratories even when not assigned to do so by a class. Usage has grown tremendously — from seven thousand individual sign-ins in the fall of 1985 to sixty-eight thousand sign-ins in the fall of 1988. The number of computers has grown in that time from 40 IBM, Zenith, and Macintosh personal computers to 160. While usage has grown by a factor of ten, the number of computers available for student access has grown by a factor of only four — growth in usage is occurring at a faster pace than access can be provided.

The installation of networks in each MS-DOS computer lab during 1986 and 1987 greatly improved service and reduced the costs of operating the labs. Service improvements occurred by changing the nature of the lab assistant's job from software distributor to user assistant and by providing faster and simpler access to software via a menu that accesses a lab file server. (A "Run Your Own Software" menu option accommodates students who bring their own software to the lab.) Networked labs are preferred not only by the students but also by faculty members and lab assistants.

Networks have also resulted in a net cost reduction. Although additional technical network management support is necessary for installation and troubleshooting, this increased cost is more than offset by reductions

In repair and operational labor costs. A lab assistant can manage a lab of twenty machines (versus approximately ten machines) if that lab assistant does not have to check out software; therefore larger labs can be operated with the same number of lab assistants. There are no diskettes to wear out — a very common occurrence even for 3.5-inch diskettes — or to be overwritten. Even greater savings occur in maintenance costs. Diskette drive replacement has been cut almost in half, in spite of aging equipment and higher levels of use.

A third unanticipated benefit of networking has occurred in the lab where much of the undergraduate instructional software from the UNC/IBM Courseware Development Project is located. Students can often be found browsing through the menus, trying different instructional software packages when time permits. Several packages engage students' interest at length, among them the history simulations, the literary terminology tutorial, the etymology tutorial, the Spanish tutorials, and the mathematical tools.

The operation of these laboratories as collaborative ventures has worked well. Scarce resources have been pooled to meet common objectives while encouraging individual lab specializations. One indication of success is the request to operate two laboratories that were previously private — with the departments continuing to shoulder many of the operating costs.

As student assignments requiring the use of microcomputers increased, so did faculty interest in being able to present the same software to students in the classroom. The result was a master classroom concept that calls for a wide array of technology in classrooms of varying sizes, distributed geographically. UNC-CH now has eight "master classrooms" equipped by the Classroom Technologies Service Center with audio-visual equipment, videotape players, Macintosh and IBM compatible computers, and videobeam projectors to display computer images on a large screen. Each classroom is connected to the campus broadband cable so that it is capable of sending and receiving video and data transmissions from remote sites. New instructional opportunities are now available — from classroom simulations managed by the computer, to improved graphics displays with three-dimensional rotation capabilities, to interactive composition instruction. Some examples of these applications are described below.

Speech Communication: Election Simulation. Professor Craig Smith uses a master classroom to teach a course on political persuasion. Professor Smith's class runs a simulated presidential election on the computer in the classroom using the software package called *Election '88*. Students act as campaign managers, making choices such as where and how to target their message and how to prepare a political advertisement. Having the master classroom available makes it possible to combine theoretical material and classroom applications. Professor Smith found that students move more quickly to the theoretical when they have extensive practical experience.

Chemistry: Presentation with HyperCard. Professor and Associate Provost John Harrison IV teaches a graduate chemistry class using molecular modeling software in a master classroom. The software runs on both a remote computer accessed via the campus broadband network and the computer in the classroom to provide full-color rotations of protein molecules. Students can now visualize important theoretical concepts in the classroom. Because material can be presented more rapidly and accurately than by drawing on the blackboard, Professor Harrison discovered it is easy to include too much material in a single lecture.

English: Presentation of Composition Concepts. For several semesters, Professors Richard Rust and James Thompson have taught English composition using a computer in a master classroom. Professor Rust found that projecting a computer screen in the classroom provided a "highly productive way to use classroom time in teaching students various strategies and styles possible in writing and ways to revise their work successfully."[4] Using a projection unit, a computer, and word-processing software, they discovered that students were engaged by the editing process and were able to focus on the text rather the author. Together, the class and instructor identified paragraph construction strengths and problems. Professor Rust found that the ability to copy text fragments quickly and use a split screen with before-and-after views allowed the class to make immediate comparisons of alternative structures. The result was an emphasis on the revision process rather than on original faults. Students also used the microcomputer laboratories to prepare their documents, submitted on diskettes.

Economics: Presentation of Modeling. Professor Michael Salemi uses a master classroom to teach advanced topics in macroeconomics. Students are assigned simulation problems using the *Fair Model*, an educational version of a commercial economic modeling software program. Student assignments begin with structured exercises, such as determining the effects of raising taxes on consumption. Later group assignments include more unstructured applications, such as developing strategies for lowering the federal deficit while minimizing social impact. In class, Professor Salemi runs the same software to discuss issues raised by student exercises and to quickly test conjectures raised in class discussions. Professor Salemi has used the software for four years, increasing his use of the model each year. Recently, at his request, the Center for Teaching and Learning provided him the capability of displaying the model's results graphically on the classroom projector. The addition of graphics makes the educational content much more readily accessible to students by giving students a clearer impression of the effects of economic intervention.

These examples demonstrate that with innovative faculty leadership, access to technology, and coordinated support services, students in a variety of disciplines can benefit from the use of technology in the classroom. The success of these and other innovative faculty members has had a cascade effect, with demand outstripping the availability of master classrooms.

Improve Local and Institutional Incentives

Two new local incentive programs were begun at UNC-CH to stimulate and encourage continuing interest and efforts: an Instructional Loaner Program and a Software Award Program. Both programs are an attempt to minimize support personnel requirements while simultaneously maximizing support for innovative faculty members. In neither case is the development of instructional software centrally supported beyond hardware and software awards.

The Instructional Loaner Program. The Instructional Loaner Program is a program currently operated in conjunction with the College of Arts and Sciences, with hopes of expansion in the future. A request for proposals is sent to all faculty members in the College of Arts and Sciences indicating what hardware and software is available for the program and the conditions for applying to the program. Proposals are evaluated and approved by a committee of faculty and instructional support staff. The successful faculty members receive the hardware and software on an extended loan basis (up to two years). On completion of the tasks specified in the proposal, and after an evaluation by the committee, the college continues the program by presenting the hardware and software to the proposal faculty members on a permanent basis and purchasing equipment for another cycle of proposals.

The Instructional Loaner Program does not provide programmer or teaching assistant support. Instead, development is encouraged using only authoring tools and, perhaps, departmental support in the form of graduate student help. After initial hardware installation, and training when necessary, design and evaluation consulting is provided.

The Instructional Loaner Program has had eleven formal and informal participants since 1987. There have been some early outcomes in several disciplines. For example, one faculty member in Greek history, and another in classics, have had the opportunity to prepare class handouts using the Macintosh Greek fonts and are currently working on *HyperCard* applications. One European history professor has been able to generate graphical illustrations of historical trends that were presented only in table data formats in the past. Music students can now use musical notation software for theory and composition classes. Chemistry students have access to molecular modeling software for their courses. A speech communication professor demonstrates the complexities of election campaigning via a campaign simulation used in the classroom. Two *Hyper-Card* stacks have been developed and used by a Law School professor in the corporate acquisitions and securities laws areas; another stack was developed for introductory chemistry courses, and another is under development in geology. An English professor is developing quiz modules using *ProPi*, and a psychology professor is evaluating Macintosh software for laboratory use.

The Software Award Program. The Software Award Program supplies faculty members with tools that hold potential for instructional purposes. *MORE* as an outlining and presentation tool was awarded in November 1987 and was followed by awards of *WordCruncher*, a concordance program; *Stella*, a dynamic and visual modeling tool; and more recently, three presentation software tools: *PowerPoint, Cricket Presents*, and *MORE II*. The first software award led to a discussion of the utility of *MORE* as both an outlining tool and as a presentation tool and thereby introduced these tools to other members of the campus. *WordCruncher* was well received when an English professor, Richard Rust, introduced this research tool to graduate students. His students immediately found this tool to be of valuable assistance in literary research and analysis. After seeing Rust's demonstrations, several librarians also took an interest in the long-range possibilities of *WordCruncher* as a library-based research tool. *Stella* is being used by several faculty members this semester to communicate concepts that would otherwise have taken two to three times as long. As a modeling tool applicable for research and instruction, it has proven useful in modeling new product adoption in the School of Business's marketing courses, in modeling geologic concepts in the geology department's courses, and in modeling environmental problems in the environmental sciences and engineering department.

Software for these awards is chosen on a basis of generic utility to a number of faculty members across several disciplines, with instructional but also potential research possibilities. Once a product is identified, the award offering is announced in campus computing newsletters and in the *Instructional Computing Newsletter.* Applicants describe how and when they plan to use the software and are expected to present or report on their experiences.

Both the Instructional Loaner Program and the Software Award Program offer tools to faculty members for instructional software use or development. Development, however, is encouraged only with high-level tools like authoring tools, rather than with programming tools. From this perspective, it has become important to permit faculty members to develop their own skills — to become self-sufficient — because they will need not only to use the developed software but also to modify it over time. Additionally, a long timeline for outcomes is acceptable, particularly since research deadlines and research leaves often intervene.

Information Dissemination

Information dissemination is a priority for all areas of academic computing mainly because of the size of the UNC-CH faculty (2,000), the complexity of distributed support, and the almost complete adoption of the microcomputer for word-processing functions by faculty and students (29,000). Applying available resources to a given function in a highly decentralized environment requires collecting information from a variety of sources and distributing it broadly. Information about instructional computing, like information about computing in general, can be found in two campus newsletters sent to all faculty, staff, and graduate students: the *Carolina Computing,* published once a year, and the *UNC-CH Newsbrief,* published weekly. Instructional computing information originates, however, in a more specialized newsletter, the *Instructional Computing Newsletter,* which is sent only to interested faculty and staff and contains greater detail than the other newsletters permit.

The *Newsletter,* edited and published by Margret Hazen, presents faculty and administrators with information on recently published instructional computing applications and award opportunities. It also features articles on examples of faculty use of instructional software; funding opportunities; information about conferences, journals, and books on instructional computing; design and evaluation information (emerging technologies such as desktop graphics, CD, and expert systems); information about disciplinary resource specialists; and demonstrations and classes related to instructional computing opportunities.

Summary

Institutional responses to the overwhelming support issues brought on by the widespread adoption of the microcomputer for word processing and other functions included the establishment of a Microcomputing Support Center. The sheer numbers of users requiring access and support created a strong, high-priority requirement for basic training, access to microcomputers, and user support services that could meet the combined needs of researchers, instructors, and administrators.

Supporting the development of instructional software from a centralized perspective has not been feasible. In spite of the innovative and extensive use of student programmers, the full costs of development are too high. Courseware Development Project support for one year (serving twenty to thirty faculty members) costs approximately as much as a small Microcomputing Support Center serving potentially the whole university community.

New Directions:
Interactive Information Technologies in the Late 1980s

There have been two global forces acting on instructional computing and its place in the organization: (1) a general tendency toward decentralization and specialization, and (2) an emerging evolution of instructional computing into a more diversified and larger perspective   instructional technology and, ever more globally, information technology.

Decentralization and specialization as trends have been increasing in many large public institutions for over fifteen years. In libraries, this is evidenced by the existence of departmental, school, and graduate libraries. Similarly, in computing, many departments have shifted a large portion of their efforts from central facilities to local or specialized facilities. Learning resource and instructional support centers also exist in central and decentralized locations.

Instructional technology is a concept that embodies all the diverse applications of the computer and other nonprint technologies for instructional purposes. Usually, information technology refers to information stored in nonprint, or analog and digital, format; and such information can consequently be used interactively for instruction. This concept has become more appealing as advances in communication technologies have extended the possibilities of interconnecting otherwise disparate units and functions.

At UNC-CH, libraries are providing access to CD/ROM discs, videodiscs, and software, and some have computer labs. Media Centers have evolved into Classroom Technologies Service Centers for classroom delivery of computing and other media. The Center for Teaching and Learning produces materials using microcomputers as well as other media; and the Microcomputing Support Center provides lab access for students. Functions increasingly overlap as computing technologies are adopted by various service organizations. From the faculty and student perspective, there is no one service that provides all their computing needs.

Communications technologies hold the potential to improve access to other technologies across institutional units and locations. Digital text, data, and graphics are in theory accessible from any terminal location on campus. Similarly, instructional software located on one hard-disk file server could be accessible elsewhere. In the future, even motion video (whether analog or digital) will be transmitted across networks. Successfully realizing the potential of these information technologies argues for larger numbers of interdepartmental collaborative efforts.

Networking and Interactive Information Technologies

If a decentralized, multimedia environment is to provide maximum instructional benefit, without costly redundancy, then an effective communications network is important. Communication needs include physical connectivity and strategic, service-oriented initiatives. There are two networking initiatives taking place at UNC-CH, one in computing services and the other in video services. In time, even this distinction will disappear. At present, UNC-CH has a campus broadband cable that connects a growing number of microcomputing laboratories, office buildings, and classrooms.

For instructional computing, the campus backbone allows terminal emulation with log-in not only to campus mainframes and libraries from the master classrooms but also, through shared high-speed gateways (asynchronous, 3270, and TCP/IP), to other computers in the state and country. In addition to terminal emulation, the network's objectives include allowing students and faculty the mobility to use shared information (software and data) from many other locations while retaining an individual owner's control of access rights and management. A related objective is to provide instructors with classroom access to exactly the same software, data, and menus that students will use in the laboratory, without having to maintain duplicate copies in the classroom. From a faculty and student perspective, using a network service is as simple as choosing a menu option to use a software package or request a connection to a mainframe computer. For personal computer service, a file server directory in a remote location appears to the local user as another disk drive. For Macintosh users, it's an icon, for MS-DOS users who bypass the menus, it's an "F:" drive.

These remote disk services provide transparent connectivity. The connections between lab networks, department networks, and classrooms are implemented with Novell network software using an Allen-Bradley token bus network on the campus broadband cable. For about six hundred dollars per network connection, this Allen-Bradley channel provides the speed necessary for remote disk access (2.5 Mbps, roughly ten times that of a floppy disk). For remote program and file-sharing services, this is a cost-effective solution today, but the speed is probably insufficient for future multimedia applications. Currently, video communications are provided by different channels on the campus broadband cable and are beginning to be used to deliver videotape materials from the library's nonprint collection directly to the classroom.

Collaboration and Interactive Information Technologies

As the use of computing increased, as networking opportunities arose, and as hardware and software improvements continued, faculty members began to evolve increasingly diverse research and instructional computing applications. The use of the microcomputer for instructional purposes took on a much more diverse nature. Faculty, staff, and students adapted the new technologies — for example, laptop computers, on-line searching, digitization of images, networked labs, new and powerful modeling tools, and videodisc medical and legal simulations — to a wide range of academic needs. As faculty usage patterns diversified, libraries, learning resource centers, and instructional support centers also became involved in supporting this diversity. Instructional computing, now encompassing videodisc (analog) as well as digital functions and database searching, could now be more accurately referred to as instructional technologies.

Some examples of this diversity of instructional computing applications can be illustrated by the School of Journalism's Macintosh lab for copy editing, which uses word-processing and networking software; the School of Medicine's digitizing cellular images for tutorials used in a networked lab; the School of Medicine's knowledge management system approach combining simulations, patient databases, and on-line searching and reference management; the School of Pharmacy and the Department of Chemistry's use of molecular modeling tools for undergraduate chemistry courses; the Law School Library's use of *CALI* software and trial advocacy videodiscs; and the psychology department's use of *HyperCard* and *DataDesk* to communicate statistical concepts in the classroom. A new emphasis on collaboration to accomplish diverse support functions is illustrated by the Medical School's TEAM project.

School of Journalism's Macintosh Lab for Copy Editing

Professor Bill Cloud, of the School of Journalism, uses a lab with twenty-one networked Macintosh microcomputers to teach advanced editing. Students use Microsoft *Word* to edit newspaper copy in class under simulated deadline conditions. Aside from classroom exercises, these students have also edited stories for the two fall issues of the *UNC Journalist.*

For classroom exercises, the networked system enables students to retrieve a story from the central network file server, but because that file is locked, they cannot write to the server and destroy the original story.

Instead, students save the story to be edited under their own file names on their own disks. After editing, students present printed copies of their work for grading; they also copy their work into a "drop box" folder on the centralized file server so that Professor Cloud can use the students' work for illustrative and comparative purposes in future classes. Another desirable feature of networking is the ability to have a centrally located glossary of preformatted headline sizes. A glossary item labeled "2-36," for example, contains the formatting for 2-column 36-point headlines. Similarly, dictionary and help files are maintained centrally on the file server not only to save space on student diskettes but also to facilitate modifications when they are required.

Medical Technology Classes with Graphics Workstations on a Local Area Network

Professor Helen Cronenberger, in the Department of Medical Allied Health Professions at the UNC-CH School of Medicine, teaches immunology, medical technology, and laboratory computer courses using interactive graphics workstations. She has received funds from UNC-CH and the Culpepper Foundation to develop a new computer technology for producing interactive instructional materials that incorporate slide-quality graphics of microscopic images. With the help of Professor Henry Hsiao, Professor Cronenberger has evolved the instructional computing project into a local area network Learning Center.

A diskette is used to initiate a lesson on the student workstation. Several lessons (each on a separate disk) have been developed, including *Cells Involved in the Immunological Response, Stimulation of T Cells, Stimulation of B Cells*, and *Auto-Immune Diseases*. On completion of the lesson, software automatically logs the student off the network.

The student workstation consists of a dual floppy, 640Kb PC microcomputer with a CGA/PGA graphics card, local area network interface card, and a multisync monitor. Development stations and the development process (digitizing, editing, and authoring) are relatively more complex. For image quality equivalent to or better than photographic slides in terms of color and resolution, images must be digitized from a video camera. The digitization station consists of a 30 Mb, 640Kb IBM-AT or compatible microcomputer, a digitizer card, a 650 horizontal line video camera, a high-resolution digital RGB monitor, a second CGA monitor, and a graphics tablet or mouse.

Once digitized, the image can be edited for instruction. The camera is no longer needed, but a Bernoulli box is useful for storing images that require from 10Kb each to 250Kb each. *PC PILOT* and, later, the *ProPi* authoring system were used to produce interactive tutorial lessons that incorporate the digitized and edited images.

Digitizing microscopic images has provided Professor Cronenberger with the capability of using high-quality microscopic images for presentation and interactive learning opportunities. Future directions and opportunities include laboratory simulations and case history simulations in immunology, hematology, and pathoimmunology.

School of Medicine's Knowledge Management System

Dr. R. G. Berger, a professor in clinical rheumatology, provides a "tool kit" contained on a Zenith portable laptop computer with an internal modem to each fourth-year student rotating on the clinical rheumatology elective. The tool kit developed by Dr. Berger has six integrated components:

- Rheumatology Knowledge Base

- Case Simulations

- Patient Database

- Clinical Communications Facility

- Medline Searching

- Reference Management

Students are required to update the patient database and query the knowledge base with new patients they work up, and they will also be required to work through case simulations. Other facilities of the system are optional.

Molecular Modeling for Undergraduates

Professor J. Phillip Bowen teaches medicinal chemistry in the Medicinal Chemistry and Natural Products Division of the School of Pharmacy at UNC-CH. He uses *Alchemy 2.0* from Tripos Associates for demonstrating molecular modeling concepts in the classroom as well as for assigning homework to be completed in the pharmacy microcomputer lab. As of the spring semester of 1989, Professor Don Jicha is also using *Alchemy* with quantitative chemistry undergraduates.

Molecular modeling is a term used to describe the generation, manipulation, and representation of three-dimensional molecular structures with the aid of computers and color graphics. *Alchemy* is a molecular modeling software program currently available for the IBM PC, AT, XT, PS/2, or compatible requiring an EGA monitor with 256Kb, 512Kb memory, a hard disk drive, and a mouse. It permits modelers to

- construct three-dimensional molecules directly by hooking molecular fragments together;

- obtain reasonable molecular conformations with an energy minimization procedure using analytical derivatives;

- fit a series of molecules to one another with a least-squares fitting routine, then compare molecular geometries;

- generate space-filling representations, with *Alchemy's* range of coloring options;

- determine the presence of and display chiral centers (and assign their absolute configuration) for a given molecule;

- modify bond lengths, bond angles, and dihedral angles interactively;

- measure inter- and intramolecular distances;

- move one molecule relative to another to manually dock or fit molecules; and

- execute a user-written program by selecting an *Alchemy* menu item and return to *Alchemy* when finished.

As a result of the availability of this tool, Professor Bowen believes students can visualize molecules far more successfully than they could by looking at textbook graphic illustrations, and he can now discuss in class how pharmaceutical companies carry out drug design. *Alchemy's* 3-D molecular rotation capabilities permit an instructor to illustrate more specifically the differences between two very similar chemical structures.

Assignments permit students to retrieve pre-entered molecular structures, like propranolol and atenolol, in order to view them; to measure distances between the ether oxygen and nitrogen, HO-C bond lengths, and N-C bond lengths; and to record the number of chiral atoms and their R/S configuration. Students also use the program to calculate the RMS fit value for the hydroxyl oxygen, carbon, and nitrogen atoms of pindolol and atenolol.

The Law School's CALI Library

The UNC-CH Law School Library has purchased site-licensed *Computer Assisted Legal Instruction (CALI)* exercises for the IBM PC or compatibles. These exercises have been added to the network menu in the Law School's PC computer lab and are available for university use. Forty-two exercises are available on the network offering a review of law in various substantive areas (e.g., evidence, torts, civil procedure). The programs involve a series of fact situations and questions on those facts. Some, such as evidence and trial advocacy, involve trial transcripts to which students must make objections. The trial advocacy course also uses several videodiscs that offer students practice in courtroom procedures.

The time of completion for each program varies, but averages two hours. Some of the programs require advance reading and preparation from manuals. Although the manuals cannot circulate outside the Law Library, they can be checked out in the library for advance reading or workstation use. *CALI* exercises are available on diskette and can be copied, with the help of a lab assistant, onto an individual's diskette. *CALI* exercises are distributed by the Center for Computer Assisted Legal Instruction, founded jointly by the University of Minnesota Law School and the Harvard Law School in 1982.

Statistics with *HyperCard* and *DataDesk*

Professor Forrest Young, Department of Psychology at UNC-CH, teaches introduction to psychological statistics. He uses *HyperCard* as a presentation tool to prepare and present lecture materials. He has found it is easier to prepare and project *HyperCard* images than to use overhead transparencies. In addition, with *HyperCard*, screens are easily modified whether in class or out of class, and retrieving screens from past lectures is possible in the classroom as students ask review questions. Students are also provided with printed copies of the *HyperCard* screens shown in the classroom.

Professor Young also uses *DataDesk*, a statistical data-handling system, to demonstrate concepts he teaches. Data sets provided by *DataDesk* can be used for hypothesis testing, but they can also be used to depict — graphically — relationships among variables. *DataDesk* can produce charts, plots, graphs, and even three-dimensional rotation to illustrate relationships between two or more variables. This permits a far more intuitive and visual approach to the teaching of statistical concepts than has been possible in the past. Students in the course purchase a student version of *DataDesk* from Kinko's Academic Courseware Exchange for use in a campus lab. Though *DataDesk* is limited in its breadth of statistical procedures, it is an ideal tool for teaching basic statistics and graphical exploratory data analysis. *DataDesk* was written by Professor Paul Velleman of Cornell, following the tradition set almost twenty years ago by John Tukey, a Princeton statistics professor.

The diversity of the six applications described above suggests the potentially high cost and difficulty of supporting all the new forms of information technology. The required technical support would include specialized expertise in networking various brands of microcomputers, in database and database searching, in digitization and videodiscs, in software tools, and in instructional computing. The breadth of technologies creates new support problems and argues for reanalyzing the nature of centralized and decentralized support. One approach, taken by the Medical School's Task Force, is to encourage collaboration among departments.

School of Medicine's Task Force

The Task Force for Educational Applications in Medicine (TEAM) was established with support from the dean of the School of Medicine in February 1988. TEAM coordinates efforts to expand the use of information technology within existing courses in all years of the medical curriculum. TEAM supports faculty with incentives, hardware provisions, technical support, and an organizational structure to integrate and coordinate efforts currently scattered throughout the School of Medicine. TEAM holds monthly meetings with presentations on information technology, offers a public seminar series with speakers from other medical institutions, and sponsors a mini–Grant Program. The following are examples of medical applications of information technology that TEAM hopes to encourage:

- Computer-driven simulations

- Computer-aided decision-making tools

- Expert systems

- Computer-aided instruction programs

- Bibliographic and full-text databases of literature to support teaching and learning

- Word-processing and file-transfer systems to support faculty and student writing

- Electronic mail capabilities to support faculty-to-faculty, faculty-to-student, and student-to-student communications

- Programs to manage the administrative aspects of the curriculum

- Databases containing information in a particular field or discipline

Patterns Observed and Lessons Learned over the Last Twenty Years

Looking at UNC-CH's instructional computing history, we see several patterns — patterns related to the university's culture and environment, to the historical patterns in the development and use of instructional computing, and to evolving trends. It is becoming increasingly clear that instructional computing cannot be logically separated from the larger umbrella of information technologies and that another wave of innovations in telecommunications is about to be incorporated into the institutional structure, facilitating the concept of collaboration and thereby encouraging planning in the broader area of information technologies. A first step in this direction was taken very recently by Professor and Associate Provost John H. Harrison IV with the establishment of a new Office of Data and Video Communications. This office consolidates many of the communications support activities that were previously scattered among many organizations. In the few months this organization has existed, it is clear that network planning and implementation is proceeding more rapidly and in a much more coordinated fashion than was previously possible.

Environmental Patterns

Certain patterns are endemic to large public institutions of higher education focusing on the research mission. These patterns have relevance to the time, funds, and efforts spent on instructional and computing projects and are therefore listed below.

The current priority of the research mission. UNC-CH is actively focusing on its research mission, creating an environment in which research projects or research grants have an implicit priority over other professional activities — for example, over instruction. How far the pendulum will swing in this direction is difficult to predict. Tenure and promotion criteria are only beginning to address the extraordinary time, effort, and expertise required to improve instruction via technology. Faculty members at UNC-CH, as elsewhere, find themselves giving first priority to research activities, particularly if they are not tenured.[5] A UNC-CH survey of seven departments indicates that about 10 percent of the faculty are interested in instructional computing and that even fewer are taking advantage of instructional computing technologies. Projects that address both research and instruction are likely to have higher faculty priority than those that address only instruction. Statistical computing is an example of the utility of such an overlap.

Faculty leadership and academic computing center budgets. When technology is used by faculty, it addresses the instructional needs of faculty members and is therefore faculty initiated and faculty led. Providing services for faculty in these instructional endeavors requires significantly more funding to support development of instructional software than to support its use. At UNC-CH, centralized development support has not proven feasible. Ongoing development support is unlikely to extend beyond the funding period, with continued use sustained by individual faculty effort and interest coupled with existing support services. Service can be twofold: support for the access of technology and support for the development of technological products. Development is far more costly and therefore not undertaken at centralized units. Faculty have therefore sought external funding. But such funding is temporary and therefore does not permit maintenance and upgrading. Lack of sufficient incentives and low academic computing budgets keep development efforts at very low levels.

The role of staff support: services versus production. Many academic computing centers find that current operating budgets barely support access to the various technologies available today. Production — or the support of software development requiring programming, design, and analysis (whether graphics, instructional, or system) — and management skills are often out of the question. Even when such cost-saving efforts as using student labor are suggested, staff support for selecting, training, and managing students must still be provided for useful outcomes. Production projects require skills and experience that differ from those needed in consulting services — skills such as troubleshooting and information dissemination. When the differences between management and skills needed for production and those needed for services staff are understood, it is easier also to understand why development projects initiated by faculty members have been difficult to sustain over time and to incorporate into institutional budgets.

Historical Patterns

Historical patterns have also had an impact on the nature of current and future instructional computing efforts.

Development funding for innovative efforts. In the early days of a new hardware device, there is the temptation to develop software, since few applications exist. As software is developed, it becomes easier to purchase what is needed rather than to develop it. Over time, commercial-quality software becomes available on a more widespread basis, and the need for development declines further. This temptation to develop when no existing materials suffice is further encouraged by external funding — either from hardware manufacturers interested in having prototype software available for demonstration purposes or from funding agencies that support the development of innovative instructional applications. While centralized academic computing centers find they cannot budget for development support, innovative faculty members find they can receive support elsewhere — granting agencies and vendors wishing to explore the potential of new technologies. These early prototype and experimental software developments often influence — but usually do not find their way directly into — the commercial market, and commercial success is usually an unrealistic expectation. Again, such projects initiated by faculty members have been difficult to sustain over time and to incorporate into institutional budgets.

Patterns of technology adoption — small incremental steps. Technological changes occur more rapidly than the academic culture can adopt and support them. Several factors contribute to the delay. The adoption of what technology offers depends on the availability of self-sufficient tools (a combination of hardware and software) and on the availability of support that promotes self-sufficiency, such as training and documentation. Although there will always be a few innovative faculty members who will seize on the advantageous features of a new technology, adoption by larger numbers depends on availability (largely a function of cost), accessibility (ease of use), and familiarity (experience).

In the process of adopting a new technology, an individual goes through several stages: a stage during which existing tasks are automated, followed by adjustment of the methodology to use features of the technology, and finally by transformation of functions. During the first stage, a new technology is used to accomplish the same task using a new tool. Word processing used as a replacement for a typewriter is a common example. During the next stage, the same function is performed, but the methods are new, taking advantage of additional features offered by the new tool. An example is the use of the glossary and the search and replace functions of word-processing software. During the third stage, the function itself is transformed, for example, using the electronic distribution of research documents for publication or comment. An instructional example of this stage is the previously described use of word processing software with a video projector to teach creative writing in the classroom.

These stages help to explain why it takes time to integrate existing technology into the curriculum — often from one to three years for faculty projects. It takes even longer to develop the materials — from two to seven years. This lengthy development timeline is due to two factors: each faculty member's fragmentary approach to the multiple functions, and the interruptions of working intensely on a research grant when awarded. This timeline can be shortened with better tools and greater leave time or with the support and time of professional staff. Without the likelihood of staff support and greater leave time for instructional functions, there is a greater reliance on better and more self-sufficient tools. With respect to computing, one major step has already taken place. Up to 90 percent of the faculty at UNC-CH have microcomputers in their offices or homes, with word processing as their nearly unanimous first application. The second or third application varies from spreadsheet, database, and electronic mail applications to instructional computing applications.

The increasing cost of support. It is seldom remembered that even in a reasonably supported operation, the price of purchased hardware and software amounts to only 40 percent of the total expenditures for computing resources.[6] Support costs can be expected to rise as new technologies coexist with the old and as diversity and sophistication increase. The relatively more costly proposition of developing new software will compete even less favorably with the need to provide support services. Additionally, access support, when amortized across large numbers, is more easily justified for the long term than is intensive support for individual faculty projects, for example, instructional software development. The professionals — whether programmers, designers, or managers — necessary for quality production and maintenance of a software product are costly. In contrast, support services that focus on and encourage self-sufficiency can continually evolve by freeing staff time for the support of new technologies.

The value of supporting innovation. Universities are usually perceived as the source of many innovative and creative ideas and activities — generating and disseminating new knowledge is a university function. Faculty members at UNC-CH have followed that tradition by producing several diverse instructional computing innovations, as the examples in this paper illustrate. The benefits of these innovations are several and include benefits to both faculty and students. Many faculty members have renewed their interest in subject matters that were previously difficult or impossible to teach. Instructional computing applications often permit greater depth into the subject matter and greater opportunities to encourage meaningful interaction with students. Students enrolled in courses using these technologies benefit from instructional improvements and from exposure to the microcomputer as a multifaceted intellectual tool. Other faculty have benefited from the experiences of their innovative colleagues by adopting, and adapting, their own instruction. Benefits are diverse and often intangible and in the long term may differ from the original intent.

These innovations have not, however, come about without a lot of effort and disruption. Effort is needed to acquire external funding, to develop materials, to change courses and teaching strategies, to manage a multitude of administrative tasks, and to cope with technical difficulties. Such effort often leads to major disruptions of other activities. Robert Taylor has expressed this tension well: "The prophetic vision alone can not be sustained long; it is too exciting and demanding and produces too much chaos. At the same time, without the periodic revelation of a prophetic vision, education becomes deadly, boring, and incapable of producing creative thinking in its products." [7]

Trends

Larger societal trends also have their impact on instructional computing. Increasing decentralization has been a trend in business and industry for several years, as it has in academia. Similarly, there appears to be a strong belief that only technology can solve many of today's problems. This has in part led to the increasing pace of technological change and the increasing sophistication of products. [8]

Increasing decentralization. The increasing specialization of faculty and staff, as well as the increasing decentralization of support units, has been an institutional characteristic for some time and is continuing. As technology costs come within the budget range of a department or external grant, decentralized facilities and support increase. Such has been the case for computing and simultaneously for instructional computing. These trends exacerbate the need to decide which support services for instructional computing operate most efficiently from a centralized perspective and which can be best provided in a decentralized fashion. Some centralized functions that have worked well at UNC-CH are site licenses, microcomputer labs, master classrooms, startup software funds, information clearinghouses, and general professional skills (technical and design) provided on a consulting basis. What has not proven feasible to implement at the centralized level, and therefore remains to be addressed in a decentralized fashion, is discipline-specific support and development.

Increasing numbers and sophistication. The number of faculty members engaging in instructional computing or instructional technology activities at UNC-CH are small but growing steadily in spite of the lack of sufficient incentives and, sometimes, support. From less than ten faculty members before 1980, the number of those engaging in instructional computing has grown to over one hundred eight years later (from 1 to 5 percent). As new hardware and software tools come down in price and become easier to use, faculty members will increasingly experiment with technology to aid their professional activities — whether instruction or research. These applications will, however, become increasingly diverse, as indicated by activities at UNC-CH in the late 1980s. Academic computing centers can expect to see a growing percentage of faculty members using increasingly diverse technology for research and for instruction.

Rapid technological changes. Improvements in technology not only can be expected to continue but also, in many instances, can be expected to occur at an increasingly faster pace. For example, the changes from the early 8-bit processor microcomputers to the near mainframe abilities of the current 32-bit microprocessors have been escalating. This type of growth in processing power can be expected to continue throughout the 1990s, as well as improvements in data storage and retrieval, data compression, and data transmission (DVI and CD-I are two emerging digitized motion technologies that hold new instructional opportunities). Hardware improvements also precede software improvements, and the time lag between hardware improvements and software that takes advantage of these new capabilities will increase. Software engineering tasks — whether analysis, design, programming, or testing and revising — remain time-intensive, creative tasks with few major productivity improvements in sight. Therefore, what is not likely to change in the near future is the inability of computer users (whether faculty or students) to perform the skills of software engineers.[9] What could improve over time is the development of software tools designed to let nonprogrammers create discipline-specific software.

Faith in technology. Another trend under way — and likely to continue — is the emphasis placed on the opportunities that new technologies offer. An example is the yet unrealized potential of improved technologies for communications, instructional access, and even distance learning. There exists today an enormous faith in technology to solve problems. More and better technologies are seen as improving productivity and reducing costs so that this nation can remain competitive internationally. Similarly, there is a faith that technology will solve the university's problems.[10] Given such an unbounded faith, support for new technologies is likely to continue unless a backlash occurs due to unfulfilled high expectations.

Taking these patterns and trends into account, we have provided several recommendations for a more successful centralized support structure in the future.

Recommendations for the Future for Similar Institutions

The priorities placed on research and technologies are increasing the need to support more diverse and rapidly changing technologies. The challenge is to adapt quickly to the technological changes of the 1990s, a challenge related to the question of how to blend new diverse technologies and old technologies, research and instructional functions, and connectivity. The institutional question becomes one of adjusting centralized organizations and functions to all these new technologies — within the research and instructional missions of the university. Although the research mission with its priority may warrant greater support, the best allocation of resources argues for encompassing both the research and the instructional mission.

Since new technologies need to be supported and since adding new, centralized staff is not the preferred option, it is safe to assume that existing staff may face retraining needs. That in turn would indicate the need to reduce the support of older technologies, that is, older technologies will hopefully become self-sufficient. The following recommendations encapsulate some of the issues presented above.

Recommendation 1

When budgets do not permit adequate software development staff support, encourage the adoption of self-sufficient technologies. At most, access to technology and access to support can be expected to be provided centrally. Access in labs is traditionally provided by computation centers. Access in the classroom is traditionally provided by media centers. Access to various media or technology products like software has traditionally been provided by the nonprint media sections in libraries. We can expect to see the budgets of these units adjust in the future to accommodate new technologies. While experimentation with the use of all the various new information technologies needs to be encouraged, faculty members need to understand that start-up project funds involving personnel may not be institutionalized and supported over time; and in the occasional decentralized case, budgeting for software development, if it occurs, has to take into account the fact that costs will increase as the technology base changes.

Recommendation 2

Promote the use of tools for instructional computing. The use of tools offers greater self-sufficiency than does the use of programmers. With the current priority on research, it is prudent for faculty members to invest time not only in a tool that permits them to improve instruction but ideally in a tool that can meet both research and instructional needs. Authoring systems are tools for the development of instructional materials, and simulation and modeling programs are examples of tools that overlap research and instruction functions.

Recommendation 3

Distribute support efforts between central and decentralized units as appropriate. Some functions that are usually best served in a centralized fashion are site licensing, information dissemination, and networking. Disciplinary-level functions are best served in a decentralized fashion, with a possible centralized clearinghouse or reference point. Decentralized locations can be expected to continue to develop highly specialized expertise that offers an opportunity to share or collaborate across decentralized units.

Recommendation 4

Continue to support innovation for its diverse and intangible benefits. Locate and support the innovators; give them seed money, leave time, hardware, software, etc., on a proposal basis and ask them to report to others, so that outcomes are disseminated. The innovators become a good source of decentralized support and are good evaluators of new hardware and software developments.

Recommendation 5

Encourage collaboration. Instructional computing can be viewed as one highly specialized version of instructional technology, one that can be subsumed under the larger umbrella of information technologies. Collaborative efforts become increasingly necessary as standard-line functions cannot address the new instructional computing, teleclass, and telecommunication functions. Without collaboration among library, laboratory, and classroom technology functions, for example, instructional computing cannot provide its fullest potential for the instructor or student.

The Role of Production

The above recommendations address the problems of effectively using instructional technologies under current budget constraints. What is in question in academia in general, and within the new information technology orientations, is the role of production. Although libraries, learning resource centers, computer centers, and media centers can provide access to technology-related products for all university members in the traditional library access model, and in most instances can also provide some support for that access, it is unclear to what extent universities can afford to support the production of print and nonprint materials. The production of high-quality videotapes, videodiscs, slides, or computer software can be a very costly institutional commitment. Traditionally, only those schools and departments with external support have been able to afford this direction, and these have often found the need to charge for the services as their expenses became evident and external support ended. Charging for production services, however, only encourages those applications that can pay — typically the research and administrative functions. Production for instructional functions becomes, therefore, at best a third-priority option, when time and money permit. It is perhaps best to openly acknowledge that institutional production of instructional materials has not been well supported in the current budgets of many institutions, including UNC-CH.

Yet the motivation to develop instructional software continues, for three reasons. First, many faculty members would like to improve the learning environment of their students. The computer offers ways to overcome difficult or impossible to teach concepts, but concepts that must be mastered before proceeding further. Second, the computer, unlike any other medium, offers an interactive environment, an environment where students are actively engaged in the learning process instead of being passive receivers of information. Third, the computer offers a way to simulate the real world and to model complex, interrelating processes.

What is needed? Four conditions must improve if better instructional software is to become available. First, incentives have to improve. Tenure and promotion criteria need to address the efforts of developing and using the information technologies and, more specifically, instructional computing. Faculty need leave time to concentrate on improvements. Second, more professional staff need to be available to manage the faculty member's ideas to fruition. Third, better information about the development process and products needs to be available so that development is undertaken only when appropriate and so that adoption is facilitated. Fourth, better self-sufficient tools and software need to be available for the faculty member's use — tools that become amplifiers of the instructor's tasks and tools that require minimum support costs.

Since the first condition is not within the realm of influence of academic computing centers, and the second is not feasible due to budgetary constraints, only the third and fourth conditions can become useful strategies. That is, academic computing centers should locate, disseminate information about, and otherwise promote and encourage the use of self-sufficient tools for the development of instructional software or for the use of instructional software as well as other information technologies. These strategies will satisfy, to the extent possible, the needs of faculty members but not necessarily the needs of students. High-quality and effective instructional software will evolve over time, but students are the ones who will have to tolerate the products of lesser quality and less effectiveness in the interim.

Notes

1. M. Hazen and T. Hazen, "Simulation of Legal Analysis and Instruction on the Computer," *Indiana Law Journal* 59, no. 2 (1984). 195-222.

2. J. Semonche, "Computer Simulations, the Teaching of History, and the Goals of a Liberal Education," *Academic Computing* 2, no. 1 (September 1987): 20-23, 46-50.

3. For further information, see F. Dominguez and M. Hazen, "CAI Development: The Experience of the University of North Carolina Courseware Development Project," *CALICO Journal* 5, no. 2 (December 1987): 55-64.

4. R. D. Rust, "Composition Instruction with Microsoft Word," *Carolina Computing* 2, no. 1 (Winter 1988–89): 5-7.

5. See, for example, D. L. Smallen, "Infusing Computing into the Curriculum: Challenges for the Next Decade," *Academic Computing* 3, no. 8 (April 1989): 8-12, 32-35, and S. R. Trollip, "Wrestling with Instructional Computing," *Academic Computing* 2, no. 4 (December 1987/January 1988): 26-29, 40-41. Dr. Robert Kozma has stated in his 1989 letter to invite faculty members to apply for NCRIPTAL awards: "Seeing few rewards or examples of success, faculty members may shy away from the development of software in preference for the established modes of scholarship. They may continue traditional approaches to instruction rather than take the time to see how computers may be used to improve teaching and learning. Thus, the potential that this new medium holds for higher education may not be realized for lack of participation by some of our brightest minds."

6. "Furthermore, as faculty members, administrators, and students become more computer literate, their demand for a wide variety of software and support services will grow explosively; like a new-born babe, it is not the initial cost but the upkeep that counts. Thus, over the next few years many institutions face the unexpected and unplanned prospect of having to provide for a significant increase in the level of expenditures for activities other than hardware" (J. C. Emery, "Issues in Building an Information Technology Strategy," *EDUCOM Bulletin* 19, no. 3 [Fall 1984]: 9).

7. R. P. Taylor, "Visions of Education and the Implementation of Technology," *SIGCUE Outlook, ACM* 20, no. 1 (Fall 1988): 9.

8. S. Berger, M. L. Dertouzos, R. K. Lester, R. M. Solow, and L. C. Thurow, "Toward a New Industrial America," *Scientific American* 260, no. 6 (June 1989): 39-47.

9. "The demand for computers and software in our society is increasing continuously. Projections of this demand, coupled with pessimistic projections of increases in the productivity of software developers, indicate that by early in the next century, every man, woman, and child in the United States will have to be a software engineer. The telephone company was faced with similar projections for operators in the 1920's, but the development of new technology allowed users of telephones to perform nearly all the duties of operators. Today, however, the technology to allow users of computers to perform the duties of software engineers is unlikely to be available in the foreseeable future. Instead, we will have to increase the productivity (and number) of the current and next generation of software engineers" (N. E. Gibbs, "The SEI Education Program: The Challenge of Teaching Future Software Engineers," *Communications of the ACM* 32, no. 5 [1989]: 594).

10. D. D. Mebane, ed., *Solving College and University Problems Through Technology* (Princeton, N.J.: EDUCOM, 1981).

Chapter 18

Western Washington University: Instructional Computing

George Gerhold

Western Washington University is representative of a large group of universities, the state-supported regionals. About nine thousand students are enrolled, and 95 percent of them are undergraduates. State support is low, since Washington usually ranks about forty-fifth in state support of higher education, and Western ranks lowest among the regionals in Washington; the annual support per student from the state is about forty-five hundred dollars. Thus the health of instructional computing has been heavily dependent on outside support and on the extra efforts of faculty and staff. Fortunately the local geography attracts a more dynamic group of faculty and staff than the legislative support justifies, and their efforts have produced most of what is worthy of note herein.

The typical teaching load at Western is thirty-four quarter credit hours per year. Although this is heavy by the standards of research universities, it does leave time for scholarly activity, and Western expects such from all faculty. The local definition of scholarly activity is fairly broad, and innovations in undergraduate education are valued, as are the more standard publications. A coterie of textbook authors has had local academic success, and several of this group have played central roles in the spread of instructional computing on campus.

Background

Western's first sizable computer purchase was made with NSF support.

Two conditions on that support had a positive effect on the development of instructional computing. At least one-third of the hardware was to be used for instructional computing, and no charges for any form of academic computing were to be allowed. Since this was in the late 1960s, suitable instructional software was in very short supply (especially for IBM 360s). To meet the one-third requirement, Western arranged for IBM to provide a special version of *Coursewriter* and faculty training in its use. The hope was that the faculty developers would create student demand for computing by writing materials for use in courses.

Faculty developers quickly outgrew *Coursewriter* and the 360-40. (Four users on a particular freshman chemistry laboratory simulation could tie up the 360-40 completely.) Western's response was to improve the systems software, a response that has been a characteristic of instructional computing at Western ever since. The first step was to meld Coursewriter with PL/1, and the second was to implement a greatly enhanced version of the *PILOT* authoring language on minicomputers. Subsequently, much of the later development of *PILOT* and the development of the *ProPi* authoring system, the Collegiate Writer word processor, and the LinkWay hypermedia system was done by Western employees, often with significant university support. Accompanying these system software developments was the parallel development of instructional application packages. In almost every case the developers of these latter packages became the leaders in the use of computing within their units.

This brief background leads to a few general conclusions:

- Institutions that combine moderation in teaching loads with moderation in publication expectations may provide the best environments for the development of instructional computing materials (and other instructional materials as well).

- An initial institutional commitment to provide hardware in excess of early demand for instructional computing is essential. Once a body of users is in place, the institution need only respond to demands — a task most administrations find easier.

- Free instructional computing avoids a major disincentive to the introduction and growth of instructional computing.

- Local development of computer-based instructional materials
  should be encouraged, not solely for the value of the materials
  — which may or may not be of significant quality and impact
  and which will never repay their development costs to the
  university — but also for the leadership that the developers
  provide within their home units. The improvements in courses
  and teaching that follow from the careful rethinking of material
  and sequence inherent in development are another,
  nonquantifiable benefit.

Two other situations were important to instructional computing at Western but are not now relevant to other institutions. The transfer of much of the instructional computing to smaller machines, particularly the transfer to minicomputers, was encouraged by the computer center staff. Second, through the efforts of a few staff members and administrators, the national office of the Association for the Development of Computer-Based Instructional Systems (ADCIS) was located on campus for a number of years. This gave one type of instructional computing local visibility, and it made Western faculty aware of what was happening elsewhere.

Computing at Western

The computer center at Western has primary responsibility for both academic and administrative computing. Whether this is good or bad is far more dependent on the judgment of decision makers at the various levels than it is on the particular structure. On the one hand, the two types of applications are placed in competition for resources within the center; on the other hand, the center provides a framework for establishing the institution's priorities for various types of computing. The two areas have separate budgets, which are not directly comparable. The tradition of no charges for academic computing has been preserved, but the center provides no programming support for academic users, other than student consultants. Thus the faculty are expected to do their own programming or to hire their own programmers. In contrast there are chargebacks for administrative computing, and programming support is supplied.

Departments frequently purchase hardware from their own equipment and operating budgets. This arrangement leads to some problems. From the point of view of the center, the departmental requests are not prioritized relative to the requests originating in the center, and there are continuing problems with incompatible hardware and with requests to the center for the repair of departmental equipment. From the point of view of the departments, the center's requests for computer equipment are not prioritized relative to noncomputer equipment requests.

The center services all equipment, regardless of how it is purchased, if it is state supported and if it appears on the center's list of supported models. The center does not restrict hardware purchases for faculty and departmental office locations, and it services such equipment, where possible, without chargeback. The center does charge for parts costing more than one hundred dollars and for repairing equipment owned by self-sustaining areas, which themselves operate on a chargeback basis.

Students are expected to do their computing at one of the clusters of computers/mainframe terminals on campus. Equipping, staffing, and regulating the use of these clusters is an ongoing problem. Older buildings are not designed with computer rooms; the demand for computing usually exceeds the supply; regulation interferes with the smooth integration of computing into coursework, and general word processing — if permitted — would push out all other uses. We have been experimenting with a system of punch cards that allow students to purchase computing time for about one dollar per hour for nonassigned use of the clusters. Clearly some standardization of equipment within clusters is essential. Most of the clusters are MS-DOS machines (the exceptions are clusters, predominantly Apple, in the education and sociology departments), and there is an attempt to preserve uniformity of display types within each cluster. The clusters vary in number between twenty and sixty machines.

Western has encouraged students to acquire campus standard equipment or compatible equipment by negotiating vendor discounts on that equipment for students and faculty. The Student Co-op administers several contracts for this equipment and serves as a sales outlet. Unfortunately, there has been a tendency to chase the "best deal" (i.e., the lowest price) in compatibles, and the identity of these "best deals" shifts rapidly. Class assignments involving instructional computing usually require the short-term use of specialized software, and no provision for loaning such software has been made. Thus there is little incentive for the students to follow the standards closely (e.g., matching graphics resolution), and they tend to buy the cheapest clone of the moment. The predominant use of personal computers by students is for word processing. Thus far we have seen little evidence of the value of computer literacy programs in the K-12 schools. Students without their own computers do not seem to know much about general software types like spreadsheets, databases, or even word processing.

The director of the computer center believes that it requires as many faculty microcomputers and terminals as public microcomputers and terminals in student laboratories to generate a reasonable workload in those laboratories. This proportion probably will shift toward the public stations now that about one-half of the faculty offices have computers (many purchased privately by faculty) and now that a body of instructional materials has been developed. It is clear that we could dramatically increase the use of public stations by giving a green light to the English and foreign language departments for increased use, and we could produce a drastic increase by allowing general word processing outside the punch-card system.

The division of equipment funds between the center and the departments is less easily systematized. Individual departments need specialized printing and graphics equipment, and the computer center has to support central timesharing, database, and data communications equipment. Our estimate is to allocate funds for instruction and research computing equipment 60 percent through the computer center and 40 percent through the departments. The distribution between these two is very dependent on the local mix of users. For example, if we did not have a computer science department, the demand for large-machine academic computing would be far less.

The computer center has played a central role in the introduction of instructional computing to a number of departments on campus. The process was straightforward. One or more machines, with suitable software, were placed in a convenient location within suitable departments. Business and technology, now two of the largest users on campus, were seduced in this way. Interestingly, some of the prior heavy users foresaw the likely result of these actions and opposed them, unsuccessfully.

As the use of computers and the number of stations increased, there has developed a predictable desire on the part of the computer center staff to monitor and regulate the use of the computers. In part this has been caused by the need to keep general word processing from consuming the resource, in part by the need to justify further purchases by use statistics, in part by the desire to provide students with access to computers outside of use assigned in courses, and in part by normal inclinations to create bureaucracy. Regardless, the result is another significant barrier to the convenient use of computers within courses. Faculty have refused to use available materials because they were not willing to commit and arrange ahead for class access at particular time. Hopefully the amount of hardware eventually available will be sufficient to handle drop-in use by students which would eliminate the red tape that currently impedes computer-based assignments.

WEST Center

In 1985 Western signed a three-year contract with IBM for the development of educational software tools. This contract led to the creation of the WEST Center, which handled the tool development and served as the resource and consulting center for CAI development on campus. The contract was for the development of tools which would simplify the writing of CAI materials. Fifteen faculty-controlled development projects served as "guinea pigs" for the new software tools. Most of the faculty members were new to CAI development, and about one-third of them continue this development as their major scholarly activity. Three of these faculty subsequently received EDUCOM software awards. The activities at the center also continue, both the tool development and the support of faculty.

In addition to the activities mentioned above, the contract provided hardware that was distributed to faculty members based on proposals for use in increasing instructional computing. These proposals were not restricted to CAI applications and did not necessarily require programming. Several of the awards supported work on integrating existing software into courses. It is hardly surprising that the level of success in these projects was mixed; less support was provided, less supervision and review was involved, and less was accomplished.

Four new clusters of public-access computers were created through this project. The benefits are open to question. The new clusters are used heavily, and — without question — they led to major changes in the way courses are taught in journalism, geology, English, and the design portions of art. However, this "big splash" of new equipment from IBM was seen by much of the administration as "meeting the demand for academic computing" for the foreseeable future, and so the regular funding of academic computing was reduced or diverted. Those not interested in developing software (mainly the business departments) felt they were shortchanged. Recently the lion's share of computing dollars has gone to administrative computing. The pattern of tiny expenditures for academic computing (versus administrative computing) has outlived the contract and is still to be reversed.

In spite of the reservations expressed, there is little question that the university benefited and continues to benefit from the contract. What, then, have we learned that may be of general utility?

- Western was granted the contract based on work that had been carried on by a few faculty and staff during the preceding decade. Western, and in particular the computer center, tolerated, advanced or promoted the participants and to a degree supported this work throughout the decade. Thus it appears that virtue may be rewarded, eventually.

- One should delay inviting faculty proposals for projects until the hardware is in hand. The frustration of waiting led to a loss of interest and to involvement in competing activities. The result of starting early on campus was a loss of momentum.

- The most effective form of faculty support is student help. The fact that the student is dependent on the income keeps the project on the top of the faculty member's desk and keeps the project moving ahead. This is doubly true close to the end of a project, when the problems are solved and the work to turn it into a transferable package is less interesting.

- Faculty do not need much support from the support center, but they do need consulting help at the start of a project. Faculty are not experienced in designing instructional materials in which they transfer control to students, and they have little experience in screen design.

- Faculty should be introduced to a new set of colleagues
  through the development process. It is unlikely that interest
  will develop among several members of a department at one
  time, so an exchange of ideas will have to occur elsewhere.
  Peer review of projects before exposure to students is
  essential. In this case the peers are others who have developed
  materials, not necessarily members of one's own department.

- The reception of a "big splash" of funding solves some
  problems but creates some new ones. We will return to this
  point later.

Current Activity

In this section we describe some of the current activities by discipline.
The list is not complete; rather we have selected those cases that illustrate
some potentially useful point.

Education and business were introduced to instructional computing
through a loan of hardware and software by the computer center. Use has
grown to the point that they have their own clusters of machines. In
neither case has there been much local development of new materials.
Instead each concentrates on using standard packages. Perhaps as a
result both units tend to teach students about software that is in use today
in their respective fields instead of teaching the more general principles
behind these packages. Thus business teaches students how to use Lotus
1-2-3 rather than the general principles of spreadsheets, and education
teaches students how to run MECC software on Apple IIs rather than how
to look ahead to what computers may mean for K-12 schools in five to ten
years. The absence of developers and the prevalence of this use pattern
may be coincidental, but we suspect not. One could debate the value
judgments implied by this description — some believe that these are
practical fields that should teach current practice — but one consequence
is not debatable. By concentrating on the use of software currently used
in the field, one makes oneself particularly vulnerable to obsolescence.

The business departments have concluded that student ownership of
computers will never reduce their need to provide access, for current
business practice will always be on more expensive hardware than the

typical student can afford. This conclusion probably applies to many other fields, for example, engineering.

Chemistry and biology offer an interesting contrast. Both had faculty in the early Coursewriter seminars. However, chemistry has become a hotbed of CAI development and of instructional use; almost half the faculty have developed sizable programs. Incidentally (or maybe not) most of these faculty have prior textbook authoring experience. Little has happened in biology, either in development or use. We do not know why the two are so different. One possibility is the greater number of graduate students in biology. Graduate students may keep the active faculty more involved in disciplinary research, thus leaving less time for new computing projects. However, other institutions show the same distribution of graduate students in the two fields but show higher computing use in biology. The chemists involved cannot account for the difference; they state that they became aware of students' problems in their courses and of the computer's potential for attacking these problems. It may be that this growth of awareness is a slow process that cannot be rushed.

One older member of the biology faculty got interested in CAI development late in his academic career. In the preceding years he had not published research and had been frustrated in attempts to publish a textbook. He recently signed a contract for the publication of a sizable instructional program. This success has brightened his prospects and offers the possibility of part- time professional activity after retirement. The development of instructional software may prove to be a suitable and stimulating activity for faculty whose scholarly activity has lapsed, and perhaps even for retired faculty.

The English department was given special funding to create a version of the entry-level composition course based on a word processor. A twenty-four-station laboratory was laid out so that students can work individually or in groups of four. An adjacent classroom was equipped with a computer and a projection TV. Two classes alternate between the rooms, so that one class meeting is demonstration and discussion of rewriting and editing and the next is hands-on. In this way the use of the hardware is maximized. What began as an experiment is now a permanent part of the curriculum. The problem is that another pair of rooms is needed to meet the demand for this course, and requests for similar facilities for other writing courses lurk in the wings. Again and again we find that efforts to introduce instructional computing are so successful that they create demands that cannot be met. By the time this became obvious, it was too late to slow the process.

The English department illustrates two other points. The resource problem is not really computers. The department would be happy with anything suitable for word processing, and there are probably enough older computers that can be shifted to that application as replacements are purchased. Space is a major problem. A computerized classroom, or in this case a pair of classrooms, is taken out of the general classroom pool by the conversion, and general classrooms are in short supply. Instructional computing leads to space demands that were not part of building designs and that are still not part of the state's space formulas. Second, although the application in English is word processing, software development is involved here too. A former member of the department, now the director of the tutorial center, was one of the principals in the creation of the Collegiate Writer package, and that package was shaped — in part — by the demands of the composition course.

The foreign language department was encouraged to replace its audio tape laboratory with a multimedia laboratory. This was funded with another "big splash" of support. In retrospect the department spent the money too quickly, and some of the equipment sits unused (notably computer-controlled tape decks and Apple II computers). The department has since found its way and is currently working on a number of quality development projects. With the exceptions noted above, the lab is heavily used and in need of upsizing, perhaps by an order of magnitude. The department's most recent new hire was in large part selected because of demonstrated expertise in the development of instructional computing materials. If the expertise had been hired earlier, the savings in equipment purchases could have paid the extra salary. The department provides further examples of the value of a developer in leading a department into instructional computing and of the propensity of successful textbook authors to enter into CAI development.

Both English and foreign language illustrate another problem caused by the growth of instructional computing. Once upon a time the sciences could count on receiving the bulk of the university's equipment budget. An occasional tape recorder or typewriter kept English and foreign languages happy. No more. And equipment budgets have not grown in accordance with these increased demands.

Psychology, computer science, economics, and mathematics are tradi-

tional users of instructional computing. Their uses are predictable and are
oriented toward large, central machines. Thus psychology uses statistical
packages and includes their application in undergraduate courses, computer science uses vast amounts of time for programming courses, economics uses large-scale simulation and modeling, and mathematics does
numerical analysis. Old applications never die or fade away; they just
continue to contribute to the demand. Mathematics would like to make
heavy use of projection terminals in its classes. The initial enthusiasm
died quickly under the strain of moving projection TVs. Mathematics
would like every classroom to be equipped with a built-in computer and a
projection TV. Unfortunately, projection TVs seem to be evolving even
faster than computers, and it costs even more to keep up in this field. Even
so, an institution building new facilities should provide for this hardware
in planning the layout and lighting of every classroom.

Western's tutorial center helps students who are having difficulty with
beginning courses. In fact its major activity is tutoring in beginning mathematics and science courses. The staff at the center has responded to the
demand by developing CAI materials in remedial mathematics. The mathematics department is glad not to be burdened with this task; it is very
supportive of the efforts of the tutorial center. This same group developed
— as a private, commercial venture — a word processor for use in
preparing term papers. This package is now marketed under the name
Collegiate Writer. It is used locally in the beginning composition courses.
Not all development of instructional software comes from the faculty, or
even from within departments.

The sociology department at Western is unusual; it has a strong demography slant. The former chair tried to make the department the first truly
computerized department on campus with a network, computers on each
faculty member's desk, computers in the classrooms, and workstations
for the students. The department chose to use Macintoshes throughout.
After some initial success, there was a change in leadership and a loss of
direction. This is frequently discovered in instructional computing: individuals, not projects, should be supported. Instructional computing projects seem not to have a life of their own; if the leadership disappears,
transfer the resources elsewhere — immediately.

Philosophy is our final example. A faculty member in the department
began a symbolic logic program. The program was never put into use
because the student assistant on the project graduated before completion.

It is very difficult to rekindle interest in a lapsed project, and it is difficult to get a student assistant interested in wrapping up someone else's project. One could probably raise the success rate in development projects by holding in reserve programming resources that could be used to finish off projects.

The continuing theme of this section is that the most effective users of instructional computing all have a developer of instructional software who has provided leadership within the unit. Such developers provide other benefits as well. They may attract outside funds that provide hardware for others within the unit; they are able to publish their work in a way that users of completed packages cannot; and the pattern of development is likely to attract the most dynamic faculty to instructional computing.

As mentioned in the introduction to this section, the list of departments and applications is in no sense complete. Other units are significant users of instructional computing, but their experiences do not add to the list of illustrations of particular points.

Institutional Reward Structure

Institutional policy is often cited as a major barrier to increased use of instructional computing. There is no question that effective use of computing requires time, whether one is just integrating packages or creating and integrating packages. If the institution does not value the activity, then the faculty member who invests time in such activity is at risk.

Western is probably the type of institution that should lead in the introduction of instructional computing. Such institutions do not risk a loss of prestige through lowered publication rates in the top research journals. Although hardware is in short supply, more faculty time is available for instructional innovation than at other types of institutions. Thus the missing ingredient is an institutional decision to encourage, or at least tolerate, instructional innovation, including computer use. At Western, although the surest way to promotion is to publish in the professional journals in the various fields, the institution seems to value instructional innovation, especially work that leads to publication in journals appropriate for that type of work. No one active in instructional computing has been denied tenure, and in at least one case promotion was probably based on it.

Without question the faculty leaders in instructional computing have
prospered at Western; promotions, merit steps, and other rewards have
been far above the average. There is no indication that these successes
were in spite of their computing activity, but the evidence that these
successes were because of the computing activity is scanty, for these
same faculty are outstanding in their other professional activities as well.

My personal impression is that the most effective proponents of instructional computing do it because they find it interesting and worthwhile. Further, they have the self-confidence to expect the institution to
value what they find worthwhile, and they will leave, without regrets, an
institution that does share or respect their academic and professional
values. Universities are changed because they first tolerate and then
follow those who are willing to rock the boat; they are not changed
because they guarantee rewards to those who — only under ideal conditions — will strike off in new directions.

A secondary reward structure could be implemented to great effect at
relatively low cost. Some fraction of the faculty that undertake software
development become quite active and successful. They should be recognized by a continual upgrading of their hardware. The institution should
set up a mechanism by which new hardware is given to the most productive faculty (productive in instructional computing), and the older hardware then trickles down to the more conventional users. Unfortunately
Western has not done this. As a result, many of the most farsighted faculty
began early, received hardware early, and now have older and less powerful hardware than the latecomers. Obviously other considerations beyond
early start must come into hardware distribution, but most institutions —
including Western — tend to distribute computers once and forever. An
annual redistribution aimed at upgrading, where justified, would be a
great improvement and incentive.

Software development is an important component of instructional computing at Western, and it is expected that much of this new software will
be distributed, in many cases commercially. This possibility caused the
university to adopt a generous and supportive policy on the sharing of
royalties. If a program is developed using the university's facilities (space,
hardware, or time), then the following division of any royalties applies:

- First $500 — 100 percent to the author.

- $501 to $100,000 — 75 percent to the author and 25 percent to the university.

- Over $100,000 — 50 percent to the author and 50 percent to the University.

This applies individually to each author of each project. Unfortunately, no one has yet reached the 50 percent range. In practice, various pressures sometimes require that a package be completed more quickly than university time allows. Thus some fraction of the development is done on weekends, etc., on privately owned hardware. In such cases the pattern has been to divide the royalties in proportion to the time invested. Thus far the university has fed at least a portion of these revenues into other development projects, but there is no formal commitment to continue this practice. In all cases the university is assumed to own a site license at no charge. The ownership of copyright is usually assigned to the university. In general an attempt has been made to anticipate problems and to resolve them in an equitable fashion before large amounts of money are involved. The degree to which this has worked awaits the test of a best seller.

Funding

There are basically two ways to fund instructional computing: either as part of the regular institutional budget or through "big splash" increments from a variety of sources. Though no one is likely to reject "big splash" increments, they are not the ideal source of funding. Perhaps the major problem is that computers have a very short lifetime, at least at the cutting edge. A major increment in hardware implies a series of major increments at regular intervals to replace the soon-to-be-obsolete computers. It is far easier to obtain supplemental funding for a new application than funding for updating an existing application. At least at Western the receipt of a "big splash" allowed the administration to reduce regular support, whereas the rational response would have been to increase the regular support, thus establishing the funding base for eventual upgrading.

It is common for the organization providing the "big splash" funding to require some form of matching funds from the institution. This may actually contribute to the pattern described above, as it makes the splash bigger. A more foresighted policy for granting organizations might be the requirement of matching funds in the form of commitments to eventual upgrading of the equipment instead of concurrent matching.

Western is just beginning to work out a pattern of replacement and transfer of older microcomputers. In fact there is an almost limitless demand for older computers as word processors. Several departments have created small word-processing centers for use by their graduate students by purchasing old CP/M machines at fire-sale prices. This seems to be an ideal use for replaced machines and an appropriate final level for the trickle-down plan described earlier.

Networks

Conspicuous by its absence is any mention of networking. The same absence is fairly conspicuous on campus; two public clusters are networked, and two departments have internal networks. Beyond that everything is in the planning stage. Time will tell whether this was evidence of prudence, as is claimed now. Like many institutions, Western is considering a structural change that would replace the position of Computer Center Director with some type of Director of Communications, integrating management of computer resources, telephone systems, and at least a portion of library services.

Acknowledgment

While the views expressed herein are the author's, many colleagues have contributed to the discussions that preceded this paper. Neither space nor memory allows a complete listing, but the following colleagues were particularly helpful: Dr. Melvin Davidson, director of computing; Dr. Donald Pavia and Dr. John Weyh, chemistry; Dr. Philip Montague, philosophy; Mr. Larry Kheriaty and Mr. Bob Urso, WEST Center.

A National Perspective

A National Perspective?

William H. Graves
University of North Carolina at Chapel Hill

To view the investments of the individuals and institutions represented in this book as investments in technology would be shortsighted, for they are nothing less than investments in faculty development, curriculum development, and institutional development. Such investments are far-sighted at a time when colleges and universities are competing vigorously for students and faculty and when the public's expectation is that technology can help solve many of the nation's problems, including its problems in education. The contributors to this book have thus described technology-based development experiences of considerable experimental and long-term value, not only to the individuals involved but also to their institutions, to their disciplines or professions, and to their students. How, then, should we respond to their successes and the issues that they raise (the most persistent of which I outlined in the introductory chapter)? My answer is that we must respond from a national perspective. We must formulate a national strategy for

- securing a more proactive role for educational priorities in shaping the use and development of affordable instructional technologies;

- gathering academic opinion in arriving at these priorities;

- supporting a representative cross section of faculty leadership on the use and development of academic tools to add value to education;

- legitimating faculty work on these issues; and

- disseminating information about exemplary educational applications supported by broadly affordable technologies.

The remainder of this book advances a rationale for a focused national response to instructional technology's challenge to higher education. The explication, however, first returns to a question posed in the introductory chapter. The question concerned the responsibility for setting directions for computing in the curriculum and asked, "From which constituency of higher education should guidance and action come?" I will draw on a variety of issues discussed by others in this book to recast this question into an argument for a national strategy to achieve the potential of instructional technology.

Complexity: One Reason for a National Strategy

The studies in this book describe exemplars of applications and support structures that buttress the claim that instructional technologies can be incorporated into the curricular mainstream of the nation's colleges and universities. Yet the diverse nature of the responsibilities of the contributing authors and their responses to the educational opportunities that inhere in interactive technology illustrate the complexity of the challenge and the depth of a perplexing line of questions. Who is responsible for infusing computing into the curriculum? The individual scholar? The discipline or profession or department? The institution? The government? The private foundation? The corporate world? The concept of a national strategy responds to my belief that achieving the potential of instructional computing not only is the responsibility of all of the above, but is impossible without their cooperative effort.

In an environment in which both academic computing and academic governance are "distributed," it is often difficult to locate a focal point for decision and action. Consensus and direction frequently must be forged from forces as diverse as collegial (peer) opinion, institutional leadership, and technical support philosophies and practices. Even in the presence of the strategic direction reported in many of the contributed case studies, the cruel hand of resource deprivation often diluted progress. An initial investment in state-of-the-art equipment at Dartmouth, for example, too quickly led to the need for a nonexistent replacement budget. Or, the high costs of individual software development projects — reported here typicually in the range of twenty five to seventy five thousand dollars and even as high as two hundred thousand dollars — cannot be sustained over time (Cornell and North Carolina). Or, institutional strategy collides with reward structures based primarily in the academic disciplines and not always immediately responsive to institutional needs. The promise of instructional technology is too great to ignore, but so too are the obstacles that are ever present in the requisite complexity of the academic process and the expense of the effort — in personal, personnel, and equipment costs.

What I have labeled *complexity,* then, argues for cooperative partnerships of the kind that EDUCOM should be encouraged to forge among the various constituencies so integral to progress on instructional computing. Indeed, the EDUCOM Software Initiative (ESI) is designed to be a cooperative, volunteer whole that is wiser and more strongly empowered than the sum of its parts. Although the EDUCOM/NCRIPTAL competition under the banner of the ESI encourages and rewards faculty attention to instructional technologies, EDUCOM and its Software Initiative remain largely inaccessible to individual scholars and academic officers who generally do not (and historically have not been encouraged to) participate in the organization and its leadership structures. The early clamor for distributed — departmentally owned — computing predated microcomputing and did not derive solely from the trend toward affordable distributed technologies. This historical reminder of the importance of faculty participation in decision making should inform any attempt to develop a national strategy around the themes of instructional computing. In any case, EDUCOM and the Software Initiative are not a source of funding for advancing instructional computing. As the studies in this book attest, however, vendor support can build the momentum necessary to overcome various forms of inertia deriving from complexity and academic budgets. I believe that vendor support of national proportions could be structured to extend to all of higher education the mutual benefits that have accrued to so many vendor-supported projects on individual campuses, such as many of those reported in this volume. A generously supported national program could assemble and support a critical mass of interest and expertise in instructional computing. The studies in this book reveal the difficulty of doing so in a single department, on a single campus, or even in a single discipline on a national scale. The goal of a national program would be to identify, demonstrate, and advance the value that academic technology can add to higher education's basic educational mission and to support and legitimate faculty effort in this new dimension of scholarship. Any plan to achieve this goal should address two related issues reported in most of the contributed articles: the effectiveness of instructional technology and its niche in academe's value system.

The Effectiveness of Instructional Technology

Is instructional technology effective? The qualitative nouns enthusiasm, commitment, and involvement often describe the behavior of faculty "technologists" and arguably correlate to their effectiveness as teachers. These qualities are fragile, however, and often require structural sustenance. The effectiveness question, moreover, is often asked with quantitative connotations and global scope. Can we expect, however, to assess the effectiveness of educational technology more readily than we can assess the other "outcomes of higher education"? How do we assess the other media and materials of teaching and learning? How, for example, do we assess the effectiveness of textbooks? We usually make qualitative judgments about individual textbooks. The costs of developing and delivering textbooks, unlike the costs of developing and delivering software, are built into current educational delivery systems. The question of effectiveness thus looms financially larger for software than for texts and is made more difficult by the relative immaturity of current mechanisms for distributing software. As the marketplace for software matures, the effectiveness issue for software may equate to success in the marketplace and may thus result in parity between texts and software.

For now, however, the issue of effectiveness has some of the qualities of a cart-and-horse dilemma. The base of high-quality software is growing through the kind of efforts described in this book. But until there is a broader base of educational software of high quality to share nationally, how can effectiveness be assessed? Until peer review of software is better understood and more widely practiced, what are the incentives, individual or institutional, to increase the software base? Peer review, after all, is a major structural means for recognizing and rewarding meritorious achievement and is an important vehicle for assessing quality and assigning rankings in higher education. The EDUCOM/NCRIPTAL Awards Program, for example, is built around peer review.

One thrust of a national strategy would be to create a better understanding of how to evaluate the effectiveness of technology-based curriculum materials in the peer review contexts that shape disciplinary and professional judgments and rewards.

Instructional Technology and Academic Reward Structures

Most of the contributed articles mention the mismatch between prevailing academic reward structures and the need for faculty involvement in instructional technology. But can software development simply be counted in rank and tenure proceedings? Perhaps justified in some institutional contexts, this oversimplified approach is largely unrealistic and unjustified. The issue at hand is part of a larger issue typically posed as a question of how to reward good teaching. But good teaching should be a baseline expectation in higher education and not a response to potential rewards beyond cost-of-living salary increases. The real issue encoded in the phrases *rewarding good teaching* and *rewarding software development* is how to encourage, recognize, and reward extraordinary achievement or innovation that either identifies or responds to special institutional or departmental needs not accounted for in existing reward structures. Lougee and Carter note in their article that removing disincentives may suffice. Gerhold suggests that one way to maintain interest in instructional computing is to reward faculty leaders with periodic equipment upgrades. A more systemic approach is to develop senior academic leadership for innovation. Must today's graduate students, who are cutting their academic teeth with technological support, mature into full professorship before such leadership can emerge and instructional technologies find a niche in academic culture? A national strategy would require strong participation by senior faculty to help move us beyond academic paralysis on this issue, and demographics suggest the timeliness of such an approach.

According to the 1988 *Digest of Education Statistics,* approximately 69 percent of the nation's tenure-track faculty is tenured, and approximately 50 percent of the tenured faculty is at the rank of Professor. There is ample opportunity, then, to nurture senior interest in the proposition that technology is affecting institutional competitiveness and the health of the disciplines and professions in two ways. It is adding value to existing courses and, in some cases, is altering the very nature of courses and curricula. That these issues are being addressed in senior ranks is evidenced by the number of scholars at the rank of Professor who have won EDUCOM/NCRIPTAL awards or have participated in major projects, such as those described in this book. Professional interest in and facility with technology are not, as they are often postulated to be, the sole domain of the junior faculty. These statistics moreover foretell an influx of fresh academic blood in the next decade. That today's senior faculty is training tomorrow's junior faculty argues for senior participation now in the development of instructional technologies. Tomorrow's curricula may otherwise evolve without the direction and continuity that mentors impart to the academic process.

A national program to support scholars from across the nation to contribute to the advancement of instructional technologies in their disciplines and professions would further legitimate participation in instructional computing. A national strategy would respond to the premises that technology is here to stay and that educational leadership demands an investment in the nation's faculty, one that incurs the kind of nonrecoverable short-term costs that typically cannot be borne by a single campus.

How could a national program be structured to support faculty from across the country and reach out to the national academic community? There are several dimensions to the answer. First, there should be an active role for recognized leaders in instructional computing in several disciplines.

Disciplinary and Interdisciplinary Leadership: Leaves and Support

Disciplinary and professional societies are the traditional vehicles for attending to problems and opportunities in a particular curriculum. Scholars gather with "their own kind" at annual meetings but are seldom freed from institutionally constrained travel and release-time budgets to sustain a collective effort, except when participating in special initiatives funded by external agencies. Inserting technology into the equation introduces additional resource constraints and further complications. A national program might support leaves of absence and various forms of short-term but sustained participation for scholars who are positioned by experience and accomplishment to shape the role of technology in their disciplines and professions, scholars such as those who have won EDUCOM/-NCRIPTAL awards.

Across-the-curriculum revisions, such as those envisioned in the chapter on curriculum perspectives, are usually rationalized around lofty interdisciplinary goals but often amount to little more than a redistribution of the feudal turf on a particular campus. Yet one of the distinguishing features of the silicon evolution in higher education is its interdisciplinary nature. Conferences and workshops often highlight computing across the curriculum, and attendees frequently describe such gatherings as refreshing and extremely valuable, in part due to an interdisciplinary atmosphere. Several of the contributors to this volume have cited the interdisciplinary synergy of projects on their campuses. A national strategy should encourage daily, not just occasional, cross fertilization in selected disciplines. The question of which disciplines and professions is one of educational priorities.

Educational Priorities

The general introduction to this book and the introduction to the section on curriculum perspectives cited both the difficulty of reaching a consensus on educational priorities on a single campus and the myriad national reports that articulate a consensus on the goals of general or liberal education. Perhaps it is easier to be a national philosopher/statesman than a campus philosopher/statesman. A national strategy should articulate educational priorities and focus resources accordingly. Such a strategy, for example, might give high priority to strengthening mathematics and science education and then might seek implementation advice from a group of mathematics and science advisors. Over time, technology could be brought to bear on a variety of educational problems strategically selected both for their importance to the nation's educational enterprise and for their amenability to technological solutions.

In a national program, what would various disciplinary groups actually do, and how would they work together in an interdisciplinary mode?

Academic Tools

Those hardware/software applications that impose no pedagogical assumptions and that can be broadly adapted to different problems and different styles of teaching and learning are often called *academic tools.* Several contributors to this book note that instructional use of software tools is often a corollary to the use of such tools in research. Their arguments recognize the contribution that software tools can make to moving the practice of a discipline from faculty offices into the classroom. Although the focus of a national program would be on instructional technology, I would not suggest attempting to distinguish too finely between research tools and teaching tools or even between tools and courseware. (Some would call Geissinger's software *courseware;* others would join EDUCOM/NCRIPTAL in calling it a *tool.*)

Some tools, such as word processors, are clearly general and interdisciplinary. Other tools appear to be interdisciplinary but may have less obvious import in some areas than in others. Hypermedia tools exhibit no disciplinary biases but presently appear to have greater application, for example, in the humanities than in the mathematical sciences. National disciplinary working groups could jointly explore the applications of general tools from their disciplinary perspectives while also identifying special disciplinary tools and, where appropriate, writing specifications for tools that are needed by the disciplines but that are either unavailable or available only in weak implementations. The goal would be to assemble and demonstrate a collection of tools that could be broadly useful in a specific discipline and that could serve as a basis for others to explore the promise of instructional technologies in their own ways.

How would those who are not participating in national research and development programs learn about the results of such programs?

Dissemination

If one thrust of a national strategy would be to build a broad consensus around a general set of academic tools and specialized disciplinary tool sets, then surely a complementary and equally important goal would be to create a national focal point for information about these tools and their use. As disciplinary groups discover thoughtful applications of existing academic tools and develop specifications for new tools, they would report these in writing and in other ways, possibly to include video tapes and satellite broadcasts. Easy access to networked classrooms and high-quality color projection would promote a variety of dissemination workshops. Such classrooms could be developed as experimental sites for studying the ways in which affordable technologies can be adapted to classroom use in a variety of campus contexts. The in-class use of technology, after all, was an important and often absent opportunity reported by several contributors to this book. What features of classroom technologies encourage faculty use? How can networks facilitate the in-class use of technology? What are the environmental features of a "model" classroom for the coming decade? These are the kinds of questions that a national program might address.

Is a National Program Feasible?

The argument for a national program has been keyed to selected academic issues reported by the contributors to this book. A rationale is not an implementation plan and, so, avoids many obvious difficulties. Which vendor(s) would ideally support a national program? How could a national program supported by more than one vendor cope with the lack of a common operating system and user interface and with the implications of such problems for identifying "national solutions"? Would disciplinary groups only develop and openly disseminate specifications for academic tools, or would prototypes or products be developed from these specifications? If the latter, how could this be accomplished in a multivendor environment? Before despairing of the feasibility of multivendor support, the reader should recall that several multivendor partnerships have been formed in the past decade, the most recent being Sematech. Where a persuasive case can be made for cooperation, partnerships have occasionally followed. The importance of higher education to the vendors of technology goes beyond the obvious market consideration to the connection between the quality of their work force and the quality of the nation's colleges and universities. The idea of adding value to education through the application of technology addresses both of these considerations. The concept of a national program created around this theme simply calls for a more focused investment in higher education than is evidenced by present patterns of vendor support, but in its multivendor format the concept also raises the issue of whether leading vendors (and perhaps other external funding agencies) can find a way to cooperate in the interest of higher education — in their own self-interest. I do not know the answer, but I can be hopeful. The concept, after all, follows the EDUCOM paradigm of cooperation between its Corporate Associates and higher education. At the very least, it helped me to focus my reflections on some of the experiences and academic issues recounted by the contributors to this book. I hope that others will be sufficiently intrigued by the idea to pursue it further.

Epilogue: A Recent Development

As a national perspective increasingly guided my thinking about this book, I began to explore with others the idea of a national program. I first publicly explored the concept of a multivendor national program with several contributors to the curriculum perspectives contained in this book, especially with Professor James Noblitt. At the 1988 EDUCOM meeting in Washington, they joined me when I broached the idea at a round-table discussion open to all vendors. One vendor, IBM, responded a few months later. In July 1989, the Institute for Academic Technology was created with support from IBM's Academic Information Systems. The Institute is operated by the University of North Carolina at Chapel Hill to meet the national goals that I have attempted to articulate here.

I recently was given the opportunity to explain how a national program supported by one vendor can contribute to the lofty goal of building a national consensus around a set of integrated general and disciplinary tools. My response, as well as additional information about the Institute, is available in the October 1989 issue of *Academic Computing*. My hope is that the Institute will succeed and either prove to be a useful model for similar ventures by other vendors or become the foundation for a multi-vendor national program for instructional technology.

Appendix A

Questions Asked of the 1987 EDUCOM/NCRIPTAL "Best" Winners

The following list of remarks and questions was presented to the authors contributing to the first part of this book, "Faculty Perspectives." It should interest any scholar/teacher contemplating the development or use of instructional software.

1. Did you choose to develop software to solve a particular educational or pedagogical problem? If so, what was the problem and how successful is your "solution"?

2. Did you investigate the availability of software suitable to your educational needs before deciding to develop your own software? If so, what did you find?

3. Discuss the pedagogical motivation and expectations that led to your work. Discuss your experience in light of your original pedagogical expectations.

4. At the time you decided to get involved in software development, was there on your campus or in your system a person leading the way — a software "champion"? If your activity was at least in part motivated or enabled by a champion other than yourself, is it likely that you would have undertaken and completed your project in the absence of the champion? Which description below best fits the champion's formal role?

- A faculty member without responsibilities either in administration or in a computing services organization

- A faculty member with administrative responsibility outside the computing services organization(s) on campus (explain)

- A faculty member with responsibilities in a computing services organization

- A nonfaculty member of a computing services organization

- None of the above (explain)

5. Did you undertake your project partly in response to a program of

tangible incentives offered by your academic unit, your campus, or your system? Is it likely that you would have undertaken and completed your project without these incentives? I refer to incentives that might or might not have relied on external funding and that might have included the following:

- A loan or gift of hardware and software

- Programming support

- Support for designing and evaluating your software

- A "grant" to supplement your salary or to release you from other duties

- Some form of career advancement (explain)

6. Was your work partly supported by a vendor or other external source(s)? If so, was the initiative for external support solely yours or was another person or group involved? If you benefited from external support, is it likely that you would have undertaken and completed your project without it?

7. What were the parameters defining the relationship between you (your department or campus) and any external source(s) of support?

8. Was your project a team effort or mostly the result of your own hard work? If a team contributed significantly to your work, was the team managed by you or by another person or group? How would you describe the management of the team on an informal-to-formal scale?

9. How "technical" were you when you decided to develop software? Have your technical skills increased as a result of your work?

10. In what hardware environment was your program developed? In which programming language, authoring language, or authoring system was your program implemented? Who worked directly in the language or system to implement your ideas?

11. Have you ported your program to other hardware/software systems? If so, discuss the experience. If not, do you expect to face this issue at some point?

12. Discuss the relative importance of any institutional support or external support to the success of your efforts.

13. If the hardware and software used in the development stages of your

program differed significantly from a single, stand-alone personal computing system, please explain.

14. Taking into account the value only of your time and any support personnel, what dollar estimate (to the nearest thousand) would you place on the development of your software? For the sake of consistency, please value your own time at forty dollars per hour and that of any support personnel at twenty-five dollars per hour. (These figures are intended as averages that reflect some overhead costs.)

15. Were there other significant direct costs associated with the development of your software that are not covered in the preceding two items? If so, explain.

16. At the time that you undertook your development work, did you believe that you were assuming an unusually high professional risk in terms of tenure, promotion, or other forms of recognition in your discipline or profession? Have standards changed since then? To the extent that you are comfortable doing so, please discuss these issues of reward and recognition as you initially perceived them and as you now perceive them, taking into account the following contexts:

- Your rank and standing on campus

- Your academic unit and campus and their standards for rewarding faculty activity

- Your discipline or profession and its standards for recognition

17. What else motivated you? Discuss the degree to which these factors were tangible, such as a publishing contract, or intangible, such as a desire to improve your teaching.

18. Putting yourself in the shoes of a publisher or commercial software distributor, would you say that your software was developed to commercial, semicommercial, or noncommercial standards?

19. Do you hold the copyright on your software? If not, who does? Is this a result of campus policy, grant requirements, a negotiation, or the absence of any ownership policy?

20. Discuss the publishing rights to your software. Explain how any royalties are (would be) distributed.

21. What legal issues have arisen or will arise in your work?

22. Does your software constitute an entire, stand-alone course or

curriculum? If not, does it target only a small portion of a course or body of knowledge or does it supplement an entire course or curriculum?

23. The continuum of books as curriculum materials includes the introductory, freshman-level text at one end and, at the other end, the graduate text or scholarly book written for specialists. Assuming that your software constitutes or supplements a substantial part of a course or curriculum, where would you place your materials on this book-based continuum?

24. Some equate the development of academic software with textbook "development." Others draw an analogy between software development and scholarly research. What are your views on this? Where would you place your work along the spectrum implied by these two extremes?

25. Did you conduct a student review of your software to address ease-of-use issues?

26. What steps have or will be taken to establish in some quantitative manner the educational effectiveness of your software? Do you consider this an important issue? Do you believe that establishing effectiveness is more important in the domain of academic software than in the domain of the academic textbook?

27. Have you used your software in your teaching? If so, how and in what part of what course(s)? Through what distribution or licensing arrangement do students gain access to your software?

28. Has any colleague on your campus used your software in his or her teaching?

29. What estimate would you place on the useful "life" of your software? Do you plan to extend its life by periodic revision?

30. Can other campuses obtain your software? If so, how and under what terms and at what cost? Has your software been used on other campuses? If so, how extensively?

31. What do you see as the most promising vehicle(s) for distributing software? What are the unsolved problems in software distribution? Do you have any advice for the distributors of academic software?

32. Did you design your software primarily for individual student use in the dorm or in a micro lab, or did you also (or exclusively) intend to use your software in the classroom, lab, or recitation section? If the latter, what are the related problems that you have encountered or that you foresee? Such problems might be related to any of the following factors:

- Projection or display technologies

- A computer in the room

- A network of computers in the room

- Control of lighting or other environmental factors

- Time to set up the classroom

- Support personnel

- Class size

33. Do you have any advice for hardware vendors that relates directly to the problems of using software in a formal teaching environment, such as a classroom or lab?

34. What were the major barriers to completing your work? How did you overcome them?

35. What might your campus do differently to encourage efforts such as yours?

36. Would you do it again? If so, what would you do differently?

Appendix B

Questions Framing the Institutional Case Studies

The following questions were posed to those who collaborated on the case studies composing the third part of the book, "Institutional Perspectives."

1. To what extent are your faculty colleagues involved in developing their own technology-based curriculum materials and tools? To what extent are they adapting materials and tools developed elsewhere (on other campuses or in commercial contexts)?

2. To what extent does your campus systematically target software development to entire, stand-alone courses or curricula? If this is not a systematic thrust, how would you describe the relationship of a typical software project to the course(s) it is intended to serve?

3. What steps have or will be taken to assess the educational effectiveness of software on your campus? Is this an important issue? Is assessment more important in the domain of academic software than in the domain of the academic textbook?

4. By rank and discipline (or profession), what is the profile of faculty participation in computing in the curriculum? Is such activity entering into rank, tenure, and salary considerations?

5. To what extent is computing in the curriculum a faculty (academic) issue that has bubbled up (or down) in various faculty committees and forums on your campus? Describe the composition and leadership of any committees that have ownership in these issues. What is the nature of the linkage between the academic program and the technical support infrastructure on your campus? Who owns what?

6. Is there institutional leadership for computing in the curriculum on your campus? Is there an institutional planning process that encompasses the issues raised here?

7. Are there technology champions on campus? If so, what is the institutional role of each individual champion and the nature of each championing academic unit or campus support service and its leadership?

8. Describe the nature, the organizational structure, and, to the extent

possible, the cost of any support mechanisms and programmatic initiatives on your campus. To what degree are these organized and funded centrally — as opposed to locally (individual departments or schools)? How are faculty encouraged to participate? Incentives might include the following:

- A loan or gift of hardware and software

- Software design support

- Programming support

- Support for pre- or post-evaluation

- Release time or a salary supplement

- Some form of career advancement

9. Which initiatives on your campus have been internal? Which have responded to externally funded opportunities, such as various vendors' grant programs? Which vendors have played a significant leadership role in computing in your curriculum? Describe the nature of this role.

10. To what extent has your campus standardized on hardware and software — languages, authoring systems/tools, productivity tools—for developing the role of computing in the curriculum? Have you attempted to coordinate development and (student) delivery environments? What are the main technical platforms for computing in the curriculum on your campus?

11. Taking into account the value only of faculty time and of any support personnel, what dollar estimate (to the nearest thousand) would you place on a typical development project on your campus? For the sake of consistency, please value faculty time at forty dollars per hour and that of any support personnel at twenty-five dollars per hour. (These figures are intended as averages that reflect some overhead costs.)

12. Putting yourself in the shoes of a publisher or commercial software distributor, would you say that much of the software on your campus was developed to commercial, semicommercial, or noncommercial standards?

13. Explain any campus policies governing the ownership of intellectual property rights (copyrights) in software and the distribution of related royalties or profits.

14. Is there a general mechanism for obtaining software developed on your campus? If so, how and under what terms and at what cost? Has

software from your campus been used systematically on other campuses? If so, how extensively?

15. What do you see as the most promising vehicle(s) for distributing software? What are the unsolved problems in software distribution? Do you have any advice for the distributors of academic software?

16. From the point of view of support for maintenance and revision of software, what estimate would you place on the useful life of software? Do you plan to meet the related costs?

17. Is your campus moving technology directly into the classroom? If so, what are the related problems that you have encountered or that you foresee? Such problems might be related to any of the following factors:

- Projection or display technologies

- A computer in the room

- A network of computers in the room

- Control of lighting or other environmental factors

- Time to set up the classroom

- Support personnel

- Class size

Index